# HUNTINGTON TOWN RECORDS

*~ including ~*

## Babylon, Long Island, New York

### 1653–1688

### Volume 1

*Charles R. Street*

## HERITAGE BOOKS
### 2016

# HERITAGE BOOKS

### *AN IMPRINT OF HERITAGE BOOKS, INC.*

**Books, CDs, and more—Worldwide**

For our listing of thousands of titles see our website
at
www.HeritageBooks.com

A Facsimile Reprint
Published 2016 by
HERITAGE BOOKS, INC.
Publishing Division
5810 Ruatan Street
Berwyn Heights, Md. 20740

International Standard Book Numbers
Paperbound: 978-0-7884-1493-0
Clothbound: 978-0-7884-6317-4

# COPY OF RESOLUTIONS.

Passed at the Annual Meetings of the Electors of the Town of Huntington, N. Y.

April 7, 1885. *Resolved*, That Hon. Henry J. Scudder, Jarvis R. Rolph and Stephen W. Gaines, be and are hereby appointed a Committee to procure edited and printed the oldest records of the Town of Huntington, and that five hundred dollars be inserted in the next tax levy to defray the expense of the same, the printing to be awarded to the lowest responsible bidder.

April 6, 1886. *Resolved*, That Judge Thomas Young, Nathaniel S. Ackerly and Charles R. Street be and are hereby appointed a Committee to have prepared for printing, and have printed the oldest town records of this town, the printing to be let to the lowest responsible bidder.

*Resolved*, That the sum of three hundred dollars be and hereby is appropriated for the purpose of preparing for printing and printing the town records of this town, the work to be done under the superintendence of the Committee appointed by the town meeting for that purpose, and that the Supervisor cause the said sum to be inserted in the next tax warrant, to be raised and paid over by the Collector to the Supervisor, to be drawn on the order of the Committee.

Town Clerk's Office, }
Huntington, Suffolk County, N. Y. }

I hereby certify that the above resolutions have been compared by me with the original records of the same, found on pages 128 and 139, Vol. IV, of Town Meetings, in this office, and are correct copies.

BREWSTER G. SAMMIS,
*Town Clerk.*

March 8, 1887.

The following resolution was passed at the annual meeting of the Electors of the Town of Babylon, N. Y., April 6, 1886. *Resolved,* That the sum of five hundred dollars, or so much thereof as may be necessary, be raised by tax for the purpose of printing the records of the Town of Babylon.

TOWN CLERK'S OFFICE, }
Babylon, Suffolk County, N. Y. }

I hereby certify that the last above resolution has been compared by me with the original record of the same in this office, and that the same is a correct copy.

JOSEPH A. MOORE,
*Town Clerk.*

March 2, 1887

# Town Clerk's Certificate.

I hereby certify that I have compared, or caused to be compared, this printed volume with the original manuscript records in my office, and that I believe the same is a correct and exact copy of said original records, "errata" excepted.

BREWSTER G. SAMMIS,
*Town Clerk.*

March 8, 1887.

# PREFACE.

The Committee appointed by Resolution, passed at a town meeting in Huntington, April 7, 1885, began the performance of their duties by selecting records and having them copied for printing; but owing to the death of Henry J. Scudder and the resignation of Jarvis R. Rolph, Stephen W. Gaines alone remained of the Committee at the end of the year. Mr. Gaines, in his report made at the annual town meeting in Huntington, 1886, says: "Many of "these (oldest records) were found to be defaced by time "and handling, with peculiarities of writing and spelling, "requiring careful copying before being in a condition for "classification or printing. For this purpose Miss Naomi "L. Street has been employed by the Committee, and has "very satisfactorily deciphered and copied manuscripts "covering a period from the first settlement of the town, "in 1653, to 1700." Mr. Gaines also resigned, as he stated, for the want of time necessary for the performance of the duties required.

The Town of Babylon having formed a part of the old Town of Huntington until the passage of the Act in 1872 creating it a separate town, and its people having a mutual interest with the people of Huntington in the printing and preservation of the records, the representatives of both towns decided to join in the common purpose and share the expenses of the publication.

At a joint meeting of the Committee representing Huntington, and George A. Hooper, Supervisor, representing Babylon, it was agreed that the first volume should contain the records relating to the territory within the present boundaries of the Town of Babylon as well as Huntington, and that the expense of printing the same should be borne, two thirds by Huntington and one third by Babylon.

The book has been edited by Charles R. Street under the supervision of the Committee.

The original spelling, capitalization and punctuation have been followed, and all the papers have been prepared for the press with great care to make them correct and exact copies of the original records.

THOMAS YOUNG
CHARLES R. STREET        *Committee*
N. S. ACKERLY        *Town of Huntington.*

GEO. A. HOOPER, *Supervisor of Babylon.*

# INTRODUCTION.

This volume covers the records of the town of Huntington from its first settlement, 1653, to 1688. Pursuant to the
plan of the work, every material paper is printed in the
order of its date regardless of the source whence it is taken,
under a brief head line, and ends with a reference to the
volume and page of the record or the file of papers where
it is found.

Originally these oldest records were in thin unbound
volumes, in paste-board covers. The entries were made
by the Recorders or Town Clerks promiscuously, with little
regard to the subject matter or the order of date; but at
the revision of the records, made by authority of the Board
of Trustees in 1873, these old paste-board covered books
were grouped together and bound in volumes, and were
entitled "Court Records," "Town Meetings," "Deeds," &c.,
according to the general subject matter of their contents,
but their titles are often misleading, as they still remain
a mixture of all kinds of records with little order as to
dates. There is also a mass of loose papers dating back to
this early period which have survived the ravages of time.
All these old records are so worn and defaced, and written
in such ancient and peculiar chirography, that it became
necessary to copy them for the hand of the printer, retain-
ing in all cases the ancient spelling, capitalization and
peculiarities of letter and form—a work of much difficulty
and magnitude.

Out of this chaos of ancient manuscript—a dead letter to
all not experienced in deciphering it—an orderly and chron-
ologically arranged record of the doings of the people of

the town at this early period is now for the first time produced, with an index pointing to the page where any given
subject may be found. Some foot notes, explanatory of
events disclosed in the records, have been added by me
with the sanction of the Committee. It is highly probable
that some inaccuracies may have crept into these notes, but
where not quite certain as to the facts, the statements are
made in guarded or qualified terms.

This book contains all the Indian deeds, all the grants
and patents from Colonial Governors, all the town meetings
and grants of land by town meetings, and all deeds and
miscellaneous records, to the date of the last paper printed.
It ends not far from where the proceedings of the trustees
of the town begin, no trustees having existed until the grant
of the Dongan Charter of 1688. A few wills and inven-
tories of estates appear, chiefly before 1665. After the
latter date, and down to the close of the Revolutionary war,
they were required by law to be proved and recorded elsewhere.

This first volume embraces what may be termed the
foundation history of the town. It tells us of the pioneers
who first settled Huntington, where they first located and
established their homes ; how they acquired title to their
lands ; their treaties and agreements with the Indians ;
what tribes of Indians they found here, and of the territory
occupied by these tribes. It tells us when and where the
early settlers founded churches and schools, built mills
for grinding their corn, and forts and watch-houses for de-
fence ; of their military system, of "train bands" for mutual
protection ; their long and bitter contests with rival com-
munities to maintain the boundaries of their town ; their
method of land divisions ; their persistent hostility to the
Dutch Government of New Netherlands, and their friend-
ship for the New England Colonies ; the laws and regulations they made at town meetings ; and it unfolds to us a
view of the social, political, religious and inner life of our

ancestors at this remote period, which cannot be otherwise
than useful and interesting to all, both in a utilitarian and
a historical point of view, and especially so to the citizens
of the towns of Huntington and Babylon.

Aside from Indian deeds, there are no records in the
Clerk's office of earlier date than 1657, and the records
from 1657 to 1660 are confined mostly to a few minutes of
civil and criminal trials. The first record of a town meeting,
now found, is dated 1659, six years after white men were
here purchasing land from the Indians. It is fair to assume
that many of the earliest records of town meetings and of
other events have been lost. They were probably kept
on loose papers, not recorded in any book, and have gradually disappeared. Many papers bound together survive;
single papers perish,—exemplifying the truth of Æsop's
fable of the bundle of sticks. An opinion prevails that some
of the events at the time of the first settlement were recorded in New Haven, Hartford, Branford or other old
towns in New England, as the pioneers considered themselves within the jurisdiction of Connecticut. A corres-
pondence, however, with those who have the custody of the
records of these towns, has so far brought nothing very
material to light, but I cannot help believing that a more
thorough search might be successful. With the exception
of the first seven years of the town's history, the records
are very continuous to the period when this book ends.
The absence of the first records of the settlement is to be
much regretted.

The first settlers of Huntington were chiefly Englishmen,
and they nearly all had sojourned for a time before coming here at one or other of the settlements in New England,
and some of them in other of the oldest towns on Long
Island. Of the exact time when, and the precise place
where the first white man, or the first company of white
people landed or located in Huntington, we have no certain knowledge. Hon. Silas Wood, in his history of Suf-

folk County, states that eleven families came here first, followed immediately by others. No names and no dates are given. He probably gave this as a tradition in his time, for there is nothing in the records of the town supporting it, and nothing elsewhere verifying the statement, to my knowledge.

After considerable research and careful examination of the records of Long Island and many New England towns, and of lists of immigrants from England to America, I incline to the opinion that those pioneers who came here during the first five years of the settlement came principally on at least three different lines. It is probable that the first and oldest company came across the Sound, perhaps under the leadership of Rev. William Leverich, from the vicinity of New Haven and Branford, landing at Huntington Harbor and locating principally along the valley where the eastern part of Huntington Village now is, this having been always called "the town spot," or "old town spot;" that the second immigration was an off-shoot from the Hempstead colony, led thither by Rev. Richard Denton soon after 1640, originally from Wethersfield, Mass., and for a time at Stamford, Conn; and that the third influx came from the vicinity of Salem, Mass., after stopping a short time in Southold and Southampton, principally in the former town. These three lines of migration are quite clearly shown by tracing the residence of these persons through successive years in more or less of the places here indicated, but the order in which they came here is not so apparent, and it may be that their arrival was nearly simultaneous. In subsequent years the settlement was undoubtedly recruited by frequent arrivals from the New England towns and from other towns on Long Island, several coming from Southold, Southampton, Setauket, Hempstead and Newtown, but few, if any, coming from the distinctively Dutch towns at the west.

The pioneers found the territory within the limits of the

old town of Huntington occupied by three tribes of Indians; the Matinnecocks holding the territory on the north
side to the middle of the Island, the Sucatogues the southeast part, the Marsepagues the southwest, each adjoining
the Matinnecocks on the north. They were comparatively
feeble tribes of Algonquin stock, their numbers having been
decimated by former wars with the New England tribes, to
whom they had annually paid tribute. The whites had
very little trouble in managing them, and gradually acquired title to all their lands.

In the first years of the settlement the pioneers built their
rudely constructed dwellings around and near the "town
spot," where they had a fort and "watch-houses," and where
the "train bands" were drilled. Their animals were daily
driven out and herded under guard, some in the "east field,"
now Old Fields, and some in the "west field," now West
Neck, and at night the cattle were driven back and cor-
ralled near the watch-house. Gradually, however, the more
adventurous pushed out in all directions, and made themselves homes where they found the richest soil and most
attractive surroundings, and at their meetings grants of
"home lots" were made. At first the women pounded their
corn in mortars and the men wrought logs and clapboards
for building with axes and cleavers; but soon dams were
constructed across the streams, small mills were built for
grinding grain and sawing lumber, rude tanneries were
constructed for tanning leather, and spindles and looms
were made or procured for the manufacture of coarse flaxen
and woolen fabrics for clothing. The ox-cart was their
only vehicle for travel and "cart paths" their only highways.
They used wooden ploughshares tipped with iron. Their
match-lock guns were even more clumsy than the old flint-
locks, but some of their swords were wrought by Spanish
artisans and were tempered with a skill that is among the
lost arts.

For a period of about eleven years, down to the English

conquest over the Dutch in 1664, the people here formed a little independent government of their own, making their own laws. From 1664 to 1691, a period of twenty-six years, with the exception of a brief hiatus of Dutch Conquest in 1673, they were governed by a code of laws promulgated by authority of the Duke of York, called the "Dukes Laws" and formed a part of the Colony of New York under successive Colonial Governors, with practically no voice in making the laws other than such orders relating to their common lands as were allowed to be made at town meetings. After 1691, under the greater freedom secured by the English revolution, they had a voice in the making of laws, and the charter given them in 1694 conferred upon them the full powers of a town corporation.

It is well to remember that nearly all the events recorded in this book occured more than one hundred years before the Revolutionary War; and that so much of this remote history of our ancestors has been preserved should be especially gratifying to the people of Huntington and Babylon, who are alike interested in its preservation.

·CHARLES R. STREET.

# HUNTINGTON TOWN RECORDS.

## [INDIAN DEED. THE FIRST PURCHASE IN HUNTINGTON.*]

[1653, April 2.]

Articles of agreement betwixt Raseokan Sagamore of Matinnicoke,† of the one part, and Richard Houldbroke, Robart Williams, Danial Whitehead, of the other party, witnesseth as followeth :

Know all men whome these present writings may any way concerne that I Raseokan do sell and make over unto the aforesaid parties Richard Houldbrock, Robart Williams and Daniel Whitehead, their heirs, executors or assigns, a certain quantitie of land, lying and being upon Long Island, bounded upon the West side with a river commonly called by the Indians Nachaquetack, on the North side with the sea and going eastward to a river

[*The origin of the name, Huntington, is involved in obscurity. Its Indian name was Ketewomoke. We have no knowledge of the signification of this Indian word. As the first settlement here was made while Oliver Cromwell was in the zenith of his power, the first Indian deed having been make in the same year and month in which he dissolved the Long Parliament, it has been suggested that this town was named after his birthplace in England, Huntingdon. On the other called Opcatkontycke, on the south side to the utmost part of my bounds ; promising, and by virtue hereof I do promise to free the above saide lands from all title off and claim that shall be made unto it by reason of any former act ; in consideration of which land the afore said Richard Houlbrock, Robart Williams and Danial Whitehead doth promise unto the said Raseokan as followeth : 6 coats, 6 kettles, 6 hatchets, 6 howes, 6 shirts, 10 knives, 6 fathom of wampum, 30 muxes, 30 needles, further the said sachem doth promise to go or send some one in twenty days to show and mark

---

hand it is generally supposed that Huntington derived its name from the abundance of game here, which made it a desirable hunting ground.]

[†The Matinecock tribe of Indians occupied all of the north shore of Long Island from the Nesequague (now Smithtown) River on the east, to Scouts, or Cow Bay, in Hempstead, on the west.

The chief of the Matinecocks then here was Raseocon, and he was called the Sagamore of Ketewomoke, then called by the English, Huntington. Wyandance, the chief of the Montauks, who resided at the east end of Long Island and claimed to be the Grand Sachem over all other tribes on Long Island, did not sign this deed, which caused some trouble later on, but is of little consequence now.

On the same day that this deed was given by the Indians to the Oysterbay men named in it as grantees, the latter assigned all their interest in the premises to certain residents of Huntington who became the proprietors, and they and their descendants, or assigns, were ever after called the proprietors of the first or "old purchase." The original assignment seems to be missing, but I think I have seen it in former years, and its execution is attested by contemporaneous papers. The boundaries of the premises described in this deed are understood to include the premises between Natchaguetack, Cold Spring Harbour, on the west, Opkatkowtycke, the stream at the head of Northport Harbour, on the east, the Sound on the north, and a line where what is now known as Country Path runs, on the south ; containing about six miles square, but afterwards construed as not including Lloyd's Neck or Eaton's Neck. It was here that the first settlement was made—what is now Huntington village being the central point, or "Town Spot" so called. —C. R. S.]

out the bounds, and in case it prove not according to expectation then this writing to be voyde & of none efectt, but in case it be, then this writing to stand in full force, power and virtue.

Witness our hands the 2th of Aprill 1653.

the mark of
RICHARD X HOULBROCK,
ROBART X WILLIAMS,
DANIELL X WHITHEAD.

the mark X
of the SAGAMOR
the mark X of HEWOIKES
the mark of X MUHAMA
the mark X of SYHAR
the mark X of POYNEYPA
the mark X of NAUAMARAWAS
the mark X of MAHENAS
the mark X of ONAMYCAS
the mark X of MANYTONY
the mark X of POANEPON
the mark X of PENETUN
the mark X of NASCORET
the mark X of SUAUSPAC
the mark X of NEMAPAPAM
the mark X of CAMPAS
the mark X of NESCEHE
the mark X of YAPACAMAN
the mark X of SCANOMY
the mark X of ANCHOPIN
the mark X of WERCOCCU
the mark X of WINHAMAS
the mark X of ASGELEUES
the mark X of MAMARAM
the mark X of WOMPOM

This is a true coppe of the origenall deed witnes our hands.

THOMAS RICHARDS.

MOSES IOHNSON

Recorded in the office at New York
11[th] day of November 1667.

Matthias Nicolls, sec[r]

(*File No. 67.*)

---

# [INDIAN DEED OF HORSE (LLOYD'S) NECK TO DANIEL MAYO AND OTHERS.]

[1654, September 20.]

September the 20, 1654.

This writing witnesseth that I Ratiocan Sagamore of Cow Harbor, have sold unto Samuel Mayo, Danil Whitehead and Peter Wright my neck of land which makes the east side of Oyster Bay, and the west side of Cow Harbor on the north side bounded with the Sound called by Indians Caumsett.   For and in consideration of which neck of land, we the aforesaid Samuel Mayo, Daniel Whitehead and Peter Wright, do promise to pay to the afore said Ratiocan, Sagamore, three coats, three shirts, two cuttos, three hatchets, three hoes, two fathom of wampum, six knives, two pair of stockings, two pair of shoes.   In witnes whereof we have interchangeably set our hands.

The Mark of × RATIOCAN, Sagamore,

The Mark of × ASPAPAM, Sagamore

The Mark of × NASTHEYE

The Mark of × ONOMICUS

The Mark of × OPATAN NATAMYE ·

The Mark of × CATANON

The Mark of × NOCONAST

The Mark of × PECHOCON

The Mark of × MOMINY

The Mark of ✕ SHONHEGON
The Mark cf ✕ MASKAN
The Mark of ✕ COPACAFF
The Mark of STAMFORD OPTAPEA
The Mark of ✕ TANSAYUSPE

SAMUEL MAYO
DANIL WHITEHEAD
PETER WRIGHT

In the presence of us underscribed this writing above written was owned and acknowledged to be the act and deed of those Indians that have hereunto signed which they promise forever to maintain.

Oysterbay 16, May 1658.

NICHOLAS WRIGHT
JOHN SAFFIN
NICHOLAS SIMPKINS

Received in part one coat one pair of breeches.

The Mark of ✕ RATIOCAN.

copy from the Records of the Manor of Queens Village "Vellum book" and entered in page 54, 3ᵈ book of Massachusetts Colony Sept. 1. 1658.*

(*File Lloyd's Neck Papers, A.*)

[*This deed was hostile to the title of Huntington, as it purported to convey a part of premises claimed to be included in the Huntington purchase a year earlier. It furnished the basis for the long litigation which followed concerning the ownership of Lloyd's, then Horse Neck. It is not strange, however, that the Indians were ready enough to sell the same land any number of times, provided they could find a purchaser who would give them wampum and trinkets.—C. R. S.]

## [INDIAN DEED—EASTERN PURCHASE.]

[1656, July 30.]

This indenture made in the yeare 1656, in or abought the Laste daye of July bee twixt Asharoken Montinnicok Sachem and the reste of the Indian owners with him, on the on parte, and Jonas Wood, William Rogers, Thomas Wilkes, for themselves and the rest of theire associates, on the other parte ; Witnesseth that I, asharoken have solld unto Jonas Wood, William Rogers, Thomas wilkes all the medoe, freshe and salte lyinge and beinge upon the north side of Longe Islande, from our fourmer bounds Cowharber brocke to Neesaquock river, all the medoe within these bounds weste and easte, and to the north sayd to as far as asharokens bounds goeth "Southwards, as the necke called Eatons Necke, Crabmedos, and all the reste of the medows within the a fore sayde boundes with all the arbige that is or shal bee heare after upon the woods, lands with in the a fore sayde bounds, to bee the afore sayd Jonas is Willans and Thomas is, to them and thare a sosiats, heeres and executors for ever, rasarvinge to the Indians Liberty to plante and hunte within thees a fore sayd bounds, and that for and in consideration of 2 coates, fore shertes, seven quarts of licker and aleven ounces of powther in witnes heeareof wee have set to our hands.

ASHAROKEN X his mark
MAKAMAH X his mark
SYHAR X his mark
FOGER X his mark
POYNEPYA X his mark
NAMEROWS X his mark
MOHEMOS X his mark
MAMARAD X his mark
MANATERORYE X his mark

JONAS WOOD
WILLIAM ROGERS
THOMAS WILKES

(*File No. 24.*)

Entered in y⁰ office at New Yorke
the 15ᵗʰ day of October, 1666
Matthias Nicolls, secr.*

---

[WILL OF JEFFREY ESTE.]

[1657, Jan. 4.]

Jefery Este deseased the 4ᵗʰ of Jenuary 57 haveing mad
his will and desposed of his estat as follueth :
  i he gave to his son Isak Easte sholld have A bedd and
all that thar unto belonging.

---

[*This has always been designated as the Eastern Purchase,
and as will be seen, began where the first purchase ended at
"Cow Harbour brooke," or as the Indians called it "Opkatkon-
tycke" and running eastward to the Nesequague or Smithtown
River. The term "To as far as Asharokens bounds goeth
southward," is rather indefinite but it was understood to go as
far south as the old Country road, where the premises joined
the lands of the Sucetogue Indians of the south side of the
Island. It was claimed afterwards by Smithtown that the part
of this purchase lying between Unthemamuck, Fresh Pond, and
the Nesequague or Smithtown River was not owned by these
Indians, but was included in valid deeds by the Nessaquague
Indians to the original proprietors of Smithtown, and Huntington lost this part of the territory by decree of the Court of
Assizes in 1675. It was also successfully contended that under
a deed by the Matinecock Indians to Theophilus Eaton, Gov'r
of New Haven, made in 1646, the Indian title had already
passed, so that as to this Neck the deed was of no effect, but it
was held valid as to all the rest. This deed, and the old purchase deed, are the only ones of much importance obtained of
the Indians by the settlers of the north side of Huntington.
William Rogers, one of the grantees in this deed, is supposed
to have been the son of Isaiah Rogers, and a descendant of
John Rogers, the Martyr, 1555. Thomas Wickes, another
grantee, left Wethersfield in 1635 ; was at Stamford, Conn., in
1641, and came to Huntington with Edmund Wood and others.
Jonas Wood, another grantee, was probably the one designated
as "of Halifax." He was the son of Edmund Wood, and came
here with Thomas Wicks about 1654, via. Stamford.—C. R. S.]

2. 20 shillings in shewes of if henry skodar so can to his dafter.

3 he bequeathed his house and lote to Jonathn Skodar the son of henary Skodar and his father to be his gardenar till his son com the age of 21 yeres and the rest of his estat to henary skodar of huntington. I henary Skodar being exetar in the presunt of thes witnesses the 23 of Jenunry 59.*

JONAS WOOD.
THOMAS BENNYDICK.

(*Court Rec., p.* 11.)

------

## [EMPLOYMENT OF THE FIRST SCHOOL TEACHER.]

[1657, Feb. 11.]

A Covenant and Agreement made the eleventh Day of ffebruary 1657, at a Corte or Towne meeting ; Betwixt the Inhabitants of y⁰ Towne of Huntington of the one p'tie ; And Jonas Holdsworth of the other p'tie, Whereby the said Jonas Holdsworth Doth engage himselfe to the said Inhabitants During y⁰ terme of ffoure yeares ; to be ex- pired from the thirteenth Day of Aprill next ensuing the Day of the Date hereof, ffor to Schoole such persons or Children as shall be put to him for yᵗ end ; by y⁰ sd. In- habitants.   And likewise the said Inhabitants Doth also engage themselves to the said Jonas Holdsworth, for to

[*Jeffrey Este was at Salem, Mass., in 1637, and afterwards at Southold. He was an old man when he came to Hunting- ton. He resided at East Neck. His children were, Tonsfield, Isaac and Catharine. Savage says that Tonsfield's wife, Mary Este, was executed as a witch, September 26th, 1692. Catharine married Henry Scudder and after his death married Thomas Jones. This is the first record of a death in Hunting- ton.—C. R. S.]

build him a sufficient house, and to give him with y$^e$ saip house, a persell of ground ajoyning to it, for accommedation thereunto.  And furthermore the said Inhabitants doth likewise engage themselves to pay unto y$^e$ said Jonas Holdsworth for and in consideration of his sd. Schooling ; Twenty five pounds (accompt) and his Diat the first yeare ; And allso to allow him what more may come in by y$^e$ Schooling of any that come from other whars.  The said Twenty five pounds is to be paid y$^e$ sd. Jonas, as followeth Three pounds, twentie shillings in butter, at six pence p. pound, and seven pounds, two shillings in good well sized Merchantable tradeing wampum, y$^t$ is well strung, or steaud, or in such comodities as will sute him for clothing, these to be paid him by y$^e$ first of October and three pounds twelve shillings in corne ; one halfe in wheat and the other in indian, at three, & five shillings p. bushell (provided y$^t$ it be good & Merchantable) to be paid by y$^e$ first of March and Teen pounds fourteen shillings, in well, thriving young cattell, that shall be then betwixt two, & foure years old ; (the one halfe being in the stear kind ; these to be Delivered him when y$^e$ yeare is expired.  And also the two next ensuing years, To pay the sd. Jonas Holdsworth Thirty five pounds p yeare ; with y$^e$ foresaid alowance of what may come in, by such as come from other places ; The said Thirty five pounds is to be paid as followeth (viz) five pounds in butter at six pence p pound, and ten pounds in such wampum as is above mentioned. or in such comodities as will sute him ; these all to be paid y$^e$ first of October ; And five pound in corne ; by y$^e$ first of March, the halfe in wheate and the other in indian, at five and three shillings p bushel (so that it bee good & Merchantable) And ffifteen pounds in well thriving young cattell betwixt two & foure years old, the halfe being in y$^e$ steare kinde ; these are to be Delivered when y$^e$ year is expired, (being vallued by indifferent men.)

And the fourth or last yeare to pay the sd. Jonas Holdsworth ffourty pounds in such pay as is above mentioned, according to the masure and quantitie proptionablely, and at the fore said times of payment.

Allso it agreed of that firewood bee gotten & brought for the school, when yᵉ seasons shall require it, by such as send theire children to Schoole ; And that the said Jonas Holdsworth shall have liberty yearely for to chuse ffoure men, that shall bee bound to him for the true performance of the foresaid engagements.*

(*Towne Metings, Vol.* 1, *p.* 343-4.)

---

## [INDIAN DEED OF FIVE NECKS, SOUTH SIDE.]

[1657, June 1.]

This writinge testifieth an Agreement and Bargaine made Betweene jonas wood off Huntington, on Long Island, the one party and meantaquit Sachem the other party : Witnesseth that the abov sd. Jonas Wood hath for himselfe and the rest of his neighboures of Huntington, afore said, Bought five Necks of meadow Ling next adjoyning to massapeags Sachems land : and the above sd. Jonas Wood Doth hereby ingage himself for and on the behalfe off his Neighbours, to pay or cause to be paid, unto yᵉ abov. sd. sachem of meantaquit, twelve coates, twenty howes, twenty hatchets, twenty knives, ten pounds of powder, ten pounde of lead and on great Cettell and on hatt, present in hand, And doth further promise to give to the

---

[*Jonas Holdsworth was an educated Englishman and, as far as we know, the first schoolteacher in Huntington. He was at one time Town Clerk. He seems to have been here at one period and in others at Southold and Southampton. His house and lands were probably located at the "Old Town Spot," the eastern part of what is now the Village of Huntington.—C. R. S.]

above <sup>sd</sup> Sachem, every yeare, a Coat for six years, next
ensuing the Date hereof:

And the abov sd. Sachem Waindance, for and in consideration of the these abov sd. goods, Doth give full Rite
and proprietie to the afore sd. Jonas and his Neighbours
and theere heyrs for ever to all the s<sup>d</sup> five Neckes of
meadow, and will free them from all Claims and titles that
any other may Lay thereto in witness whereof Booth parties Interchangably put to thir hands this fist day of June
1657.*

In the presents of
LION GARDENER
THOMAS TALLMAGE
BENJAMIN PRICE

WAINDANCE X Marke
Sachem of Meantaquitt

This may witness to all that:

keeossechok the sachem of <sup>t</sup> secoutok have Resigned up
all that Right or Interest hee might any wayes lay unto
the neckes of medowe expressed above in this wrighting
and so confirm the bargan and full of the mantakit sachem
as witness my mark.

KEEOSSECHOK X
his mark.

[*This was the first Indian deed of lands on the South Side
of Huntington. It was made by Wyandance, the Grand
Sachem of all Long Island, residing at Montauck, and by the
Chief of the Seucatogue Indians, in occupation. This deed,
like all others conveying Necks only, took in the meadow lands
lying between the "Old Indian Path" and the South Bay,
being the Necks extending into the Bay. The grantee was
Jonas Wood "of Halifax," and the purchase was for the benefit of a number of persons to whom the lands were afterwards
divided   These Necks were located on the Great South Bay,
about midway of the shore line of the present Town of Babylon, between Sumpwams and Copiague Necks   The value of
the premises was chiefly in the salt grass these meadows produced, and as "English hay" was unknown to this country for
the first century after its settlement, salt hay was highly valued
and was carted to all parts of the town from the South
Meadows—C. R. S.]

In p^resents of
JOHN STIKLINGS
SAMUELL FFERMAN
as witness the mark of
AMBRUS SUTTON X the mark
of RICHARD BRUSH X
Recorded in the office in New York the 2^d day
of November 1667 Matthias Nichols Sec.
(*File* 25.)

---

## [INDIAN DEED OF HALF NECK.]

[1657, July 23.]

This Writing testifieth an agreement and bargain made
between Jonas Wood of Huntington, Long Island, the
one party, and Wyandance the Sachem of Mantokett and
Keetoseethok Sachem of Secotaug the other part Witnesseth that the abovesaid Jonas Wood hath bought for
himselfe one Half neck of Medow Lying betwixt a river
that bouns the Necke bought by the Inhabitants of Huntington eastward and so to Trees that are marked being
next joining to Massapegs Sachems Land and the aforesaid sachem Wyandanse and Keetoseethok, for and in Consideration of one new gun and one Pistol and two pounds
of powder received now in hand as in full satisfaction for
the aforesaid Meadow, doth hereby give full right and
propriety unto the aforesaid Jonas Wood, and unto his
Heirs, executors, administrators or assigns forever, unto
the aforesaid Half Neck of Medow, and the aforesaid
Sachem doth engage themselves and promise that they
will free the said Meadow from all Claims and titles or
Chalinges whatsoever that any other Indian or Indiens or
any other may lay thereunto, that so the aforesaid
Jonas Wood and his Heirs may enjoy the said
Land peacably in Witness whereof both Sachems have

set to their Marks and signed this bargain and sale this 23ᵈ July 1657

Signed in the presence of

JOHN STICKLINE
JOHN LUM

his mark

WYANDANCE Sachem ✕ of Maun-takett

his mark

KEETOSETHOK Sachem C, of Seguc-taug.

This further doth witness and confirm that the aforesaid Sachems, spacified in this writing, hath granted and doth give the aforesaid Jonas full right to fence, build or plow or sow, English grain or Corn upon the foresaid Half-neck herein specified, as witness their own hands and marks with their own hands.

his mark

In the presence of          WYANDANSE A. A. Mant-

his mark

CHRISTOPHER ✕ BUSH          okett Sachem

This is a true Copy of the original deed extracted by Thomas Powell, recorder.*

(*File No. 26, a. and Court Rec., p. 294.*)

----

[COURT RECORD. MATHEWS AND WOOD.]

[1658, (about).]

The deposition of mark mags taken befor Jonas wood, this deponent sayeth that about agust in the yere 58 or when we ware a weding of indian corn, Thomas mather

----

[*This neck was west of and adjoining the five necks heretofore purchased.—C. R. S.]

cam to this deponent and desired hem to hellp abord a but of rum and a pip or 2 of windes that jonas wood and Edward highbe had bought of his cosen and this deponent went to mr mathues house and he desired him to hellp in with pipe of rum and a pip or 2 of windes which jonas wood and Edward higbe had bought of hem and so this deponent did goe and hepe in with them then this deponent asked mr mathers if he had don and Mr Mathewes answered stay he colld not tell and this deponent and jonas wood and Mathews sate downe and Mr. Mathwes sayd to Edward higbe com hellper and they 2 went a sid that is to say Mr Mathews and Edward higbe and we sate to gethar and take a pip of tobackow so when Mr Mathews and Edward higbe had ended thayr discorse thay had them hoyst in the rest of the wine and this deponent furthar sayeth that he undar stod no partnarship betwixt them thre but only that Ead higbe and jonas wood had boute a pip of rum and a pipe or 2 of sacke and that without referanc to any partnarship with Mr mathues.*

(*Court Rec., p* 13.)

---

[*This item, in connection with others, shows that a trade had already sprung up between Huntington and the East India Islands in which the return cargo was rum, wine and sack. Mathews, Higbee and Wood were engaged in this trade. Mark Mags, or Megs, was a noted character. He was the son of Vincent Megr, who settled in Mass., and died there in 1658. Savage says that Mark, being rather wild, removed to Long Island and is not mentioned again. His wife's name was Avis. He once owned the first mill here. In a subsequent paper he states: "Whereas I Mark Megs have grown ancient and desire peace and quiet and desire to move to Stratford," &c. He prboably ended his days in Stratford.—C. R. S.]

## [CONFIRMATION OF INDIAN DEED OF HORSE (LLOYD'S) NECK.]

[1658, May 14.]

I Wyandanck, Sachem of Meantacut do confirm the sale aforementioned of the tract or neck aforementioned, commonly by the English called Horse Neck, sold by Ratiocan, Sagamore unto Samuel Mayo & Comp'y aforementioned, and do promise and oblige myself and successors to maintain the said sale and title thereof forever unto Samuel Andrews, his heirs, administrators or assigns, as being the true repurchasers thereof from said Samuel Mayo and Comp.y; and at any time upon demand to make unto said Samuel Andrews, his heirs, executors administrators or assigns a more firm deed according to law if required, and in witness of the truth and for full confirmation hereof, have hereunto set my hand this 14th day of May, 1658 at Shelter Island.

> This is the mark of × WYANDANCK
> Sachem of Maantacut.
> This is the Mark of × SUSAKATUCAN
> This is the Mark of × SAIMOP
> Indian Witnesses.

Witness by us
JOHN OGDEN
RICHARD ODEL
NATHANIEL SYLVESTER.

This Confirmation, together with the within written deed from the Indians were entered and recorded with record of the Massachusetts Colony of New England the first of September, 1658.

> Per ROBERT HOWARD.

Recorded in New York in the office the 3ᵈ day of October 1685.

Matthias Nicholls, Secry.

Copy from records of the Manor of Queens Village "vellum book" and entered in page 54, 3ᵈ book of Massachusetts colony Sept. 1, 1658.*

   (*File Lloyd's Neck Papers, B.*)

---

[INDIAN DEED OF THREE NECKS, SOUTHSIDE.]

[1658, Aug. 17.]

Agust the 17 day 1658.

Bee it knowne untoall men By this writing That I, wyandance, sachem of pammanake, or by the English called Long Island, doe By these acknowledg to have sould to Henry Whitnee of huntington, for the use of the whole

---

[*The way that Samuel Andrews acquired title to Lloyd's Neck appears by the following extract from the records of the Manor of Queens Village "vellum book :"

"1658 May 6. At Oysterbay Samuel Mayo, Daniel Whitehead, and Peter Wright convey Horse Neck to Samuel Andrews, Merchant of London, in consideration of the sum of one hundred pounds. The witnesses to this were John Saffin, John Pickenson, and Anthony Wright. The deed is entered and recorded in the office of the Notary Public of the Mass. Colony, Sept. 1658 in page 54 of 3rd book of Records."

Huntington was at that time, and had been from the first settlement, in possession of this Neck and so continued until 1665, claiming it all the while under, and as within the description, of its first or "old purchase" deed by Ratiocon, or Raseocon as often spelled, the local chief of the Matinecock tribe. Huntington, however, had no confirmation of its deed by the Grand Sachem Wyandance, though it sought in vain to procure it. It was the above confirmation by Wyandance to Mayo and others, that was subsequently made the chief pretext for defeating the title of Huntington to the Neck. Andrews, as soon as he bought the Neck of Mayo and others, immediately procured this confirmation.—C. R. S.]

Town of Huntington, I say, I have sould to him for them three whole necks of medow Land Lying on the southward side of theire towne and westarly from the six necks which wee Bought Befor, these three necks of messepeake Land I say I for my selfe, and my heirs for ever, have sould, as above mencioned, and have sent my agent Cheaconoe to deliver, upon condicions as followeth : first they shall pay, or cause to bee paid to mee, or my assigns, these ffollowing goods punctually, that is, first twelfe coats ech coate Being too yards of tucking cloath, twenty pounds of powder, twenty dutch hatchets, twenty dutch howes, twenty duch knives, ten shirts, too hundred of muxes, five paire of handsom stockings, one good dutch hatt, and a great fine Loking glas, and for Choconoe, for his wages and going to marke out the Lande, shall have for himselfe one coat, fower pounds of poudar, six pound of led, one dutch hatchet, as alsoe seventeen shilling in wampum, thay must send by Chockanoe, which being punctually paid, then shall I declar this deed, which shall bee for the free and quiet possession of them and theire heaires forever and in the mene time it shall Remaine in the hands of Lyon gareden: in witnes where of wee have here to set our hands the day above written.

Witness
RICHARD BRUSH
AMBROS SUTEN
Huntington, Receved this 23 of May 1659, from the Inhabitants of Huntington full satisfaction and payment for the medow I sould Last to them which my man Chochenoe marked out ffor them which joynes to that neecke that Belongs to Mr Stikland and Jonas Wood and soe goes west ward soe ffar as Chakenene hath marked being purchased In august Last which was 1658 witnes

CHEKENOW ✕ his mark
SASAKETAWUH ✕ his mark,

the mark of
AMBROS✕SUTTEN,
the mark of
RICHARD✕BRUSH

WYANDANCE
mark  o  o
✕
The mantak
Sachem
TACPOWSHA his
✕
mark.*

(*File No. 27.*)

---

## [DIVISION OF LANDS]

[1659]

1659  After wee yᵉ Inhabitants of huntington by means of
maineta——sachem had bought a sertaine number of
necks of medowe at yᵉ south side of yᵉ Island : of
seaquetauke & massapage Indians and have paid for
them.  The towne then disposed of these necks to
particular men of the towne by yᵉ hundreds as there
Rule of dissposing of Land was : and that haulf neck

---

[*Takapousha was the chief of the Marsapeague Indians who
occupied the Southwest part of Huntington.  In another
paper he put it on record that it "grieved his heart" to make
this deed, but he was compelled to do so by Wyandance, the
Montaque chief and Lyon Gardiner.  It was necks of meadows
only, but was soon followed by a deed of the uplands.  Henry
Whitney, the grantee, was a man of note among the first settlers here and he officiated in the church here before there was
any regular minister employed.  These three necks of land
were located west of and adjoining the six necks previously
purchased and extended westward to the Oyster Bay line.
The one adjoining Oyster Bay Town was the subject of litigation, further on.—C. R. S.]

which was massapage Indian land called by them
tatamunehese weare for thomas weeks, william
Rogers, Richard ogden, Jonas wood, bartholoma
smith and Henry whisson amounting to sixteen hundreds this haulf neck did belong to y$^e$ above named
men to devide amongst them selves for their share
which they did : sum amendment was afterwards
given upon santipauge by the town to Jonas wood,
thomas weeks and Henry whisson of the same haulf
necke above said.*

(*Town Meetings, Vol. 1, p. 143.*)

[1659, Jan. 13.]

Mr leverg cleared the town of their ingagment conserning thar not doing the dam at the tim be for the cort the
13 of january ; 59.†

(*Town Meetings, Vol. 1, p. 344.*)

[*This was a valuation in a certain number of hundred
pounds upon a given tract and a division proportionate to the
amount of money, goods, or services paid or rendered. The
land was not immediately divided and the separate parcels
taken possession of, but certificates or records of the divisions,
were issued or made, which entitled the holder, to his share,
to be vested in him, or his heirs or assignees, at a future time,
by either resolutions at Town Meetings or by action of the
trustees of the town in later years.—C. R. S.]

[†Mr. William Leverich was the first minister in Huntington. He was born in 1608. He came in the "James" from
London to New England in 1633. Preached at Boston, Pisqua-
tagua, Plymouth, Duxbury and Sandwich, and came from the
latter place to Oyster Bay about 1653. He first came to Huntington about 1657, possibly earlier, and was the only minister
here until 1670. He died at Newtown, 1694. He built the
first mill at Huntington, and this paper refers to an agreement
concerning the construction or repair of the mill dam, connected with this mill, and it was on what is now known as Mill
Dam Lane, at the head of Huntington Harbour.—C R. S.]

## [FURTHER CONFIRMATION OF INDIAN DEED OF HORSE (LLOYDS) NECK.]

[1659, February 1.]

Oyster Bay Feb'y the first 1659.
Whereas it manifestly appeareth by sundry and clear by
due proof that Wyandank my father, Great Sachem of
Meantieut and also of Long Island did confirm and subscribe unto a bill of sale made betwixt Samuel Mayo, Peter
Wright and Daniel Whitehead of the one part and Ratiocan and Aspapam of the other part concerning a tract of
land lying and being to the north side of Huntington
bounds, commonly called, distinguished and known by the
name of Horse Neck. Thes are therefor to certify all and
every person and persons whatsoever that I Rioncom, son
to the afors$^d$ Sachem, being by both English and Indians
ordained and acknowledge Chief Sachem in his place, do
by virtue hereof, ratify and confirm all and every act and
acts by my father formerly confirmed.

The mark × Rioncom [seal.]

Testes : The mark of × Chacanico. The mark of × Pocan-
acke, Anthony Wright, John Richbell."

Copy from the records of the Manor of Queens Village
"vellum book," and entered in page 54, 3$^d$ book of the
Massachusetts Colony, Sept. 1., 1658.*

(*File Lloyd's Neck Papers C.*)

---

[*Wyandance, the great chief of all Long Island, a shadowy
and broken power, had passed away, and his son Rioncom
had succeeded him, and the people of Huntington still held
possession of Horse Neck in spite of all hostile deeds. Andrews, to still further strengthen himself, procured this further confirmation.—C. R. S.]

[TOWN MEETING.]

[1659, March 10.]

Record of Johnathon Rogers

At a Town meeting of y$^e$ Inhabitants of huntington : March y$^e$ 10th 1659 It was granted Jonathon Rogers That he should have all y$^e$ medow that fals within y$^e$ Range of his hous Lott : To him and his heirs for ever. This a true Copy taken out of y$^e$ old book by me John Corey Clerk : Aprill 27th 1683.*

(*Deeds*, *Vol.* 1, *p.* 147.)

---

[INDIAN DEED, CONFIRMATION OF

HALF NECK.]†

[1659, May 12.]

May 12th 1659.

Bee it known unto all men by this present writing y$^t$ I Wiandance Sachem of paumanuck doe grant and confirm unto Jonas Oood alias hallifax, that halfe neck of land which hee all Ready hath in possession and hath built upon I say I doe fully sell and Confirme unto him and his heires for ever so to act and dispose off as hee shal best see cause soe that he may improve y$^t$ halfe neck from y$^e$ water along

---

[*Some of the descendants of Jonathan Rogers claim to trace his ancestry as follows : son of Noah, who was a son of Joseph, who was a son of Thomas a passenger in the Mayflower, 1620, who was the son of John of Dedham, who was the son of Noah of Exter, who was the son of John the Martyr, 1555.—C. R. S.]

[†The premises here described seem to have been included in the former purchase by Jonas Wood from the Secetaque Indians of what was called "that half neck." It probably involved a dispute between the Massepagne and Secetaque tribes as to ownership.—C. R. S.]

y$^e$ Creeke unto the high way y$^t$ headeth it and for Confirmation hereof wee eave sett our hands and markes.

signed sealed and                        The Sachem ✕ his mark
delivered in y$^e$ pre-                                    his mark
sents of us.                           WEEAYCOMBONE ✕
   DAVID GARDINER              The mark of
   JEREMIAH CONKLING                      ✕
   LION GARDINER               BEBESECHACK
  This is a true Coppy of the orriginall extracted   By
                                Thomas Powell
                                        Rec$^r$

*(File No. 26, and Court Rec., p. 295.)*

---

## [TOWN MEETING.]

[1660, Feb 4.]

At a towne meting the 4 of February 1660 : it was a greed
that Timothy Conklen shalle keepe both his own hom lots
and his fathers and to lay down all Comonig and medowe
be longing to his own hous.*

  It wase all so a greed at the sam Town meeting that the
widow portar should have one acare of medow joyning to

---

[*Timothy Conklin was the son of John Conklin who came
from Nottinghampshire, England to Salem ; from Salem to
Southold, and thence to Huntington. Timothy and his brother John, Jun., and perhaps others settled in Huntington and
were the ancestors of those of the name here now. John Strickland (called Goodman or justice), was in Massachusetts as early
as 1630, and probably came with Winthrop. Thomas Benedict
was the son of William Benedict who came from Nottinghampshire, England, about 1639, and married Mary Bridgham, a passenger in the same ship he came in. Thomas Benedict came
from Southold to Huntington but soon moved to Norwalk,
Conn., where there are now numerous descendants. These men
were practically nominated justices here and appointed at Hartford, Conn., as Huntington at this time acknowledged the
juгisdiction of Connecticut.—C. R. S.]

Tho. Skudars 2 akers occupying it so longe as she liveth in the towne.

Mr. Stricklon and Jonas wood and Thomas Benidicke ware chosen magistrates and Jonas Holdsworth Clarke for Towne and Corte and Joseph Jeninges marshall.

*(Town Meetings Vol. 1, p. 347.)*

(1660, April 5.)

The 5th of aprell 1660 old latern tole Mr. wood it **wase** well if he did not sit in the stockes first.*

*(Court Rec. p. 27.)*

[TOWN MEETING. JOINING CONNECTICUT.]

[1660, April 10.]

The 10 of aprill 1660

in a town meeting it being put to vote conseining joyning to a jeurisdiction, the major vote was for to be under coniticot jeurisdiction.

Mr. Nicklos wright of osterbay do acknowlleg that whar as i sed Mr. Salltan of osterbay was a knafe and that I would prove hom so I do in for this presenc acknowleg that i did do hen rong in speaking so unadvisedly in speaking that which had no ground for and do forth with promis to pay in part

_____

[*According to Savage, Richard Latten, or Latting, came from England to Boston in 1638. He was in Hempstead in 1653, afterwards in Oyster Bay, and here in 1660 with his son Josiah, and remained here until about 1660 or 1663, when he was expelled from the town for refusing to acknowledge the supremacy of the New Haven Government. He had offended Mr. Wood, a Justice of the peace, who claimed the office under the Connecticut jurisdiction, was threatened with punishment in the stocks, but boldly intimated that Mr. Wood would get there first.—C. R. S.]

of the charg and trobell i have put hem to that is to say
Mr. Sallton 10 shilling toward the charges.*

*(Town Meetings, Vol. 1, p. 345.)*

---

[COURT RECORD—TRIAL OF MARY SUTTEN.]

[1660, April 13.]

Aprill the 13 : 1660.

Mary suten indited to the corte for kepenig and alltaring
the property of the goodes of lide higebe and likewise for
having corispondence with Mr. Mattnes his negar in pill-
faring.

gorge sotton indited likewise of being acesary thare unto
is conserning the goods of Lide higbe.

the deposition of mary tites this deponent sayeth when she
com to the mell she mete with mary soten which wase a
making a cote which the deponent take to be all coten and
it was in 2 peses and she asked mary soten what she make
that cot of and she sed it was a curtayn and the deponent
teke so much notes of it that it was not all to gathar news.

the deposition of Lide higbe this deponent sayeth that she
went to her bedestede and found 4 bisketes and she asked

---

[*From the first settlement down to this time, and a few
years later, Huntington was practically free from the control
of any outside government.  New Netherlands, with its head-
quarters at New Amsterdam, Manhattan Island, tried to en-
force its authority here but the people had never acknowledged Dutch authority, and had managed their affairs in their own
way.  The claim was now put forward that Long Island was
within the grant to Connecticut and the people here gladly
sought the protection of the Connecticut Colony from Dutch
pretensions ; sent deputies to Hartford and acknowledged its
authority until 1664, when the English conquered aud over-
threw the Government of New Netherlands, and under a grant
and charter to the Duke of York, Col. Richard Nicholls took
possession and enforced the obedience of the people here to
the Colonial Government of New York.—C. R. S.]

her dafter mary how thos bisket came thar she sed she
colld not tell but mary soten cam and sed they ware herses
but this deponent knoweth not how she com by them and
further she testifieth she herd mary soten speke to gorge
for bisket sevriall times and he sed he had none about him
then she spake to him to bring som the next tim he com
and he toulld her it may be he would.

The confession of Mary seton before Mr. Sticklon jonas
wood, thomas——wase her waskot wase made of a cote
an that her cote was mad parte of a pece of cloth broute
out of the tray by her mother and the other parte of a
pese of cloth boute of Mr. leverige and likewise she owned
that she had a cortayn that was lade higbes but she sed
she boroud it and likewise confesed that she never cared
it home agayne but sed it wase borent by her fathers
menes being at worke nere the fir with his ax strok it in
the fiar and so it wase borent in parte and the rest wase
throwen a bout the house and so lost she knew not what
became of it.

the verdit of the corte thay find threw her own confesion and
witnes broitin to the corte it is ordered that Mary seton
shall make full satisfackcion for the curtayn detayned
acording to the worth of the other curtaynes and that
mary soten shall be brout forth the next trayning day and
that on to be apinted by the magestrates to proclayme be
for the towne the crimes proved against her 1. her keping
away and alltaring the proparty of the goodes of lide
higbee and 2 that she have intesrted and used arguments
with a manes sarvant to play the thefe and stell from his
mastar that she might be the reserver.

and the cort se case to find good man seton gilltie in to he
up houlld his dafter in so sinful and evell a way and mayn-
tayneing her thar in by arguements of fallshod and for
which he is to give publick satisfackcion befor the trayn
band next, or this, pay 20 shilling.

(*Court Rec. p.* 14, 5.)

## [COURT RECORD. EDWARD HIGBEE'S ESTATE.]

[1660, May 12.]

the 12 of may it wase agreed by the Corte to demand the
will out of Jonas wood his hand which will belonged to
Edward higbee it wase allso agreed by the sam corte that
Thomas weeke Edward Tredwell John Tilot shall take an
inventary of the estate which is eqlent belonging to
Edward Higbee which inventory is to be taken the next
second day being the 14 of may in the yere 1660.

it was allso agreed by the sam cort that thos that are to

[*" Lide " Higbee was the wife of Edward Higbee who then
resided at the head of Huntington Harbor near where George
W. Scudder now resides.

This is inserted as a sample of the Court proceedings of the
times ; and not as having any special value otherwise. There
are in the book entitled "Court Records" the recorded minutes
of about thirty trials between 1659 and 1664, before Justices of
the Peace. Such as relate to title to land are printed in this
volume, but the most of them relate either to civil actions for
debt, or contract or criminal prosecutions for assault, slander
or other minor offences, of no interest now, except purely in a
historical point of view. The Court also exercised power of
probate, the proof of wills and settlement of estates.

There is no intimation in the records that the courts of this
period were controlled by any written laws unless it might be
some town meeting regulations.

They certainly did not recognize the Dutch laws. The
magistrates, being Englishmen, recognized the New England
jurisdiction,and at this time probably applied the unwritten common laws of England, as far as they understood it, and adopted
its methods of procedure. After the conquest in 1664, when
Gov. Nichols entered Manhattan Island and promulgated the
" Duke's Laws,"—an elaborate system of jurisprudence, under
the authority of the Duke of York,—these laws controlled the
courts, and there are a large number of cases of which minutes
are found in the volume above referred to, entitled Court
records, covering the period between 1664 and 1690. The
"Duke's laws" continued to be the laws here with a few modifi-
cations until about 1690. The well thumbed volume containing
them in manuscript, is now in the Town Clerk's Office, and
was used in all Courts here for a long period of years.—C. R. S.]

prise the estat of Edward higbee that thay shall leve
sufisient unprised as to leve his wife on sent of clothes for
evry day and on seute for Lordes dayes and allso that
which is convenient to cloth the children that is to say to
paralel with thar mothar.

it wase allso ordered by the same corte that Thomas
skidmor Junear wase to have the disposing of Edward
higbees 4 children tell thay are of age to provide for them
sellves in case theyr father by his coming se not; case to
allter what the cort hase don.*

(*Court Rec. p. 16.*)

[TOWN MEETING. RICHARD LATTING

BANISHED.]

[1660, June 28.]

the 28 of June 1660

It wase voted and agreed at a town meetin that ould
Laten† shalle take away his catell out of this town bounds
within a fort night or 14 days or pay to the town 10
shilling a head.

[*Edward Higbee seemed to have been engaged with Capt.
Mathews and Jonas Wood in a vessel trading with the West
India Islands, carrying barrel staves thither and bringing back
rum, sack &c. Probably he was absent on a voyage and was
assumed to have died abroad, hence the proof of his will &c.
That he did return is shown by the fact that he was afterwards, in the same year, a party to two lawsuits in the town,
unless, as is possible, it was his son Edward who was the
litigant.—C. R. S.]

[†This is Richard Latting, referred to, who was expelled for
refusing to recognize Connecticut's authority over Huntington.
The Court at Hartford subsequently made an order expelling
him from its jurisdiction on account of "turbulent conduct."—
C. R. S.]

All so itt wase ordered at the sam meting that oulld lating is to bring his catell and show them to 2 men home the town shall apint be fore he drive them away or to pay 5 poundes.

it was all so voted that Thomas Skidmore and jonas alldar shall make a rate for the skull house† and for wolf‡ * * * and all detes as consarn the town.

(*Town Meetings, Vol. 1, p. 344.*)

---

### [TOWN MEETING.]

[1660, Oct. 15.]

it was a greed at a towne meting the 15 of Ocktobar 1660 .that goodman* brush shall keepe the ordinary so long as hee do carry on his p * * * as he ought that thar be no just caus for the town to chaing thar mindes likwis————further ordered that ' no man shall w————this town drawe any lickars by re * * * * salle of it unless it be————and not under upon the forfet of * * * * * * that thay shall so drawe.

*Town Meetings Vol. 1, p. 347.*

---

[†This is the first mention of the building of a school-house. It was probably located at "the Old Town Spot" near where "Goose Green" now is.—C. R. S.]

[‡The wolf rate was an annual tax raised out of which to pay rewards for killing wolves, the skins of the animals having to be produced to entitle the party to the reward.—C. R. S.]

[* "Goodman" was a term, or prefix, indicating that the person was of more than ordinary prominence as a citizen and was usually applied to persons of considerable age. Thomas, or Goodman Brush was born about 1610, and came from Southold to Huntington about 1656-7. He left children; Thomas, John, Richard and Rebecca, who all settled in Huntington. Thomas, Sr., is believed to be the ancestor of all the persons of the name of Brush, now in Huntington. The "ordinary" was in those days a public house or hotel. He was the first keeper of the "Ordinary" mentioned and this is the first excise law here of which we have any record.—C. R. S.]

## [COURT RECORD. THOMAS SCUDDER vs. EDWARD HIGBEE.]

[1660, Oct. 17.]

Thomas Skodar plainive against Eadward higbe defendant in an ackcion of defamasion to the damag of a hundred pound the plaintive declaimeth that Eadward higbe hase charged hem that he and his wife are both in fere of thur lifes of the plantife.

the defendant ownes the cnarg.

the 17 of ocktto. 1660.

thomas skodar plaintive against Eadward higbe defendant in an ackcion of slandar to damag of twenti pound the plaintive declameth that the defendant charged hem with the houlding of hem by the throt hallf an oure, the deposition of good Laten he deposeth that good higbe sed that thomas skoddar tok hem by the throt and helld hem hallf an ouar or thar about and all most throtelled hem.

for the first ackion of the cost Thomas skodars Eadward higbe is to give publick satisfackcion or pay the Skoddar five poundes with the cost and charg of the cort.

for the second the cort finds for the pla$^t$ that the defendant shall give publock satisfac$^t$ or pay 20 shilling and all so to pay 10 shilling for his ly with the cost and charge of the cort.*

(*Court Rec., p. 28.*)

[*This was Thomas Scudder, Jr., son of Thomas Scudder, Sr., who is believed to have been a son of Dr. Henry Scudder, who presided at a Convention of clergymen appointed by order of the King, at Westminster Abbey, England, in 1643. Thomas Sr., came from Groton, England, in 1636. His wife's name was Elizabeth; and he settled at Salem, Mass. in 1642, and died there in 1657, leaving children, John, Thomas, Henry and Elizabeth. John, Thomas and Henry came to Huntington via. Southold about 1653 to 6. Thomas was a farmer and tanner. He settled near the head of Huntington Harbor and died in 1690. His homestead has remained in his descendants to the present time and is now owned by Geo. W. Scudder and John R. Scudder.—C. R. S.]

## [TOWN MEETING.]

[1660, Oct. 18.]

The 18 of ocktober 1660
it was a gred that the towne will mend the hywaye between
the towne and the south and to begin on the marow so far
as the hyway is in generall and who ever is wanting for
everi days work thay shall do a days work and a halfe in
such worke in the towne as shall be apointed to them by 2
men agreed upon by the towne and if any man refeus being
abell to go to marow he shall pay fife shillinges.

(*Town Meetings, Vol.* 1, *p.* 345.)

## [TOWN MEETING.]

[1660, Oct. 19.]

it was voted and agreed at a town meting the 19 of ocktober 1660 that the inhabitans shall have libarti to fall whit
ookes in any part of the towne bounds exsept in any manes
propriaty for the making of pipstaves.*

(*Town Meetings, Vol.* 1, *p.* 345.)

## [COURT RECORD.   WILLIAM LUDLAM vs.
## HENRY WHITNEY.]

[1660, Oct. 25.]

at a courte held in huntington octobar 25. 1660:
William ludlam in an action of the case against henery
whitne defendant.

---

[*Quite a trade had sprung up with the Barbadoes and other
Islands for the sale of barrel staves about this time.   The staves
being used in the manufacture of casks for rum and other
liquors.—C. R. S.]

The plantif declars aganst the defendant for breach of covenant or covenants made by the defendant to or with Mr. Leverich his eyers or assigns concerning the mill the non-parformance whereof hath bin to his greate Damage to the valou of one hundred pound starling :

first branch of the second covenant found broken formrly : second brance pleaded as broken by the defendant that he had not eused all posable menes to goodman web or som other men the defendant answer he did git a work-man in the spring to ben the mill.

the plaintiff pleads the 2 brance broken because the defendant did not git good man Webe to be the man or at leaste one of them that did ben the mill.

defendant answer he was not bound absolutely to good man webb but to any other suffeciant work man : and therefore he did erly in the Spring send to henery lininton by Mr. Stickling to come to ben the mill : atested by him the defendant presents the detarmynasion of sargant hubbard and John simons, touching the mill and ther detarminasion.*

The vardit of the Courte in this acsion runs thus they finde the tenor of the covenant runs expresly boeth in the first and second branch of it that the defendant is bound to git goodman webb to ben the mill if posable he cann & obtayne him therfore we thus conclude that the defendant must still euse all posable menes to obtayne him and to doe it according to his direction or else git him to doe it for him unles good man ludlam and the defendant can agree otherwise or the defendant cannot git goodman webb then any other approved workman, which we finde answers the covenant

---

[*This was the first flour mill built in Huntington and was located on "Mill Dam Lane." "Goodman" Webb was a millwright living at Stamford or Norwalk, Conn. The Mr. Leverich referred to was William Leverich, the first minister in Huntington, he having sold the mill to William Ludlam. The latter brought the suit for damages for breach of contract.—C. R. S.]

and that the defendant must pay so much charge of courte
as he must have payd at the quarter courte namely 6s. the
acsion and other charge, the rest must be borne by the
plaintif as unnessesarry charge.

(*Court Rec. p. 29.*)

---

[1660, Oct. 26.]

a second acsion. comenst by William ludlam plainetif
against henery whitne defendant in an acsion of trespas for
breking the mill and grinding severall times without his
leve to his greate damage.

the defendant deny the breking of the mill but confesed
he opened the dore : and went and ground his corne, his
famely being all sick none abell to beate, he went to inquire
for the kei but could not her of it for he was gone to the
south and his famely with himselve, being like to famish he
was constraynd to do it : yet notwithstanding he gave the
miller his just towle : the vardit of the courte in this acsion
is this they finde the defendant was nessisitated to y$^t$ he did
and the plaintif sufered no damage.

(*Court Rec. p. 30.*)

---

## [WILL OF HENRY SCUDDER.]

[1661, Jan. 25.]

The last will and Testament of Henry Scuddar late of
Huntington, Deceased, Made the 25 of January 1661.

I Henry Scudder being in right understanding and per-
fect memory, Do Dispose of my estate as ffolloweth : first I
make my wife Catherin Scudder my whole and sole executor and to foure of my Children (viz) Moses, David, Mary
and Rebeccah Scuddar, I do give ten pound a peece ; to
each of them And to my oldest sonne Jonathan Scuddar I

do give a Duble portion (to wit) twenty pounds together
with yᵉ house and Lands wᵗʰ his Grandfather* left him (by
will) And all this their severall portions I do appoint to be
paid to them out of my Estate by my said Executor, as
they shall come to age or at the Day of their Marriages.
This is my whole minde & will.
Witnessed upon Oath
by HENRY WHITNEY
    EDWARD FFRENCHAM.
    (*Court Rec. p.* 50.)

[INVENTORY OF GOODS, &c. OF EDWARD
               TREDWELL.]

[1661, Jan. 30.]

The 30th of January 1661.

An Inventory of the goods & estate of Edward Tredwell
late of Huntington Deceased ; given in by his Wife beeing
upon Oath ; And valewed by ffoure Men Chosen, and appointed by Authority, (viz) William Smith, Thomas
Weekes, John Conklin, & John Titus, The vallew where of
amounteth to two hundred eighty five pounds, (sterling)*

The Widow having a third part thereof, commeth to
Ninety five pounds, And the six Children having the resȝ
divided among them, each Childs portion cometh to thirty

[*The "Grandfather" was Jeffrey or Geffrey Esty, whose
daughter Catherine married Henry Scudder, the father of Jonathan Scudder.—C. R. S.]

[†Edward Tredwell is believed to have been a son of Thomas
and Mary Tredwell, who came from London to New England
in the "Hopewell" in 1635. Edward came here ,via. Southold
about 1659, perhaps earlier. He married Phœbe, a daughter
of Epenetus Platt. John Tredwell was a brother of Edward
Tredwell.—C. R. S.]

one pound, thirteen shillings foure pence his oldest Sonne having had som thing given him by his ffather in his life tiem,

Doth in this estate but share equally with y<sup>e</sup> rest of the Children.

*(Court Rec. p. 50.)*

_____

## [TOWN MEETING.]

[1661, Feb. 8.]

at a Town Meeting of the Inhabitants of Huntington. Feb. 8, 1661 it was concluded and agreed that all the rates now made shall be gathered and payed between this day and the 15th of March next insueing upon the penalty of ten shillings to be forfeited to the rate gatherer if he discharge his trust by making demand of every inhabitant; & for his neglect in his office in not making seasonable demand, he is to forfeit five pounds to the town ; at which time Jonathan Rogers was chosen Rate-gatherer.

[Copied from original, bound with C, Records.]
    *(Town Meetings, Vol. 1, p. 351.   Court Rec., p. 52.)*

_____

[1661, March 30.]

It was ordered by the Court March y<sup>e</sup> 30th 61.

            s    d                    d
That a warrent shall be 10 ; 4 y<sup>e</sup> making & 6 serving.

            s    d                d
A Tachment 18 ; 6 y<sup>e</sup> making, & 12 y<sup>e</sup> serving An Exe-
        s    d  d                d
cution    2 ; 6, 6 y<sup>e</sup> making, & 2 y<sup>e</sup> Destress.

    *(Court Rec., p. 30.)*

## (COURT RECORD. ESTATE OF SAMUEL WHEELER.)

(1661, May 1.)

Bee it known unto all Men by these pr<sup>s</sup>ents That I Moses Wheeler of Stratford in the Jurisdicktion of Connecticut, (having taken administration of the goods and Lands of Samuell Wheeler my kinsman late of Huntington Deceased) Doe hereby binde my selfe my heairs, Executors, and administrators to y<sup>e</sup> Court of Huntington, in the Summe of eighty pounds sterling to Dispose of the sd. estate of y<sup>e</sup> sd. Samuell Wheeler (his kinsman Deceased) according to his minde and will so farre forth as hee Did expresse it, at, or before his Death; (viz) to Mariem Wheeler y<sup>e</sup> Daughter of y<sup>e</sup> sd. Moses Wheeler five pounds; to his sisters Children if shee have any; or to her if shee have none twenty pounde; and twenty shillings to a Neiger Boy of Mr. Mathews; And to secure the rest of his estate, (all Just Debts being Discharged) in his owne hands (if no further Demande be made by any that are nearer of kinne) the terme of three years; ffor the true performance whereof I Do hereunto set my hand, this twenty first Day of May 1661.

MOSES WHELER.

---

The 12th of Aprill 1661.
An Inventory taken of the Estate of Samuell Wheeler late of Huntington, Deceased, by Richard Ogden & Joseph Smithe, both of y<sup>e</sup> same plantation; being prized by them as ffolloweth.

| | £ | s. | d. |
|---|---|---|---|
| Imprim, the house, Lande & accomodations | 20 | 00 | 00 |
| "     one two yeare Mare | 08 | 00 | 00 |
| "     one horse | 09 | 00 | 00 |
| "     two Cowes | 10 | 00 | 00 |
| "     one yeare old Calfe | 01 | 10 | 00 |
| "     one two yeare steare | 02 | 10 | 00 |
| "     five swine & a halfe swine | 05 | 10 | 00 |
| "     one Bed & wearing Cloths<br>      with some other small things | 09 | 10 | 00 |
|                   Suma. | 66 | 00 | 00 |

*(Court Rec. p. 51.)*

---

## (COURT RECORD. ESTATE OF JONATHAN PORTER.)

(1661, May 1.)

Know all men by these p^rsents, that I Giles Smith of ffair-
field ; doe binde my selfe, my Heires, Executors and Administrators to pay unto the three Daughters of Jonathan
Porter late of Huntington Deseased (viz) Elizabeth, Eunis,
and Mary ; or to their Heires (in Case that any of the sd.
three sisters Die before their Mother) the full and Just
summe of twenty pounds sterling, at the Decease of their
Mother Eunis Smith. Which sd. twenty pounds the sd.
three sisters, Elizabeth Eunis, and Mary, with the Approbation of their Husbands ; Do accept of, for full satisfaction for what portions was left them by their ffatheres last
will and testament ;*

---

[*Jonathan Porter died in Huntington iu 1660. He was at
Salem, Mass., in 1636, and came to Huntington about 1654.
Eunice Porter married James Chichester ; Elizabeth married
Edward Harnet, and Mary married Stephen Jarvis, all then res-
idents of Huntington. The widow of Jonathan Porter, Eunice,
married Giles Smith.—C. R. S.]

In witnesse whereof I Do hereunto set my hand, this twenty first of May 1661.

Testese GILES SMITH.

Jonas Houldsworth Clerk.

*(Court Rec. p. 49.)*

---

(TOWN MEETING.)

(1661, Dec. 2.)

At a towne meting the 2 of desambar 1661.

Mr. Sticklen and William Smith, thomas benidick ware chosen by the townes consent to end any differance between naybar and naybar in and by every waye untell the next court of election (or session) at harford and in case the delinquent refuse to apare before them to answar, it is the townes mind that either of them shall have power to grante a warant or warants to compell him or thay to make thare aparance and stand to the a ward and all so it is agreed that the plantive and defendant shall have liberty to chuse either of them a man to have the hering and thar vote desiding the mater in difference betwext them and in case thare bee any crimmall case committed by any person or persons of the towne or any stranger that shall com to towne and any way transgrese thay above menciond have powr to send for examin and punish ackording to the quality of the crime and allso these three above mencioned to have power to call in such as they thinke mete to asist them in the matar depending. and also it was agreed that in habitans shall have against strangers and strangars against inhabitants the benefit of this authoryty will so fere as they authoryty will reache.

*(Town Meetings, Vol. 1, p. 346-8.)*

## [TOWN MEETING.]

[1662, Feb. 10.]

ffebuerary the 10th 1662.

at a town meetting it was this day ordered that the bootte should bee sent to Conitucott Rivers mouth to fech Captine Seele* to this Towne upon the Townes choose and that to be sent the first opurtunity. Secondly it was the same day ordered that Thomas weekes and Thomas Joanes† should doe their best to by a house and land in the Towne to be and continue the Townes for the use and beniffit of yᵉ ministrey there in to enttertain a minisster

at the same Towne meting Thomas Skudder wase chosen by the Towen To calle for an atachment and deliver it to the Cunstabell for to * * * * prize or Seese upon the house and Land which wase Samuell whellams desesed for an order broken by moses whellar whidh ordar wase made the 6 of July 1661

(*Town Meetings*, Vol. 1, *p.* 354.)

---

[*Robart Seely, at one time owned Eaton's Neck and land on West Neck. His wife, Mary, was a sister of the celebrated Capt. John Manning. He was killed in an Indian War in New England about 1675.—C. R. S.]

[†Thomas Joanes is believed to be identical with a person of this name at Elzing, in Norfolk, England, who left Ipswich for N. E. with William Andrews 1637, in the "John and Doratha," as appears in "Hotton's Lists." He married Catharine Esty, widow of Henry Scudder. He was probably a brother of Rev. John Joanes. See Trumbull's Colonial Records.—C. R. S.]

[TOWN MEETING.]

[1662, Feb. 19.]

At a towne meting being The 19 of febary 1662. John
lome Jeames Chichester* were chosen deputies for to send
to the Corte of election helld at harford next may being in
the yeare 1663.

(*Town Meetings, Vol. 1. p. 350.*)

---

[TOWN MEETING.]

[1662, Feb. 19.]

At a Towne meting the 19 of feberary 1662. it was agreed
by the magar vote that if any of the inhabitants of huntington shall aftar the last of march next insewing shall
ither by way of gifte or paye do give or selle entartane-
ment to Richard Laten for more than the spase of on
weeke every person so ofending shall pay forty shillinges
fine for every time he shall ofend in brakeing this order
made for the pease of the Towne.

(*Town Meetings, Vol. 1, p. 353.*)

---

[TOWN MEETING. GRANT TO REV. WM.
LEVERICH.]

[1662, June 7.]

at a towne meting of the inhabitents of huntington aboute
the 7th of June 1662 : it was agreed and by vote granted :

---

[*James Chichester was the son of James Chichester, Sr.,
who was at Taunton, Mass., in 1643, and Salem in 1650. The
name was originally spelled "Circencester." James, Jr., resided at Huntington Harbor.—C. R. S.]

that Mr Leverich shall have all the meddow y$^t$ lyes aboute cowharbor on boeth sides the creeke, for his yerly benifit, so lang as he continue the minester of huntington.*

(*Town Meetings, Vol. 1, p. 350.*)

---

## [TOWN MEETING.]

### [1662, June 7.]

June the 7th 1662 : it was this daye ordered that thar shall be no foote way through goodman chichesters lot ; nor shall any person or persons have liberty to pass y$^t$ waye as formerly withoute leave : upon the penalty of paying all damages that shall be done in the same house lott in corne or otherwise :

(*Town Meetings, Vol. 1, p. 346.*)

---

## [TOWN MEETING. APPLICANTS FOR SETTLEMENT TO BE APPROVED.]

### (1662, July 6.)

July the 6th 1662.
it is this day ordered by the townesmen of Huntington that no man possing house or lands in this town shall not at any time sell or lett or any way alinatte any part of such houses or lands to any man or woman but such as shall be aproved of by such men as the towne have chosen for that purpose p.vided they receit not such men as are honest as are well approved of by honest and xpditious men only such men as have bene freely entertained into

---

[*These salt meadows were probably located about the head of Northport Harbour.—C. R. S.]

the towne as inhabitants have thar libertie to by and whomsoever shall breake this above mentioned order shall pay 10 ten pound to the towne. the men chosen by the towne to aprove of such as shall be presented to them are as followeth.

Mr Leverge.    Will Smith

Thos. Weekes,    John Lum,

Goodman Jones,    James Chi-

chesler   and   Jonas Wood.

Likwis it was ordered at the same towne Metting that James Chichester shoulld keep the ordinary the town Chos him and he exepted of it.

(Town Meetings, Vol. 1, p. 354.)

## [TOWN MEETING.]

[1662, July, 16.]

At a towne meting of the inhabitants of huntington July 16th 1662. it was ordered that what man soever of our inhabitants being legaly chosen to the ofice of a constable shall refuse to serve for the yer insuing shall forthwith pay for his refusall thre pounds as a fine to the towne.

(Town Meetings, Vol 1, p. 350.)

## [COURT RECORD. THOMAS MATHEWS vs. JOANNA WOOD.]

[1662, July 29.]

At a Courte held in huntington July 29th 1662 :
Mr Thomas Mathus plaintif against Joanna wood widdow adminestratix to Jonas wood defendant; in an acsion of

debt for fifty four pound two shilling two pence.

the plaintif declareth in writing

Mr John simons of hemstead apered to the case as an atorny for Joanna wood widdow he denyes the charge.

Thomas powell deposed sayth, y$^t$ the writings y$^{ts}$ in his masters books was redd to good higbe or good wood one or boeth of them he cannot tell which : viz : that partecular accountes his master good wood and good higbee : touching the 6 pipes of wine and the pipe of rum : when it was writ his master red it to him or them and ast if it wer well, and one of them answered yes and this was at oyster baye in danill whiteheds house and he furder sayth, he knew no other entery in his masters books aboute wines as touching them but that before menshoned and furder sayth that liveing with his master almoste nigne yers he never knew his masters books questioned in the leaste.

Mr Mathus tooke his oath that the entery in his booke touching the case above entered is a true entery and that the winds ther menshoned was delevered aborde the boate upon acount for Edward higbe Jonas wood and him selff.

The verdit of the jury they finde for the plaintif that the debt demanded is just and due which the defendant must pay and forty shillings damage and court charges.

The jurymen upon this acsion wer Tho. wicks, Jams chichester : Tho. Jones : Richard williams, steven Jarvice : Samwell Titus.

(*Court Rec. p.* 34.)

----

## [DEED.  WILLIAM JONES TO ROBERT SEELY.]

[1662, December 22.]

Know all men by these presents that I Wm. Jones of New Haven in New England Planter, in the Right of my wife Hannah Jones otherwise Eaton Daughter of Theophilus

Eaton Esq. late Governor of New Haven Colony, deceased, unto whom the lands herein mentioned were given or granted by Rusurocon Sagamor of Cutunomack in the presence of sundry Indians ———

Have, for and in consideration of the sum of Fifty pounds Sterling, Bargained assigned sold and set over and by these presents do bargain assign sell and set over unto Captain Robert Ciely All that Island commonly called Eaton's Neck on the Eastward of Oyster Bay otherwise Huntington Bay together with a parcel of land upon Long Island joining thereunto to the Eastward called Oyster Bay otherwise Huntington Bay as follows, viz: All Meadows, Woods, ways, water courses, passages, privileges, Immunities and appurtenances thereunto belonging to have use and occupy possess and enjoy to him the said Robert Ciely his heirs and assigns for ever for and in consideration of the said fifty pounds by him the said Robert Ciely to be paid to me the said William Jones my Executors Administrators and Assigns as follows—viz. Ten pounds sterling of the said sum in good current Pay with the Merchant on or before the 25th of March 1664 and ten pounds of like pay yearly on the said 25th of March (at his house in New Haven) every year until the said sum of fifty pounds be fully satisfied and paid and I do give the said Captain Ciely full power to enter upon and possess the said lands and premises and by law to sue for and recover the same from any person or persons unduly claiming or detaining the same or any part or parcel thereof.

In Witness whereof we have hereunto interchangeably set our hands and seals this 22nd day of December 1662.

(Signed) WM. JONES.

Sealed and delivered }
in the presence of }

WILLIAM CUBBELL
THOMAS HEWETT or JEWETT

Recorded in the Office at New
York the 12<sup>th</sup> day of August 1667.*
Matthias Nicoll, Secy.

*(File Eaton's Neck Papers, A.)*

---

## [DEED.  EDWARD HARNET TO JOHN SAMMIS.]

[1663, Jan. 20.]

This bill Testifeth that I Edward harnit off huntington
on Long eiland and inhabitant in huntington have Bargoned and sould unto John Samwayes of the same towne
a house and lot lynig at the Reare of Thomas brush,
Reareing at the mil pond for the some of ten pounds with
al the accomidacons Belonging there unto as a lot of too
hundred pounds : And doe here by alinate it from my self
eaires and assignes ffor ever to bee the proper Right of the
afore said John Samways his heirs and assignes for ever
and Doe Confirme the same by seting unto my hand this
20th Day of Jenuary in the yeare of our Lord 1663 in the
presence of these witnesses.

ROBERT SEELY scrib                    EDWARD HARNETT
CONTENT TYTUS
this is a true Coppy writen
by mee, Joseph Bayly
Rec<sup>r</sup>
*(Court Rec., p 322.)*

---

[*This is the first in the order of date of a series of papers
relating to the title to the soil of Eaton's Neck, a title which
was subsequently disputed and litigated in the Courts.  From
the papers and documents on record it appears that the Matin-
necock Indians sold Eaton's Neck to Governor Theophilus
Eaton in 1646.  A certificate signed by the Indians, that such a
deed was given was recorded in New Haven, dated in 1663, but
the original deed is not found   A copy of the certificate is filed
here.  The grantor in the above deed, William Jones, married,
as therein stated, Hannah Eaton, a daughter of Theophilus Eaton, and he thereby acquired the title and by this deed conveyed
Eaton's Neck to Robert Seeley —C. R. S.]

(TOWN MEETING.)

[1663, April 6.]

at a towne meting the 6 of Aprell 1663 Captaine Selle Jonas Wood, Thomas wekes were chosen by the towne to
send thar names to harforde for the Corte to Electe of them
for magestrates.
at the sam Towne meting John Lome was chosen constable
at the sam towne meting Isack plate wase chosen to be the
mesengar to Mr bonaws.
at the same meting Jonas wood, Tho. wekes, Thomas
Jones, Jone lome, Edward harnet Jeames Chichester ware
chosen to chose fremen and Jonas wood Tho. wekes.,
Thomas Jones, Tho. Skidmor were chosen to wright the
letar to Mr bonaws.  Mr. Jones his son
        (*Town Meetings, Vol. 1, p. 353.*)

---

[TOWN MEETING.]

[1663, April 27.]

At a towne meting the 27 of Aprell. 1663 it wase ordered
that all fenses that are in generall either about felldes or
hom lotes are to be sofisently mended within 3 days after
this meting or else for every rode thatt shall be found de-
fetetive by the men that are chosen to vew the fense for
every rode being not jodged sufisent the owenar of the
fense shall pay 5 shilling fine it was furthar ordared the
sam meting that for time to com all fenses shall be sofisently repared by the 10 of March or for every rod that
shall be found defeteive by the vewares thos that thar
fense shall be unrepayred the 11 of march shall pay 5 shilling a rod.

and at the sam meting willam Lodlom and Jonathan Rog-
ares ware chosen to vew the west end fenses and Thomas
skuddar and henary whison to vew the este end fenses.
the 27 of aprell 1663.  goodman Chichester wase chosen
to be the ordinary keeper and none but he for the entar-
taynement of straingares and that no towns man shall sell
any strong drinke to straingares by or sell but the towns
men have libarty to by or sell on of a nothar or of a stran-
gar to the quantity of a quart but not undar upon the forfet of dubell the vallue of what thay so selle or drawe ithar
straingar or towen dwellar.
   (*Town Meetings, Vol.* 1, *p.* 355 )

[TOWN MEETING.  BOUNDARIES  OF LANDS
         TO BE RECORDED.]

[1663, June 1.]

At a Towne meting the 1 of Jeune 1663.  Captain Sele,
Thomas weekes, Thomas brush Isacke Plate* were chosen
by the Towne to take a vew of all landes allredy layd out
in feldes and to record the ownar and the quantity he has
taken up in the town booke and allso thes fowar men have
power for to lay out and to dispose of the land a cordin to

[*Isaac and Epenetus Platt were brothers and sons of Richard Platt, who is claimed to have been the common ancestor of
all of the name in this country.  Richard came to America in
1638 from Hertfordshire, England.  He was at New Haven in
1638 and died there in 1684.  Isaac and Epenetus first make
their appearance here about this time, 1663, and probably came
to Southold and then to Huntington.  Isaac married Elizabeth,
daughter of Jonas Wood and left children as follows : Elizabeth,
Jonas, Joseph, John, Mary and Jacob.  He died in 1691.  Epenetus Platt married Phœbe, probably a daughter of Jonas Wood,
and left children Phœbe, Mary, Epenetus, Hannah, Elizabeth,
Jonas, Jeremiah, Ruth and Sarah.  He died in 1693, after holding many official positions.—C. R. S.]

fellds or hom Lotes so as may condus to the most advanc-
ing of thos as need land to inprofe and so to lay out as it
may not prof presidiciall to the comanes (as nere as they
can) or town plat and to record all such landes so layd out
in the towns booke and for every acar layd out by thes
men the person imploying them are by the magar vot of
the towne epoynted to pay six pence the acare.

(*Town Meetings, Vol.* 1, *p.* 356.)

## [TOWN MEETING.]

[1663, June 6.]

at a towne meting the 6th of Juene it was agreed at the
sam meting that the towne plat shall be fenced in for the
generall good for keping calfes and shepe and horses and
for the keping hoges out of the towne and tow men to be
chosen to mesur the ground to give in what quaintity of
fence it will amount to and Captain sely and good Finch
ware chosen to mesuar the fence.*

(*Town Meetings, Vol.* 1, *p.* 353.)

## [COURT RECORD.]

[1663, July 3.]

this ordared by the Cort, hild the 3th of July 1663 for the
wrighting a warant 4 pence. and it is furthar orderd for
the sarving a warant eight p$^{nc}$ an atachment eighteen pence

---

[*John Finch, according to "Hotton's Lists," came from London in the "George" in 1635, then aged 27. He died here in
1685. Some of his lands were sold at an "out cry" to pay rates.
—C. R. S.]

and sirving six pence writing an execution tew shilling
six pence.

for entring an axion. for the clarke 2 shillings six pence, for
witeneses for a man to shillings and for a woman twelfe
pence.

for the Jury for evry Action six shillinges and for evry
Action hered by the magestrates or Commisonars ten
shillinges and to the Cort six shilinge.

  (*Court Rec., p.* 37.)

---

## [DEED JONAS WOOD TO JOHN COREY.]

  [1663, July 7.]

 this writing witnesseth that I Jonas wood inhabitant in
huntington have sold and made over to John Core* of the
same town all the housing and land both home lot and
comonedg so fare as belongeth to a hundred pound lote
that was formerly my father Edmone woodes the medow
now belonging to it excepted, I the afore sayd Jonas wood
do by thes presenc and according to the premises above
expresed fully make over from me my eyers executers
administrators or assines unto John Core his ayers, executors administrators or asines the afore mentioned hous and
home lott with all the priveledges there unto belonging
the medow excepted to Remain free from any clayme or
molestation of me or my ayers for ever, and the afore sayd
John Core is to take possession of the hous now and of
the land at mikellmus or so soon as the crope is of, witnesse
my hand this 7th of July 1663 JONAS WOOD, witnesse

---

 [*John Corey seems to have been a man of considerable
influence. He came from Southold to Huntington. He married Mary Cornish, who survived him. His children were
Mary, Abigail, Elizabeth, John, Martha, Elnathan, Thomas
and Abraham.—C. R. S.]

ROBART SEELYE, THOS. SKIDMOR; this is A true Coppye
Extracted out of the originall by me.　　　John Core.

　　　　　　　　　　　　　　　　　　　　　Recor<sup>d</sup>.

(*Court Rec., p.* 327.)

---

[CERTIFICATE THAT A DEED OF EATON'S
NECK WAS GIVEN TO THEOPHILUS
EATON IN 1646.]

[1663, Aug. 17.]

This Recorded at y<sup>e</sup> Desire of Robart seelie.

We whose names are under written doe afirme & testifie
that Resorokon sagamore of Ketanomocke of Long Island
now called by the English Huntington Did give & grant
to Theophilus Eaton Esq<sup>r</sup> and Goverher of Newhaven,
(now deceased) to hime his heirs and assignes forever a
Neck of land lying on y<sup>e</sup> east side of Huntington Harbor
next y<sup>e</sup> sound towards the Mayne, together w<sup>th</sup> a tract of
land adjoining to y<sup>e</sup> Bay called Cow bay, on the east side
of it, Reaching Westward to a Runlet of water y<sup>t</sup> cometh
into the same Bay southward, w<sup>ch</sup> Runlit hath a gr<sup>t</sup> Hole
w<sup>th</sup> a gr<sup>t</sup> Rock in y<sup>e</sup> bottom, hard by the path way y<sup>t</sup> goes
from Huntington unto Neseguanke & from the head of y<sup>e</sup>
Runlit south into y<sup>e</sup> Island to y<sup>e</sup> middle of a gr<sup>t</sup> Plaine
halfe——Breadth of y<sup>e</sup> Island, and from y<sup>e</sup> s<sup>d</sup> Cow Bay
eastward it lyeth by the sea or sound four or five miles or
thereabouts reaching to a little river west to Nesseynank
great River of y<sup>e</sup> west side of it called the fishing River.
and from y<sup>e</sup> end of y<sup>t</sup> River southward it Runs on y<sup>e</sup> point
soe to y<sup>e</sup> Middle of y<sup>e</sup> playne toe y<sup>t</sup> Line upon the Plaine
w<sup>ch</sup> is y<sup>e</sup> Reare of the land lieth east & west. We doe
all affirme that Resorocon above sd. was the sole Propretor
of it as his owne proper Right, and did freely give it to

theophilus Eaton then Govero$^r$ of Newhaven as above sd. with all the lands, trees, meadows, springs. Rivers, water courses & all other preveledges & appurtenances belonging to y$^e$ sd. land, or any pt of it, we affirme was given as above sd. to Mr Eaton, his heairs & asignes for ever, and that this guift was given as above sd. in y$^e$ yeare 1646, one thousand six hundred forty & six, and to the truth heere-of we Confirme the same by setting to o$^r$ hands In the presence of these English Wittneses this 17th day of Aug$^{st}$ 1663.*

Test
ABIELL TITUS
her
ELEASER × LEVERIGE
mark

his
MUS × QUAT
mark

his
NOSCOSIT × mark
his mark
WARING × TOWN
his mark
SAUGHT × GRUM
his mark
NEAMSE × MAYE

---

[*As will be noticed by the description, this deed included, with Eaton's Neck, all the territory east of Northport Harbor to Smithtown River, and south to the middle of the Island. This was, as far as we know, the first purchase from the Indians in the boundaries of Huntington, and, with the exception of Southampton and perhaps Southold, the first within any town in Suffolk County. The circumstance that this deed was made to the Governor of the Colony of New Haven reminds us that the Indian deed to East Hampton was given to Theophilus Eaton, as Governor of the Colony of New Haven, and Edward Hopkins, Governor of the Colony of Connecticut, in 1648. Mr. Pelletrau, in his history of Southold, thinks that the lost Indian deeds to that town were made to Governor Eaton under the auspices and direction of the general court at New Haven. Such may have been the case here. There is no evidence of any settlement under it until after the Indian purchase of 1653, embracing the territory on the southwest, but it is possible there might have been inhabitants there at an earlier time.—C. R. S.]

This writing above specified & that therein was wittnissed by these p,tyes whose names are subscribed & marks, the day & yeare above written.

Before me.

ROBART SEELY

This is a true Record of the Originall examned p mee James Bishop

secretary.

Extracted out of New haven towne Records begun Augᵗ 1662-page 3 at yᵉ end of sd. book & agrees there of as attested.

By me Wᵐ Jones, Recorᵈ

(*File Eaton's Neck papers, B.*)

---

[TOWN MEETING.]

[1663, Oct. 2.]

at a towne meting the 2 of ockto. bar 1663.

Calebe Cornell and Tho. Skidmor were chosen to make the rate for the pay for the house* wase boute of Mʳ Leveridg.†

---

[*This refers to the house which the people had at a town meeting voted to build for Mr. Wm. Leverich in which "to entertain the ministry."—C. R. S.]

[†The first settlers of Huntington, like those of other towns in Suffolk County, were Puritans, and formed a part of the immigration to New England, impelled chiefly by religious persecution occasioned by acts of conformity enforced by Star Chamber Courts, the Conventicle and Test Acts, and other harrassing acts of Parliament, which continued until the Toleration Act in 1691. They held to the doctrines contained in the Confession of Faith adopted at Westminster, 1642, and were in church government Congregational and so continued until 1747, when there was a change in part to the Presbyterian form. After the English revolution of 1688, the colonial governor, members of his council, and other officers, sent here from England, were members of the established church, Episcopalians, and their

at the sam meting it wase voted and agreed that Mr Wood
should be fre from paying to the charg of sending depetyes.
(*Town Meetings, Vol.* 1, *p.* 356.)

---

## [TOWN MEETING.]

### [1663, Nov. 2.]

at a towne meeting the 2ⁿ of november 1663 it was ordered
and agreed on by vote that thos that bring in estates for
the making of rates that they shall bring in show what
estat of catell horse cind or swine and if any do not bring
in all what they leve out shall be forfited the on half to the
town and the other half to him or them that give intilegence
conserning any that shall be defecent provided it be aprov
by thos that give inteligence.
(*Town Meetings, Vol.* 1, *p.* 1.)

---

## [DEED.  JOHN GOSBY TO JAMES MILLS.]

### [1663, Nov. 27.]

Be it known to all men by thes presents that wee John
and Mary Gosby of Huntington one Long Island ffor a
valuable consideration have bargened and sould and by

---

official power was exerted in most of the towns to compel a
support of the established church by taxation. They never
succeeded in this as to Huntington, tbough Episcopalians,
Quakers and others bitterly complained that they were compelled to pay taxes on their property to support a Puritan
church. The struggle against compulsory taxation for the
support of any particular church establishment continued until
it was finally overthrown and church divorced from the state.
—C. R. S.]

thes prsents doe bargin sell and deliver, unto James Mills
of Hipscoebay in James River in virgina all oure Right,
title and Intrest that wee have or had in oure new Dwelling
house, and home, Lott in the afforsaid towne, bounded one
the south with the Lott of Samuell Titus, on the west with
the woods one the North with the Lott belonging to wattels
& on the east with the Highway, together with all Rights
priveleges accomondations proffites and Revenues belonging there to deriving there from as alsoe a sectsond parsell of
Ground about three akers being and Lying in the west
Commons ffield belonging to the said towne, being bounded
one the south with such a parsell of land belonging to Tho.
Brush of the sade towne & on the north with shuch a parsell of Ground belonging Caleb Curwithy of the sade towne
and one the easte & west with the ffence of the sade ffield,
as alsoe a certayne parsell of Meddowe on the south side
of the Island to the number of twelve akers lying in three
parsells that is to say ffour Akers on the west neck bounded
on the east ward with the medoe belonging to Timmothy
Conkling & to the west ward with the Crick and fowr akres
of Meddoe on the next neck to the estward lying betwext
the meddoe belonging to Steven Jarvis and Josiah Latten,
and alsoe fower akers one the second Neck to the Eastward
of the west neck bounded one the est with Timothy Conklin,
Meddow & to the west ward with wattles his Meddow all
which the afforsaid Lands Meddows, housengs and accom-
mendations and preveleges we the affore saide John & Mary
doe by these prsents sell alinate and estrange from us our
hires, executors & administrators all our right, title and
Intrest unto the affores said James Mills his hires exsecutors
administrators and assignes to have and to hould ffor ever
and we doe allso by these prsents Ingage our selves oure
heires executors, administrators & asignes to save harmless
and Indemnefied the said Mills his hires, executors, administrators & asignes ffrom any person or persons what so ever
who may or shall lay any Clame or title to the af. said house

or Land or any parsell of the afore sade Land to the In_
demnefieng the sade Mills or his sucksessors in his or eithere
or quiett possesion of the afore sade Lands or hous in
wittnes whareof wee have here unto sett our hands and
seles the twenty seventh day of November one thousand
six hundred Sixty and three.        The Mark of
sealed, signed and                          JOHN✕and
delivered in p'sents of                   MARY✕GOSBY*
     WILLIAM LUDLAM
     EDWARD CONQUEST
          (*Court Rec.*, p. 55-6.)

---

[DEED.  JOHN STRICKLAND TO GABRIEL
FINCH.]

[1663, Dec. 2.]

March the 2 : 1663 :
     Be it known unto all men by these p'sents that I John
stiklan, widower, of the towne of Crafford, alias Jemeco,
on long Iland, have bargnd & sould and by these p'sents
doe bargin and sell unto gabriell Finch, all my acomeda-
tions in huntington, onely my halfe neck of meddow, excepted :  I say have sould to him, his eyers, exseketers, adminestrators and assigns, all my right and titell of house,
house lott, barn yards, garden, frute trees, with all previliges and apurtenances thereto belonging, lying and being
betwixt Thomas Scidmore and the lott yᵗ was formerly

---

[*John Gosbee came from Southampton to Huntington before
1658.  He was sent with others by this town that year to procure the confirmation of the deed by the Matinecocks of the
"first purchase," but arriving after Wyandance had given his
ratification to another deed, of a part of the same lands, the
mission failed.  His home lot seems to have been in West
Neck.—C. R. S.]

Joseph Smiths : with all Right of Comonage and meddow as namely : a lott of meddow upon the neck called negun-tetake, contayning six acars more or less, lying betwixt the lott y$^t$ was formerly Thomas Smiths and william ludlams, and also what shall fall to the share of a third lott upon the east neck, with all previliges thereunto belonging, except before excepted, with waranty against, me my eyers, exec-utors, administrators and assigns or any other clayming any right titell or interest to any part or parcell thereof In witness whereof I have sett my hand and seale the day and yere first above writen.

Witness THOMAS BENNYDICK
ZECHARIAH WALKER

JOHN $\times$ STIKLAN [Seal]
his mark

(*File No.* 37.)

---

[TOWN MEETING.]

[1663, Dec. 7.]

at a towne meeting the 7th of desember 1663 at goodman finches house it was a greed to prevente the great damage don that at the south to the medowes by swine that every man shall do his best in dever to fech home and kepeing his swine between this day and this day to night and in cace he or they can not find them if after warde they be found in or about the medowes by ani other thay bringing intelygence to the owner of them thay shall have ten shilling of the owner of the swine for thare labor and the owner fourth with the next day shall go or send to fech them home and in case such swine as are feched home returne to the south againe the owner shall pay to thos as bring intelligence as such fine exprest and in case the own-er do not forthwith upon inteligence given fech his

swine hom from the south for every such swine found at
the south 2 days after inteligence given ——————————

—————————————————————————————————————

—————————————————————————————————————

to the owner, there shall be ten shilling forfit which the
owner of the swine shall pay; five shillings to him or
them that find them at the south after notice given and the
other five shillings shall be the town's, to dispose of as
they think good.

[Copy from original bound with the C. Records.]
(*Town Meetings*, Vol. 1, *p.* 1-3.)

———————————————

## [DEED. JOHN WESTCOTT TO THOMAS POWELL.]

[1663, Dec. 8.]

Know all men by these p^rsents that I John Westcott lat of
fairfield Bargained and sold and doe by these p.sents make
over from mee my heirs executo^rs administrat^rs and assignes
for ever to Tho. powell* his heyers executo^rs administrat^rs

[*Thomas Powell was prominent in all the earliest history of
this town.  He was a Quaker, and, though his religious belief
and practice differed so widely from the dominant Presbyterian
faith here, he exercised great influence, and at one time or
another held nearly every office in the town.  After considerable research I am of the opinion that he was the son of Thomas
Powell, who, pursuant to a warrant of the Earl of Carlisle, was
sent from London to the Barbadoes Islands in 1635.  He
probably came from those Islands to Huntington with Jonas
Wood, of Halifax, when the latter was on a voyage to those
Islands in the rum and sack trade, for it appears by the Court
records that he had, when younger, lived with Jonas Wood
nine years.  Near the end of his life he acquired and occupied
a large tract of land on the border of Queens County, near, or
including what is now Woodbury.—C. R. S.]

and assignes for ever all my accomedations which Moses Hayte and my selfe bought of Richard ogden in Huntington that is to say my house home lot meadow and hollow Comonage and all previledges belonging to y$^t$ accomodation as alsoe land upon y$^e$ plaines which belonged to Richard ogden when I bought the accomodations of him I y$^e$ afore$^{sd}$ John doe bind my self my heires and assignes to Clear all Rate and taxations that shall bee demanded and found from the beginning of y$^e$ world to this day as wittness my hand this 8th of december 1663.

Witnesses                      JOHN WESCOTT
THOMAS SKIDMORE
CALEB WOOD

This is a true Coppy of y$^e$ orriginall deed extracted by
Thomas powell, Recorder.

(*Deeds, Vol.* 1, *p.* 27.)

---

## [CAPT. JOHN SCOTT'S PRETENSIONS DENOUNCED.]

[1663, Dec. 26.]

Propounded and voted this 26 of the 12 month 1663:

It was propounded that, if Capt. John Scott* should come and command the constable to warn a town-meeting, the said constable should not obey him without he shew

---

[*Capt. John Scott was a bold and seditious adventurer, whose name appears more or less in the records of all the towns on Long Island at this period. He pretended to have authority to adjust the boundaries of this town in its controversy respecting Lloyd's Neck. He made himself notorious by his denunciation of the King's authority and of the Connecticut govenment, until he was finally arrested at Setauket and taken to Hartford, tried, and his lands sequestrated. Huntington made short work of him.—C. R. S.]

his commission impowered by his majesty King Charles the Second.

2. It was voted that if Capt. John Scott should command to see our title to the lands of this town that he should not see them unless he shew his power to be from King Charles the Second.

It is voted that when Chiskanoli come that Mr. Wood shall have power to agree with him and the towne to gratifie him to shew the boundaries of the necks of meadow at the South bought by the Town.

[Copy from the original recorded at p. 43, of the Court Records. Copied in the revision of the Town Records, 1873.]

(*Town Meetings, p. 5 and Court Rec. p. 27.*)

---

## [ORDER OF GOV. NICHOLS CONCERNING THE SOUTH NECKS.]

[1664, March 6.]

Att the Generall Meeting of yᵉ Deputyes ot long Island held before yᵉ Governer at Hempsteed march 6th 1664.
Huntington
Oyster bay

It is this day ordered yᵗ yᵉ Towne of Huntington shall possesse & enjoye three necks of meadow land in Controversy between yᵐ: and oysterbay as of Right belonging to them they haveing yᵉ more anncient Grant for them, but in as much as it is pretended that Chickano marked out foaer Necks for Huntington in steed of three, if upon a joynt view of them it shall appeare to be soe, then Huntington shall make over the out most neck next to oysterbay to yᵉ inhabitants thereof and their heirs forever, the Indians or some of them of whome each towne made their purchase, being personally present when the view is to be made*

. R. NICOLLS

(*File, No.* 11.)

---

[COURT RECORD. JOHN RICHBELL AGAINST
JOHN CONKLIN. THE TITLE
TO LLOYD'S NECK.]

[1664, March 10.]

Mr. John Richbell ⎫ At the general meeting of the deputies
John Conklin ⎰ of Long Island held before the Governor at Hempstead March 10, 1664.
Upon hearing the differences between John Richbell of Oyster Bay, and John Conkling of Southold concerning a certain neck of land near Oyster Bay, called Horse Neck, Mr. Richbell making his right appear by several deeds & testimonies, and no sufficient right or title appearing to be in the said John Conkling or those from whom and in whose name he claims ; it is this day ordered, that Mr. John Richbell is to have possession of the said Horse Neck with its

[*This is the first positive indication of outside governmental authority in Huntington. Township independence had come to an end. The Dutch power in New Netherland had just been broken and the country conquered by the English. King Charles II had made his grant and charter to the Duke of York granting New Amsterdam, including Long Island. Col. Richard Nicholls, Governor of the Colony of New York, had taken possession and issued his proclamation commanding obedience to King Charles II. The flimsy allegiance to Connecticut ceased. Henceforth the Duke's Laws were to prevail here, and his charter and grants by his governors constituted the foundation of all title to lands. Indian deeds availed nothing except that it was made a condition of procuring the governor's grant that the Indian "right owner" should be produced and his release given.—C. R. S.]

appurtenances as of right belonging to him & the said John
Conkling nor any other by or under him are to disturb
him the said Mr. Richbell, or his assigns in the quiet and
peaceable posesssion & enjoyment thereof:

RICHARD NICOLLS——

Whereas the matters in difference between Mr. Jno.
Richbell and John Conkling concerning a parcel of land
near Oyster Bay, called Horse Neck, were at the General
Meeting at Hempstead heard on both parts and concluded
that Mr. John Richbell had the right to the said land, for
which he had then order of possession : These are to require and command you that you immediately put Mr.
Richbell or his assigns into possession of the premises, and
that no person be permitted to keep possession of part or
parcel thereof who pretend any right or title from or
under the said John Conkling ; for which this shall be your
warrant.  Given under my hand at Fort James in New
York this 29 day of June 1665.

RICHARD NICOLLS.

To all Justices of the Peace High Constables, Constables
Overseers, or whom Elce this may concern.*

*(Copy from the Records of the Manor of Queens Village, "Vel-
lum Book."—File Lloyd's Neck papers D.)*

---

[*This was the first suit of importance to Huntington under
the "Duke's Laws," and as it was decided adversely, although
Huntington people had held possession of Horse Neck for
eleven years, the people here were not well-disposed toward
the new government and tried unsuccessfully to get annexed to
Connecticut.  Possession of Horse Neck was only nominally
given up and more suits soon followed.—C. R. S.]

## [BOND. JAMES MILLS TO JONAS WOOD.]

[1664, April 6.]

Aprill ye 6ᵗʰ 1664.

this¹ ingadgeth mee James Mills of Pisquategue Bay in James River Virginia                   and my assinee to pay or caus to bee paid to Mr Jonas wood of Huntington or his assignees the full and just sum of six pounds and eaighteen shillings sturling —— bee paid in Huntington att my Return from virginia or within fower months from this time in som curraut   *   *   pay to his content and att prise   *   *   and is in for and consideration of a Debt to him that said   *   *   the widoe of John Casbr late of the said towne deaseased the said sum is attached by the assise of the said towne in my hands as alsoe   *   shillings and six pence for the said attachment as witness my hand.

Witness                                          JAMES MILLS
THOMAS BRUSH.
THOMAS SCUDDER.

(*Town Meetings, Vol.* 1, *p.* 7.)

---

## [TOWN OF HUNTINGTON vs. ROBERT SEELY.
## TITLE TO EATON'S NECK.]

[No Date.]

The Declaration of the towne of Huntington Beeing Against Capt Robart seely Defendant in an action for trespas.

May it please this honorable Cort now mett wee being   *   *   Doe Declare against Captn Robart seely in an action   *   *   *   *   for selling and giveing posession of our medow land   *   *   Right of upland on a neck on the east side of huntington harbour which is to our great Damage the Defendant having nothing off the townes Right by

their Lawfull purchas  *  *  *  *  *  forewarned from
giveing or takeing any possesson  *  *  *  Land and that
by the consent of the towne in generall  *  *  *  *  bee
made apeare to this Coort by sufficient prooffe the wa  *
*  *  *  *  the Defendant made slite of and for all that
could bee said on the towns part in a mild and naybourely
way.  *  *  *  *  hee proceeded and gave possession to
the man that hee  *  *  sould it too: which occasoned
the towne ffurther troble and charge: Being Deprived of
the use of theire owne Land as upon the 7ᵗʰ of february
1664 which caused the towne to send men to the neke
gorg & Balding had fenced in and bilt upon: wch was to
in  *  *  *  *  *  said balding that hee was there Contrary to the townes mind and that there hee should not Remaine  And further  *  *  *  men ware to protest against
his further preseeding  *  *  *  our men Did as will bee
made apeare to this honorable coorte by prooffe all which
will not efect the end  *  *  *  which wee ware att this
troble which was only  *  *  *  wee might peasabley
Injoye that which is our  *  *  *  bought and paid for as
may appeare to this honor*  *  *  *  cort by our Deed
wᶜʰ was assigned to us by the true p'prietors owners of the
afore said land Now in contriverse and there fore wee
humbley crave the helpe of this honorable coort for the
Determination of our cause according to law

(*Court Rec.*, p. 261.—*Loose leaf.*)

---

[No Date.]

that which I have Written conserning the bargan between
John davis and abigall Samons is don with out the know.
of either of them: aftar I came home for feare difference
could arise I have written it as I am Recorder upon oath:
John Core.

Record.

(*Town Meeting, Vol.* 1, *p.* 356.)

## [TOWN MEETING.]

[1664, June 6.]

at a towne meting the 6<sup>th</sup> of June 1664 it was voted and agreed by the magar vot that Jery wood* shall have libarty to perchas heare in this towne and to be reseved as an in habitante.

(*Town Meetings, Vol.* 1, *p.* 356.)

## [TOWN MEETING.]

[1664, Dec. 13.]

at a towne meeting the 13 of Desember 1664 Thomas weekes Isaac plat were chosen to gather Mr Jones his rate and to take as fair what may be for his comfort so far as consernes the towne so long as Mr Jones dos stay or the towne se case.

(*Town Meetings, Vol.* 1, *p.* 1.)

[*Jeremiah Wood no doubt came from Hempstead, and was the son of Jeremiah, Sr., who died in Hempstead in 1686, as appears by deed recorded in Hempstead Records, Liber 1, p. 283, County Clerk's office, in which it is recited that "Jeremiah Wood, Joseph Wood and Jonas Wood are brethren and sons of Jeremiah Wood, lately deceased." Again, in deed by Jonas Wood, Vol. 2, p. 172, it is recited that Jonas "resigns his interest in lands that belonged to his grandfather, Edmond Wood." Probably this is the "Edmond" who died in Huntington.—C. R. S.]

## [DEED. THOMAS MATTHEWS, &c., TO GEORGE BALDWIN.]

[1665, March 6.]

Know all men by these p'sents that I thomas powell of huntington upon Long eiland attornie to Mr Thomas Mathews Merchant have for the vallue of thirtie five pounds to bee paid in mannor and forme following viz: fifteene pounds at or uppon the 29 of September 1666 and twentie pounds the 29th of september 1667 for which I have Bargon sould and by these p'sents doe bargon sell and Deliver unto gorge balding of huntington aforesaid all the Right title and Intrest that Mr thomas Mathews, Marchant have in an acommendations that lieth at the harboure in the afore said huntington north to the woods and west to the harboure or that I have from him by aughthoritie of an Attornie from him that wee have or had in hous and lott aforesaid together with all the Improved lands priviledges accommendatons proffits Revenews thereto belonging or accureing therefrom as alsoe A certaine parcell of ground about six acars ling in the east ffeild the lott of nathaniell foster on the east side and the lot of Gabrell Linch on the west the lott of thomas Scudder and henry whitson on the north and the south side the woods as alsoe A certaine p'sell of medowe on the south side of the Iland about the number of sixteene acars bee it more or les lying on the eastermost neck now purchased of the bounds of huntington all which the aforesaid Lands Meddows housings and accomendac. and priviledges I the afore said thomas powell attorney to Mr thomas Mathews doth by these p'sents sell alienate and estrainge from us or either of us our heires executors administrs. and assignes all our Right title and intrest unto the aforesaid gorge balding his heires executors administrators and assignes to have and to hould ffor ever and I doe also by

these p<sup>r</sup>sents Ingadge my selfe my heires executors administrators and assignes to save harmeles and Indemnified
the said balding his heires execut. administrs. and assignes
ffrom any person or persons whatsoever whoe maye or
shall laye any claime or title to the afore said hous Lands
or any part or parsell thereof to the Indemnifieng the said
belding or his sucksessors in his or either quiett possession
of the aforesaid hous or lands in witnes whereof I have
here unto sett my hand this six Day of march in the yeare
of our lord 1665.

signed and delivered        THOMAS POWELL
in the p<sup>r</sup>sents of
the mark of
ALES ✕ BAYLY
    Joseph bayly* Rec<sup>r</sup>
    *(Conrt Rec., p. 320.)*

---

[COURT RECORD. JONAS WOOD vs. JAMES
MILLS.]

[1665.]

1665 Mr Jonas Wood plaintie against James Mils def.
found upon due examination as is made appear by bill ——
in James —— his own hand of James River Virginia that
seaven pound six pence —— due to Mr Jonas wood from
the said mils for wich wee the said townmen doe grant an
attachment upon the any goods or estate that can bee found
of the said mils and to men then to prise the said estate
which men is Tho. Scudder and Tho. skidmor.
    *(Town Meetings, Vol. 1, p. 7.)*

---

[*Joseph Bayle is supposed to have been the son of John
Bayle, who was born in England in 1617. Came from London
in the "True Love" to the Bermudas in 1635, and afterwards
settled at Southold. Joseph came to Huntington from Southold.
He was Captain of the "Train Band" and Town Clerk and
Recorder several years.—C. R. S.]

## [TOWN MEETING.]

[1665, April 26.]

At a Towne Meeting the 26th of Aprill 1665. ——— it is
voted and agreed by the trustees of the said towne that
Sam- * * and Jonathan Rogers shall bee the men to
vew the west end fenseˢ feild fence and it to bee Repaired
sufficiently within too Days aft- * * and for the este
end of the towne John Rogers and henry whit * men to
vew the east end fence and east feild and see it bee *
don within to Dayes after this meeting and it is further
agreed by * * said * * that yᵉ men or either of the
said men or men * * shall reffuse the viewing of the
said fenses for the year ——— that they shall * * for
such Refusing, fortie shillings.*

*(Town Meetings, Vol. 1, p. 7.)*

---

## [DEED.   CALEB WOOD TO SAMUEL DAVIS.]

[1665, May 12.]

Know all men By these pʳsents that I Caleb Wood off
huntington upon Long eiland in yorkesheere husbandman
have for the vallue of seaven pounds to bee paid in a young
mare that is to be a yeare ould and ——— vantadge when
shee is Delivered which is to bee in July next ensuing and
More at Large is exprest by A bill of Debt under hand
signed ffor which I have Bargoned sould and by these
pʳsents Doe Bargon sell and Deliver unto Samuell Davis

---

[*The Duke's Laws required what was called a "perambulation" of the boundaries of farms and "home lots" once every
year under a penalty of seven shillings for each day of neglect.
A "perambulation" of the boundaries between towns was also
required to be made every three years in the month of February, under a penalty of £5 for neglect.  The law also required
the constable and overseers to appoint fence viewers to examine
the fences and order necessary repairs made.—C. R. S.]

of southhamten upon Long eiland and yorkesheere aforesaid all my Rite tytell and Intrest that I have in a como-
dacon which is a too hundred pound alotment that lyeth
and being in huntington aforesaid the Lott of henry whitson on the south side and the Lott that was given to
trustram hodges on the north the Reare Running to the
woods and frunted with the highwaye together' with all
Lands priveledges accomidacons proffits and Revenews
there to Belonging or accrueing therefrom as also A Certaine p'sell of Meddow Lying on the south side of the eiland
which containeth eaight acars which is the pporsion of a
too hundred pound Lott lyeng and Being on the eastermost neck now purchased all which the afore said Lands
Meddows and accomidacons and privelledges I the afore
said Caleb wood Doe by these p'sents sell allenate and
estrainge from mee my heires executors administrators
and assignes all my tytell and Intrest unto the aforesaid
Samuell Davis his heires executors administrators and
assignes to have and to hould for ever and I Doe by these
prsents Ingadg my selfe my haires executors administrators
and assignes to save harmeles and Indemnified the said
Davis his heires executors administrators and assignes from
any parson or p'son whatsoever whoe may or shall Laye
Any claime or title thereto or Any part or p'sell there of to
the Indemnifing the said Davis or his sucksessors in his or
either of thaire quiet possession of the aforesaid Lands
Meddow or any part or p'sell there of and the aforesaid
Lands and every part and p'sell thereof to bee free from
all Rites and tacksacons from the Begining of the world
untill June 1665 as witnes my hand this twelfe Daye of
may in the yeare of our lord 1666
Signed and Delivered           CALEB WOOD
in the p'sents of
    JOHN FINCH
      Joseph Bayly, Rec'
      (*Court Rec. p.* 321.)

## [TOWN MEETING.]

[1665, May 30.]

Att a generall Town Meeting held the 30th of May 1665.

it was voted and Agreed the Daye aforesaid that all young Cattell or all Cattell exsept working oxen and Milsh Cows should be drove out to horse neck on thursday being second of June and if all can not be got — by that then the Rest should bee drove on the last Day of the same week and that thomas brush and Joseph whitman were the men that  *  *  appointed to keepe the cattell on the first week and thomas weeks jun[r]  *  Caleb wood the next week and soo they to keep the Cattell as long as the towne see accasion and to have for their satisfaction A *  *  for 1 day and it is further agreed that if any inhabitant will not drive his cattell their that hee or they shall pay their equall preportion towards the satisfaction of the men so appointed to keep.*

(*Town Meetings*, Vol. 1, *p.* 7.)

## [AGREEMENT.   JOHN SCOTT AND GEORGE WOOD.]

[1665, June 15 to 1671.]

Know all men by these presents that whereas by vertue of an order from John Scott George Wood was seized of one hundred ackers of land by lease to have fowerteen ackers of the land at the expiration of six yeares, there fall-

---

[*This bold act of the people of Huntington in occupying Horse Neck was doubtless the cause of John Richbell, to whom it had been awarded in the preceding suit, bringing an action to recover possession, which he did in September of the same year.—C. R. S.]

ing out in y<sup>e</sup> time acting of affaires such obstructions from
John Richbell of oysterbay marchant, who Clames the
whole necke as well in the Right of major generall John
Leveritt as his owne, and othere causes by which the said
John Scott becomes disinabled of the performance of the
lease formerly made from the said John Scott to the said
george wood upon the which matter as an Issue of all def-
ferences it is Concluded by & betwixt both parties that
george wood shall have in full sattisfaction of y<sup>e</sup> said non-
performance of his lease and saile of 15 acors, all y<sup>t</sup> house
orchard hom lott land in the feild meaddow att South with
all Rights, members & appurtanances belonging to y<sup>e</sup> accomodation which the said John Scott bought of James
miles formerly John gosbies all which the said George
Wood his heires and assignes shall injoye for ever to the
performance of y<sup>e</sup> premises y<sup>e</sup> said John Scott & george
wood doe put to there hands this 15<sup>th</sup> of June 1665.

Signed & delivered                                  JOHN SCOTT.
in y<sup>e</sup> p<sup>r</sup>esents of                                  the marke of
SIMON LANNE                                  GEORGE X WOOD
witt. JOHN TREDWELL

Entered in the office of Records att fort James in new
yorke this 21<sup>st</sup> of ffebruary 1670 Matthias Nicolls, sec<sup>r</sup>

Whereas I the within named James miles did Impower
Capt. John Scott of seatocit one long Island to dispose in
my behalfe of a house land and other apperrtenances &
accomodations there to belonging which formerly I purchased of John Gosbe deceased, situated & being in huntington and the boands & limetts thereto beelonging and
where as the said Scott hath disposed to george wood the
said house land and other, the apperrtenances as by this deed
with in writen may more at large appeare and whereas
James Chitester of y<sup>e</sup> said towne pretended I the said milles
am Indebted to him hath unjustly molested the said george
wood in the quiet possdsion of the said house and land

These there fore wittnes y$^t$ I the said miles doth avouch and affeirme y$^t$ y$^e$ said Chichester is about 20$^{lb}$ sterling in my debt the which I shall sufficiently prove in time and place Convenient & I doe here by ratefie & confirme & allow of this within deed made by Cap$^t$ Scott for my use & behofe to georg wood his heirs & assignes for ever disowning for myself my heirs and assignes all right title clame or Intrust in or to the said house and land & I doe hereby Impower Theophilus phillips of newtowne on long Island to bee my attorney to accknowledge this deed in Court and to have it recorded as wittnes my hand & seale the 30$^{th}$ Decm. 1670.

JAMES MILLS.

wittnes                          acknowledged before
RALPH HUNT                  RICHARD BEETTS
✕ his mark                      Justice of y$^e$ peace.

Entered in y$^e$ office of Records att fort James new yorke this 21$^{st}$ of ffeb 1670

Matthias Nicols, sec$^r$.

I george wood of new towne of long Island doe assigne all my Right & tittle of this bill of sale to william osburne of long Iland from mee my heires and assignes to him his heirs and assignes peaceably to Injoy for ever as witness my hand & seale this 5$^{th}$ may 1671.

his mark

GEORGE ✕ WOOD

Signed and delivered
in the presence of us.
    JOHN MARSHALL
    SAMUELL MORE.
    This is a true Coppy out of y$^e$ orriginall.

Thomas powell, Rec$^r$.

    (*Court Rec. p.* 297–8.)

I william osbourne of hempstead one long Iland doe heer by assigne over all my right and intrust in this within written bill of sale assigned from gorge wood to me my heires and assignes I say I doe assigne the same fully and absolutly from mee my heires and assignes to Jonathan Scudder of Huntington one long Iland his heirs. and assignes peaceablely to injoy for ever as wittnes my hand this 24 of August 1674.

Test. JONAH FORDAM            WILLIAM OSBOURN.
     SAMUELL TITTUS.
This is a true Coppy out of yᵉ originall by me.
                              Thomas Powell. Recʳ

(*Court Rec. p.* 299.)

---

## [DEED. CALEB WOOD TO SAMUEL DAVIS.]

[1665, June 24.]

Records off Alottments :

1665.

June yᵉ   Sould By Caleb wood off Huntington uppon Long
24ᵗʰ Esland  unto  Samuell Davis off  South hampton
     uppon Long eiland all his Right title and intrest in
     a Lott that Lyeth in huntington and adjoyneing to
     A lott off Henry Whitsons on the south sid and A
     lott  that  was  Late  in the posession of  William
     whitemore on the North sid and the higeh way to
     the harbor on the west sid which lott is in the pos-
     session of the said Caleb and according to the
     Name of A too hundred pound lott with eaight
     acers of Meddow at the south on the eastermost
     Neck which I the said Caleb wood have delivered
     up unto the said Samuell Davis for and in Consid-
     eraton of seaven pounds to bee paid at or before
     the twentie on of December next ensuing.

p mee Jos: Bayly.

By George woods Report and none els.

Made over By John Scott Late of hempsteed all his Right titel and Intrest in a Lott that was on Cosbis Desesed in huntington and Late in the possession off James Mils off James River Verginea which hee the said scott owned By A deed of sale ffrom the said James Mils which lot is A three hundred pound lott with all the apurtinances or privilidges that doth there unto belong which hee the said John scott doth ffully and ffreely acknowledge to have Resind to gorge wood his heires and assigns entird cominad. adjoyneing to Samel titus on the south and watels on the north and the street on the east feeld land calib coronthos on the west and tho. brush on the east:

p mee.

Joseph Bayly.
Record.

(*Court Rec. p.* 319.)

---

## [TOWN MEETING.]

[1665, July 2.]

July the 2nd 1665.

Att a towne Meeting held the day and yeare abovsd By the Constable and Overseers of Huntington conserning the Common medder: at the south that noo inhabitant shall Mowe any gras fres or salt upon any of the s$^d$ Comon Meder without leve from the Counst. and tho. weks and John Kettcham upon the forfeitture of seven shillings for esh loade soe Mowed or cut without leve and to be levied to the use of the towne.

(*Town Meetings, Vol.* 1, *p.* 8.)

# [DEED. HENRY LUDLAM TO NATHANIEL FOSTER.]

[ 1665, Oct. 3.]

Know all men by these p'rsents That I Henry Ludlam of Southampton one Long Iland in new England plan[t]. have and by these p'sents doe alienate bargaine & sell and for and in consideration of a valuable consideration in hand recived have & hereby doe (as afore. sd.) alienate & sell unto Nathaniell ffoster of easthampton on y[e] sd. Iland all y[t] my messuage or tenem[t] in y[e] towne of Huntington one y[e] sd. Iland with all y[e] houseing yards orchards, gardens, fences, & easem[te], with all y[e] upland & meadow or marsh ground y[t] there unto belongeth with all y[e] p'fitts & comedities or enlargments there to doth or here after may belong the said accomodations, goeing at y[e] sd. Huntington under or at y[e] Denomenation of an two Hundred pounds or second allottm[t] to him y[e] sd. Nathaniell foster his heyers executors administr[rs] & assignes. for ever. To have and to hold, and peaceably and quietly to possesse & enjoy for ever with out the least lett hindarnce mollestation or desturbance of mee the sd. Henry Ludlam my heyers executo[r] administrat[rs] or assignes or any other claimeing any right, title or intrest in y[e] premisses or any part thereof in my name or by vertue of any former saile bargaine mortgage or any act of mine whatsoe ever In witnes where of I have here unto sett my hand and seale this third day of october Ano. dom. 1665.

signed, sealed        HENRY LUDLAM.
and delivered in          [Seale O.]
the p'sents of us.

  HENRY PEIRSON.

JOHN DICKERSON

    This is a true Coppy of the orriginall Deed extracted by me.        THOMAS POWELL
                                                 Rec[r]

(*Court Rec. p.* 293.)

## [JOHN RICHBELL AGAINST HUNTINGTON.
## THE TITLE TO LLOYD'S NECK.]

[1665.   Sept. 28 to Oct. 4, inclusive.]

The proceedings at the General Court of Assizes held at New York on the Island of Manhattan before the Governor and his Council and the Justices of the Peace of Yorkshire, upon Long Island, on the 28th, 29th and 30th days of Sept., and the 2d, 3d and 4th days of Oct., in the 17th year of his Majesty's reign, anno domine 1665.  Sept. 28th.

John Richbell, Plt.

The inhabitants of the Town of Huntington, Def'ts.

The names of the Jurors :—Richard Gildersleeve, Foreman of the Jury, John Symonds, Henry Pierson, Thomas Smith, William Hallet, Edward Titus, John Burrows.

Mr. John Rider, Att'y for Pl't.

The pl't declares upon an action of trespass, for that the def'ts have given him unjust molestation in possession of a certain parcel of land commonly called Horse Neck to his damage &c.; whereupon he brings his suit.  To prove his title the plaintiff produces a bill of sale of the said land from Richard Russel and Nicholas Davison, who were appointed by the General Court at Boston to administer upon all the estate, both real and personal, of Samuel Andrews who died intestate at Charlestown in New England.  The plaintiff proves the purchase of the said Neck of land for a valuable consideration by Samuel Andrews, from Daniel Whitehead, who was the first purchaser thereof from the natives, Sept. 20th 1654.

After that Samuel Andrews had made his purchase from Daniel Whitehead, he obtained a confirmation thereof from the Grand Sachem, Wyandanck, which was produced.

Nathaniel Sylvester declares in Court that he is a witness to the confirmation and that he disbursed the pay for it at the request of Mr. Andrews.

Richard Woodhull, sworn in Court says, he accompanied Samuel Andrews and Daniel Whitehead to Shelter Island, where the Grand Sachem met them and confirmed the same, and that returning home, he met one John Gosby of Huntington, who said he was employed by the town to purchase the said Neck of land of the Sachem, for their town, but hearing of the said confirmation, he said he was come too late, and so returned homeward. John Scudder (not sworn) declares in court, that he being then an inhabitant of the town of Huntington, knoweth that Mr. John Gosby was so employed by them, and that he returned with the answer that he was too late.

Capt. John Underhill sworn, says that he ther living at Southold, Mr. Andrews came and told him, he was going to get Horse Neck confirmed by the Sachem; returning he called on him again and said he had done his business, and that awhile after, John Gosby coming to him told him what he came about, but was come too late.

The Attorney for the plaintiff, pleaded likewise a verdict obtained by the plaintiff at a General meeting held before the Governor at Hempstead, in the beginning of March, 1664, whereupon he had judgment given for him, against John Conkling, who sued for the same land in behalf of his wife and some orphans, and had an order for possession accordingly.

Mr. Leveridge, attorney for the defendants, in answer to the plaintiff's declaration, denies the unjust molestation—pretends the want of timely benefit of the declaration, and alleges that the judgment and order at the General Meeting at Hempstead concerned only Conkling's pretences, not theirs.

He argues the defendant's title to Horse Neck to be more valid, as being more ancient than the plaintiff's.

He produces an assignment from the inhabitants of Oyster Bay of all their rights to the lands at Huntington, &c., bearing date 2d April, 1653, wherein he says Horse

Neck is included (though not by name mentioned) as not being excepted, and that it comes within their line; for proof thereof, two depositions are read in Court, the one from Thomas Benedict, sworn before Justice Denton, the other from John Corey, sworn before John Strickling who lives out of the government. They are both to this purpose, that after the first purchasers had sold their lands to those of Huntington, some of them bethought themselves of Horse Neck, and desired that they might have half of it, and if not the one-half then they might have liberty to put their horses on it, but both were denied them.

Mr. Leveridge alleges that the desire of the first purchasers, after their resignation, implies that they were sensible they had parted with their rights; he likewise pleads possession of the said Neck, near double four years, without any legal demant or just molestation.

The attorney for the plaintiff offers to prove that Horse Neck was not included in the resignation made by the first purchasers.

Daniel Whitehead, one of the first purchasers of the lands at Oyster Bay and Huntington (not admitted to take his oath, it being alleged he was a party) declared that Horse Neck did never belong to either of the towns, it being reserved by the Indians at their first sale for hunting, and Mr. Leveridge being told by a chief Sachem, he wrote to the said Daniel Whitehead to buy it, otherwise he should not come to live at Huntington.

Robert Williams, not sworn, one of the first purchasers, declares that Horse Neck was excepted by the Indians, in their first sale, as reserved for their hunting. So Oyster Bay could not resign what they had not. He says moreover, that they being sensible of their want of title to the said Neck, he struck a bargain with an Indian for it, and delivered him a coat in part payment for it, but the Indian coming no more, he could not go through with his bargain, which afterwards, Daniel Whitehead did perform.

Deposition—Richard Holbrook, another of the first purchasers, deposeth to the Indians reserving Horse Neck when they bought their lands at Oyster Bay and Huntington.

Attestation—Anthony Wright, Thomas Hermitage, attest the same under their hands.

Nicholas Wright, sworn in Court, declareth the same and that he knew that Mr. Leveridge had written a letter about the purchase of it.

As to the possession, the attorney of the plaintiff declares that the plaintiff had possession given him by an order of the General Meeting at Hempstead, before which he knew not where to have recourse for law or justice. The attorney for the defendants objects against the taking possession by the plaintiff to be legal, it being not done by the Sheriff, a *forma ejectionis*.

He finds a difference in the oaths, depositions and attestations made for the plaintiff; some calling that which Mr. Andrews purchased at Shelter Island, a confirmation, others a sale, and he questions the Sachem Wyandanks power to do either.

The attorney for the plaintiff alleges that notwithstanding Mr. Leveridge questions Wyandanck's power, yet the town of Huntington would have purchased Horse Neck of him and had a confirmation of their land from him likewise which was allowed of by them.

After a long debate of the cause on both parts, it was refered to the jury, who the next morning, being Sept. 29, brought in their verdict as followeth, viz:

VERDICT.

That upon serious consideration of the cause depending between Mr. Richbell and the Town of Huntington; weighing all the evidences, we find for the defendants, we finding that the ancient deed is the right of Huntington, wherein we find by the bound of Huntington's deed, and by evidence that Horse Neck (which is in controversy) lyeth within the bounds of Huntington's deed, except further light can be made to appear unto us by the Hon. Gov'n. and Council, and that plaintiff shall pay all costs and charges depending upon this suit.

The plaintiff appealed from the verdict to the Governor and Council.

### THE APPEAL

At the Court of Assizes held at New York the 28th of Sept. by his majesty's authority in the seventeenth year of the reign of our Sovereign Lord, Charles the Second, by the grace of God of Great Britain, France and Ireland, King, defender of the faith, &c, and in the year of our Lord God 1665.

John Richbell, Plaintiff, the Inhabitants ⎫
of the Town of Huntington, defendants. ⎬

The Court having heard the case in difference between the plaintiff and defendants debated at large concerning their title to a certain parcel of land commonly called Horse Neck, and having also seen and perused their several writings and evidences concerning the same, it was committed to a jury who brought in their verdict for the defendants; upon which the Court demurring, did examine further into the equity of the cause, and upon mature and serious consideration, do find the said parcel of land called Hors Neck doth of right belong to the plaintiff, it being purchased by the said plaintiff for a valuable consideration and by the testimony of the first purchasers under whom the defendants claim, was not conveyed or assigned by them to the defendants with their other lands; upon which, and divers other weighty considerations, the court doth decree that the said parcel of land called Horse Neck doth of right belong and appertain unto the plaintiff, and his heirs, and it is hereby ordered that the high Sheriff or Under Sheriff of the north riding of Yorkshire upon Long Island do forthwith put the said plaintiff or his assignes in possession thereof and all persons are hereby required to forbear the giving the said plaintiff or his assignes any molestation in the peaceable and quiet enjoyment of the premises.*

Signed by order and appointment of the Court.

RICHARD CHARLTON,
Clerk of the Assizes.

Whereas the Hon. Col. Richard Nicolls, Esq: deputy to his Royal Highness James Duke of York, together with his honorable council did upon the 28[th] of Sept. 1665, pass judgment in the Court of Assize, that I, John Underhill, Under Sheriff of the north Riding should by virtue of the said power, possess Mr. John Richbell, marchant of Horse Neck, adjudged by the Honorable and y[e] said Council of right belonging to him the said John Richbell; these are, in obedience to the said authority and do by these presents and upon y[e] 24[th] day of October, 1665, give unto the said Mr Richbell, possession of the said Neck, with all appurtenances thereunto belonging and for full assurance according to the laudable custom of order, possession, I do as aforesaid in the presence of two subscribed witnesses give him the said Mr Richbell possession of the said neck by turf and twig, Signed in the name and authority of the

---

[*This is probably one of the most fully reported cases in this country, a record of which has come down to us from this remote period, and its chief value, now, consists in the facts and circumstances which are related, and which have in this way been rescued from oblivion. It was only a few months before this that the English had captured New York from the Dutch, and when Gov. Richard Nicholls landed, the common law came with him. The Court of Assize had only just been established and this was probably one of the first land trials that came before it. It was a sample, however, of a Star Chamber Court reversing the verdict of a jury. Whether right or wrong, it placed Lloyd's Neck out of Huntington and barred off one-third of its seashore front; and from that day it remained out, until the passage of the act of the Legislature of the State of New York in 1886 annexing it to the town of Huntington—a period of 221 years.]

honorable aforesaid; together with the honorable council, day and date above said.

Pr. me JNO. UNDERHILL, as aforesaid
RICHARD HARROT, RICHARD LATTEM.

This is Recorded in the Secretarys office in the Book of Records of the several Courts of Assize beginning Anno. 1665 No 2. page 7 to 14 inclusive.

(*File Lloyd's Neck Papers, E.*)

---

## [MARKS AND BRANDS ON ANIMALS.]

[1666.]

Imp

John Samways 1666 Record of horses. A Baye mare aboute eaight yeare ould her eare marke is the tips off Booth eares Cropt off Branded on the neare Buttoke with I S and the off buttoke with the towne Brand E.

tt

A too yeare ould hors in Coullor a Browne Baye with a white face and too white feet his owne marke with the tip off Booth eares cropt off and Branded on the neare Buttoke with B.

tt

A yeareling mare in collor Blacke her eare marke with a swallow forke on the neare eare and a niche under that yeare. Branded on the off buttocke with the towne Brand E.

Bought By John Samway off Huntington off Richard williams off the same towne A paire off steares on Browne and the other Blacke the on som ffive and the other som fower yearrs of age their eare marke is too half pence o the off eare the on on the uper side the other under that.*

Joseph Baiely, Rec^r.

(*Court Rec. p.* 210.)

Sould unto Jonathan Lewis by Thomas Whitson a colored horse with little star on his forehead a crop on ye left year a black main and tail four white feet, one walle eye it being ye left Eye. The said horse is in part pay for his man sarvant which yea said Tom Witson bought of yea said Lewis.†

(*Court Rec. p.* 10.)

---

[*These items, showing the marks John Sammis put upon his horses, are printed as specimens showing the custom of the period founded on the Duke's Laws, and are taken from the large manuscript volume of similar records of marks, but which are omitted as having little value. It will be noticed that the town mark is here given as the letter E. It so appears in all the records. The letters of the alphabet were applied to each of the old towns, beginning at the east end of the Island with the letter A. and ending with E. for Huntington. Animals were branded with a hot iron with the Town Mark and the initials of the owner, or a monogram. A record of the mark was then made in the town book, and a statement of the age, color and all " observable " marks on the animal and a date of the brand. It was an offence punishable by a fine of £5 to sell, exchange or give away any horse, ox, cow or bull not marked, and the penalty was £10 for a failure to record the sale or exchange of such animal. If the animal was taken to another town and sold, the brand of that town and the marks of the purchaser were put on over the other marks.—C. R. S.]

[†Slaves were held from a very early period of the Dutch settlement of New York, and it is believed that the first importation of negroes in America was by a Dutch vessel which brought them from the African coast and sold them in Virginia. In 1655 a cargo of slaves was brought from Guinea in the " White Horse " and sold in Manhattan Island. Many cargoes of negroes were afterwards landed and they were bought and sold under both Dutch and English authority in the Colony for more than one hundred years. Slaves found their way into Huntington at an early date, and nearly all the prominent families held more or less of them. As late as 1755 there were as many as 82 slaves (47 males and 35 females) distributed

## [DEED. GABRELL FINCH TO EPENETUS PLATT.]

[1666, Feb. 24.]

Know all men by these p'sents that I Gabrell Finch off huntington uppon Long Eiland in yorkesheare weaver, have
from mee my heires executors administrators and assignes
Bargoned sould and made over unto Epenetus platt off
huntington on long Eiland in yorkeshere afore said his
heires executors administ[rs] and assignes all my Rite title
and Intrest in all my accommindacon sittuate and lying in
huntington afore said formerly in the occupacon of Mr
Stiklin together with all houses out housses Barne
orchards gardens Lands Meddows or whatsoever there to
Belongeth or Appertaineth as alsoe to alotments in the
east ffeild off huntington late in the tener or occupacon off
thomas skidmore and Samuell wood Containeing seaven
Acars and a halfe bee it more or les as alsoe A certain
p'sell of Meddow on the south side of the eiland part
thereof lyeth on A neck Called nagunttatauge Lying Betweene the Alotment of John Ketcham and william Ludlam
Containeing six acars Bee it more or les the other p-porcon
of Meddow lying on A necke of Meddow Called By the
name of the east necke it Being the halfe p-porcon of a
three hundred pound Lott, Too have and to hould for ever
all the said houseing Barne orchards home lott Booth
Meddow and upland together with all singular the appurtinances, Rits title or intrest that now is or ever here after
shall Belong or Appurtaine unto the aforesaid Epenetus
Platt his heirs or assignes ffurthermore I the said Gabrell

among 53 families. By an act of the Legislature of 1799 and
later. provision was made whereby slave-owners might voluntarily free their slaves when under fifty years of age and capable
of supporting themselves. Under these acts slavery soon disappeared.—C. R. S.]

Finch Doth Covenant and promise to save harmeles and indeminified the said epenetus platt his heirs and assignes ffrom any person or persons whatsoever whoe maye or shall Laye Any Claime of Rite or title to any p'ᵗ or parsell thereof and allsoe I the saide gabrell Finch Doth fully and abseelute make over and estrainge from mee my heires execut'ˢ administrat'ˢ and assignes every pte. and p-sell thereof unto the above said Epenetus platt his heires and sucksessors as alsoe to be free from all Rates and tacksatons ffrom the Beginning of the world to the Daie of the Date hereof as witnes my hand this twentie fowerth of frebruary in the yeare of our Lord on thousand six hundred sixtie and six.

Signed, sealed and dal.

in the presents of

the Mark of

GABRELL ✕ FINCH

RICHARD SMITH
CALEB WOOD
Joseph Baiely Recʳ.

Memorandᵃᵐ I the saide Epenetus platt Doth promise not to molest nor hinder Samuell wood of the privilidg of his commonadge of that lot that gabrell Finch Bought of the said samuell wood lying in the este feilde which is not to bee made us of untill the feilde b cleare of Corne or any usefull nessesaryes and hee the said Samuell is but to have his equall p'porcon according to that lote unto which I the sade Epenetus plat have hereto set my hand the Daye and yeare within written

this is A true
Coppie of the originall
Deede. extracted p mee
Joseph Baiely, Rec.
(*Court Rec. p.* 314.)

EPENETUS PLATT

## [DEED.   JOHN STRICKLAND TO JONAS WOOD.]

[1666, March 8.]

Jonas woods Deede of sall for Coppiage know all men by
these presents that I John stickland of Jamaick In the
North Riding of yorksheer on Long Island have fully and
absolutly sould unto Jonas wood of Huntington In the east
riding of york sheire on Long island afore said a certain
passell of medow on y$^e$ south side the saide Island In y$^e$
bounds and Limittes of the Towne of Huntington Lying
and being in A necke comonly called by the Indians Coppiage bounded on the west with a river called Yatamunti-
tahege on y$^e$ east bounded by samuell wood and thomas
Powell parted by and ogke tree by the path marked so H.
ranghing to a lone tree standing In y$^e$ medow on y$^e$ east
sid the hassackes and soe upon a line to y$^e$ south water I
say y$^e$ affore said John stickling have for my selef my heairs
&c fully sould and made over unto Jonas wood aforesaid
his heirs &c. the above sd. medow with all y$^e$ preveledges
and apartenances there unto belonging to have and to hold
and peaceably In joye for ever free from any just Claime
or Incumbrance of any person or persons what soever and
Do hereby acknowledge that In consideration of y$^e$ premises I the affore sd. John stickland have reseved full and
valluable consideration to my full satesfaction and to the
confirmacion of the premises I y$^e$ affore sd. John stickland
have subscribed my name & set to my seale this eight daye
of march in y$^e$ eighteenth yeere of his magiestes Raine
Charles y$^e$ second & in y$^e$ yeare of our Lord god 1666
signed sealled and Delivered              his marke
In y$^e$ presents of                                ✕
WILLIAM SMITH ✕ his marke          JOHN STICKLAND
Anthony Waters
    clerk of y$^e$ sessions of y$^e$ north riding of yorke shiere
long Island.
        (*Deeds, Vol. 1, p, 294.*)

# [AFFIDAVITS OF JONAS WOOD AND THOMAS TOWNSEND.]

[1666, May 10.]

in the yeare of yᵉ Lord 1665 after the first Coort heald att hempsteed the Constable of oysterbay caused us to goe to hors neck as witnessess for Mr John Richbill to give him possession of the neke and gorge wood being setled by the order of John Scott was by the said Richbill displaced and John Richbill gave unto gorge wood ten akars of up- land and five akars of Meddowe in Reference to noe man at all but A free gift where gorge wood lived then and was setteled and the said John Richbill said that hee would never Dispossess him without hee sould the neke and the said gorge wood promised in so Doeing not to bee his hindrance and Mr John Richbill said that hee would make it in quanttitie and quallitie a like as that is att hors neck this I witnes that this is the truth and nothing but the truth.

Huntington may the 28th 1666.

John Coles,
Joseph Bayly,             swoorne Before
         Recʳ             Mr Jonas wood

Thomas Townsen of oysterbay affermeth as aforesaid Be- fore mee John Underhill undersherif of the north Riding oysterbay 28th of June 1666

Thomas Towsend.

Jos. Bayly Recʳ.
  (*Court Rec. p.* 319.)

## [RECORD OF JOSEPH BAYLEY'S LAND.]

[1666, May 27.]

All the peice of Land that lyeth beelow the lote that was
suttons next unto the Run off water allmost from the path
or waye that goeth through the swampe which is almost
straite from the Lot fence unto the Run of water and soe
from thence unto the mil pond and from the Run of watter
all thee hill ffrom the Lott to the mil pond untoo thee side
off the first hollow that is neare against the Middell off the
Lott of Mr Mils Late in the possession of goodman sutton.
this peece of Land was a gift given by the towne too Joseph Bayly of huntington uppon the twentie seaventh
Daye of Maye 1666 and Layed out by Mr Jonas wood and
Thomas wilks senior.

(*Court Rec. p.* 322.)

---

## [COURT RECORD. INHABITANTS OF HUNTINGTON vs. ROBERT SEELY. TITLE TO EATON'S NECK.]

[1666, Sept. 27 to 29.]

The proceedings of the Genall Court of Assizes, held at
New Yorke, on the Island of Manhatans, before the Govern-
or and his Councell and the justices of the peace of Yorkshire, upon Long Island, the 27th, 28th and 29th dayes of
September and the first and 2d dayes of October, in the
18th yeare of his Majesty's Raigne, Annoq Domini 1666.

September 27th, 1666.

The Inhabitants of the Town of Huntington, Plts.

Robert Ceely, Defendt.

Mr. John Rider, attorney for the Plts.

Hee produces a Copy of the heads of two tryalls had at

the Court of Sessions; the first by way of Accord, the Second by review, by the Governors Speciall Warrt. Hee likewise putts in a Declaracon for the plts, wherein is alleged That the Person under whom the defendt, Claymes, had no Right to the land in question, comonly called Eaton's Neck, having never beene in Possession, or given any consideracon for it, but that the Plts Purchased the same from the true Proprietors, and paid for it.

To prove their declaracon severall deposicons were read in court—vizt., one of Mary, the wife of Samll. Davis, who affirmeth; That if Mr. Eaton had any Right to the Land it was only by Guift; and yt Mr. Eaton resigned the Guift of the said Land to the Indyans.

Mr. Jones, the Sonne in Law to Mr. Eaton; his letter is also produced wherein hee Confesses the uncertainty of his title.

The Plt's deed was shewen and read, bearing date iu or about the last day of July, 1656, wch is a great uncertainty in a deed, besides there are no Christian Testimonyes to it.

The Deposicon of Richard Smith, of Nesaquack, but excepted agst hee being concerned.

The Deposicons of Henry Jackson, John Cole, George Baldwin, John ffinch, as also the Testimonyes of Thomas Weekes, Thomas Scudder, John ffinch, Joseph Whetnam and others, with the like of Thomas Scudamore and others, were read in behalfe of the Plts.

Mr. Sharp, attorney for the Defendt.

Hee puts in an Answer declaring That ye Plts have already had two Legall Tryalls upon the same acct, and had been overthrowne in both, yet the Plts continue their vexatious Suites agst the Defendts in Appealing to the Court of Assizes agst all Law and Equity.

The Attorney for the Defendt delivers into ye Court a writing, wherein severall Indyans acknowledge the Land in controversy was freely given to Mr. Theophilus Eaton. It is witnessed by foure Christians.

The Plts object that the witnesses deny their hands, but Samuell Titus, who is one of them, acknowledges his handwriting, but Saith that hee was surprized, & that there was no good Interpreter betweene them.

A Deed is read in Court, wherein Theophilus Eaton, the Sonne of Theophilus Eaton, to whom the Guift was made, resignes all his Interest to his ffather's Lands in New England unto his sister, who is Marryed to Mr. Jones. It's dated March ye 28th, 1659.

Mr. Jones, his Bill of Sale of Eaton's Neck to Robert Seely, for the consideracon of 50lb. Sterling, is also read; it beares date the 22d of December, 1664.

To prove the Land did belong to Mr. Eaton the Deposicons of these Persons following were read—vizt. Samll. Edsalls, John Dickensons, Nicholas Wright, Anthony Wright, Thomas Benedict and Daniel Whitehead, Together with the Testimony of Capt. Thomas Willett, given in Court by word of Mouth.

The Court after having at large heard the matter in controversy, debated on both parts, thought fitt to make this following Order and Decree—vizt. :

At the Genall Court of Assizes &c.

The inhabitants of the Town of Huntington, Plts. Robert Seely, Defendt.

The Court doth Decree that the two former Verdicts given in by the jurges at the Courts of Sessions, in the East Riding of Yorkshire upon Long Island, do stand good, and that the Land in question, called Eaton's Neck, bee adjudged to ye Defendt. That the Plts do pay or cause to bee paid the Sume of ten pounds to the Person or Persons who received the Damage, in having their ffence pluckt up by them. And that the Plts do also pay or cause to bee paid the Sume of tenn pounds more to the Defendt for the damage hee hath Susteined by them. And likewise that they Pay the Costs of Court and Charges.

By order of the Governor and Court of Assizes,*
Matth. Nicolls,<br>Secty.

STATE OF NEW YORK, OFFICE OF THE ⎫
  SECRETARY OF THE BOARD OF RE- ⎬ ss.
  GENTS OF THE UNIVERSITY. ⎭

I, David Murray, Secretary of the Board of Regents of the State of New York, do hereby certify that the foregoing is a correct and true copy of the procedings of the Court of Assizes of the Province of New York, in the matter between the Town of Huntington and Robert Seely, as recorded on pages 55 to 58 in book "Court of Assizes 2, 1665–1672," on file in the State Library, and of the whole thereof.

Witness my hand and the seal of said Board of Regents this 18th day of April, 1882.

DAVID MURRAY,<br>Secretary.

(*File Eaton's Neck papers C.*)

---

### [TOWN MEETING.]

[1666, Oct. 17.]

October 17. 1666

Voted and agreed, this day and year above said by the major part of the inhabitants of this town of Huntington that no inhabitant, whether proprietor or renter, shall sell let or set any of their lands of commonage or meadow in any

---

[*The inhabitants of Eaton's Neck having been successful In establishing their title to that neck under the Theophilus Eaton purchase by three successive suits with Huntington, the result was acquiesced in and Huntington never gave any grants or deeds or other conveyance of land in any part of that neck, though for all jurisdictional purposes of town government it seems to have been regarded as within the town.—C. R. S.]

part or parcel of that land lying Eastward or Northward
from Cow harbor to any person or persons that are or shall
be proprietors of the neck called Stony Neck or Balding's
Neck; and whomsoever shall act or do contrary to this
order shall forfit ten pounds sterling for every hundred
pound commonage, upon demand, to the constable and
townsmen.*

[Copied, from the original in Court Records p , in the
Revision of the Records in the year 1873.]

(*Town Meetings Vol.* 1, *p.* 9.)

---

[CONFERENCE BETWEEN HUNTINGTON MEN
AND THE MESSEPEGUE SACHEM
CONCERNING SOUTH NECK.]

[No date.   Between 1664 and 1667.]

The afermation of John Ketcham, Thomas Brush and
Thomas powell being sent by the Inhabitants of huntington with an Indian called Chickeno too The south meadowes according to the order of the generall asembly at
hempsted.   When wee came to the south to our meadows
wee went ovar too neckes to our naybours who had called
massapeege Indians About the number of twentie, whoe
opoased us about the space of an ower and would not suffer the Indian too goe and shew us the marked tree, then
wee shewed the sachem the writing to which hee had set
his hand which was our acquitance and yet hee would not
suffer the Indian to goe, when wee see nothing would pre-
vaile, wee tooke our leave of them and said wee should

---

[*This prohibition against inhabitants of Eaton's Neck grew
out of the bitter feeling engendered by the previous litigation
between Robert Seeley and George Baldwin on the one part
and the people of Huntington on the other.—C. R. S.]

carry backe this anser to them that sent us : but they not willing that wee should, tooke up the matter as wee did apprihend, spake to the Indians whoe after gave leave to the Indian who was Chickemo to goe and shew us the tree, many off massapauge Indians went with us. Thomas Brush went before and not taking notise off the tree went past it then a massapauge Indian called him backe and shewed him the tree before Chickenoe came neare it. when Chickenoe came to the tree hee said that was the tree hee marked, as his master Commanded him. Massapauge sachem said by his Interpriter that hee told muntaulke sachem that hee was grived at his hart that hee had sould that necke upon which then wee was, but muntalket sachem tould him that it was sould and it could not bee hoped and therefore bid him goe and Receve his paye and soe hee said hee did : and alsoe massapauge sachem owned his Land and that hee had Receved the goods :

Recorded in the office at New Yorke<br>
the 2<sup>d</sup> day of November 1667.<br>
Matthias Nicolls, Secr.

(*File No.* 13.)

---

[CHICKINOE'S AFFIRMATION CONCERNING

THE SOUTH NECKS.]

[1665, Oct. 7.]

7 : Oct. 1665.

The day and yeare above said, wee undersubscribed, being in Huntington where Chickinoe came and Instified the matter following in relation to y<sup>e</sup> reference or order made at Hympsted Generall meeting, touchinge three necks of meadowe wh. Huntington had formerly purchased of Muntaukatt Saichem, and he informs true properiet<sup>y</sup> as also

in responsion to Oyster Bay inhabitants, who lay a claime
to part of the said three Necks, saying thare are fouer
necks & one thereof belongs to them, the said Chickinoe
now did playnely and cleerly demenstrate before us that
the Tree he first marked by his Master Muntakett Sachems
order, and hath a second tyme denied according to order,
is noe other but that w$^{ch}$ ought justly to be owned by him
and so marked as aforesaid, and comprehends only Huntingtons just Purchase of three Necks of Medow and in
truth is three necks of medowe & not four according to the
present relation of Chickinoe,*

THOS. TOPPING<br>WILL WELLS.

*(File No. 19.)*

---

## [THE NICHOLLS PATENT TO HUNTINGTON.]

[1666, Nov. 30.]

The People of the State of New York, by the Grace of
God, Free and Independent: To all to whom these presents shall come, Greeting: Know ye, that we, having inspected the records remaining in our Secretary's office, do
find therein Book of Pattents, No. 1, page 99, certain Letters patent recorded in the words and figures following
to wit:

A Patent granted unto the Inhabitants of Huntington,
Richard Nicolls, Esq., Governor Generall under his Royall
Highness, the Duke of Yorke and Albany, etc., of all his
territories in America.

To all to whom these pr'ts shall come, sendeth Greeting:

---

[*This, in connection with the action of the Governor and
Council at Hempstead the year before, closed the controversy
with Oysterbay about the three hecks.—C. R. S.]

whereas there is a certain Town within this Government commonly called and known by the name of Huntington; situate and being in Long Island, now in the tenure or occupation of several Freeholders and Inhabitants there residing, who having heretofore made laufull purchase of the lands thereunto belonging, have likewise manured and improved a considerable part thereof and settled a competent number of familyes thereupon. Now, for a confirmation unto the said Freeholdr's and Inhabitants in their enjoym't and possession of the premises, know y$^e$ that by virtue of y$^e$ commission and authority unto me given by his Royal Highness, I have ratified, confirmed and granted, and by these pr'sts do hereby ratify, confirm and grant unto Jonas Wood, William Leveredge, Robert Seely, John Ketcham, Thomas Scudmore, Isaac Platt, Thomas Joanes, and Thomas Weeks, in the behalfe of them-selvs and their associates, the Freeholders and inhabitants of the s'd Towne, their heires, successors and assigns, all y$^t$ land that already have beene or hereafter shall bee purchased for and in the behalfe of the Towne of Huntington, either from the natives, proprietors or others within the limitts and bounds herein exprest, (vizt) That is to say; from a certaine river or creeke on the West com'only called by the Indyans by the name of Nackaqnatok and by the English the Cold spring, to stretch eastward to Nasaquack River; on the North to bee bounded by the Sound running betwixt Long Island and the Maine; and on y$^e$ South by y$^e$ sea, including there nine several necks of Meadow Ground, all which tract of land together with the s'd necks thereunto belonging, within the bounds, limitts aforesaid, and all or any plantacon thereupon are to belong to the said Towne of Huntington, as also all Havens, Harbors, Creekes, Quarryes, Woodland, Meadows, Pastures, Marshes, Lakes, Fishing, Hawking, Hunting and Fowling and all other profitts, commodetyes, Emolum'ts and Heriditam'ts to the said land and premises within limitts and

bounds aforementioned, described, belonging, or in any
wise appertaining, to have and to hold the said Lands and
Necks of lands Hereditam'ts and premises with their and
every of their appurtenances, and of every part, part and
parcell thereof to the said patentees and their associates,
to the proper use and behoofs of the said patentees and
their associates, their Heirs, Successors and assigns forever and I do likewise hereby confirme and Grant unto
the said Patentees and their associates, their Heires, successors and assigns all the privileges belonging to a Towne
within this Governm't, and that the place of their present
Habitacon shall continue and retaine the name of Huntington by which name it shall be distinguist and knowne in
all Bargains and sales, deeds, records and writings. They,
the said patentees, and their associates, their Heirs, successors and assigns rendering and paying such dutyes and
acknowledgem'ts as now are or hereafter shall be constituted and establist by the Laws of this Colony under the
obedience of his Royall Highness, his heirs and successors.

Given under my hand and seale at Fort James in New
York, the 30th day of November, in the 18th year of his
Majesties reign and in the year of our Lord, 1666.*

RICHARD NICOLLS.

[*This is in many respects the most important paper held by
the town. It embodies all the qualities of a grant, a patent,
and a charter, and is the basis upon which all title to lands
and all local government as a township rested under the government of Great Britain. Though comparatively brief, it
contained all the essentials necessary to enable the people to
maintain title and carry on a town government. The two
subsequent patents only amplify the powers, and rights here
granted, vest the title in Trustees and change, somewhat, the
boundaries. In effect it would seem to have swept away all
private ownership in undivided and unoccupied lands or commons founded on Indian deeds, and to have vested such lands
in the town, as a public, municipal corporation; but whether it
was so construed at the time or not, the rights of the first
purchasers from the Indians still continued to be recognized, as
divisions continued to be made at town meetings, based on such

All which we have exemplified by these presents.

In testimony whereof we have caused these, our Letters, to be made patent, and the Great Seal of our said State to be hereunto affixed. Witness our trusty and well-beloved George Clinton, Esquire, Governor of our said State,

---

exclusive purchases and the holders of these ancient rights, continued to assert them, and they descended from father to son and were bought and sold for more than a hundred years after this and subsequent patents were granted.

The Indian title, which the people here had then acquired, in part was nothing more than occupation for fishing and hunting, or, as Aaron Burr decided many years afterwards, a mere "right of earbage." The settlers, it is true, had for some thirteen years occupied lands and made divisions and conveyed to and from each other on this flimsy Indian title, without the special authority of any sovereignty, but it was a precarious title, liable to be challenged at any time and always open to the question whether the consent of the "right owner" had been obtained. This grant of Gov. Nicholls at once vested in the town of Huntington, as a political corporation, the full title held by the sovereignty of England, subject to the condition that the consent of the Indians be first obtained. There was a wide extent of territory in the middle of the town, far back from the shore, which the town had not then acquired, but the grant provided that upon the purchase of these lands of the Indians the title should rest in the town, and it was finally all purchased of the Indians. The grant was made to certain individuals named " in the behalf of themselves and their associates, the Freeholders and inhabitants of the said town, their heirs, successors and assigns." This was clearly a grant to the town, in behalf of all the people, the commonalty as well as the freeholders. However it cost something to procure the patent and procure the "Earbage right" of the Indians, and those who contributed for the purpose were held to be entitled to receive a proportion of the lands corresponding with the amount they had thus contributed. For this purpose a whole purchase was estimated at a given value and "hundred pounds rights" were given, or fractional parts of such rights, and were held from generation to generation, as representing a definite share in the common land, the title to which still continued in the town. Probably the persons who held these certificates or records of "rights" in undivided lands held no legal title whatever, the legal title being in the town or its trustees, but they had an equitable right to claim of the town a deed or conveyance to them of their

General and commander-in-chief of all the Militia, and
Admiral of the Navy of the same at our city of New York
this twelfth day of September, in the year of our Lord one
thousand seven hundred and ninety-three, and in the
eighteenth year of our Independence.

[L. S.]                                    GEO. CLINTON.

(*File No.* 69)

---

## [TOWN MEETING.]

[1667, Jan. 24.]

At a Towne Meeting January the 24<sup>th</sup> 1667, it was voated
and Agreed by and with the Consent of the towne that

---

proportionate share.  If they obtained such a deed, very well ;
but if they never procured such a conveyance they would have
no legal title.  Down to as late as the beginning of the present
century the descendants and assigns of these holders of " hundred pound rights " in the old or first purchase, in the eastern
purchase and other purchases, seemed to claim a legal title as
tenants in common of the common lands in the town, and
through committees made sales in some cases—some small and
some great ; but it is difficult to see how they gave any legal
title, unless such conveyances were afterwards ratified by the
town or its trustees.  The lands under tide water in the town
were acquired under this grant of Gov. Nicholls in the same
way as the uplands and, except what has been sold, constitute
the remains of the town's commons, and these old " hundred
pound right " claims adhered to such lands under water as well
as to uplands, but as the claims are now so widely distributed
among the descendants of the early holders, and their precarious nature has become better understood in the light of
decisions of the courts in this State, there seems to be no
disposition to further assert them, and the legal title is admitted
on all hands to be in the town trustees.

These observations only refer to common lands, or those
which had not been duly alienated at the time this grant was
made.  It did not disturb grants made at town meetings to
individuals prior to its date.  On the contrary it confirmed
such titles, and under the Duke's laws, then in force, four years
of quiet possession, immediately before Sept. 1, 1665, was
declared to give good, fee simple title.—C. R. S.]

Content Tytus* shall have that lott that was formerly given to John Ketcham it beeing a too hundred pound alotment, too acars of medow on the little neck and the rest on the west neck.

All above is entered in the new Book A. page 35.

(*Town Meetings. Vol.* 1, *p.* 13.

---

[TOWN MEETING.]

[1667, Jan. 24.]

January the 24 1667.

it is agreed that what land is found usfull for tilling at the end of Jonathan Rogers swampe henry sooper may take up not prejudising any watering or highway.

it is alsoe agreed that Nathaniell foster shall take up 4 akere of land neare to the Long swamp at the up side of Tredwells plaine.

Nathaniell foster have layd Downe that four acare.

(*Town Meetings, Vol.* 1, *p.* 12.)

---

[TOWN MEETING.]

[1667, Jan. 29,]

January the 29th 67.

it was agreed by and with ye consent of the townesmen Mark Megs shall have the swamp below the mill Dam to

---

[*Content Titus and his brothers Abial, John, Samuel, Henry and Edward, whose names often appear in the records, were sons of Robert and Hannah Titus, who came from near Stanstead Abbey, England, to New England in the "Hopewell" in 1635. I think they all came here by the way of Stamford, Conn. They probably went there from Wethersfield, Mass., with the Rev. Mr. Denton and came with him subsequently to Hempstead and Newtown, where their names appear at an early period.—C. R. S.]

Jonathan Rogers so it—pevided hee grind for the towne for twelfe part of the bushell wheat and Indian he clearing it in som convenient time.

(*Town Meetings, Vol.* 1, *p.* 29.)

---

## [DEED.   SAMUEL DAVIS TO JOHN FINCH.]

[1667, March 23.]

This writing testifieth that I Samuell Davis now off fairefeild have sould to John finch of huntington on home lot in huntington uppon Long eiland containing six acars more or les Bounded on the south by the Land of henry whitson on the north with the land that was Trusteram hodges with all the privilidges and devidents Booth of upland and Meddow there unto Belonging that I the saide Davis hath sould for a valiable Consideracon all redye paide and Doe binde my selfe heires and assignes to ffree it from all Bargons sales Morgidges executions or Incumbrances whatsoever only the said ffinch is to cleare any Damadge Whitson hath sustained since it was the said Davis and alsoe to cleare all Rates that is unpaide since that time in witnes whereof I set too my hand this 23th of March 1667.

the marke of

Witnes                                          SAMUELL × DAVIS
  CORNELIUS HULL }
  STEPHEN JARVIS }
This is A true Coppie of the Deede p mee

Joseph Bayly

Rec<sup>r</sup>

(*Court Rec. p.* 311.)

[TOWN MEETING.]

[1667, April 2.]

1667 at a towne meeting Aprell the second given Mr Jonas
wood 12 acars of Land on the littell necke against Cow
harbor by a towne voet as allsoe 8 acars of Meddow on
a neck called santipauge the on half too Mr Jonas wood
the other halfe to thomas seniors as alsoe fower acars lying on the easter most side of the said neck the on halfe
to Isack platt and the other halfe to henry whitson p
mee.

Joseph Baiely, Rec[r]

(*Court Rec. p.* 322, & *T. Meetings Vol.* 1, *p.* 15.)

---

[DEED. JOHN MATTHEWS TO THOMAS WEEKS.]

[1667, May 1.]

Know all men by these p[r]sents that I John Mathews of huntington uppon Long eiland victular have from mee my
heires executors administrators and assignes Bargoned
sould and made over unto thomas weeks sen[r] off huntington afowr said all my Rite title and Intrest that I have in a
too hundred pound Lot that I the said John Mathews Late
purchased of John Lum off fairefeild sittuate and Lying in
huntington afore said the Lot of the widow Rogers on the
south side, the frunt east towards the Run of water the
north side the high waye the Reere next to a hundred
pound Lot that the said Mathews lives in together with all
Lands priviledges Accomindacons profits and Revenues
thereto belongiug or accureing therefrom except halfe of
a hollow that was John Lums lying on the west side of
tredwels playne which I the said Mathews doth Reserve
for mine owne use and allsoe fower akars of Medow that

is uppon a necke of medow on the south side of the Iland
called by the name off siases necke which I doe Reserve in
the Roome of that fower akers that lyeth on the estermost
neck of Land now purchased of the bounds of huntington
which fower akers or A hundred pound Lotment of medow
I the said Mathews sell alinate and Make over unto the said
weekes and his sucksessors els all Lands Medows and
Accommidasons and privilidges I the aforesaid John Mathews Doe by these pʳsents sell alinate and estrainge from
mee my heires executors administrators and assignes all
my Rite title and Intrest that I had in that to hundred
pound Lot that I purchased of John Lum or ought to have
by any waye cr Meanes of that purchas I Doe Make over
unto the afore said thomas weekes his heires executors
administrators and assignes To have and to hould for ever,
further I doe by these pʳsents ingadge my selfe and my
assignes to Save harmeles the afore said weekes and his
assignes from any parson or parsons whatsoever whoo
maye or shall Laye any Clayme or title thereto or any part
or parsell thereof except Before excepted to the Indemnifing the said weekes or his sucksessors in his or thaire
quiet possession of the aforesaid Lands Medows or any part
or parsell thereof and all the said Lands to bee free from
Rates from the begining of the world untill the Daye of
the Date further more I the above said John Mathewes for
my selfe my heeres and assignes doth ingadge that if any
part or parsell of my fine that is Due to Lum to bee paid
yearely at fairefeild that is to saye fifteene pounds to bee
paid in five yeares by equall proportion yearely beginning
1668 the on and thirtie of march if any part or parsell bee
Lefte unpaid that the Lots should bee forfited to John Lum
as is spesified in the bill of sale of the said Mathews that the
above said thomas weekes should bee Damnified that then
it shall bee Lawfull for the said thomas weekes to enter
seaes poses and Injoye all the said mathews now liveth in
and every part and parsell thereof without Let or hindrance

of him the said mathewes his heires or assignes in witnes
whereof I have here unto set my hand this first Daye of
maye in the yeare of our Lord 1667.      the marke of
signed aud ddl.                          JOHN × MATHEWS
in the p^rsents of
JOSEPH BAYLY
JOHN KETCHAM.
        (*Court Rec. p.* 315.)

---

## [DEED. WILLIAM LUDLAM TO MARK MEGGS.]

[1667, June 13.]

know all men by these p^rsents that I William Ludlam of
the towne off huntington within the east Riding husban
man have and by these p^rsents doe sell assigne allinate and
make over ffrom mee my heirs executors, administrators or
assigns all my Right in and unto my mill* att huntington
Bought of Mr will Leverich of huntington aforesaid with
all the Right there unto Belonging or that heareafter may
belonge or appertaine and all preveledges what soever unto
marke meggs off oyster Baye his heires executors administrs or assignes for ever Really to have hould ocupie
and Injoye without any ffraude troble emison or molestation

---

[*This is the mill before referred to as having been built by
Rev. William Leverich. It was located at the south-west
corner of a lot on the north side of Mill-Dam Lane about five
hundred feet westerly from where the brook crosses the highway. The spot where the mill stood and the mill wheel was
located was often pointed out to the writer by his grandfather,
Gilbert Scudder, nearly fifty years ago, Mr. Scudder then own-
ing the land and being about 80 years old. The mill race,
though partially filled up, can now be traced. The dam which
flooded the lands far to the south was on the same site as that
now occupied by the highway—Mill-Dam Lane—and the gate
of the mill pond was where the bridge over the brook is now
located.—C. R. S.]

off any p'son or psons whatsoever ffirmely by these or as ffully
as maye bee made by any deede or convayance whatsoever
and as ffully Largely and amply as I the said Willi hade
might or could by any purchas grant or bill off sale ffrom
Mr William Leverich or the towne as Doth and maye appeare by the said Leveriches Bill of sale, dated the Twentie
on Daie of December anoe—1659 and all and other grants
ffrom the said towne or Townesmen what soever as alsoe the
Lands Inclosed Lande houesing or houses Barnes orchards
Meadows pastures gardings or all and singular my Rights
Titeles or my claimes whatsoever Belonging or done uppon
the said premises or any parte or parcell thereof with all
my Right unto A Certaine p'sell of Land Lying and being
in the west ffeild adjacent to the Lott of thomas Brush and
the Lande of the Townes in Comonadge with the ffeeding
and entradgements heareafter with Meddow According to
an Allottment off three hundred pounds allotment as ffirmely and fully as it was made to mee or mine all the Rits and
 *   *   *   not possessed or brought into possession I doe
heareby Deliver and ffurther what I maye or can deliver
as Belonging to my said mill or any of the said p^rmises and
all the fflooring and planking off the said house or houseing
hee the said Marke meggs sattisfing for the said Land the
full and just some off seaventie pounds to bee paid as followeth vizt : in Cattell and Mares as will more plainely : In
Wittnes I have heare unto sett my hand in oysterbaye this
Thirteene day of June in the Eaighteen yeare of the Raine
of our soverend Lord King Charles The second By the
grace off god off England scotland, ffrance and Ireland
Defender of the faith etc and in the yeare of our lord god
on thousand six hundred sixtie & seaven according to the
Church of England the above said mill and message it to
be Delivered at or about the ffeast of St. Michaell next.
the date five weeks more or les before or after not exceeding.                                        WILLIAM LUDLAM

signed, sealed and
delivered in the p$^r$sents of
  RICHARD HARKAR
  SIMON LANE
  this is a true Coppie of Marke meggs Bill of Sale from
william p mee

Joseph Baiely, Rec$^r$

(*Court Rec. p. 323.*)

---

## [THE NICHOLLS GRANT TO GEORGE BALDWIN OF EATON'S NECK.]

[1667, June 22.]

A conformation of Eaton's Neck, granted to Geo. Baldwin,* Richard Nicolls, Esq., Governour Gen., all under his Royall Highness, James Duke of Yorke and Albany, &c., of all his Territories in America.

To all to whom these presents shall come sendeth, Greeting : Whereas Mr. William Joanes, ot New Haven, deriving a right and title from Theophilus Eaton of the same place, Esq., did upon the 22d day of December 1662 for the consideration therein expressed, Bargain, sell, assign and set over unto Capt. Robert Seely of Huntington a certain parcel or Neck of land commonly called Eaton's Neck, lying and being in the East Riding of Yorkshire upon Long Island on the North side of said Island to the East of Huntington Bay where striking out into the sound it is thereby Bounded to the North East, and South, and on ye West with Hun-

---

[*This grant to Baldwin was made about seven months after the grant by the same Governor to Huntington. As the grant to Huntington was bounded on the west by Cold Spring harbor, on the east by Smithtown, and on the north by the Sound, it would seem to include Eaton's Neck ; but on the theory, we presume, that the inhabitants of Eaton's Neck had in three suits maintained their title as against Huntington, the Governor made this grant.—C. R. S.]

tington Harbor, from whence it goes on East to the Beach wch divides it from Crabb Meadows, the middle of which said Beach is Bounded betwixt the said Neck, and Crabb Meadow which also Joynes it to the Island. The Neck of land aforesaid containing by estimation about one thousand five hundred acres bee it more or less and whereas the said Robert Seely did by Bill of Sale bearing date the 29th day of July 1663 sell and make over all his right and title in the said Parcell or Neck of land commonly called Eaton's Neck as aforesaid unto George Baldwin of Huntington aforesaid who doth secured to pay a valuable consideration for the same unto the said Robert Seely having likewise cleared his Right and title to the premises at Law ; Now for a confirmation unto the said George Baldwin in his En-joyment of his Bargain for the premises ; Know Ye, That by virtue of the commission and authority unto me given by his Royal Highness I have ratified, confirmed and granted and by these presents do ratify, confirm and Grant unto the said George Baldwin his heirs and assigns the afore recited parcel or Neck of land called and known by the name of Eatons Neck as aforesaid. Together with all the lands, Woods, Meadows, Pastures, Marshes, Creeks, Waters, Lakes, Fishing, Hunting and Fowling and all other profits, commodities and emolum'ts to the said Parcel or Neck of land and premises belonging or in any wise apper-taining to have and to hold the said Parcel or Neck of land and premises unto the said George Baldwin his heirs and assigns unto the proper use and behoofe of the said George Baldwin his heirs and assigns forever Binding, and Paying such duties and acknowledgements as now, as or hereafter shall be constituted and established by the Law of this Government under the obedience of his Royal Highness his heirs and successors, given under my hand and seal at Fort James in New York the 22d day of June in the 19th year of his Ma'ties Reigne Annoez Dm 1667.

RICHARD NICHOLLS.

*(File Eaton's Neck papers D.)*

# [THE NICHOLLS PATENT TO NATHANIEL SYLVESTER AND OTHERS OF HORSE (LLOYDS NECK.]

[1667, Nov. 20.]

> The Patent to Nathaniel Sylvester, Thomas Hart and Latimer Sampson for Horse Neck neare Oysterbay.

Richard Nicolls &c. Whereas there is a certain Parcel or tract of Land in the North Riding of Yorkshire upon Long Island, Lying and being in a Neck on the north side thereof streaching out in the Sound or East River comonly called and known by the name of Horse Neck, bounded to the West with Oysterbay to the east with Cowe Harbour, towards the North with the sound and towards the south with a Beach extending to the head of a certain creek which parteth or divideth the bounds of the town of Huntington and the said neck which said parcell or tract of land hath been heretofore purchased of the Indian proprietors and due satisfaction given for the same and whereas John Richbell late of Oysterbay in the foresaid North Riding, Merchant, did make good proofs of his title to the said Hors Neck at the generall meeting held att Hempsted in the beginning of the Month of March 1664 against John Conkling on the behalf of his wife and some orphans who lay claim thereunto and also at the general Court of Assizes held in this City in the month of September 1665 against the inhabitants of the Town of Huntington and hath since sold and conveyed the said premises together with a neck of meadow called the fort Neck lying upon the South side of Long Island and belonging to the Town of Oysterbay unto Nathaniel Sylvester of shelter Island,

Thomas Hart of the Island of Barbadose and Latimer Sampson of Oysterbay on Long Island aforesaid Merchant. Now for a further confirmation unto the said Nathanel Sylvester Thomas Hart and Latimore Sampson in their possession and enjoyment of the premises Know $^{ye}$ that by virtue of the commission and authority unto us given by his Royal Highness thee Duke of York I have ratified, confirmed and granted and by these presents do ratify confirme and grant unto the said Nathanill Sylvester, Thomas Hart and Latimer Sampson, their heirs and assigns all the afore recited parcell or tract of land called Horse Neck aforesaid togather with all woods beaches marshes, meadows, pastures, creeks waters, lakes, fishing, hawking, hunting and fowling and all other profits comodities and imoluments to the said parcell or tract of land belonging and next or appertaining with their and every of their appertnances and of every part and parcell thereof and in regard of the distance of the plantations settled or to be settled upon the said Neck from any Towu the persons inhabiting or that inhabit thereon shall be excused from ordinary attendance at trainings and other such ordinary duties in the Town but in matters ef assessment public rates and the like they are to be taxed by the officers of Oysterbay to which Town they are adjudged to belong and they are likewise to give due obedience to all such warents as shall be sent from any Justice of the Peace or executions granted by any of the Courts of judication which shall be served by the sheriff or his deputies. To Have and to Hold the said parcell or tract or Neck of land with the Neck of Meadow afore mentioned and premises with all and singular the previlege and appertenances to the said Nathanill Sylvester, Thomas Hart and Latimer Sampson, their heirs and assignes to the proper use and behoofe of the said Nathanill Sylvester, Thomas Hart and Latimer Sampson their heirs and assigns forever as free Land of inheritance. Rendering and paying as a quit

Rent for the same the Value of four bushell of wheate yearly upon the 29 day of September, if Demanded unto his Royal Highness the Duke of York and his heirs or such Govornor and governours as shall from time to time be appointed and sett over them. Given under my hand & seal at Fort James in New York on Manhatans Island the 20 day of Nov. in the 19 year of the Reign of our Sovereign Lord Charles the second &c. Annoy Dom in 1667.*
Exam'in
by J. SPRAGGE, Lieut.

(*File Lloyd's Neck Papers F.*)

## [TOWN MEETING.]

[1667, Dec. 24.]

Att a towne Meeting December the 24th 1667 it is voated and agreed the same day that Epenetus platt and John Sammis† and Noah Rogers shall take up there first———

[*This patent of Horse Neck was given by Gov. Nicholls about one year later than the date of his patent to Huntington, and is open to the same charge of inconsistency noticed in the Eaton's Neck patent of the same year. The grant to Huntington was bounded on the north by Long Island Sound and no exception was made of Lloyd's Neck. Gov. Nicholls probably had in mind the decision he and his council had made awarding title to the Neck to Richbell as against the claim of Huntington.—C. R. S.]

[†John Sammis was the common ancestor of the Sammis family in Huntington. He is believed to have come here via. Southold among the first settlers. His homestead was at the Cove, West Neck, and it remained in the family down to about 1880, when it was purchased and is now owned by Jenkins Van Schaick. The first John Sammis married a daughter of John Corey. His children were John, Isaac, Silas, Jeremiah, David, Deborah and Hannah. The line of ancestry in Huntington may be stated thus, as to one branch of the family : John Sammis I, John Sammis II, John Sammis III, Platt Sammis, John Sammis IV, now living here, aged about 80 years.—C. R. S.]

---


of land against Samuel Ketchams hollow on the east side of the south path with what they find good alsoe to take up towards the second division not exseeding what they are to take in by the towne order which is 12 acares to a too hundred alottment.

Alsoe it is agreed the same day that Mr Wood and Epenetus platt and thomas weeks is to have six Acares a peese on the east side of the south path on tredwells plaine towards there Division of land that is their second division.

Also it is agreed that Tho. powell Samuell wood and thomas ———— shall take in six acars apees toward their second division on the west sid of the south path on tredwells plaine

Alsoe it is agreed that Noah Rogers shall take up fower acars on the hether side of Mr Woods feild at Cow harbour towards his second Division of land.

Alsoe it is agreed that Thomas Powell and Henry whitson shall take up what good planting land they can find on the hill by the side Cowharbor swamp the swamp is to the south ———— of the planting land it being toward their seconddivision of land being on the south of the path.

Alsoe it is agreed that Nathaniell foster samll ———— and John Rogers shall take what planting land is found good in the mouth of the little neck below at the path it being toward their second devision of land they not exseeding their division their request being but 12 acare.

Alsoe it is agreed that James Chichster shall take up six acres on the east neck adjoyning to that three acres that hee hath allready taken up provided hee fense in the swamp westward it being toward his second division.

Alsoe it is agreed that thomas Scudder shall take up four acers of land adjoyneing to his six hee hath already taken up on the east neck, it being toward his second devision of land.

And alsoe it is agreed that mark Megs shall take up six acars of land on the east neck on the north side of thomas Scudders it being towards his second division of land

Alsoe it is agreed that Mark Megs shall take up som more of the swamp below the mildam as the townsmen or any appointed by them shall judge meet consideration it shall bee cleared in som convenient time and alsoe hee grind wheat & indian corne for the twelfe part of the Bushell for the whole towne and to make good meal when there is water enough to doe it for which the towne hath committed to every man to noe their wish.

(*Towne Metings*, Vol. 1, *p*. 11.)

---

[TOWN MEETING.]

[1667, Dec. 24.]

Alsoe it was voated and Agreed 24 of December that———— Simond Lane shall have that lott that was formerly given to Benjamin Jones lying on the north side of Capt. Thomas fleitts* home lott, provided hee improve it according to

---

[*Thomas Fleet was here as early as 1660, and there is a tradition in the family that he came here direct from England, bringing his family with him in his own vessel, and that he first landed in Cold Spring Harbor at a place which has ever since been called "Fleet's Hole." There is also a tradition in the family, said to be supported by good authority, that he was descended from Admiral Fleetwood of Cromwell's time, and that the name was shortened from Fleetwood to Fleet. He was largely engaged in commerce, and is said to have had as many as forty vessels on the high seas. He was the ancestor of all the Fleets in Huntington.—C. R. S.]

the custome of the towne.

Alsoe it is agreed the same day that Samuell Titus Thomas Conklyne and Richard floyd shall take in six acares of land apeece on the west sid of the west neck to make up that they take in on the north sid of Timothy Conklynes home lot to make up their second devision of land.

Alsoe it is agreed that Joseph Bayly shall run the fence at the west end of his home lott to the mill pond hee there to making a suffissiont gate for a horse with a sack it being the townes gift to Joseph bailey.

Alsoe it is voated and agreed that Joseph Bayly shall take up what good planting land is to be found on the left hand of the path——hether side of stony brook hee prejudising not the way of cattell to water it being to his second division of land,
see old Book No. 3 : page 61 : and in New book A. 35.

Alsoe it is agreed that Epenetus plat shall take in what land is found fitt too plant on the east end of Mr woods feild hee prejudising not the high waye and not exceeding his second division.

(*Town Meetings Vol. 1, p. 13.*)

---

## [TOWN MEETING.]

[1667.]

Constable and overseers chosen for the yeare 1667.
    Thomae powell Constable
    John Teed* and ⎫ overseers.
    John Rogers   ⎭
    (*Court Rec. p. 267.*)

[*John Teed's homestead was at West Neck, near what is now called Bouton's Point. He came from London as a servant in the family of Samuel Gunseld in 1637, when 19 years old. (See Hotton's Lists). He married Mary Jennings and had one son, Samuel. The name long since disappeared from this town.—C. R. S.]

## [AGREEMENT BETWEEN MARK MEGGS AND SIMEON LANE.]

[1667, Dec. 24.]

Whereas it was Agreed in the 24[th] of December 1667 that Marke Meggs should take up six Acars of land on the north side of thomas scudders on the east neck the said meegs giveing Libertie to Simon Lane for make use and improve the said six acars of Land as Long as the said Lane lived provided the said Lane did not Lett it to any or parson to Improve nor give any leave or lysence to any parson or persons whatsoever directly nor indirectly the which made appeare the said Land and every part and parsell thereof to Returne to the said megs or his Assignes without troble or molestacon This marke meggs ordered mee to Record soone after the Land was granted.

Joseph Bayly Rec[r]

(*Court Rec. p.* 190.)

## [ORDERS BY THE CONSTABLE AND OVERSEERS.]

[1667.]

Orders made By the Constable and Townsmen in 1667.
Constable Thomas powell : oversears, Thomas Skidmore : Joseph whitman, John Tedd, John Rogers.

first, for the Fireing off the woods.

it is ordered and agreed by the Constable & overseers that thomas wilke sen[r] and tho : Jones shall for the next yeare 1668 warne the whole towne Inhabitants at such a season as they doth judg fit to fire and burne the woods and every Inhabitant shall spend the whole Day in that

worke it any p'son Doth not com at the time appoynted he
shall forfit 2$^d$ and if any com not att all 4$^d$ this order to
Remaine yearely and every Constable and townsmen for
every yeare insuing shall so appoynt to men for that purpos.*

Secondly

it is ordered and agreed by the Constable and townesmen that every Inhabitant having suffictient warning to a
towne meeting every man shall com to the place appoynted
at the time Appointed : and for neglect hearein thay
shall pay as ffolloweth for not coming at the ower six pence,
for not coming at all three shillings and for goeing away
without Leave from the Company twelpence and on them
that is found Delinlquent and Denies to pay it shall bee
taken by Destres forth with.

(*Court Rec. p.* 195.)

---

## [TOWN MEETING.]

[1668, Jan. 1.]

January the first 1668.
it was ordered and agreed at a town Meeting the same Day

---

[*Under the Duke's Laws, promulgated when the English
took possession in 1665, eight overseers were to be chosen the
first year to hold office two years, and four to be elected every
two years afterwards, and a constable was to be elected every
year out of the overseers of the previous year.  The constable
and overseers managed the town affairs and had power to
make orders and rules concerning fences, highways, and similar
matters.  Constables were to attend courts, and they had
power to make arrests of those " who were overtaken with
strong drink, or found swearing or Sabbath breaking.  Va-
grants night walkes provided taken in sight of constable or
provent information from others or if in bear houses or disorderly places."  " Every constable shall have a staff six feet long
with the King's arms on it, as a badge of his authority."—
C. R. S.]

that John Cory shall take up 2 acars on the south sid of his hom lot and 2 acars or more if fond in the hollow, it not prejudicall to wayes it being towards his second Devision.

the same Daye it was ordered that Robart Crandfeild shall take up six acars on the east neck it being p$^t$ of his second Devision.

the same Daye it was ordered and agreed that Richard Brush shall take up 5 or 6 acars of Land by the side and at the Reare of his Lot it being not prejudicall towards his second, Devision.

John ffinch is to have six acars of Land on the bottom of the east neck, stephen Jarvis six acars second, Thomas powell six acars third Robart Cranfeild six acars fowerth.

(*Court Rec. p.* 180 )

---

[TOWN MEETING.]

[1668, Jan. 13.]

I John Jones* of huntington Doth Ingage to Bare all Charge of lawe sute that may arise by oyster Bay or Smith of Smithfild and what Damage or loss may fall uppon that Alotment I Bought of Richard floyd I promise to Bare and that Richard floyd nor his successors shall not bee Damnified.

Joseph Bayly, Re$^r$

---

[*A writer in the *Stamford Herald* in 1879 says that three brothers, John, Benjamin and Ebenezer Jones, came from Wales to New England ; that John settled in the town of Huntington, L. I., another on the Hudson, and the third, Ebenezer, at Poundridge, near Stamford, where his descendants now reside. It is worthy of note that the father of Rev. Eliphelet Jones, who preached in Huntington from about 1667 to about 1732, was named John Jones. He was also a minister of considerable note. We have no facts, however, sufficient to identify the John Jones of Huntington with him. Benjamin Jones, above mentioned, was probably the same Benjamin whose name appears often in these records.—C. R. S.]

1668 Imp<sup>r</sup> these two orders
\* \* \* that came from o<sup>e</sup> governer came unto Mr
Woods hands and the Constable the eight daie of January
that is tuching the prise of graine and also touching a new
election of military officers† and were publised wendesday
the 13<sup>th</sup> of January 1668.

Joseph Bayly Re<sup>c</sup>

---

[†The Duke's Laws had established an elaborate military
system. All able-bodied male persons over sixteen years old
were required to do military service, and were to meet at
appointed times for training, under a penalty of five shillings
for default. Each man was required to have, at his own expense
if a freeholder, and if a servant, at his master's expense, one
good gun, fit for present service, a powder horn, worm, prime
rod wire, one pound of powder, seven pounds pistol bullets,
twenty pounds bullets fitted to the gun, four fathoms of match
for a match-lock gun, and four good flints fitted for a fire-lock
gun, subject to a fine of five shillings for neglect as to each;
and captains were required to examine the arms every three
months and make yearly reports to the Governor of the State of
the equipment. Those who wilfully refused to provide arms were
to be put to service by the constable and their wages applied
for the purpose. There were four regular training days in
each town every year, and in each riding one general training,
occupying three days, and once every two years there was a
general training of all the soldiers in the government, the
Governor to appoint the day. A troop of horse consisted of
fifty, a captain, lieutenant, cornet, quartermaster and three
corporals, each to have one horse, saddle, bridle, holsters,
pistols or carbine, and a good sword, under a penalty of five
shillings; and if a trooper sold his horse without leave of his
captain, he was subject to a penalty of £5. The penalty to a
soldier for sleeping in his watch in time of peace was £5; in
time of war, death. Every town was compelled to have a
watch house and to have in it one barrel of powder " English
wraught," 150 lbs. of bullets, and 30 lbs. of matches. If there
were forts, the constables and overseers were to mount the
guns and provide appurtenances, and assess the cost on the
inhabitants. A company consisted of sixty men. The constables and overseers nominated three men for captain, lieutenant
and ensign, and the Governor appointed them unless objected
to, in which case they were appointed by him after being
chosen by a plurality of the soldiers in the company. This

[TOWN MEETING.]

at a town Meeting January the 13ᵗʰ 1668 it was voated and agreed with the generall Consent of the town that the Constable and overseers shall geet a pitition drawn up and presente to the governer to Manifest the towns grevence concerning the prise of corne and what els the towne see cause and to send a messenger with the petison as soone as possable.‡

(*Town Meetings, Vol.* 1, *p.* 23.)

---

[DEED. WILLIAM LEVERICH TO JOHN TEED.]

[1668, March 2.]

Know all men by these presents that I William Leverich of huntington in yorksheare uppon Long Island doe heareby sell and alinate to John Tedd off the same towne A peice off Land with the Meddow Belonging to the same the Land lying uppon the west necke and the Meddow Bounded by the head of the Creeke lying by it which said land and Meddow was sould to me by John Ketcham the

---

system was enforced in all its details by severe penalties and punishment for disobedience or neglect. From the records we learn that Huntington had its military company, troop of horse, watch house, and fort, and its training days. The "town spot" was the place where the train bands met.—C. R. S.]

[‡Under the Duke's Laws the Governor and council fixed the price of grain and they had power to prohibit its export. About this time an order was made prohibiting its export and fixing the price so low as to seriously affect the interests of the people here and they protested against it. The government not only controlled the price of grain, but made it a legal tender in payment for all work done at the price so fixed, unless otherwise provided by special agreement to be paid in some other commodity.—C. R. S.]

said land and meddow I doe hereby sell and alinate ffrom my selfe and heires to the said John Tedd and his heires for ever witnes my hand this second Daye of March one thousand six hundred sixtie eaight in the p,sence of,

BENJAMIN JONES                    WILLIAM LEVERICH

                    his
SAMUELL ✕ W. WOOD
                    mark

                    this is A true Coppie of the origgin-
                    all p, mee Joseph Baiely, Rec<sup>r</sup>

(*Deeds, Vol. 1, p.* 19.)

---

## [DEED.    SAMUEL DAVIS TO JOHN FINCH.]

### [1668, March 23.]

This p<sup>r</sup>sent writting Testifieth y<sup>t</sup> I Samuell Davice now of fairefeild have sold to John finch of Huntington one home lott In Huntington upon Long Island Containeing six accars more or less bound (one the South by the land of Henry whison one y<sup>e</sup> north with y<sup>e</sup> land that once was trastrum Hoges) with all previleges and Devidents both of upland and meadow there unto belonging. Thus I the said Davis hath sold for a valueable consideration allredy received doe bind myself heirs and assignes to free it from all bargaines sales mortgages executores or Incumberances what soever, only the said finch Is to Clear any damages y<sup>t</sup> y<sup>e</sup> said whison hath suffered since it was the said Davices and all soe to clear all Rate that were due since that time In wittness whereof I sett to my hand this 23 of march 166$\frac{7}{8}$

witness                              the mark of

CORNELUS HULL                    SAMUELL ✕ DAVICE
STEVEN JARVICE

This is a true Coppy of y^e originall deed extracted by
Thomas powell, Recorder.

*(Deeds. Vol. 1, p. 9.)*

---

[TOWN MEETING.]

[1668, April 1.]

At a towne Meeting the first day of Aprill it was voated
and agreed that Nathaniell Foster shall take up fower
Acares of land on the hetherend of tredwels plaine on the
east sid of the south path it being like unto a hollow it be
ing towards his second division.

Also it was voated and agreed the same Daie that Joseph
Whitman shall take up ten or twelve acars of land on the
west sid of the south path on the hether side of Samuell
Ketchams hollow, it being toward his second division.

*(Town Meetings, Vol. 1, p. 12.)*

---

[TOWN MEETING.]

[1668, April 1.]

April the first 1668.

At a general town meeting it was voted and agreed that
Joseph Baiely shall run the fence at the west end of his
home lot to the mill pond or drain ; he making a sufficient
gate for a horse with a sack to come in and go out ; it being the town's gift to Joseph Baiely.

Joseph Baiely, Re^r

[Copied from the original in the Court Records, p.——,
in the Revision in 1873; also Book of Transcription, p.
70.]

*(Town Meetings Vol. 1, p. 25, & Court Rec. p. 322.)*

Constable and overseers chosen in 1668. was,
Thomas Scudder, Constable ;
James Chichester
        and                    Ovarseers.
Epenetus Platt,
[Copied from the original Court Records p.      , in the
Revision in 1873.]
        *Town Meetings Vol. 1, p. 27.)*

---

## [TOWN MEETING. CATTLE TO BE DRIVEN TO CRAB MEADOW.]

[1668, April 14.]

Att a Gennerall towne meeting Aprill the 14th
it was voted and Agreed that all the drie or young cattell
Belonging to the town shall be driven to Crab medder or
beyond toward the Sunken Meadow the first day of May
next and that the said cattell shall bee keept the first weeke
by too men day and night and then three weekes by on
man and if need require longer and if men can bee hired
then the Constable and overseers to hire them and see a
Rate to bee made and every man to pay according to the
proportion of Cattell and if men cannot bee procured then
men to take their tearnes in keeping and the Constable to
apoynt whare to begin and if any Inhabitant shall Refuse
to drive his Cattell or steares Dry cows, ox yearlings that
he shall pay towards the Cow heard for every yearling as
a cow if not more and alsoe such Inhabitant so Refusing to
bee looked on as a contemner of authoritie.

                                        pe mee Joseph, Rer
    *(Town Meetings p. 14.)*

Alsoe it was voated and agreed the same Day that the towne shall bee fensed in in generall between this and the later end of June next and if any man shall Refuse or neglect soe to doe by that time hee shall pay for every road five shillings of his due portion it being equally devided how much every mans sheare shall bee and after it bee fenced according too the voat and Agreement noe inhabitant to exceed three creatures for on hundred pound alotment swine excepted.

per mee Joseph Bayly. Re<sup>r</sup>

(*Town Meetings Vol. 1, p.* 14.)

----

## [COURT RECORDS. MARK MEGGS vs. SARAH SOPER. SARAH IN THE STOCKS.]

[No date.]

Marke Meges plaintive Against Sarah Sooper wife of henry Sooper Defendant in an accon of Molestacon.

the plaintive Declareth that shee Coming to my house in a violent mannar Contrary to order given her by y<sup>e</sup> Aughtoritie to the Contrary betterly Raileing and vehemently prevoking me by words saying shee was come to dame mee and that I was a damde ould devill and A Rogue if I did not throw her into the fire and her husband stood by her and did not Rebuke her for it which I shall prove.

The Court finds for the plaintive in every Branch of the Declaracon that the Defend hath Raishly and unreasonably ansured Marke Megs for which the defendant is to give public sattisfaction.

secondly. in slanderous Lyes against Mark Megs as hee proved ffor which offence the Defendant is to sit in the stoks.

Lastly for Molesting the plaintive in Coming to his hous and Raileing Against him in A very unreasonable mannor when shee was Commanded By aughthoritie to the Contrary ffor which Contempt the defendant to sit in the stocks.

The plaintiff to pay Cost of Court in Respect the Defendant suffers the Law.

and if alsoe if the defendant p'sist in such a Raileing and Revileing mannor that the Complaints coms in the like Manner to Aughthorytie that then the Defend. to Bound to her good Behaviour or els to give good securitie or to Bee sent to prisson.

the Defendant sarah Sooper Charged Marke Megs the plaintive that hee would Murder her and that shee now gave notice of it that after it was Don it might bee knowne.*

( *Court Records, p.* 268.)

---

## [MARK MEGGS'S BOND FOR APPEARANCE.]

[1668, May 19.]

Know all men By these prsents that I Marke Meggs of Huntington on Long eiland in New Yorksheere Miller doth Bind my selfe and my goods unto our Sove^r Lord the

---

[*The law of the period required that every parish should have stocks for offenders and a pound for cattle, and prisons and pillories at the places of holding Sessions. The Town Court had jurisdiction of assault, slander and disorderly conduct amounting to minor offences generally. One offence was defined as "giving false news and lying about another." The penalty was a fine of 40 shillings, and if not paid, to sit in the stocks not exceeding seven hours, or be whipped not exceeding forty stripes, and give satisfaction. If the law was in force now the town whipper would have abundance of employment. —C. R. S.]

King and to his inferior offecars in the towne of huntington to anser the Complaints of Thoman wicks Isacke platt
Cap<sup>tn</sup> ffleete and Nathaniell ffoster Inhabitants of huntington aforesaid att the next sessions att south hampton which
will bee on the ferst wensdaye of March next ensuing then
and there too personally appeare and to abide the order
of the Courte and not to Depart without Lyceanse given
under my hand this 19<sup>th</sup> of January in the twenteth yere
of his Ma<sup>tis</sup> Raine and in the yeare of our lord 1668.*

(*Court Records p.* 185.)

[TOWN MEETING.]

[1668, July 1.]

per mee Joseph Bayly Re<sup>r</sup>
Att a towne Meeting July the first 1668 it was ordered and
agreed the same day by and with the Consent off the
whole towne that Thomas skidmore shall have the Reed
Pond on the south sid of the east field leaving some part
of it for watering for Cattell and a Bridg for people to goe
to cow harbor for a pathwaye and alsoe his preportion of
land adjoining to the pon as convenient as can bee found.

[*Courts of Sessions were at this period held three times in
each year in the East Riding—Suffolk County—in March, June
and December, not exceeding three days in one term. Courts
were required to be opened by a crier "who shall make
proclamation and say O, yes! O, yes! O yes!. Silence is
commanded in the court while his Majesty's Government and
Justices are sitting, upon peril of imprisonment." The fee of
Jurois was three shillings and six pence per day. Under the
Duke's laws juries consisted of not more than seven, nor less
than six men, and, except "in case of life and death" a majority
of the jury was sufficient to convict.—C. R. S.]

Alsoe it was ordered and agreed the same Daye that all the
Inhabitants of ye towne from sixteene upward of male
shall for this year all meete together when they shall bee
cald thereto for to cut downe Brush or under wood in and
about this towne at such seasonable times as shall bee
thought fit to destroy it and for the carring on of this work
to overseers to be chosen by the towne for carring on of
this expedison and every Inhabitant is then and there to
appeare and to work the whole Daye or dayes and not to
depart untill the whole Company departe uppon the pennaltie of five shillings for esh dayse neglect or too shillings
six pense halfe a dayes neglect.*

(*Town Meetings, Vol.* 1, *p.* 29.)

---

[TOWN MEETING.]

[1668, July 1.]

July the first 1668.
it was ordered and Agreed the same Daye that thomas
mills shall have the Boggie Meddoe that is at the Reare of
his lott on the east necke square with his lotte and to give
fortie shilling for it to the use of the towne this Medder is

---

[*There is every reason to suppose that Huntington at its
first settlement, like all new countries where they are not low
and marshy, was clear of undergrowth, as the annual fires running over the country destroyed it, or prevented its growth ;
but as soon as the lands became populated and fenced in, and
the spread of fires was prevented to a great extent, underbrush
grew up and covered the premises in all directions. This is
the experience in all new countries and Huntington was
probably no exception. Probably the elevated lands of Huntington, before the advent of white men, was an open park of
scattered trees, and the thick forests were confined to low and
wet grounds. Fifteen years' of settlement had no doubt
changed the face of the country considerably and it became
necessary to cut away the underbrush.—C. R. S.]

to bee fenced in in some Convenient time, it is to bee understood y$^t$ it is all y$^e$ boggie medder y$^t$ lies at y$^e$ rear and east side of y$^e$ fenced land y$^e$ wish bee paid for.

it was ordered and Agreed the same Day that Abiall Titus shall have fower acars off land on the north side off a small pees of land of Richard Watels it not Being found preiadicall to any high way it being in part towards his second devision.

the same day
it was ordered and agreed that thomas Scudder shall take in that boggie medder on the south side of his lot on the east necke from the spring to the harbour as his fence goeth and it to bee toward his third Devision.

it is ordered and agreed the same Day that Stephen Jarvise and Robart Crandfeild shall Run their fense to the Beech all above entered in Book A. p. 35.
(*Town Meetings Vol. 1, p. 30.*)

---

[DEED. MARK MEGGS TO JONATHAN ROGERS.]

[1668, July 1.]

Know all men by these p$^r$sents that I Marke Megs off Huntington upon Long Eiland in New Yorkeshire, Millare Have and by these p$^r$sents doe sell alinate and Make over ffrom mee my heires executors & administrators and assignes all my Rite title and Intrest in A parsell off Land sittuate and Lying in the south est end off the West ffeild Containeing six acars bee it More or les unto Jonathan Rogers off huntington upon Long Eiland in new yorkeshire planter his heires executors administrators assignes ffor ever, Too have hould occupie and Injoye with out any fraude troble or Molestation of any pson or persons what soever with all

priviledges proffits and Revenows thereunto Belongeth or
Appertaineth therefore I the aforesaid Marke Meges Doth
By these sell allinate and Make over unto the aforesaid
Jonathan Rogers his heires and assignes to have and to
hould for ever and I doe further Ingadge my self my heires
and assignes to save harmles and Indemnified the said
Jonathan Rogers his heires and assignes ffrom Any p'son
or p'sons whatsoever that shall or may Laye Any Claime
or title to any p^t or p'sells thereof  In witnes whereof I
have heare unto sett my hand this first Daye of July in the
twentteth yeare of the Raine off our sovr Lord Charls the
second king of England scotland france and Ireland defender of the faith etc^r and in the yeare of our Lord 1668·
signed and ddld

in the presents of
the mark of
GEORGE × BALDING
Joseph Baiely Rec^r

the mark of
MARK × MEGGS

*( Court Rec. p. 324.)*

---

## [DEED.  GEORGE BALDWIN TO ALEXANDER AND RICHARD BRYAN.]

### [1668, July 11.]

Know all men by these presents that I, George Baldwin of
Huntington on Long Island with the consent of my wife
Mary Baldwin late Demison, granted bargained sold and
made over unto Alexander Bryan and his son Richard
Bryan both of Milford in the Colony of Connecticut—mer-
chant—a certain parcel or neck of land commonly called
and known by the name of Eatons Neck, lying on the East
side of Huntington Harbor bounded as is specified in the
Patent granted for that neck of land by Richard Nicolls
Esq Governor of New York unto the said George Baldwin

as also as doth appears by a bill of sale of Captain Robert Siely made over unto the aforesaid George Baldwin of Huntington to him and his heirs and assigns forever bearing date the twenty ninth day of July one thousand six hundred sixty and three with all the appurtenances privileges profits and commodities or what so is specified particularly in the Patent—and the aforesaid George Baldwin does by these presents grant bargain sell and make over unto the aforesaid Alexander and Richard Bryan* to them their heirs and assigns forever—All that neck of land, commonly called and known by the name of Eaton's Neck with all dwelling houses, barns, outhouses, land wood meadows, pastures, marshes, rivers, waters, lakes, fishing, hunting, fowling and all other profits commodities and all appurtenances there. unto belonging—for and in consideration of the sum of two hundred pounds in hand paid by the aforesaid Alexander and Richard Bryan unto the aforesaid George Baldwin, and I do by these presents promise and engage unto the said Alexander and Richard that I will furnish the building of the Barn that is to be done by agreement and likewise to leave there those plants that * * * * further I do promise and engage to secure and deliver every particular in as good * * * on the first of May next ensuing as is at this present sealing and delivering, the aforesaid George Baldwin for himself his wife and heirs and assigns does covenant and grant ; for himself and either of them to and with the abovesaid Alexander and Richard Bryan their heirs, executors and assigns by these presents shall and law fully may well and in peace have hold and enjoy the aforesaid neck of land and all appurtenances thereunto belonging

[*Alexander and Richard Bryan came from Milford, Conn., to Huntington. Alexander was probably the ancestor of those of the name of Bryant now in Huntington and Smithtown. We shall find that Alexander and Richard Bryan, several years after this deed, procured a Manorial grant of Eaton's Neck from Gov. Dongan to them.—C. R. S.]

and unto their use and behoof of their heirs and assigns
forever and for the true performance of these conditions
I have hereunto set my hand and seal this Eleventh day of
July one thousand six hundred sixty and eight 1668.
Signed, sealed and delivered )                    ✗ mark of
in the presence of                   )        GEORGE BALDWIN
    THOMAS OVIAT                            ✗ mark of
    SAMUEL BALDWIN                        MARY BALDWIN
    Recorded in the Office in New York 8th day of August
1668.
                                    Matthias Nicolls.
                                            Secy.

    (*File Eaton's Neck papers E.*)

---

## [DEED.  JONAS WOOD TO JOSEPH BAILEY.]

[1668, July 16.]

know all men by these p'sents that I Jonas Wood senr of
huntington uppon Long eiland in new yorksheare have and
Doe by these p'sents Doe sell allinate assigne and make
over ffrom mee my heires executors administrators and
assignes ffor A Considerable some in hand paid all my
Rite title and intrest in an Allotment By denomination off
a too hundred pound lot fformerly in the Tenor or occupation off George Sutton since Allinated ffrom him the said
Sutton unto Mr James Miels off vergenia and since attached
and prosicuted in lawe by mee Jonas wood afore said and
given too mee By the Courte of sessions in the east Rideing
ffindeing my prosekeucon to bee just and leagall I saie all
my Rite title and intrest in and to the p'meses I have sould
and made over unto Joseph Baiely off huntington uppon
Long eiland in yorkesheare afore saide his heires executors
administrators and assignes ffor ever to have hould occupie
and injoye without any fraude Trouble or molesstacon off

any parson or parsons whatsoever firmely by these p<sup>r</sup>sents or as ffully as maye bee made by any Deed or Convayance whatsoever with all Lands privelidges accomindacons proffitts and Reveneues thereto Belonging or accrueing therefrom as allsoe all houseing out houseing orchards Barnes, gardens pastures Medows, and privilidges I the afore said Jonas wood Doe by these p<sup>r</sup>sents sell allinate and estrainge ffrom mee my heires executors administrators and assignes all my Rite title and Intrest unto the afore said Joseph Baiely his heires executors administrators and assignes Too have and too hould forever and I Doe by these p'sents Ingadge my selfe my heires executors administrators and asssignes to save harmeless and indemnified the said Baiely his heires and assignes from any p'son or p'sons whatsoever whoe shall or maye Laye any Claime or title to the afore said Lott or any p<sup>t</sup> or p<sup>sell</sup> thereof to the indemnifying the said Baiely or his sucksessors in his or either of thaire quiett possession as witnes my hand this sixteene Daye of July in the twenteth yeare of the Raine of Charles the second. King of England, scottland ffrance and Ireland et. cet<sup>r</sup> and in the yeare of our Lord on thousand six hundred sixtie and eaight according to the computacon of the Church of England.

signed sealed and                         JONAS WOOD.
dlld. in the p<sup>r</sup>sents of

JOHN FFINCH sen<sup>r</sup>
TIMOTHY CONKLOYNE

This is a true coppie of the originall Deede extracted p mee Joseph Baily Rec<sup>r</sup>

{*Court Records, p.* 312.)

## [THOMAS POWELL'S LANDS.]

[1668.]

The Records of the Lands and Medowes of Thomas Powell.

Imp[r] his hous Lot, situate and Lying Betweene the Lot of samuell wood on the southeast side of samuell wood and the norewest Jonathan harnit frunting towards the high waye and Rearring to the woods the Breadth at the frunt 18 Rod the Reare 20 Rod as alsoe a certaine parsell of Land Lying neare to Cowharbor Brooke.

alsoe a parsell of Land in the east feild Containing 3 acars bee it more or les the Land of thomas wititson on the east side and the Land of thomas weekes on the weest this Land was Laide out to James Chiehester and was part of his Division of Land.

more alsoe too Acares on the west side of Robart Cranfeild which was Land bought of Samuell Blackman and part of Devision of Land belonging to his lot.

More alsoe A Certaine parsell Lying on the Bottom of the east necke Bounded on the east side with the sound on the south with the Land of Stephen Jarvis and the west side the high way going through the midell of the necke.

more alsoe a hollow lying and being on the west side of tredwels plaine Containeing six acars bee it more or les Bounded on the east side with too acars of land Belonging to Samuell wood.

Joseph Bayly [then] Rec[r]

(Deeds, Vol. 1, p. 29.)

---

## [THOMAS POWELL'S SOUTH MEADOWS.]

[1668.]

Record of the Lands and Medowe of Thomas Powell ordered by a towne acte in 1668 to B Recorded.

Imp^r A Certaine parsell of Medow lying and Being on the south side of the eiland on a necke caled by the name of the greate necke Lying in too parsels the first devision Bounded on the east side with the meddow of Mr wood and on the west side with the medow of thomas weeks only Mr wood to have fower Rod wide in the fresh medowe. the second Devision of medow Bounded on the east side with the Creeke as far as the Clamsheals then with Mr Woods and John weeks on the same side this Devision Runs to the sounde alsoe Bounded on west side with the meddow of the widoe Rogers.

More alsoe A Certaine parsell of Medow Lying and being on a neck called By the name of Copiage Being the third part of upland and Medow the ather too parts Belonging to Samuell wood and Calib wood.

Joseph Bayly ^then Rec^r

*(Deeds Vol. 1, p. 28.)*

---

[DEED. JOHN PLATT TO JOSEPH WHITMAN.]

[1668, Oct. 21.]

October the 21^th 1668·

Bargoned and Agreed the Daye and yeare above said as ffolloweth:

Imp^rs I John platt of Huntington uppon Long Eiland have Bargoned sould and made over unto Joseph Whitman of huntington afore said all my Right titell and intrest in my Accomindacon that lyeth and being in huntington afore said formerly in the tennor or occupacon of John Bud of Southhould I say I have sould and made over as aforesaid all my Right titell and Intrest unto the said whitman his heirs and assigns for ever all and singular the Appurtinances there to belonging and every part and p'sell thereof with all Devisions of land that may hereafter Belong thereto

except that parcell or allotment of meddow that lyeth on a
neck of Meddow called nagunttatauge which is the halfe
Devision of a three hundred pound Lott which halfe  Devision I the said John platt Reserveth for my owne use and
Behoufe But all the Rest of the Accomondation and every
part and p'sell thereof I have sould and made over as
aforesaid for A Graye mare and A cow that is now in the
teneer of Joseph whitman Boath to be delivered unto John
Platt aforesaid.  By the Last of november next ensuing
for the true pformance hereof the p'ties above said have
enterchangably sett our hands the Daye and  yeare above
said.

JOHN PLATT.
JOSEPH WHITMAN
Joseph Bayly, Rec<sup>r</sup>

(*Court Records, p.* 181.)

---

## [DEED.   HENRY SOPER TO JONATHAN
ROGERS.]

[1668, Nov. 2.]

know all men by these p'sents y<sup>t</sup> I Henry Soper* of Huntington upon Long Island, planter, have Barganed sold and
made over from me my heirs executors administrators and
assignes part of my swoomp y<sup>t</sup> did belong to my home
Lott, a joyning to y<sup>e</sup> lot of Jonathon Rogers By Estmiation
three acres be it more or Lesse.   I say I have sold and made
over unto Jonathen Rogers his heirs executors adminis-

---

[*Henry Soper resided near the head of Huntington Harbor.
He was a brick maker.  He was the husband of the notorious
Sarah Soper, a woman of violent temper and speech, who kept
the neighborhood in an uproar.  She was often prosecuted for
slander, assault, &c., and was sentenced to " sit in the stocks."
—C. R. S.]

trators and assignes to have and to hold, for ever. as witnesse my hand this 2ᵗʰ of Novembʳ : In yᵉ 20ᵗʰ yeare of yᵉ Raigne of Charles yᵉ second, king of England, Scolland france, and Ireland : etc, and in yᵉ year of our Lord, 1668 :

the mark of

HENRY × SOPER

Witnesse
JOSEPH BAILY, Recʳ

This is A true Coppy
taken out of yᵉ old Book
By me John Cory, Clerk :
Aprill the 28 : 1683.

(*Deeds Vol.* 1, *p.* 147.)

---

## [ORDER OF THE CONSTABLES AND OVERSEERS AGAINST CUTTING TIMBER.]

[1668, Dec. 29.]

December the 29ᵗʰ 1668.
Impʳ it is ordered and Agreed By the Constable and townes men that noe pipestavess, hogshed stavess nor any other timber trees shall bee fallen or wrought up for sale within three miles of this towne Becaus By it much timber hath Been spild thereby and soe townes Ruened By such Ruin off timber and ffurther it is ordered that Noe Inhabitant within this towne shall give leave or Impower Any alian or strainger to fale and worke out any timber for pipe staess, hogshed staves Barrell staess or any timber for Any other use what soever within the Limits of the towne of huntington uppon the pennaltie of five shillings for every such tree fallen and wrought out uppon the said Commons of this townes Bounds alsoe five shillings for the faling and working out of every tree for pipe staves or Any other

use for sale by any Inhabitant as is above spesified within
three miles of the towne on the townes Commons.

Joseph Baiely, Rec<sup>r</sup>

(*Court Rec. p.* 269.)

---

## [TOWN MEETING.   AGREEMENT ABOUT THE MILL.]

[1669, Jan. 24.]

At a towne meeting January the 24<sup>th</sup> 1669.

I Marke Meggs hath given the mill hee bought of
william Ludlam too the townes use if hee die whilest hee
live being in the towne and if hee happen to sell the said
mill in the time off his life he the said marke meges have
Ingadged to sell the said mill to the towne or that the
towne shall have the Refusall thereof.

this gift is to bee understood if marke meggs Doe leave
that mill.

(*Town Meetings Vol.* 1, *p.* 29.)

---

## [DEED.   RICHARD DARLING TO BENJAMIN JONES.]

[1669, March 3.]

Know all men By these p<sup>r</sup>sents that I Richard Darling
off Huntington uppon Long eiland in new yorkesheere
Carpenter have for the vallue off thirtie and six pounds to
bee paid as is more at Large exprest in A Bill of Debt
Bareing Date with these presents have Bargoned sould and
By these p<sup>r</sup>sents Doe Bargen sell and Make over unto
Benjamin Jones off huntington uppon Long eiland in new

yorke sheare a fore said all my Rite title and intrest that I
have in an accommindacon which is A too hundred pound
Lottment lying and Being in huntington afore said the lot
of thomas powell on the east side the lott off Isack plat on
the west side the Reare with the woods in Comonadge
the frunt with the street or high waye as alsoe all houseing
Barnes out housing gardens orchards, Together with all
Lands privilidges accomindacons profits and Reveneus
thereto Belonging or accrueing therefrom as alsoe A Certaine parsell of Meddow lying and Being on the south side
of the Iland Containeth eaight Acars bee it more or Les it
beeing the p'porsion of A too hundred pound Lott according to the nomination of the towne lying and Being on A
necke called By the name of siasses necke all which the
aforesaid Lands Meddows and accommonda. and priviledges
thereto Belonging I the afore said Richard Darling Doe by
these presents sell alinate and estrainge ffrom mee my
heires executors administrators and assignes all my Rite
title and intrest unto the afore said Benjamine Jones his
heires executors administrators and assignes to have and
to hould for ever and I Doe by these p'sents ingadge my
selfe my heires executors administrs and assignes to save
harmeles and Indemnified the said Benjamin Jones his
heires executors administrs and assignes from any p'son or
p'sons whoe maye or shall laye any Claime or title to the
afore said Lands or medows or any pt or psell thereof this
Lande and meddows was fformerly in the tennor or
occupacon of Richard letten thence estranged to Josias
Letten his son and so to John Robins and thence to Richard
Darling whoe ingadgs to save indemnified the said Jones
or his sucksessors in his or either of their quiet possession
of the afore said Lands or any pt or p'sell thereof as witnes
my hand this third Daie of march in the on and twentie
yeare of the Raine of our sovr Lord Charles the second By
the grace of god of england scotland france & Ireland

King defender of the faith ect. and in the yeare of our Lord
1669.
signed & ddl. in                    RICHARD DARLING
the p^sents of
  NICK. RIDER.
  JOSEPH BAIELY Rec^r

                            this is A true Coppy of the
                            originall, extract, p mee
                            Joseph Baiely Rec^r
        (*Court Rec. p.* 316)

---

[DEED. NOAH ROGERS TO THOMAS WICKS.]

[1669, April 19.]

Know all men by these presents that I Noah Rogers off
Huntington uppon Long Eiland in New Yorke shire
plantter. Doe Bargen sell and Make over all my Rite title
and Intrest in my alottment off Meddow Lying and Being
on the south side of the Island on a neck Called santtapauge
beeing the parportion of A too hundred pound Lott ffor a
valiable consideration in hand paid I saye I have and Doe
By these presents alinate and estrange ffrom mee my heires
executors administrators and assignes all my Right title
and intrest unto thomas wicks off huntington in new yorke
sheare afore said his heirs executors administrators and assignes for ever too have hould ocupie and injoye without
Any fraude troble or Molestacon off Any p son or psons
whatsoever with all and priveledges proffitts and Revenews
thereto Belonging or Accrueing there from : and I doe
ffurther ingadge my selfe my heirs executors, administrators and assignes to save harmeles and indamnefied the said
thomas wilks sen^r his heirs executors administrators and
assignes from any person or persons what soever whoe
may or shall Lay any Clayme or title to any p^t or ps.ell.

there off to the Indemnifing the said wilks or his successors in his or either off theire quiet possession in witness whereof I have hereto sett my hand this Nineteene Daye of Aprill in the one and twentie yeare of the Raine of Charles the second King of England scottland france and Eireland etc[r] and in the yeare of our Lord 1669.

NOAH ROGERES.

Signed and Delivered
in the presents of
JAMES CHICHESTER JR
the marke of ✕
HENRY SOOPER.

Joseph Bawlys.
Rec[r].

( *Court Rec., p.* 262.)

---

## [DEED. WILLIAM LEVERICH TO JONAS WOOD.]

[1669, April 20.]

Know all men by these p[r]sents y[t] I Mr W[m] Leverich* of Huntington upon long Island in new yorkeshare Clarke have for a valueable Consideration in hand paid bargoned sold & by these p[r]sents doe bargon sell & make over from mee my heires execut[ors] adminest[rs] & assignes in & unto my accomodations or alottment sittuate & lieing in Huntington afore sd. unto M[r] Jonas wood of Huntington one long Island in new yorke-share afore s[d] his heires executo[rs] administ[rs] & assignes for ever to have hold use occupy &

---

[*Rev. William Leverich, as has already been stated, came to Huntington among the first, and continued to be a minister here until about the date of this deed. He now sold all his lands here and early in 1670 moved to Queens County, settling finally at Newtown. He was succeeded here by Rev. Eliphelet Jones. His son Eleaser remained here, for a time at least.— C. R. S.]

enjoy with out any trouble eviction or molestacion of any
person or persons w$^t$ soe ever & as fully largely & amply
as could bee made by any deed of sale w$^t$ soever togather
with all lands improved outlands houseing barn orchard
gardens out houseing previledges accomodations proffits
& revenews there to belonging or accuring there from, as
alsoe a certain parcell of meadow lying one south side of
this Iland on two severall necks of meadow part one a
necke called neguntataug & y$^e$ other part on a necke Called
bp y$^e$ name of the east necke both parcels Containes twelve
accors bee it more or lese which is the porportion of a
three hundred pound alottment all which the afore sd.
lands meddows accomodations & p'vilidges I y$^e$ afore s$^d$
M$^r$ W$^m$ Leverich doe by these p'sents sell allinat & estrange
from mee my heires executo$^rs$ adminis$^trs$ & assignes unto y$^e$
afore s$^d$ Mr Jonas wood his heires executors administ$^rs$ &
assignes To have and to hold for ever & I doe by these
p'sents ingage my selfe my heires & assignes to save harmless & indamnified y$^e$ said Mr wood or his sucksesers in his
or either of there quiet possession of the afore said lands &
every part and parcell thereof which lands was formerly in
y$^e$ occupation of Edw. Tredwell, thence estranged to Calib
Carwithy from Carwithy to John Kitcham & from Ketcham to mee W$^m$ liverich which land & every part & p cell
herein spesified I promise to Clear unto Mr Wood from y$^e$
beginning of y$^e$ would untill y$^e$ day of y$^e$ dat here of as
witness my hand y$^e$ one & twenteth day of aprill in y$^e$ one
& twenteth yeare of his maj$^{tls}$ Raine & in y$^e$ year of our
lord according to y$^e$ Computaton of England one thousand
six hundred sixty nine

                                        WM LEVERICH

Signed, sealed & deld$^r$
in y$^e$ p'sents of
ELIASER LEVERICH
    his ✕ mark
CALIB LEVERICH

This is a true Coppy of y^e origenal deed extracted p me
Tho: powell.

Rec^r

*(Court Rec., p. 302.)*

---

[DEED. MARY SEELY, WIDOW OF ROBERT
SEELY, DEC'D., AND JOHN MANNING
TO ANDREW MESSENGER.]

[1669, July 15.]

Know all men By these p^rsents that wee Mary seely, widdow, of the Cittie of New Yorke and Cap^tn John Manning,
off the Cittie of new yorke, aforesaid, executor in trust
unto the afore said widdow have for A valiable consideration in hand paid Before the sealeing and delivering hereof
have Bargoned sould and by these presents doe Bargon
sell and make over unto Andrew messenger off Jamacoe
on Long eiland in new yorke sheare yoeman all our Rite
title and Intrest in an Accomindacon or alottment sittuate
and Lying in huntington uppon Long eiland in new yorke
sheare afore said formerly in the tenor or occupation off
Cap^tn Robart seely deseased and since Confirmed unto mee
Mary seely widow Late wife off the said Cap^tn seely deseased and to my trusty and welbeloved Brother Cap^tn
John Maning executor in trust unto mee the afore said
Mary widow aughthorised by the Honorable Governor
and his Counsell at a jenerall Court of assizes at new yorke
wee saye all our Right title and Intrest in and to the same
and every part and parsell thereof as housing Barne, gardens, orchards home lote Meddow or Meddows, out Lands
devided or that hereafter may bee Devided according to
the parporcion of a to hundred pound Lot to hould occupie and Injoye without any fraude * * * * troble or
Molesstacon of any p'son or p'sons whatsoever firmely By

these p'sents or as fully Largely and Amply as can Bee
made by any Deede or Convayance whatsoever Bounded
on the east side with the lotte of Abiall Tituss and on the
west side with the Land of the widow Titus and the Reare
with the land of John Tedd and frunted with the high waye
as alsoe a cairtaine p'sell off Meddow Lying and being on
the south side off the Iland Containeing eaight acars Bee
it more or les which is the parporcon of A too hundred
pound Lott all which the afore said Lands Meddow and
accomindacons and privelidges wee the afore said Mary
seely widdoe and Cap^tn John Manning Doth alynate and
estrainge from us and every of us our heires executors
administrators and assignes all our Right title and intrest
unto The afore said Andrew Messengar his heires executors
administrators and assignes To have and to hould for ever
and wee Doe by these p'sents Ingadge our selfs and our
assignes to save harmeles and Indemnified the aforesaid
Messengar and his assignes ffrom any p'son or p'sons whoe
may or shall laye Any Claime or title to the afore said
houseing Lands or any p^t or p^sell thereof to the Indeminfing
the s^d Messengar or his suksessors in his or either of
thaire quiet possession in witnes whereof wee have here
unto set our hands and seales this fifteene Daye of July in
the on ane tweneth yeare of the Raine of our sover^nd Ld.
Charles By the grace of god of england scotland france
and Ireland king, and in the yeare of our lord on thouson
six hundred sistie nine.

signed, sealed                           JOHN MANNING
and ddl. in the
presents of.

THOMAS BURRAMANS
JOHN PRATT
This is A true Coppie of the originall extracted p mee

                              Joseph Baiely
                                   Rec^r

(*Court Rec., p.* 318.)

## [DEED. ANN ROGERS TO SAMUEL MESSENGER.]

[ 1669, Aug. 9.]

The Record of Jonathan Harnuts Land and medowes.

Know all men by these p<sup>r</sup>sents y<sup>t</sup> I An Rogers* of huntington upon Long Island Widowe, have for y<sup>e</sup> vallue of twenty pounds in currant pay to be made as is more at large expressed in a bill of debt under hand seale given: have barganed sould & doe by these p<sup>r</sup>sents bargan sell & make over unto Samuel Messenger of huntington uppon long Island afore sd. All my Rite title & Intrust in and to my accommondation situate & being in huntington as housing barn out housing orchyard, garden trees home lot frame for a hous alredy hewen Bounded as heere specified the lot of Tho<sup>s</sup> Wicks on y<sup>e</sup> north side and y<sup>e</sup> lot of Noah Rogers on y<sup>e</sup> south side y<sup>e</sup> Rear with y<sup>e</sup> lot of John Corey & frunted with y<sup>e</sup> high way as also a certain parcsell of land lying & being in y<sup>e</sup> east feild: by estemation fower acres be it more or less: Bounded with y<sup>e</sup> land of Thomas

---

[*Genealogists have expended a great deal of effort and time in endeavoring to find out who Ann Rogers was, but as far as I know without an entirely satisfactory result. She is called in these records the widow of George Wood, but it is presumed that she was the widow Rogers when George Wood married her, as she had children bearing the name of Rogers, as follows : Obadiah, John, Noah, Samuel, Mary and Hannah, and a large share of the Rogers family now in Huntington undoubtedly descended from these, her children. She came from Setauket to Huntington and died here soon after this deed was given. The record of the Court of Assizes held in New York City, Oct. 2, 1665, states that one Ralph Hall and Mary his wife were brought to the bar on indictment for witchcraft in having, in the town of " Seatalcott," caused the death of George Wood and an infant child of Ann Rogers. The indictment reads as follows, as to the charge of murdering the child :

" Morover the constable and overseers of the said town of Seatalcott in the East riding of Yorkshire upon Long Island

Jones on yᵉ west side and yᵉ Rear yᵉ woods in Comonadge
yᵉ frunt to yᵉ cart path wᶜʰ goes throw yᵉ feild Is also halfe
my proportion of medow sittuate & being on yᵉ south side
of yᵉ Island by estimation six acres be it more or lesse wc'h
is yᵉ half proportion of a three hundred pound lot all which
Lands, medows, priviledge accomandations, profits, belonging thereto or accuring there from, or ever here affter
shall be : except foure acres lying in yᵉ north of yᵉ littell
neck neer Cow harbour alredy in Records & half my Right
of Comondage wich my half part of medow I resarve to
my only use & behoof, elos all Lands medows pastures, ac-
comindations profits and Revenues there to belonging or
ever here after shall bee. I yᵉ afore sd, An Rogers doe by
these p'sents sell, allynat and estrange from me my heirs
executirs administraters and assignes all my Rit title and
intrust unto Samuel Messengar his heirs, executors, ad-
minˢᵗʳ & assignes, To have and to hold for ever ; furthr I
yᵉ afore sd an Rogers doe Ingadge my self my heirs and
assignes to save harmelesse and indamnefied yᵉ fore sd.

---

aforesaid do further present to our sovereign lord the King that
somewhile after the death of the aforesaid George Wood the
said Ralph Hall (did as is suspected) divers times by yᵉ like
wicked and detestable acts commonly called witchcraft and sar-
cery maliceously and felonously practice and exercise on the
person of an infant child of Ann Rogers widow of yᵉ aforesaid
George Wood deceased by which wicked and detestable arts
the said infant child (as is suspected) most dangerously and
mortally sickened and languashed and not long after by the
said wicked and detestable arts (as is likewise suspected) died.
And so yᵉ said Constable and overseers do present that the
said George Wood and the said infant child by the ways and
means aforesaid most wickedly maliciously and felonously
were, (as is suspected) murdered by the said Ralph Hall at the
times and places aforesaid against yᵉ peace of our sovereign
lord yᵉ King and against the laws of this Govrment in such
case provided." Both pleaded not guilty. The jury found as
to Mary Hall: "There are some suspicions by the evidence of
what the woman is charged with but nothing considered of
value to take away her life:" and the court gave sentence that,
"the man shall be bound body and goods for his wifes appear-

Samuel Messenger his heirs and assignes from any person or persons who may or shall lay any claim or title to y^e fore sd. accomindation or any part or parcell there of except before excepted in witnesse where of I have here unto set my hand and seale y^e 9 of august: in 21^st yeare of Charles y^e second of England, Scotland france & Ireland, king &c and in y^e year of our lord 1669: The mark of

ANN X ROGERS

Signed sealed and
ddl. in y^e presence of
JOHN BARTRAM
JOSEPH BAIELY Rec^r.

This a true Coppy Compered with y^e originall by me John Corey Rec^r March the 31: 1682.

The assignment of this Bill of sale is on y^e back side of this leafe

John Corey Rec^r.

*(Deeds Vol. 1, p. 107.)*

---

ance at the next session and so on from session to session so long as they stay within this Goverment in y^e mean while to be of y^e good behaviour."

It will be noted that this "witchcraft" record belongs to Setauket and not to Huntington, and is only given here as connected with the death of a child of the mysterious Ann Rogers. There is no record, I think, anywhere that an arrest was ever made in Huntington on a charge of witchcraft. It is highly probable that Ann Rogers was the widow of William Rogers, one of the earliest settlers here, and one of the grantees in the eastern purchase Indian deed in 1656, and whose name disappears soon after. As George Wood was living in Brookhaven town after the date of the witchcraft proceedings it is difficult to see how Ann Rogers could have been his widow at that time.—C. R. S.

## [DEED. JONAS WOOD Jr., TO JONATHAN ROGERS.]

[No Date.]

This writing testifieth yᵗ I Jonas wood Junʳ of Huntington in yᵉ east Riding of yorkeshire on Long Island have
Barganed sold & made over three acars of Land unto
Jonathan Rogers of yᵉ above sd. town & Riding: the above
sd. three acars of land is lying in yᵉ old West feild in yᵉ
west neck and was formerly in yᵉ tenure or occupation of
John Conkling, thence to timothy Conkling thence to
Caleb Cornethy & from thence to me and is Bounded on
yᵉ north with yᵉ woods: on yᵉ east with yᵉ land of John
Scudder and on yᵉ south with yᵉ woods and on yᵉ west
with yᵉ Land of Richard wilams for which Land I yᵉ above
sd. Jonas Wood doe acknowledg my self to be fully sattisfied contented and payed and doe by these pʳsents bargan
sell & make over all my Rite & title yᵗ I yᵉ afore sd. Jonas
Wood Junʳ have in and to yᵉ above sd. 3 acars of Land
from me my heirs, executors, administrators & assigns:
unto Jonathan Rogers his heirs executors, administrators
& assignes to have hold use & peacably to Injoy with out
any lett or mollystation by mee or any means öf mine for
ever as witnesse my hand this ———— of————

(*Deeds, Vol.* 1, *p.* 53.)

---

## ]JONATHAN ROGERS' LANDS.]

[No Date.]

The Records of the Lands and Meddows of Jonathan
Rogers his house and hom Lot Lying and Being in Huntington the Land of henry sooper on the south side the

north side part with Land of the towne in Commonadge
and part withe the Medow of thomas scudder the frunt to
the Common the Reare to the woods in Commonadge as
alsoe 9 acars of Land at the est end of the west feild as
alsoe 5 acars on the north side of the hether end of the
west feild as also a hollow containeing 3 acars Lying in
setalket Rode more on smale hollow Betwene the towne
and the other hollow formerly in the ocupacon of thomas
Brush thenc estranged to Eliazar Leverich thence to John
teed.

as also 8 acars of Meddow Lying on A neck called Santipauge Being the Medow of his owne Lot.
more alsoe six acars be it more or les on a necke called
the great neck Being halfe the parporcon of Meddow that
lot Belongeth to the Lott formerly in the ocupacon of
william Rogers.

as alsoe the halfe part of the Comonadge of that Lott that
is to be Devided or all that ever heare after shall bee Devided is to Remaine unto Jonathan Rogers* his heirs and
assignes.
        (*Deeds Vol. 1, p. 53.*)

[*The law of this period was very strict concerning the record
of all conveyances of land, and the record of transfers of land
that had been made prior to the English Conquest in 1663. It
provided that no sale of land should be good unless by deed in
writing under hand and seal acknowledged, and a particular
form of words was prescribed for the granting and other
clauses in deeds, not, however, to apply to wills or grants by
towns to individuals. It provided that no mortgage, bargain
and sale of lands, where the grantor shall remain in possession,
shall be of force against any person except the grantee unless
acknowledged and recorded within one month, and grantors
were compelled to acknowledge under penalty of imprisonment.
—C. R. S.]

## [RICHARD BRYAN'S LANDS.]

[1669.]

A Record of the Lands & Meadow
off Mr Richard Bryan* in the yeare 1669.

Imp$^r$ his home Lott sittuatte and being in Huntington
bounded as heare named the highe waye or buring hill on
the east side the Land of thomas Brush on the west side
the ffrunt south to the highe waye the Reare the land off
John Sammeses alsoe a Certaine parcell off land in the west
ffeeld Containing too acers bee it more or less the Land of
Andrew Messenger on the east side and the land of Samuell
Titus on the west side the Le  *  * north and south with
the woods in Comonadge as alsoe a Certain parsell of meddow on the South side of the Iland on too necks the on
halfe on a necke called nagunttatoug it beeing 4 acars bee
it more or les Bounded on the east side with the Meddow
off Joseph whitman and the west with the Meddow off
Marke Megs in Lengh north and south which is the halfe
p.porcian of a too hundred pound lott alsoe the other half
parportion on a necke called the east neck which part is
not Layd out or divided.

Joseph Ba—ly

*(Deeds, Vol. 1, p. 1.)*

[*Richard Bryan was a son of Ann and Alexander Bryan, the
latter a merchant of Milford, Conn.  Richard came to Huntington from Milford among the first settlers.  He and his
father at this time (1669) owned Eaton's Neck, having purchased it of George Baldwin it 1668, and they held it until they
sold to John Sloss in 1710.  As very few conveyances of lands
on Eaton's Neck were recorded in the Huntington records, the
title not coming originally from the town,  no mention is made
in this record of Richard Bryan's lands on  Eaton's Neck.
Richard had brothers, Alexander and Samuel; and his first
wife's name was Mary, second, Elizabeth.  His children were
Alexander, Samuel, John, Robert, Joseph, Mary, Hannah,
Abigail, Frances, Sarah, and Elizabeth.—C. R. S.]

## [JAMES CHICHESTER'S LANDS.]

[1669.]

The Records off the Lands and Medows off  *  *  *  *
Chichester sm<sup>r</sup>, off Huntington 1669.

his house and home Lott sittuate att the harboure in huntington the frunt off the Lott faceing to the harboure nore
*   the Reare soufh to the townes Land in Commonadge the
east side Bounded with the high waye the west side Bounded
with a Boggea : Meadowe off the towns in Commonadge
as alsoe A Certain Parssell off Land Lying and Being on a
necke caled by the name off the east necke—Runing from
the harbour norward Bounded the east side with the
Land off Stephen Jarvis and on the west side with the
highwaye going on to the necke the south side or frunt
with the woods in Commonadge Running to the great
harboure almost to the Beach it Being eaight Acars bee
it more or Les as alsoe fower acars Be it more or les Lying
and Being in the west feild the Land the Land off Jonas wood
Junr on the east side the Land off Thomas Brush on the
west side ffrunt and Reare with the woods in Commonadge
alsoe fower Acars on the Littell east necke.

(*Deeds Vol.* 1, *p.* 3.)

---

## [ISAAC PLATT'S LANDS.]

[1669.]

A Record of the Lands and Med  *  *  *  *  *  *
Isacke platt in the yeare 1669
Imp<sup>r</sup> home Lott lying and beeing in Hun  *  *  *  *  *
*  *   Josias Laten on the east side the west side  *  *  *
*  *  *  *   into the woods and to the east feilde a  *  *

\*   \*   \*   \*   \*   off Land lying in the east feild the La \* \*
\*   \*   \*   on the east side the west side and Reare   \*   \*
\*   \*   \*   \*   Commonadge frunted as other lots: as als   \*
\*   \*   \*   \*   off medowe lying on the south side off   \*   \*
\*   \*   \*   \*   \*   necke caled the great necke on p.sell by
the   \*   \*   \*   \*   the name of the Iland bounded with the
gr   \*   \*   \*   \*   east side off it a littell creeke and good
man wood   \*   \*   \*   \*   \*   side off it the other parssell
bounded on the east by   \*   \*   \*   \*   \*   \*   creeke on the
west by Andrew Messenger on the s \*   \*   \*   \*   \* thomas
powells: alsoe too more parsels of Meddow   \*   \*   \*   \*
on a necke caled santtapauge the Lot of henry sooper on
ye north side the meddow off thomas wilks on the south
side the Reare to the Sounde west and soo Running east to
the woods the other p sell Lying on the eastermost side off
that necke by estimacon 4 acars bee it more or les the Meddow of Thomas wilks on the south and runing as far by the
Creeke side as mowable

Joseph Baiely, Rec<sup>r</sup>.

(*Deeds, Vol.* 1, *p.* 4.)

---

## [ROBERT CRANFIELD'S LANDS.]

[1669.]

The Record of the Lands and Meadow of Robert Cranfield in this year 1669.
Home Lott Lying and Being att the Harboure the Lott of
Thomas   \*   \*   on the South side, and the Lott of Stephen
Jarvis on the north side in rear with the woods, the frunt
to the Harbour; as also, a certain piece of Land Lying in
the east field, The Land of Thomas Weekes on the east
side, and the Land of Thomas Powell on the west as also a
Certain parcel of Land Lying on the East Neck Containing four Acres and one Half Be it more or Less.

The Land of Thomas Wilks on the East side, and Land
of Stephen Jarvis on the West side the Rear toward the
Great Harbour, the frunt to the woods in commonage.
That parcel of Land In the east field is by Denomination
three acres be it more or Less, as also a Certain parcel of
Meadow Lying on the south side of the Island on a Neck
Commonly called by the name of Josias his Neck and is
the Westermost Lott on that Neck Bounded on one side
with the Creek and other side with the Lotts of James
Chichester, and Stephen Jarvis not yet Divided

Joseph Baiely, Recorder.

(*Deeds, Vol.* 1, *p.* 5.)

## [NATHANIEL FOSTER'S LANDS.]

[1669.]

The Record of the Land and Meadow of Nathanial Foster In the year 1669.
Imprimus, House Lott sittuate and beeing in Huntington
the woods in Commonadge on the south side and the Lott
off Thomas Scudder on North side the Reare to the woods
east the frunt too the harboure west in Length east & west
as alsoe a certaine parsell off land in the east ffeild containing three acars Bee it more or Les the land off Thomas
wilks senr. on the east side and the Land off Cap^tn Thomas
fleet on the west side the Reare to the woods south.

as allsoe A. Certaine parsell of Meddow lying on the south
side of the Iland on a Necke called santtapauge by estema-
con eaight acars bee it more or les in length it Runeth
north and south, Bounded on the north end with a Ranke
of small trees by the Indian path, on the west sid with the

creek the east side with the woods the south end with the meddowe of henry sooper:

Joseph Baiely<br>Rec<sup>r</sup>.

*(Deeds, Vol.* 1, *p.* 7.)

---

## [JONAS WOOD'S LANDS.]

### [No date. Probably 1669.]

The Record of the Lands and Meddows of Mr Jonas Wood.

Imp<sup>r</sup> his housing orchard and hom Lott sittuate and lying in huntington Bounded as is heare mensoned the frunt to the streit west ward the south east side to a Lane that Leads to the woods the Reare to the woods in Common-adge the west side bounded with the Land of John weekes Containeing seaven Acars Be it more or les: as alsoe fower acars and a halfe lying and being in the east feild the east sid to the woods the south side adjoyning to the woods in commonadge the west-side bounded with, the land off John weekes the north side to a high waye that leads through the midell of the sd. feild as alsoe a certaine parsell of land lying and being on a smale neck of land beyond Cowhar-bour brook Containeing twelfe acares bee it more or les Bounded on the north. and norewest side with the salt water and on the east side with the Land of Eppenetus platt and on the west side with the Land of Jonathan Rog-ers on the south side with the woods in Commonadge as alsoe six acars lying and being on tredwels plaine the frunt to the highwaye that leds to the south side of the Iland Reareing to the woods in Commonadge bounded on the north sid with the Land of John weekes and the southside with the Land of Isacke platt as alsoe an acar of Land be

it more or les lying in a hollow on the west side of tredwels plaine bounded on the southest side with the Land of
John weekes. as alsoe Certaine parsels off Medow Lying
and being on the south side of the Iland twelfe acars bee it
more or les lying on a neck off Meddow Callcd by the
name of the great necke being the porporcon of a three
hundred pound lot and belongs to the lott Mr wood now
lives in lying in three particular parsels as alsoe fower
Acars be it more or les lying on a necke of Meddow called
santapauge Bounded on the south sid with the Medow of
John weeks on the north side with the medow of henry
sooper the southwest with the sea and the nore-east with
the woods which fower acars of medow was a gift from the
towne to Mr wood: as alsoe fower acars of medow lying
and Being on a necke of medow called by the name of
siases necke bounded east with the Creeke north and west
with the woods formerly in the Tenor or accupacon of
Edman wood father of Mr Jonas wood Deseased. as alsoe
the westermost side of a necke of medow called by the
name of Copiage which Containes the halfe of the said
necke formerly in the tennor or occupacon of Mr Sticklen
thence allenated to Mr. Jonas wood Bounded on the west
side with a Creeke that parts the greate necke and it the
south with, the sea: what medow I have on the great
necke Bounded as hereafter specified on acare Lying
Betwne thomas powell and John weeks on other parsell
Bounded on the west with thomas powel the norest with
the medow of Jonathan Rogers ser lying north and south
the north with the woods the south to the sound the part
of Common medow the west and north with the medow
of thomas powell the east with the medow of John Weekes
the south By the Sound.

(Deeds, Vol. 1, p. 11.)

## [THOMAS SCUDDER'S LANDS.]

[1669,]

A Record off the Lands and Meddowe of Thomas Scudder
off Huntington in the yeare 1669.
home Lott Lying and Being Betweene the Lott off Nathaniell foster on the south side and the lott off Robard Crandfeild on the north side the Reare with the woods east the
ffrunt west to the harbor as alsoe A Cairtaine p.sell off Land
lying in the east ffeald containen three acars bee it more or
les the Left off Joseph Baiely on the east side and the lott
off Henry whitson late Deseased on the west side the Reare
with the woods north and ffrunted with a high waye as
goes through the middell of the ffeild.
as alsoe a Certaine p.sell off Land Lying on the east necke
containing sixteene Acars bee it more or les Bounded on
the north side with a lot off six acars that Marke Megs
tooke up but improved by Simond Lane the west side
bounded with the harboure the south side with the woods
Commonadge the Reare with a high waye that goes into
the necke as alsoe too certaine parsells off Meddow on the
south side off the Iland, the on parsell Lying and being on
the westermost neck but on some time caled by the name
off siases neck it being eaight acars bee it more or les
Bounded on the east side with the sea and the west side
with a lott of Josias Letten and y$^t$ of the common meddow
not yet Divided as alsoe a certaine p,sell off Medow lying
on a necke called nagunttatauge by estimacon six acars bee
it more or les it beeing the halfe parpouson off a three
hundred pound lotte formerly in the tenor off W. Whitnie
thence alinated to John budd off southhould thence too John
platt of huntington Bounded on the east side with the
creeke and the south with the Sound the west side with
the medowe off Jonas wood Jun$^r$ and the ffrunt with the
woods now: as alsoe A Cairtaine p-sell off meddowe lying

and Being on the head huntington harbour Joyneing too
the Meddow off Jothan Rogers on the south side it beeing
too acars bee it more or less fformerly given too thomas
skidmore off huntington by the said and since purchas by
mee the above said thomas scudder and is my proper Rite
too mee and my heires fforever

Joseph Baiely Rec[r].

(*Deeds, Vol.* 1, *p.* 13.)

## [JOHN TEED'S LANDS.]

[1669.]

The Records of the Lands and Meddow of John Tedd
of huntington 1669.

This Bill Doth testifie that I Eliazar Leverich have sould
pased over all my Rite and Intrest from my selfe my heirs
and assignes forever unto John tedd of huntington on Long
eiland his heires and assignes for ever to bee his proper
Right to posses plant or desspose of at his pleasure my
Dwelling house and barne and home lott in huntington
eaight acares off meddow at the south with all the priviledges and appurtinances belonging unto the said lotment
of too hundred pounds that Doth or shall belong thereto
I the said Eliazar Doth Bargan sell and alinate from my
self eaires and assignes for ever unto the said John tedd
his heires and assignes to bee his proper Right for ever in
and for the sum of seventeene pounds paid in the yeare
1665 or then Discharged.                        the mark of
Witnesses                          ELIEZAR ✕ LEVERICH
    ROBART SEELY
    EDWARD HARNET

the Meddow of this accomindacon is fower
Acars the west neck the other part on the

halfe neck the meddow of John Jones on the
est sid and the medow of Samuell Titus on the
west sid another parsell on the said neck
the Meddow of John Jones on the east side
and the Medow off James Mils formerly John
Scuder on the west.

Joseph Bayly, Recr.

As alsoe six acars of upland lying in huntington the Lot of
Richard Wattles on the south sid and a smale lot of the
said Richard Watels on the north sid.

(*Deeds, Vol.* 1, *p.* 19.)

---

## [HENRY SOPER'S LANDS.]

[1669.]

The Records off the Lands and Medow of henry sooper
the yeare 1669

Imp$^r$ his home Lott sittuate and lying in huntington the
highe waye as coms out off the woods too Jonathan Rogers
on the east side the west side to the woods in Comonadge
the ffrunt south towards the Mill the Reare Bounded with
the Lott off Jonathan Rogers as alsoe A certaine parsell off
Meddowe Lying on the south side of the Iland on a neck
called santtapauge by estimacon eaight acars bee it more
or les the Meddowe of nathaniell foster on the north side
the meddow of Isacke on the south side the west too the
Creeke east to the woods, more alsoe a smale parsell of
ffresh medowe on the west side of the said necke betweene
the swampe and the Indian path.

Joseph Baiely<br>Recr.

(*Deeds, Vol.* 1, *p.* 15.)

## [ABIAL TITUS' LANDS.]

[1669.]

The Records of the Land and Meddow of Abiall Titus in the yeare 1669.

Imp[r] hous and home lott sittuate and lying in huntington, Bounded on the east sid with the high waye that goes to the mill frunted with the street the Lott of Andrew Messengar on the west side the Reare with the Lot of John tedd as alsoe to parsells off Land lying in the west feild too acars in the middell of the feild the Land of Jonathan Rogers on the east side and the Land off Richard willams on the west sid the other parsell on the being three acars the Land of Richard Williams on the west sid and the Land off Benjamine Jones on the east sid as alsoe A certaine parsell of Meddow on the south side of the Iland on a necke called Nagunttatauge John Sammayes on the west side and thomas Brush on the east Running south to the sound and north to the woods the other parsell being 4 acars bee it more or les Lying on the east side of the same necke Bounded on the east sid with santipaug creeke and the other side with the woods.

Joseph Baiely, Rec[r].

*(Deeds, Vol. 1, p 21,)*

---

## [JOHN SAMMIS' LANDS.]

[No date.  Probably 1669.]

The Records of the Lands and Meddow of John Samwayes
his hous Lott Lying at the Reares of the Lots of Thomas Brush and Richard Bryan Bounded with the high waye

goeing too the mill on the north the Reare to the milpond
as alsoe a certaine parcell of Meddow on the south side of
the Iland part on a necke called nagunttatoug the meddow
of abiall Titus on the east side and the Meddow of Joseph
whitman on the west side and a smale parcell of ffresh
Meddow on the east end of the said neck and the other
parsell lying on a necke called by the Indians Guscomquo-
rom and by the English the east necke w$^{ch}$ meddow is not
yet Devided.

Joseph Bayly, Rec$^{r}$.

The above said medow: belonging to John Samweys y$^{t}$
lyeth on the east neck above sd: Is now layed out this first
of July: 1681 and bounded as followeth: the first devision
is in y$^{e}$ sault marsh y$^{e}$ lot of Jonas wood Jun$^{r}$, on y$^{e}$ north:
y$^{e}$ Town lot on y$^{e}$ south with the creek on y$^{e}$ west: and to
y$^{e}$ middell of y$^{e}$ neck east ward it being six Rods Broad:
Also another parsell of medow on y$^{e}$ same side of y$^{e}$ neck
being: fower Rods broad: and Running east and west as
before: with the lot of Thomas Brush on the south and the
lot of John Bats on y$^{e}$ north.
it is to be understood that the twoo above sd lot both of
them ly on y$^{e}$ west side of y$^{e}$ neck: And also on y$^{e}$ east
side of y$^{e}$ neck are twoo lots more the lowermost lot is
Bounded on the east with A creek: the west to y$^{e}$ middill
of y$^{e}$ neck: with the lot of Epenus platt on the south: y$^{e}$
lot of John Bate on the north: it being six Rods Broad—
also the other parsell of medow lying on the east sid of the
neck: and Bounded on ye east & west as afore sd: with y$^{e}$
lot of Joseph whitman on ye south side and the lot of
Epenetus platt on y$^{e}$ north.
it is further to be understood that the lower end of the
neck of medow is not yet layed out: whare John Samways
hath also according to his proportion yet unlayed out.

By mee John Corey, Rec$^{o}$r.

(*Deeds*, *Vol.* 1, *p.* 31.)

## [JONATHAN AND DAVID SCUDDER'S LANDS.]

[No date. Probably 1669.]

the Record of the Lands and Meddow of Kattren Jones Made over to Jonathan Scudder:

The hous orchard and home lot lying and Being in huntington the Lot of John Jones on the north side the Lot that was given to Jonathan Scudder on the south side the frunt to the streete the Reare to the woods as alsoe a Certaine parsell of Land in the west feild containeing fower acars be it more or les: more fower Acars and a halfe in the east feild lying betweene the land of Joseph Baiely and Samuell Messengar as alsoe A Certaine parsell of Meddow on the south side of the eiland containing eaight acars bee it more or les fower on the halfe necke and fower acars on the wester most necke.

Joseph Baiely: Rec[r].

the Lott of David Scudder formerly in the occupacon of Jeffrey thence given to Jonathan Scudder since Resigned to David Scudder by the consent of Katteren his Mother and Jonathan his Brother the Lott off Jonathan scudder on the north side the frunte to the streete the south side and Reare to the woods in Commonadge as alsoe a certaine parsell off Meddow Lying on the south side of the eiland containeing eaight acars bee it more or les fower acars on the halfe necke and the other fower acars on the westermost necke of huntington purchas.

Joseph Baiely Re[r].

(*Deeds, Vol. 1, p. 35* )

---

## [WILLIAM BROTHERTON'S LANDS.]

[No date. Probably 1669.]

The Record of Lands of William Brotherton situate on

y^e freshpond necke lying one east sid of Crab meadow
which containes 6 acars toward his halfe part of farm which
Containes 20 acares the which 6 acars is onely bounded by
y^e woods butt Laid out and tres marked        *     *     *
and alsoe about 2 acars of swamppy land in y^e same place
according to y^e towne grant & Record        *     *     *
also another parsell of land containg fower acars lying on
the north sid of his hous lott: The hie way Runing between them.            *          *.          *          *
also another persell of land containing fower accars and
lying on the west side of the freesh pond hollow against
the head of the boggey medow neer the fresh pond.
and also six acars of medow in the eastren part of crab
medow.

(*Deeds, Vol.* 1, *p.* 36.)

---

## [THOMAS JONES' LANDS.]

[No date.  Probably 1669.]

The Records of the Lands and Medow of Thomas Jones
situate in huntington the Lot of Samuel Tytus on the north
side the lott of Jonathan Scudder on the south side the
frunte to the streete the Reare to the woods in Commonadge as alsoe a certaine parsell off Meddow lying on the
south side of the eiland Containeing eaight acars Bee it
more or les the on fower Acars Lying on the westermost
neck now purchased the other fower acars lying on the
halfe necke adjoyneing to the Meddow of John Teed.

Joseph Baielye, Re^c.

(*Deeds, Vol.* 1, *p.* 37.)

[THOMAS WICKS', Sr., LANDS.]

[1669.]

The Records of the Lands and Meddowes off thomas wilks* sen$^r$ in the yeare 1669.

Imp$^r$ home Lott Lying and being in Huntington the lött off Mr Jonas wood on the east sid the lot of henry whitson late deceased on the west side the Reare to the woods in Commonadge the ffrunt to the streete as alsoe ttoo parsells off land lying on the east ffeild the Land off Mr Jonas wood on the east side the Land of Nathaniell ffoster on the west side it beeing 4 acars and halfe bee it more or les the other parssell lying on the hether side of the cast ffeild the Land of thomas powell on the east side fformerly in the tenner off James Chichester and the Land of Robert Crandffeild on the west side the Reare to the woods the front as other Lots it being 3 acars bee it more or les as alsoe a Certaine parsell Land lying and beeing on the east necke containeing six acars bee it more or les the Land of the townes in Commonadge on the east side the Land of Robart Crandfield on the west side it lyeth in Length north and south as alsoe on acore be it more or les of hollow lying betwene Mr Jonas wood and Caleb Wood as alsoe a certaine parssell of meddow lying on the south side of the Iland on a necke called the great, the meddowe off Henry whitson late Deseased on the west side and the medow of thomas powell on the east side it lying north and south alsoe

[*Thomas Wickes was at Wethersfield in 1635 and at Stamford in 1641. He came to Huntington with Edmond Wood and others. His homestead was at the "town spot" and probably included the open space at the east end of the present village of Huntington, as his descendant, Thomas, subsequently made a deed of it to surrounding owners on certain conditions. He died in 1671 and left children Thomas, John, Rebecca, Martha, Elizabeth, Mary and Sarah. The name is spelled in the records many ways but generally Wicks.—C. R. S.]

another parsell of medow on the same necke the Meddow
of Isack platt on the east side the meddow of John wood
on the west side : as alsoe too Certaine parsels of meddow
lying on a necke called santtapague 4 acars bee it more or les
lying Betwene the meddow off Joseph Baiely on the south
side and a p-porcon off meddow off Isaac platt on the north
side the Length east and west the other parsell Containeing
8 acars bee it more or les late in the tenor or ocupacon of
noah Rogers but since estrainged to thomas wilks the
Meddow of thomas Skidmore on the south the east side
the brooke, the west the woods the north end the Meddow
of Isaac platt.

Joseph Baiely, Rec<sup>r</sup>.

(*Deeds, Vol. 1, p. 47.*)

## [THOMAS WHITSON'S LANDS.]

[1669.]

The Records off the lande and Meddowe off Thomas Whitson in the yeare 1669.

Imp<sup>r</sup>  hom Lott sittuate and being in huntington the Lott
off Thomas wilks senr on the east side the Lott off John
ffinch on the west side in Length north and south as alsoe
a certaine parsell Land in the east ffeild the Land off
Thomas Scudder on the east side and the Land off thomas
powell on the west side in Length north and south as alsoe
a hollowe lying on the west side of tredwels plaine on the
north side off a hollow of Thomas wilks and Mr Jonas
woods as alsoe a parsell off Land lying at Cow harboure by
estimacon three acars and halfe bee it more or which is the
halfe part of that Land that was fenced in betweene thomas
powell and henry whitson late Desessed as alsoe a certaine
parsell of meddow Lying on the south side of the Iland on

a necke called the great necke the Meddow of thomas wilks senr on the west side the east side of the creeke in Lenght north and south the south to the sound and the north to the woods.

Joseph Baiely. Rec.

(*Deeds, Vol.* 1, *p.* 51.)

## [LAND OF THOMAS WICKS, Jr.]

[1669.]

The Record of the Lands and Medow off thomas wilks Junior in the yeare 1669.
Imp.rs the home Lott lying and beeing in huntington the ffrunt east to the streat thea south side the Land off Samuell Messenger the North the high waye as alsoe A certaine parselle off Meddow ling on the south side of the Iland fower acars bee it more or les on a neck caled by the name of siases necke which is the halfe sheare of a too hundred pound lott late in the tener of John Lumee the other fower acars bee it more or les lying on the eastermost neck now purchased of the Meddowe of huntington.

Joseph Baiely Rec.

(*Deeds, Vol.* 1, *p.* 49.)

## [JOHN FINCH'S LANDS.]

[1669.]

The Records off the Lands and Meadow off John Finch Late in the Tennor or ocupacon off Trustram Hoges, but since by * * * Made by severall Naybours adjoyneing whose Lands adjoyned the Lotte of the sd. trustrum aforesaid which hade Receved great Dammag By Reason the

said Lott Lay oppen unto the Common ffor such Dammage
Complainte was made unto the Counstable and overseers
By the sufferer ffor Redres therein the Constable and
townsmen Desired Instrucksion ffrom supperior offisars
which advis was too put those lands soo trespasing to an
out cry att A publike Towne Meeting and those that
proffered most have and injoye it Cleareing all aReareedges
of Rates and soe By the said sale peasably to injoye it and
every part and parcell thereof provided the fformer pos-
sessar appeared not in on whole yeare or an Agante ffrom
him ffor the sale of which Lands and Meddow and every
part and parsell thereof wee the Constable and oversears
have proseeded in the waye of sale According to order
given in the nineteene yeare of his Magis$^{tis}$ Raine and in
the yeare of our Lord 1669 and after the expireacon of on
whole year noe owner nor agent appeareing wee have given
unto the said John ffinch peasable possession as witnes our
hands the said John ffinch paying or Causing to bee paide
the just some of fower pounds and on shilling to the
Constable and townsmen ffor the use of the towne as more
at Large exprest in a Bill of Debt given under his hand.

THOMAS POWELL, Const.

Joseph Bayly Rec$^r$.
(*Deeds, Vol. 1, p. 9.*)

[COURT RECORDS.   SAMUEL HAGKURNE vs.
WOOD.]

[1670, about.]

Att a Court held in huntington the 19$^{th}$ of November by
the Constable & the fower townes men.
Mr Samuell hagkurne, Marchant, plaintife Against wood
defend. in an acttion off Debt to the vallue off three pounds

nine shillings and eaight pence, the Defendantt Confesed the debt.

The Court find for the plaintive that the Defendant shall paye unto the plaintive the some of three pounds nine shilling and eaight pence in paye according to his judgment viz poorke at three pounds and ten shillings the Barrell beiff at too pound ten shillings the barrell, wheat at three shillings p bushell peas at three shilling & six pence p bushell, Indian Corne at too shillings p bushell or other pay equivelent there too.*

Debt 03—09—08
Court Charg 01—00—00
————————
04—09—08

*( Court Rec., p. 264 )*

---

## [DEED. JOHN ROBBINS TO BENJAMIN JONES.]

[1670, Jan. 6.]

Know all men by these prsents that I John Robines of oysterbay on long Island in york sheeir Cordwinder have for a valiable Consideration in hand payed : have & doe by these prsents sell alinate assinge all my Right title and intrust in an Accomondation or alotment : sittuate and lying in huntington : on long eiland aforesaid, formerly in the tenur or occupation of Timothy wood : thence estranged unto Richard latin thence to Josiah latten : son of the sd. Richard from thence unto John Robins : I say all my Rite, title and Intrust in and to all the prmises I have sold and made over unto Benjemine Jones of huntington upon long

---

[*At this period the law provided for imprisonment for debt and if debtors had property they were provided for in prison out of their own property ; at the same time the rule was that " No man shall linger in prison for debt if he can find sureties for answering the suit or debt."—C. R. S.]

eiland in york sheer a fore said : his heirs executors administrators and Asings for ever to have and hold occupie and
injoy with out any fraud trouble or molistation of any
person or persons, what so ever firmly by these prsents, or
as fully and amply as may or can be made by any deed of
Convaiance whatsoever together with all lands In clossed
or not in clossed that doth or hath belonged theretoo as
out land meddows devided or not devided with all priviledges, accommandations pr-fits and Revenues there to
belonging or acureing there from as also all housing gardins, orchards, pasturs as also A sartin parcell of meddow
lying and being on the south side of the Iland : on a neck
of meddow called by the name of siases neck lying between
the meddow of Thomas Scudder and James Chitchester,
by estimation aight acars, be it more or lesse, which is the
proportion of A two hundred pound lot, all and singuler
all these lands meddowes, priveledges, I the afore said
John Robins doe alinate and astranges from me my heirs
and asinges unto Benjemen Jones his heirs executors,
adminstrators and asinges  To have and to hold forever
and I doe by these prsents ingage my selfe my heirs and
asinges to save harmlesse and indamnefied the afore said
benjemen Jones his heirs and asinges from any person or
persons what soever who may or shall lay any Claime or
title by any way or means whatsoever to any part or parcell thereof to the indamnifing the said Jones or his
sucksessors in his or either of their quiett possesion as
witnesse my hand this sixt of Jeneuary in the two and
twenty yeer of the Raine of Charles the second of Ingland,
Scotland, france, Ireland King, defender of the faith et
cetr. and in the yere of our Lord 1670.

sealed, singed and ddld.                    the mark of
in the presence of the                    JOHN X ROBINS
marke of
    JOSIAH X LATTEN
    JOSEPH BALY, Recorder.

This is a true Copie compared with the originall by me
John Core Recorder.
the hollow that did belong to the within named p'micesses
is not neither doth it belong to the p'meses therefore
excepted by John Robins: before the delivering as witnesse my hand.

Joseph baly, Rec<sup>r</sup>

(*Court Rec., pp.* 200–1.)

---

## [DEED. BENJAMIN JONES TO JONATHAN HARNETT.]

### [1673, Jan. 22.]

Know all men by these presents that I Benjamin Jones
with in named have assigned and made over all the within
named pr'messes from me my heirs and assinges unto
Jonathon harnut of huntington upon long Island in York
sheer Cordwinder his heirs and asinges to have and to
hold forever as witnesse my hand this 22 of Jan. in the
year of our lord 1673

BENJEMEN JONES

signed and delivered in the presents of
Joseph Bayly Recorder.

(*Court Rec., p.* 201.)

---

## [THEY REFUSE TO REPAIR THE FORT.]

### [1670, Feb. 21.]

Huntington february the 21. 1670.

To the Honarable Court of sessions houlden at south
hampten in the towne of huntington humbly Manfest thair

Agrevences touching the order Conscerneing the Repaireacon of the fort James at new yorke.

. May it please the worshipfull Bench.

wee of the towne of huntington Cannot see Cause to Con-
tribute any thing to wards the Repaireacon, of the forte*
for these following Reasons, first because wee conceve wee
are Deprived of the liberties of english men secondly wee
conceve we have little or noe benifits by the Law : thirdly
wee cannot conceve of any benifite or saftie wee can expect
from the forte : fourthly wee finde our selves soe much
Desinabled by Manyfould trobles when wee thought our
selves in peace that wee Cannot Imparte with any such
Desburstments nither was there any such p$^a$sedent in
the      *      *    .

(*Court Rec., p.* 187.)

---

[*The order for repairing the fort at New York was made by
the Colonial Governor and the Court of Assize.   There was
much discontent in all the Long Island towns about this time,
owing to the dictatorial policy of the Government.   When the
English came in power six years before great promises were
made as to the benefits to be derived from it, but instead of
deriving advantages therefrom the people chafed under the
restraints and impositions of the Governor and council.   They
had been promised a Colonial Assembly, made up of delegates
to be elected by the people, but such an assembly no longer
existed.   They were taxed without representation   This protest was a beginning of that long and bitter contest between
the people and the arbitrary authority of Great Britain, which,
with similar protests elsewhere, finally led to the Revolutionary
War.   The people of Huntington refused to help repair the fort
and the Governor had to content himself with denouncing their
protest as "scandelous, illegal and seditious,' and having it
publicly burned before the town house in the City of New
York.   This document was Huntington s first declaration of
independence.   Unfortunately the paper is so worn and
tattered that a few lines at the end are lost.—C. R. S.]

# [A CARTWAY DISCONTINUED AND A WATER-ING PLACE PROTECTED.]

[1670, March 9.]

At the Complaint of the widdoe Jones unto M$^r$ Wood March the 9$^{th}$ 167$\frac{0}{1}$ Conserning a peace of Land the widoe Jones is to take up on the north side of Samuell Titus Lott which John Tedd founde himselfe agrived conscerning a waye Betweene the Lot of Samuell Titus and the Lot of the widow Jones.  Mr wood Appoynted Thomas Skidmore and Joseph Bayly to vew the Land to see if that place Required a waye which was don acordingly wee finding it soe that that place Required noe Cart way By Reason there was noe Considerable parsell of Land for ffeid for Cattell but what was Appoynted ffoor a Lotments neither Doe it priduce any wattering.*

Joseph Bayly, Re$^c$.

(*Court Rec.*, p. 180.)

---

[*At this period roads and watering places were established and laid out by the constables and overseers, subject to the town meeting, and this continued until 1691, when by a change in the law "Surveyors and Orderors of roads" were elected at town meetings.  The principal roads in the town probably followed Indian paths.  The road to Lloyd's Neck is called in the records "Horse Neck path;" that running easterly from the "Town spot" "Nassequague path;"  The principal road leading to the "Town spot" from the south "Sabbath day path;"  The principal road across the south side necks, now through the village of Babylon, "The Indian path;"  The road running westerly from the "Town spot" "The Oysterbay path."  It is not probable that these, and many others in use at the date of the above paper, were ever formally laid out.  They became roads by usage.  There were also the "Sumpwams path," the "Neguntetogue path," the "Santepague path," roads leading to the south necks, and "Nichols path," not far from the present boundary line between Huntington and Babylon, and also the "country road" near the centre of the town and the "country road" where "Rogue's path" is located.—C. R. S.]

## [TOWN MEETING.   VOTE TO PROCURE A MINISTER.]

[1670, April 4.]

April 4. 1670.

At a town meeting it was voted and agreed this day that if Mr Leverich went from the town, that it was the town's mind that they would have another minister, and that there should be some speedy course taken to seek out for some other to supply us.

Joseph Baiely, Re<sup>r</sup>.

1670

Thomas Brush, Constable ;

Capt. Thos. Fleet and } Overseers ;
Jonathan Rogers

Thomas Brush deceasing in his room was chosen Sam¹ Wood, Constable.

Layers out of land for the town's use :

Thomas Powell } for the east end of the town.
Joseph Bayly

Richard Williams } for the west part.
Content Titus

[Copied in the Revision in the year 1873 from the original in No 2. p. 11.]

(*Town Meetings, Vol.* 1, *p.* 31, *and  Court  Rec., p.* 183.)

---

## [ORDER BY CONSTABLE AND OVERSEERS.]

[1670, April 26.]

Ann order Made By the Constable and overseers the 26 Daie off Aprill Anno 1670 it is ordered and agreed the Daie and yeare above said that Mr Will Leverich shall in some shorte time Deliver in unto us whose names are under writen or unto some on of us all those Rates that hath Been made ffor his paie since the yeare 1665 that wee maie take some speedie cors ffor the parfiting thereof that this Last Rate for the yeare 1669 may bee forth with gathered.

THOMAS BRUSH.

THO. FLEET

THO. SKIDMORE

the marke of

THO: ✕ WILKS

JONATHAN ROGERS.

Joseph Baiely

Rec.

*(Court Rec., p. 189.)*

---

## [RECEIPT. RICHARD FLOYD TO JOHN JONES.]

[1670, May 12.]

Know all men By these pʳsents that I Richard floyd of brookhaven uppon Long eiland in yorkeshere Tayler doe acknowledg to have Received of John Jones of Hunting-ton uppon Long eiland in yorke sheare afore said the some of eleven pounds and on shilling which is in parte of A Bond of twentie three pounds I saye Received by mee the some of eleven pounds on shilling as witnes my hand this twelfe of maye in the yeare of our lord 1670 the mark of

his

witnes                                    RICHARD ✕ FFLOYDE.

JOSEPH BAIELY Recʳ                          mrrk

*(Court Rec., p. 317.)*

## [THOMAS POWELL, GUARDIAN FOR THOMAS WHITSON.]

[1670, June 17.]

June the 17<sup>th</sup> 1670.

Whereas henry Whitson off hunting Deseased in the yeare of our Lord 1669 and after the will was proved according to the Law of this Jurydickson the estate Being Devided By order and Consent of the widoe off the said Henry Deseased and thomas whitson son of the said Deseased which said thomas whitson Being under adge hce with the Consent of his granfather ffoster and the Rest of his ffrends have thought good to make Choyc of Thomas Powell of huntington to bee the Trustee and Garddian of him the said Thomas whitson : for the care and p-servacon of the estate of him the said thomas until hee Accemplish the adge of on and twentie yeares. Dureing which time the aforesaid thomas whitson Doth promise not too Bargan sell or Impart with any of his estate without the leave and consent of his said gardian but in all things expedient bee searvall too his advise and Counsell as witnes my hand the Daie and yeare above writon.

THOMAS WHITSON

Joseph Baiely, Rec<sup>r</sup>
(*Court Rec., p.* 271.)

---

## [DEED.  JOHN MATTHEWS  TO  MARK MEGGS.]

[1670, September 6.]

This writting witnesseth that I John mathews of huntington have for a valluable Consideration sould and made over all my Right & tittle in y<sup>e</sup> farm at Crabmedowe I say all my Right from mee and my heairs to marke megs his heairs for ever both my own Right beeing one hundred pound lott : and John Cores beeing A. too hundred pound lotment in all y⁰ Right of three hundred pound lotment & doe by these presents ingage that y⁰ fore sd. marke megs his heairs shall Injoy it Peacablely free from y⁰ Claime of any as wittnes my hand this : 6ᵗʰ septembar : 1670

Witnes

TH0 : SÇIDMORE
the marke of
CHARLES × ABRAHAMS.
*(Deeds Vol. 1, p. 205.)*

the mark of
JOHN × MATHERES

Witneseth, These pᵣsents That I marke meges with in mentioned doe heer by allinate asigne and make over all my Right title intrest and Clame to the within mentioned Bill of saile from mee my heirs executors Administrators and asigens unto Edward Bunce of Crab meddow his heairs executors Administrators or Asignes for ever wittnes my hand at Crab meddowe this thirteenth of Aprill 1674.

MARK × MEGS
his marke

signed and delivered
in presence of SIMAN LANE
1674.

the mark of
JOHN × INKERSON
JOHN PAGE.
*(Deeds Vol. 1, p. 205.)*

---

## [ORDER BY GOV. NICHOLS AND COUNCIL CONCERNING THE SMITHTOWN BOUNDARY.]

[1670 Dec. 1.]

At a Counsell held in y⁰ Fort at New Yorke Decembᵣ y⁰ 1ˢᵗ 1670 :

Upon a Petition p^rsented by M^rs Smith, of Nesaquake, on y^e behalfe of her selfe & husband, desiring an Explanation of the Verdict of y^e Jurye & order of y^e Court of Assizes, as to y^e bounds of y^e Land w^ch y^e Inhabitants of Huntington had gotten their suite for, Declaring and offering to prove that y^e Nesaquake lands lay on both sydes of y^e Ryver, & that parte lyeing on y^e west syde, comonly called Nesaquaque Accompsett, did extend as farre as y^e fresh pond westward, and so to y^e Hollow Southward, The w^ch, together w^th that on y^e East syde, was y^e proportion on w^ch they were to settle y^e ten familyes, and y^e oth^r Ten families, in consideration of y^e Land westward of y^e fresh pond, if they had made good their title thereunto.

Upon consideration had hereupon it was ordered that y^e Towne of Huntington should have notice hereof to y^e w^ch they are to returne an Answer to y^e Governer and w^th all its recomendes that a faire comp * * * be endeavoured between both p^tyes, that there be no furth^r trouble or molestation concerning this matt^r By Ord^r of y^e Governe^r & Councell.*

Matthias Nicolls, Sec^r.

(*File No*, 60.)

---

[*Richard Smith was at this time claiming all the territory between the head of Cow Harbor (Northport) and the Nassequague (Smithtown) river. He was called "Bull" Smith, as distinguished from "Rock" Smith and "Tangier" Smith. In the interesting history of Smithtown, written by Judge J. Lawrence Smith, in 1882, "Bull" Smith is made the son of Richard Smythe, of Mireshaw, Bradford Parish, Yorkshire, England, who with his son were soldiers in Cromwell's army. They afterward came to Boston, then to Southampton, L. I., then to Setauket. An interesting story is told of how the daughter of the grand Montauk sachem Wyandance, who had been captured by the Narragansett Indians, and recaptured by Lyon Gardiner, was restored to her father at Richard Smith's house, and in gratitude Wyandance granted Richard Smith, Lyon Gardiner's friend, the territory of Smithtown, or all the land Smith could ride around on a bull in one day, and that he took his lunch in a hollow, ever since called "Bread and Cheese Hollow."—C. R. S.]

## [SUMPWAM'S INDIAN DEED.]

[1670, Dec. 2.]

Know all persons by these presents that wee whose nams are subscribed, namely pompott & mamascokan, secakatake Indians, being deputed and apointed by the Rest of our asosiate to Receive the payment of huntington men for a sertaine neck bought of y⁰ said Indians, commonly called and known by yᵉ name of sumpwams, wee say wee have Received of Epenetus Platt in behalf of huntington: for our selves and all the Indians that have any right, their full satisfaction acording to our bill of sall by us made as witnes our hands & seals yᵉ 2ᵈ December 1670.*
the word right interlined was before signing and sealling.
pwamas, sachems sun, acknoledg yᵉ sam as witness my hand and seall.
signed and sealled in presence of
us JOHN BRUSH.

EPENETUS PLATT     the mark of×WAMAS [L. S.]
the mark of×WILL    the mark of×MAMASOP [L. S.]
   Indian
DANIELL×MARKEN    the mark of×POMPOTT [L. S.]
his mark

(*File No.* 28.)

## [DEED. CATHERINE JONES TO JONATHAN SCUDDER.]

[1670.]

the 28ᵗʰ 1670
the day and yeare above said katteren Jones Widdoe wife

[*This deed was from the Sucatogue Indians and embraced only the meadows below the Indian path. Part of Babylon village is now located within it, and it was the easternmost of all the necks purchased of the Indians in behalf of Huntington. —C. R. S.]

off Thomas Jones Late Deseased Doth hereby these presents give assignie and make over unto my son Jonathan
Scudder that house and lott with all the priviilge and
appurtinances thereto belonging or ever here after shall
belong to the premises: after my Desease but dureing the
time of my naturall Life to injoye it and every part and
parsell thereof : which Lott was fformerly Henry Scudder
father of the said Jonathan Scudder to remaine to him and
his heirs forever for which I the said Jonathan Scudder
doth wholly and ffully Resigne up unto my Brother David
Scudder all my Righte title and interest that I have in that
Alotment or accomidacon which was my grand-fathers Jeffery esties lott and given to mee before his disease I say
I make over unto my Brother David Scudder his hcires
and assignes ffor ever and Doth estrainge it ffrom mee my
heires and assignes ffor ever : But this Lot and every parts
and parsell thereof to Remaine and bee at the Desposal of
my Loveing mother Katteren Jones untill my Brother
David coms to adge or shee see cause to Resigne it unto
him : ffor the parformence of which wee have enterchainge-
able sett our hands the Daie and yeare Abovesaid.

Witness                              the mark of
JOHN JOHNS                    KATEREN ✕ JONES
JOSEPH BAIELY Re⁰

        Another Record behind this.
    (*Deeds Vol.* 1, *p.* 34 )

---

## [TOWN MEETING.   THE MILL POND TO BE LET OUT.]

[1671. Jan. 6.]

At a town Meeting January the 6ᵗʰ 1671 it was voated
and agreed the Day and year aforesaid that the Constable
and townse men and Mr. Wood and Thomas Skidmore and

Epenetus Platt, Joseph Bayly shall Consult together to consider of a way that the water may be let out of the mil-pond and see if the parties aforesaid can agree with mark megs upon termes whereby the towne and marke megs doth joyntly agree for the Removall of the said mill and before a full agreement bee made too give the Result of what they have Don to the Remainder of the towne this to bee Don in some short time.

it was voated and agreed the same day whether the towne was willing that the water might bee let out of the mill-pond and they so agreed for the mill, if mark megs could bee agreed with, all whereby this agreement might bee effected, if by it it may please the Lord the towne might injoye their health to which the towne joyntly agreed and proseeded in a way as aforesaid.*

(*Town Meetings Vol. 1, p. 33.*)

[TOWN MEETING.]

[1671, Jan. 16.]

January yᵉ 16th, 16⁷⁰⁄₇₁
It was ordered and agreed the same Daye By the pluaral-litie off voats at a towne Meeting that Jonathan Rogers Jonas wood junir and thomas weekes shall take up and equally devide betwene them what good planting land is on the south sid of Isaac plats on the little neck leaving a

[*This mill pond undoubtedly occupied the swamp and low lands south of its dam where "Mill Dam Lane" (Huntington village) now is, flowing southerly to near Main Street. That it should have occasioned sickness is entirely reasonable. After this pond was let out another was constructed further north and adjoining. The land occupied by the old mill pond was subsequently divided to those holding common rights in the "old purchase," as will be seen further on.—C. R. S.]

sufficient highway or hindering not high ways and water
ings it being part of their devision.

Tha same Daie it was ordered as A Boursaid that Beniam-
in Jones shall take up six Acars of land on the north sid of
nathaniell fosters on the littell necke it being part of his
Devision hee hindering not high ways and waterings.
these two Below entered in Book A page 36.
(*Town Meetings, Vol.*1, *p.* 30.)

---

## [DEED.  MARK MEGGS TO JACOB WALKER.]

[1671, Feb. 3.]

Know all men by these p'sents that I Marke Megs of huntington uppon Long eiland in yorkesheare Millar have for
the value of fower pounds by the yeare theareby to bee
paid the on halfe p' in wheate the othere halfe p' in Indian
Corne : Dureing the naturall Life of Mark Megs and Avis
his wife for which Consideracon I have Bargoned sold and
made over and by these presents Doe bargon sell and make
over unto Jacob Walker of Stratford within the Collony
of Coniticott Marchant all my Rite Tittle and intrest that
I have of Land & medows sittuate and being in huntington
aforesaid I saye all my Rite tittle and intrest in and to the
same and every part and parcell thereof as Dwelling hous,
orchards, gardens Barne home lot or lots swompe and
hassokie Medow as alsoe twelfe acars of Medow bee it
more or les lying and being on the south side of the Iland
on too severall necks of Medow that is to saye six acars
bee it more or les on a necke called by the name of nagunttatauge bounded on the north side with the Medow of
Epenetus platt and on the south side with the medow of
Mr Richard Bryan the other half part on a necke called
by the name of the east necke not eat layd out nor devided

being the parporcon of a three hundred pound Lott the
hous Barne orchards gardens home lot or lots with p-porc-
cond of Lands in Comondge or that ever heare after shall
or may belong there unto, was formerly in the tenor or
occupacon off william Leverich clerke thence alinated unto william Ludlam thence to marke Megs now to Jacob
Walker the swamp and hassokie Medow was given to him
the said Marke by the Towne of huntington I say all my
Rite in and to the same I have Made over unto the afore
said Jacob walker his heires executors administrators and
assignes for ever to have hould occupie and injoye without
any fraude or Mollestacon of any person or persons whatsoever formely by these p'sents or as fully Largely and
Amply as can or may bee made by any Deede of sale or
Convayance whatsoever all and singular those Lands
Medows and pastures I the aforesaid Marke Megs have
estrainged from mee my heires executors administrators
and asignes unto the afore said Jacob walker his heires
executors administrators and assignes Too have and to
hould for ever and I doe by these p'sents ingadge my
selfe my heires executors administrators and assignes to
save harmeless and Indemnified the afore said Jacob
walker his heirs executors administrators and assignes
from any parson or parsons who may or shall Laye Any
Clayme or title to the aforesaid houseing orchards Lands
or Any part or parcell thereof to the indemnifing the afore
said walker or his sucksessors in his or either of their
quiet possession in witnes whereof I have heare unto set my
hand and seale the third daye of february in the three and
twentie yeare of his Maj$^s$ Raine and in the yeare of our
lord on thousand six hundred seaventie and on.

signed and deld.                                    the mark of

in the presents of                              MARK X MEGS

JONAS WOOD                                          the mark of

ISACK PLAT                                      AVIS X MEGS.

JOSEPH BAYLY.

This is a true coppie of the originall Deed compared
p mee Joseph bayly
Rec<sup>r</sup>.
(*Court Rec. p.* 310.)

---

[TOWN MEETING.   HUNTINGTON TAKES
POSSESSION OF THE DISPUTED
TERRITORY.]*

[1671, Feb. 15.]

February the 15. 71.
it was voated and Agreed the same Daye that these towne
should bee Divided into ten parts and ech part to have a
farme and soo bee ingadged to settell them and every
farmer that went forth soo to settell that the towne
approved of should injoye all the Remaining parts besids

---

[* This was the beginning of a plan for the occupation and
settlement by the people of Huntington of the disputed territory lying between Cow Harbor (Northport) and the Smithown
River.   The method pursued was peculiar to the time and was
probably borrowed from old English customs.   Richard Smith
was vigorously pushing his claims to the land in the courts, and
Huntington acting on the theory that "possession is nine points
in the law," determined to get a firm hold of the territory.
The part of the premises· considered of the most value was
that adjoining the Sound.   This was parcelled off into ten parts,
or farms so called, and ten families were chosen to settle thereon, one to each farm.   The selection of these ten, who were to
"go fourth" and settle there, was determined by dividing all
the inhabitants of the town into ten parts or hundreds, so called, and each part or hundred chose the man from their number to go and occupy, and upon building, fencing and planting
within a stipulated period, and paying the expenses of litigation, these ten farmers were to own the lands.   This plan was
not carried out until the summer of the next year, 1672, when
the writings were drawn and the persons "went forth."—C. R.
S.]

theire owne paying all Charges of sute of law or ether just Charges

Joseph Bayly Re$^r$

this one Below is Entered in Book A page 38.

(*Town Meetings Vol.* 1, *p.* 33.)

---

[DEED. RICHARD WILLIAMS TO JONATHAN ROGERS.]

[1671, February 16.]

Know al men by these p$^r$sents y$^t$ I Richard Williams of Huntington upon long Island Husbandman have Barganed sold and made over from me my heirs & assignes ; for a reasonable vallue in hand payed. all my Right title and Intrust in two acers of Land Lying in y$^e$ west feild lying between a lot y$^t$ was Joseph Whitmans : And a Lot y$^t$ was Jonas wood Jun$^{rs}$ unto Jonathan Rogers of Huntington on Long Island afore sd. his heirs and assignes for ever : As also two acres more Lying in y$^e$ same feild Ad joyning to y$^e$ Land of Abiell Tittus for a consideration in hand payed to have and to hold for ever unto Jonathen Rogers and his assignes for ever as witnesse my hand this 16$^{th}$ of febuary 1671 :

RICHARD WILLIAMS

Joseph Bayly Re$^r$

This is a tru coppy taken out of y$^e$ old Book per mee John Corey Clerk Aprill 27. 1683

(*Deeds Vol.* 1, *p.* 147.)

---

[TOWN MEETING.]

[1671, April 12.]

April 12. 1671.

At a town meeting it was agreed the same day that

James Naibour shall have what land as shall be thought
fit by those appointed to lay out land for to make a home
lot, not prejudicing any highway or watering (place) for
cattle, provided it be cleared within some convenient time;
this lot to be on the south side of Sam¹ Woods last lot
taken up.

[Copied in the Revision in the year 1873, from the original in No. 2, p. 19.]

(*Town Meetings, Voi.* 1, *p.* 37.   *Court Records, p.* 189.)

---

## [TOWN MEETING.  FOREIGNERS PROHIBITED FROM KILLING WHALES OR OTHER "SMALL . FISHES."]

[1671, April 12.]

April 12. 1671.
    Chosen for the year above-said
        Content Titus, Constable ;
        Isaac Platt, and
        Thomas Powell, Overseers.

It was voted and agreed the same day by and with the
consent of the whole town that any man or every man
that have meadow upon any neck at the south side of the
island may have liberty to purchase what upland they can
of the Indians according to their proportion of meadow
provided it be on the neck of that their meadow lieth on.*

                                Joseph Bayly, Reʳ.

---

[*This was soon followed by purchases from the Indians of
lands adjoining and north of the south necks of meadow heretofore purchased.   Under Gov. Nicholl's patent such extin-
guishment of the Indian title vested the title to such lands in the
town.—C. R. S.]

It was ordered and agreed the same day by and with the consent of the whole town that no foreigner or any person or persons of any other town upon this Island shall have any liberty to kill whales or any other small fish within the limits of our bounds at the south side of the Island neither shall any inhabitant give leave directly or indirectly unto any such foreigner or other town's inhabitants whereby the companies of whalemen or fishermen may be damnified except any such foreigner or (other town's inhabitant) comes into the said company or any of them as a half-share man.†

[Copied in the Revision in the year 1873 from the original in No. 2, p. 16.]

(*Town Meetings Vol. 1, p. 35.*)

---

## [TOWN MEETING. THE SMITHTOWN BOUNDARY QUESTION.]

[1671, July 3.]

July 3. 1671.

It was voted and agreed the same day that whether the town would send two men to Governor concerning the difference between Smith and the town ; the generality of the town voated not to send men but to write to the Governor.

Joseph Bayly Rr.

---

[†This is probably the first order or law made by the town concerning the fisheries. It indicates that the people at that early day understood their rights over the waters as well as the lands, under the colonial grant. At this period the government claimed and received one fifteenth of the oil out of whales cast up on the shore, and "the right of drift whales" was a privilege bought and sold.—C. R. S.]

It was voted and agreed the same day by and with the
consent of the town that the Constable and Towns [men]
shall send in writing to the Governor the minds of the
town touching the Governor's letter to the town touching
Rich^d Smith and the town.

Joseph Bayly Re^r.

It was ordered and agréed the same day that Thomas
Brush shall take up six or eight acres of land upon the hill
at the rear of Sam^l Titus lot or neare thereabout provided
the layers out see it convenient.

Joseph Bayly Re^r.

[Copied in the Revision in the year 1873 from the original
in Old Book 2 back p. 30 or 42.]
(*Town Meetings Vol.* 1, *p.* 39.)

---

## [DEED, THOMAS SKIDMORE TO EPENETUS PLATT.]

[1672, Jan. 22.]

Bee it known unto all men by these p^rsents y^t I Thomas
Skidmore of Huntington y^e east Riding of yorke share
Blacksmith have bargoned & sold alinated & made over
unto Epenetus Platt of Huntington one Long Iland in the
east Riding of yorke share husbandman I say I have sold
from mee & mine my heires, executors adminst^rs & assignes
unto y^e afore sd. Epenetus Platt to him & his heires execu-
tor^s administ^rs & assignes I say I have sold all my Right
and intrust, y^t I have to houseing land & all othere my
accomodations in huntington y^t is to say my house and
shop my home lott Consisting of six accors bee it more or
lees seittuate in huntington bounded on the south by the
street one the west by the home lott of Epenetus Platt one

the north by old mile Pond one the east by Jno. wickes his
swamp as allsoe all fruite trees & fences as they now are
together with 8 accars of meadow bee it more or less lieing and beenig one a neck Comonly called and known by
y⁰ name of Santepaug bounded one y⁰ south by y⁰ Sound
one y⁰ east by y⁰ lott of Thomas wickes & one west by y⁰
lott of Jn⁰ ffinch one the north by wood land alsoe, all
othere lands that doe or at any may here after appertaine
or any way belong to a two hundred pound allottment, as
alsoe all and every percell or p'ticuler peece or peeces of
land yᵗ have been att any time given to mee by the towne
of huntington as disstinte from my p'ticular Right by
allottment with all and singuelar appertunances previlidges
Rights and Emunities that either hath or at pʳsent doe or
hereafter shall belong thereto To have and to hold to him
the said Epenetus Platt and to his for ever, always except-
ing and reserveing to my selfe and to my owne p'per use
and behoufe my Right of my farme with all the previlidge
there unto belonging as at large is exprest in the generall
covenant and agreement made by the Inhabitants of Huntington the said farme lieng and being in that land east
from Cow harbour alsoe it is to be understood that 3 accars
of land in y⁰ east feild which I formerly sold and y⁰ two
accars of meadow lieing att the harbour sold by mee to
Tho: scudder is not in this saile intended alsoe I doe by
these p'ents Covenant p'mise and engage to deliver unto
Epenetus Platt or his assignes free, quiett and peaceable
possission free from all Clames or disturbance by any person or persons whomsoe ever the first day of may next
ensueing the datt hereof onely reserving the use of the
shop to my selfe till the first of octoᵇʳ next ensueing the
date hereof and alsoe the fruite of one apple tree this next
ensueing yeare and noe longer, and I doe here by promise
and engage my selfe to discharge all Ratts yᵗ are or will
bee due eithere to y⁰ towne or County att the forementioned time yᵗ I doe engage to deliver possission unto the

trueth of w$^t$ is here inscribed I doe sett to my hand & seale
this 22$^{th}$ day of Jan : & in y$^e$ yeare of our lord 1672

sealed signed &                THOMAS SKIDMORE
delivered in p'sents of
  JONAS WOOD, Jno$^r$
  THOMAS LAWRANCE
    This is a true Coppy of the origenall extracted by mee.
                  Thomas Powell. Re$^c$
    *(Court Rec , p. 308.)*

---

## [DEED OF THE OLD MILL FROM MARK MEGGS TO THE TOWN.]

[1672, Jan. 23.]

Know all men by these p$^r$sents that I Marke Megs of
huntington upon Long Island in yorkshire, miller, have
Barganed sould and made over unto the Constable and
townsmen of the towne of huntington all my Rite, title and
intrest in and to my mill, mil hous, mil pond, mildam, and
all and singular the sd. nessesaryes that properly Belongs
to the mill, lying and Being in huntington, aforesaid formerly in the tonor & occupation of Willam Leverich,
Clerk, thene alinated unto wille Ludlam, thene to Mark
Meggs with milpecks crow or crows of Iron, or any other
nessesary, what soever Belonging thereunto as alsoe a high
waye of too Rood wide from the gate that is att the north
west end of the hom Lott of Marke Meggs, unto the brinke
of the water in the mill pond, unto A Crooked white oake,
thence to the mill Dam, with the same Alowance. Derecktly
provided they stur not an apple tree  *  *  *  *  *  *  *
said marke Megs have excepted who shall  *  *  *  *  *

and Remaine in its place as it grows, although * * * *
* * the fence Runeth Crooked, and alsoe a foote waye
to com from the waye of henry sopers hous unto the mildam that now is, Reserveing the swampe Below the mildam,
the hassekei meadow, and my proporcon in the mil pon,
according to my alottment, unto my proper use and Behofe,
w<sup>ch</sup> swamp and hassehei meddow was given mee by the
towne of huntington, these and alsoe my house, Barne,
home Lot, Land in Comonadge, Meddow at the south, and
all and singular the Appurtinances thereto belonging, I
Reserve unto the desposing of my selfe, my heires and
assigns for ever, But the mil with the Dam and pond with
other usfull nessesarieyes, I have sould and made over unto
the Constable and townsmen, as aforesaid, for the vallue
of five pounds yearly for eleven years, to bee paid in manner and formie following, that is to say : 20 Bushels of
Indian Corrne, fower bushells of wheate, the Remainder in
pease, Dureing yearely the said tearme as aforesaid, y<sup>t</sup>
Mark Megs and Avis, his wife, chance soe Long to live, y<sup>t</sup>
Booth of them chance to Dye within the said terme of
yeares then what is unpaid to Remaine to the use of the
towne of huntington forever, and further I Doe ingadge
my selfe and my assignes to save the Constable and over
sears of the towne of huntington ; free from the Claime of
Any person or persons what soever ; as witnes my hand
this 23<sup>th</sup> of January in the 23 year of his magis<sup>tis</sup> Raine and
in the year of our Lord 1672.

Memorandd<sup>m</sup> the yearely payment of five pounds by the
yeare, as is within specified, to Begin at or Before the 20<sup>th</sup>
of february next ensuing, at which tender of payment in
Corne as is within specified, I promis and Ingadge to surrender and Deliver up unto the Constable and overseers,
the mil, mildam, with the nessaryes as within specified, as

we the p.ties within named have interchaingably set our
hands the Day and yeare within spesified.

signed sealed and
Delivered in the pᵣ.
  JACOB WALKER
  JONATHAN SMYTH

the mark of
MARK × MEGS [Seal.]
the mark of
AVIS × MEGS [Seal.]
THO: FLEET
JONAS WOOD
THOMAS POWELL [Seal.]
ISAAC PLATT
JONATHAN ROGERS.

(*File No.* 48.)

---

## [MARK MEGGS S TAXES.]

[1672, Jan. 25.]

        January yᵉ 25ᵗʰ 167½
  it is Agreed by the townesmen of huntington that Marke
Megses yearely paie shall bee Rated for this yeere 1671 by
the hundred that is to saye thirteene pence halfe peny the
hundred 9c hundreds and it is to bee paide in to Jonathan
Rogers and hee to paie it into Marke Megs and to take an
Aquitance of Mark Megs and if any over plush of paye
Remaine Jonathan Rogers to bee Responsable unto the
townesmen this paie to bee made forth with and not to
Remaine but this yeare to paie by the hundred except the
towne in Jenerall see cause and consent thereunto and if
Any person or persons Refuse to paie thaye Loose thaire
intrest of Land in the milpon furthermore it is Agreed that
noe person or persons shall Claime Any Intrest in the pond
Land by the payment of this Rate this pᵣsent yeare 167½

                    Joseph Bayly Recᵣ

(*Court Rec. p.* 182.)

## [COURT RECORDS. MARK MEGGS vs. SARAH SOPER—FIFTEEN STRIPES TO BE INFLICTED.]

[1672, March 13.]

At a Court held in huntington on the 13th Daie off march in the twentie fowerth of the Raine of our souvr. Lord Charls the second King of great Briton france, and Ireland etc. Anno: Dom. 167½. By Captn John Maning Justice of the pease and high Sheirfe off York sheare and Mr. Jonas wood Justice of the peace and the oversears of the sd. towne Whereas Marke Megs and Avis his wife p'sented A Complaint against Sarah sooper wife off henry sooper for her veyarious carradgcs towards the com plainants and for formor miscarradges and abuse of Aughthoritie whereby the said Sarah sooper Laye under the sentance off a towne Coort for Corparall punishment and it was not inflicted. This Coort have therefore ordered that is the sd. sarah sooper wife of henry sooper parsist in turbelence of sperit without Reformacon that for the first offence whether contempt of Aughthoritie or abuse of her Naighbours for the first offence committed by her the sd. Sarah to Receve fifteene strips forthwith after Complaint Bee made to Aughthoritie at the Most public place in the towne.

Alsoe Whereas henry sooper Complained Against Marke Meges for provokeing him the Coort see cause to Lay a fine of six shillings and eaight pence uppon him the sd. megs for his Breach of the peace.

Alsoe that henry sooper for his abuesfull carradge and provocacons against Mark megs in his hous and against the said megs this Court hath ordred that him the sooper shall

paye all Charges herein that it may for the future time take
warning that hee Commit noe more such ffolly.

(*Court Rec. p.* 329.)

---

## [THE OLD TOWN PARSONAGE.]

### [1672, April 15.]

Aprill the 15, 1672

The day and yeare abovesaid the Constable and townsmen meeting at Mr Woods sent for Martha nabor, Dahter
and executrix to James nabor Deceased to know what shee
would allow unto the reparatcion off the ruings of the
towne hous or parsonadge hous and land and fence the
townsmen asked £50 and som labour that was Bestowed
by the sd. James nabor on a hous lot that the towne gave
the sd. nabor towards his Incouridgment to supply the
towne nessessittie hee being a Cooper the sd. Martha nabor
being silent touching the townsmen demands then the overseers spake to Thomas Scudder and too Joseph Bayly to
walk forth with Martha nabor and consider together
what damage was don to sd. hous land fence and what shee
would willingly give thomas scuder Joseph Bayly and
Martha naibor came in to Mr woods hous with our consent
and freely offered 40ˢ and the labor that was bestowed on
the aforesaid lott the Constable and overseers excepted their
offer and demand was mad what the 40ˢ should bee paid in
Martha nabor Replied shee would paid it in salt which
was excepted with a full Resignation of labour land and all
priviledges that did or might belong thereunto Considering the towne and could not bee answered by Reason the
aforesaid nabor did ingadg to keep an ordinary.

Joseph Bayley Reʳ

(*Town Meetings, Vol.* 1, *p.* 41.)

## [THE TEN FARMS.]

[1672, April 16-17.]

The Account off what was Doun by James Chi-chester, Samuell Tytus Jonathan Rogers and Joseph Bayly, Conscerneing Laying out those ten farmes from the head of nesaquage River unto Crab med-ow Littell necke. By the appoyntment off the towne and was Don and parformed by us aforesaid the 16th and 17th Dayes of Aprell 1672 p'sented unto the towne in Jennorall and exsepted and the farmes Devided by Lot with a joynt consent and therefore Recorded by mee.

Joseph Bayly Re[r]

Imp[r]   the River head farme from the Littell Run of water on the left hand of the parth 56 Rood by the side of the River the north side 60 Rod the west 56 the south side 60: that parporcon 40 acars the owners Joseph whitman John Samwayes, Samuell Ketcham, Richard Williams and Timothy Conkloyne.

H 2   farme on the east sid of the littell necke against Mr Smiths 60 Rod in Length and 56 Rod in breadth, the owners thereof by lot is Thomas Scudder John Budd, Stephen Jarvis, Robart Crandfeild.

H 3   farme by the side of the scompe on the s[d] littell necke in Length 60 Rod and breadth 56 the owners Jonathan Rogers and Samuell titus.

H 4   farme by the side of a Run of watter on the west side off sunken Meddow 60 Rod in length and 52 in breadth the owners epenetus platt Jonas wood John weekes thomas whitson:

H   the 5 farme on the west sid of the fresh pond the Length by the sound 52 Rod the bredth 24 Rod the owners thomas skidmore Mr wood James Chiches-

ter and thomas powell whoe have given thaire Rite
and intrest unto thomas skidmore.

H    the 6 Lot of the same Length and breadth adjoyneing to that the Remainding part of those farmes of
the fresh pon Lyeth south and west of the hous Lots
the onnor of this farme Samuell wood Joseph bayly
nathaniell fostar, John Ted, Jonathon harnett :

H    the 7. farme on Crabmedoe littell necke which is
cald the first on that neck which is next to the gut
the Length 80 Rod the bred 24 Rod the oners thereof J. green and Is. plat, Mr bryan, tho : weeks Rich.
brush.

H    the 8 farme adjoyneing to that of the same breadth
oners Captn fleet John finch Mark Megs.

H    the 9 farme of the same breadth adjoyneing to that,
the owners Abiall titus Content titus John Cory
John mathews

H    the 10 farme of the same breadth bounded with the
other on on sid and the Round swampe on the other
the oners, widoe Jones thomas Brush John Jones.
every of the sd. farmes to have 40 acars of upland
and the benifitt of what medow there was neareast
to them.

(*Court Records, p.* 305.)

---

[CONTENT TITUS'S LANDS.]

[1672.]

The Records of the Lands and Medow of Content Titus,
Rec[e] in 1672.
Imp[r], hous orchard gardens sittuate Lying and Beeing in
huntington aforesaid Bounded as Discribed the frunt to
the streate faceing Richard Williams the east side with the
Lot that was formerly in the tenner occupacon of Cap[tn]

seely the Rcare with the Lot of John Teed the west side
with the streete or high waye alsoe six acars of Land in
the west feild Lying in too severall places 3 acars Bounded with the Land of samuell Titus on the east side and the
Land of thomas Brush on the west the other 3 acars
Bounded with the Land of Richard williams on the east
side and the Land of Jonathan Scudder on the west as alsoe
a certaine parcell of Meddow Lying and being on the south
side of the eiland on too severall necks that is to say fower
acars Bee it more or les Lying and being on a necke called
by the name of the great neck in the severall parsels on p$^t$
which was called the Comon meddow bound with samuell
Ketchams on the east sid and Richard Williams on the
west the other parsell Bounded as aforesaid the other p,cell
Lying on A neck called by the name of the Littell necke
Bounded with the Medow of those as aforesaid.

p. mee Joseph Baylye.

(*Deeds Vol.* 1, *p.* 25.)

[DEED. JOHN RICHBELL TO NICHOLAS AND
JOHN FINCH.]

[1672, April 28.]

Know all men by these p$^r$sents y$^t$ I John Richball formerly liveing in Oyster Bay and now at momerinock have
formerly made over unto sd. Nickolls and John finch of
huntington A. certain parcell of beach which formerly I
did purchase and had possession from Tackapousha sachem and y$^e$ Rest of your Indians of masepege the beach
lying between huntington gutt eastwards : And masepague
gut westwards : I doe confirme and grant y$^e$ afore sd.
premises unto y$^e$ afore sd. Isack Nickolls And John finch
as witnesse hand this 28 of Aprill 1672.

JOHN RICHBELL.

witnes. ROBART CUTT
    ✕ WALTER NOCKES
The above sd. are true copies of yᵉ originall by me John
Corey Recʳ

                            Agoust yᵉ first 1682.

    *( Court Record p. 395.)*

---

## [DEED.  SAMUEL MESSENGER TO JOHN GREEN.]

[1672, May 18.]

Bargoned, sould and Made over ffrom mee my heires and
assignes unto John greene of huntington uppon Long
Eiland, husbandman his heires and assignes all my Rite
title and intrest in my Accomindacon sittuate and Lying
in huntington afore said both housing barne orchard
medow and upland that doth or ever heare after shall belong there unto which was halfe medow and upland and
halfe the Comonadge formerly in the tener of An Rogers
widoe for the some of twentie pounds to bee paid by Mr
Richard Bryan of milford as is more at large exprest in a
bill of Debt bareing date with thes presents I saye all my
Rite title and intrest in and to the same I have estranged
from mee my heires and assignes unto John greene his
heires and assignes To have and to hould for ever in witnes whereof I have heare unto set my hand this 18th Daye
of maye in the yeare of our Lord 1672.
signed and Deld.          SAMUELL MESSENGER
in the presents off
JOHN FFINCH
    Joseph Bayly Recʳ
     *(Court Record p. 309.)*

## [ABIAL TITUS TO BEAT THE DRUM SABBATH DAYS.]

[1672, June 3.]

Monday, June 3rd, 1672.

Being a training day it was then agreed by the consent of the whole company that Abiell Titus should beat the drum Sabbath days in the fore and afternoon; and for his pains therein the company consented to buy a new drum which drum the said Abiall is to keep in repair and beat at all needful times, as training days and times aforesaid, for which the said Abiall is to remain rate-free as long as the town see cause.*

Joseph Bayly, Re<sup>r</sup>

[Copied in the Revision in the year 1873, from the original in No. 2, p. 5.]

(*Town Meetings, Vol.* 1, *p.* 43 *and Court Rec. p.* 179.)

---

## [DEED, EDWARD BUNCE TO CONTENT TITUS.]

[1672, Sept. 2.]

Know all whome it may conserne y<sup>t</sup> I Edward bunce of eatons neck one Long Island doe by these presents Ingage to deliver to content tittus of Huntington a cow fowr̄ yeers old past. y<sup>e</sup> cow being now in y<sup>e</sup> custitie of Edward bunce called & known by y<sup>e</sup> name of Cherey this fowr sd. cow to bee delivered to content titus or his assigencs at or before y<sup>e</sup> last of octobar and for and in consideration of y<sup>e</sup> afore sd. cow the fore sd. content tittus doth Resigne all his Right in that farme hee belonged to in crabmedow

---

[*This practice of calling the people together for public worship was common to the period. I incline to the opinion that there was no church bell in Huntington until the erection of the church on the site of the present First Presbyterian Church in Huntington village, about the year 1711, perhaps· later.—C. R. S.]

neck soe far as belongeth to a five hundred pound alottment as it is agreed one by yᵉ town I say I doe fully make
over from mee my heairs to yᵉ sd- Edward bunce his
heairs with out any nolestation for ever: the sd. Edward
bunce cleering all charge as hath been exspended as wittnes our hands this second of September 1672.

The Mark of EDWARD × BUNCE
Witnes                                    CONTENT TITTUS
  THOMAS SCIDMORE
  The mark of MARK × MEGS

A true Coppy by mee<br>
John core Clerk.<br>
may yᵉ 27ᵗʰ 1684.

Taken out of an old booke by order from Edward bunce
yᵉ 25ᵗʰ of octobʳ 1686. p mee        Isaac Platt. Recʳ
  (*Deeds, Vol. 1, p.* 205, *and Court Rec., p.* 266.)

---

## [DEED.    HENRY SOPER TO JONATHAN ROGERS.]

[1672, Sept. 17.]

this writing testifieth that I henry sooper of huntington
uppon Long Eiland have Bargoned and sould from me my
heirs and assignes unto Jonathan Rogers of huntington
* * *    and his heires and assignes all my Right title and
intrest that I have in that farme and              between
Cowharbor              and nisaquage River that I had of
my mother in law the widdoe wattles to have and too hould
for ever as witnes my hand this 17ᵗʰ of september 1672

the marke of<br>
HENRY × SOOPER

Joseph Bayly. Rc·
  These Two above Entered Book A 71.
    (*File, No.* 69.)

## [LAYING OUT A HIGHWAY.]

[1671, Sept. 18.]

Septembr y$^e$ 18$^{th}$ 1671.
it is agreed by marke meggs & y$^e$ towne of Huntington
that y$^e$ towne should have their first high way bettween
the pond & his lott & soo through over the Dam the towne
taking y$^e$ dam for their owne.

(*Court Rec. p.* 187.)

---

## [THE SETTLEMENT OF THE TEN FARMS, WITH-
IN THE DISPUTED TERRITORY.]

[1672, Sept. 23.]

This Writing Witnesseth to every on Before whome
these Presents may at any time come that whereas the
town of huntington have Bine by Richard Smith, of Nese-
puage Molested in their Right of Land Betwixt Cowharbour & Nesaquage river & have bine by him the sd :
Smith forced to Defend our rights from court to Court,
both at Southampton and also at high Court of assises, &
at Both the said Courts we have Reseaved Both verditt &
Judgment for us, and Being by the high Court of assisses
& their Judgment there Injoyned to settle Families one y$^t$
Land in the space of three years after that Judgment or
else to have no Benefit by that verdit, & in order to the
fullfilling of that Decree, we the Inhabitants of huntington
have thus far Proceeded, first we have Laid out tenn farms,
consisting of forty acres of upland to each farm, together
with meadow & commonage for Cattle : we have Divided
the town into ten parts as they consist of hundreds, according to our manner of Division of Lands & a ptucular men

of each Company of hundreds to Drawe Lotts for which
farm each Company should have, Begining with the first
at the head of Nesequage River and so going north to
the mouth of the river, from thence westward by the
sound to Crabmeadow Neck, the particular men to whome
these Particular farms are by Lott fallen to are as followeth the first farme next the river head Belongeth to Joseph
Whitmen, John Sammis Sam. Ketcham, Richard williams,
Timothy Conklin ; the second farme, by the river side, Belongeth by Lott to Stephen Jarvis, Tho : Scudder, Robert
Cranfield, John Budd henry soper : The third farme Lying
on the west side of the little Neck, Belongeth by Lott to
Samuel Titus, Jonathan Rogers ; the fourth farm Lying at
the sunken meadow Belongeth by Lott to John wickes,
Epenetus Platt, Jonas wood Juner, Tho : Whitson ; the fift
farm Lying on the fresh pond Neck Belongs by Lott to
Tho. Skidmore, Jonas wood sen$^r$ James Chichester, Thom-
as powell; sixt farm Lying on the fresh pond Neck Be-
longeth by Lott to Sam wood Nath. foster, Joseph Baylee,
Ben Jones, John teed ; y$^e$ 7$^{th}$ farme one Crab Neck Belong-
eth By Lott to widdow Matthes, Jacob Platt, Tho : wickes
John green, M$^r$ Briant, Richard Brush ; y$^e$ 8$^{th}$ on Crab
Neck Belongeth to widow Jones, Tho : Brush, John Jones;
y$^e$ 9$^{th}$ Lyeth on Crab Neck, Belongeth to Capt. fleet, Mark
Megges, John ffinch ; y$^e$ tenthfarm Lyeth on Crab Neck
Belongeth by Lott to Abiel Titus, Content Titus, John
Cory, John Matthias ; now to the end we may fully & absolutly Performe all that Judgment of the high Court
have injoyned, according to the true intent & meaning
thereof we the inhabitants of Huntington and every one of
the fore mentioned Compeny es Partaining to every particular do joyntly and severally By these Prsents Bind our
selves each to other our heires, executors and assigns, in
the sum of five hundred pounds in currant Pay that we will,
our selves, or by some other by & from us, settle every
one of the afore said farmes By Building fencing & plant-

ing soo many Portons in each farm as may Propperly be a family according to the Courts Judgment, Betwixt this & the 15th of September 1673 : and if any of the afore mentioned companyes fail of the true Performance of what is aforementioned so that we come to losse the Benefit of the Courts verditt, they shall pay or cause to be paid to the rest of the Companyes afore mentioned ye full sum above, request upon demand : and to the full & true performance hereof we jointly and severally subscribe our hands.

| | | |
|---|---|---|
| CONTENT TITUS | JONATHAN ROGERS | JOHN FFINCH |
| SAM. WOOD | JOHN TEED | ROBERT CRANFIELD |
| RICHd BRUSH | JOHN MATTHEWS | NATHANIEL FOSTER |
| THOMAS BRUSH | HENRY SOOPER | EPENETUS PLATT |
| JOHN GREEN | ABIEL TITUS | STEPHEN JARVIS |
| THO : WICKES | | THO : POWELL |
| JOHN JONES | | JOHN SCUDDER |
| | THO : SKIDMORE | JONAS WOOD |
| | JAMES CHICHESTER | JOSEPH BAILY |
| | SAM. TITUS | ISAAC PLATT |
| | JONAS WOOD | THO : WHITSON |
| | THO : WHITSON | MARK × MEGGS |
| | | THO. SCUDDER. |

These also further Witnesseth yt we ye Inhabitance of huntington have given and granted to any Person of our town not Been atteched nor suspected upon fellonious accounts, to go & settle all or any of these farms, they paying to the rest of the Proprietors Intrusted in such farms, all such charges as have Been expended in or about our Defending of our right to that Land viz Betwixt Cowharbor and Nesequage river, and so Doing, every such Person shall be the true Propriator of such farms to have and to hold to them their heirs and successors forever, they paying all rates and Dutys as men in the town that is or shall be By Law required, and all such Propriators or owners of all and every such farms do hereby engage them selves their

heirs & successors to the town of Huntington, first: that
they & every one of them shall make and maintain sufficient fences about all such grounds as any of them shall
take in from the Commons, to mannure that so their fruits
may be Preserved: 2$^{ly}$ that none of those farmers shall at
any time Directly or indirectly, by themselves children,
servants or Dogs hurt or chase or Disturb any Beast, either
cattle, horses or hoggs, Belonging to any men of the town
of huntington, from any place where it may be for the
Cattles safty or the owners Profit: 3$^{ly}$ that all such owners shall for all such Land as they shall take in by fenc to
till for their Profit, we say they shall satesfie the Indians
just Demands and so free the Town from all such Demands
and Indians Complaints; 4$^{ly}$ that all & every such farmer
shall not at any time sell or Lett any part or parcell of any
of these farms to any person of a vitious Life or truly of an
evil reporte, and if at any time any of the Farmers shall
alienate or Dispose of any of those farms to any other
it shall in all Particular be according to what is here
exprest in the afore mentioned tearms: 5$^{ly}$ that all and
every of these Particular farmers shall have a Distinct ear
mark for them selves with which ear mark they shall mark
all their cattle and Beasts Markable, and that every farmers ear mark shall be recorded in the Town Book: 6$^{ly}$ that
all and every of these farmers shall from time to time Duly
mark all their calves, Lambs and Piggs within the space of
14 or 20 Days after they be fallen: 7$^{ly}$ and that all those
afore mentioned farmers shall not at any time marke any
horse kind that runeth wild in the woods untill they have
first Brought them into the Town and made appeare to
the Constable & overseers that they are there own, or that
they have orders from some other so to Do.
September y$^e$ 23. 1672
the mark of GEORGE BALDWIN
is instead of THOMAS BRUSH.

THOMAS SCUDDER
ABIEL TITUS
THOMAS BRUSH
JONATHAN SCUDDER
THOMAS MARTEN
   his ✗ mark

JOSEPH BAELEE
THO SKIDMORE
THO. SCUDDER
   his
THOS. ✗ WHITSON
   mark

   his
EDWARD ✗ BUNCE
   mark

JOHN ROGERS
WILLIAM BROTHERTON

A True Copy By mee
  Solomon Ketcham, Clerk.
  (*File No.* 64 *and Court Rec. p.* 274.)

---

## [ORDER OF COURT OF ASSIZE CONCERNING THE HUNTINGTON AND SMITHTOWN BOUNDARY.]

[1672, Oct. 7.]

At a Genr¹¹ Court of Asizes held in new Yorke by his Maitie Authoritie beginnig on yᵉ 2ᵈ and ending on the 7ᵗʰ Day of ocktober in yᵉ 24 yeare of the Raigne of our soveren Lord Charles yᵉ 2 king of great briteane, france and Ireland Defendar of the faith  Anno: Domini 1672.

uppon the peticon of Richard Smith of nesaquage to yᵉ Govenʳ wherein hee alledges that at yᵉ Tryall had in yᵉ Court of asizes held in Anno: 1670 severall false evedences ware produced at the Tryall by yᵉ inhabitants of huntington whereby ye Court and jury ware mesled the same being debated in Counsell and Refered to this Court to give thaire judgment and opinion whether upon the grounds afore specified as well as the reasons and suggestions to

bee brought in there were a sufficient cause of a Re hearing
or Review of the accon it is Adjudg and ordered that if
the said Richard Smith can uppon the first thursday in
December next when a specall Court is to bee heald here
in this Cittie p^rvaiel w^th Thomas Bennadict and henry
whittng of norwalke in his mai^ties Collony of Coniticott to
Appeare at the sd. Court in person or cause sufficient
evedence then to bee p'duced to cleare the matter in difference concerning wch thaire Testimonyes are said to bee
soe materiall or can detect any fraud or foule practice in
the sd. Inhabitants of huntington wch y^e occasion of their
carrining the sute that then a Rehearing of the Cause betwene the sd. Richard Smith & the inhabitants of huntington shall be had when the Court will give such further
Determination therein as will bee Consonant to law and
good Conscience.

this is a true                by y^e order of y^e Goven^r and
Coppy.                        Court of assizes
                                  Mathias Nicols secret^r.

  (*Court Rec. p.* 253.)

---

## [TOWN MEETING.]

[1672, Nov. 23.]

          November ye 23^th 1672
it was voated and agreed the day Beformentioned the
Thomas Wilson shall take up the Remaining part of his 40
Acers of planting land Belonging to his farme on the north
side of his lot running by the side of the Meddow toward
the sound.

Edward Bunce is exepted as a farmar to improve on the
farms on Crabmeder neck.
   these 2 Below entered in New Book A. page 37.
     *Town Meetings, Vol. 1, p.* 23.)

[COURT PROCEEDINGS. THE SMITHTOWN
BOUNDARY SUIT.]

[1672, Dec. 5.]

At a specall Court of assizs held in new yorke by his
Magiet. Authorytie on y⁵ first thursday in December being
the 5ᵗʰ Day of the sd. month in yᵉ 24 yeare of the Raine of
our Soveren Lord Charls yᵉ 2ᵈ by the Grace of god of
England Scotland france and Ireland King Defender of the
faith &c Anno : Domini 1672.
Richard Smith plant.
yᵉ Inhabitants of huntington Defend.
This Cace being taken into consideration & fully Debated
in Court wherein yᵉ plf. Desired to bee heard in Equitie
for yᵗ part of nesequake Land on the west side of the River
which hee alledgeth to bee part of the land on which hee
was obliged to settell the first ten families although now
claimed by the Defd. by vertue of the verdicts thay obtained at Comon Law against the plnt. for other land as
hee Concieves, it is ordered that for the p'sent Respite
shall be made of any proseeding in this matter. untill the
spring when some time in yᵉ month of may next his honᵒʳ the
Governor intends to have a Generall Trayneing & a meeting of the two troops of hors at the east end of hempsteed
playnes from whenc some indifferent person from the east
end of Long Island whoe will bee there & some others from
the west end shall bee appoynted to goe & view the sd land
called nesaquake Land on yᵉ west sid of the River & to
make inquiry there in to in the best mannor thay can & if
possable to make a Conclusion therein Betwene yᵉ plf : &
Deft : wch. if it Cannot be Attained unto that then the plf.
shall have Libertie to p'fer. his Bill in Equitie against yᵉ
Deft. at ye next Genʳ Court of assizes as to that Land called
nesaquake Land where a Definite time Determinacon shall

bee made there uppon according to Law & good conscience·
This is a                              By order of the Governer and
True Copie                             Court of Assizes.

Mathias Nicols sec[r]

(*Court Rec., p.* 254.)

---

## TOWN MEETING.   [PROCURING A MINISTER.]

[1673, April 7 ]

April 7. 1673.

It was voted and agreed the same day by and with the
consent of the town that the Constable and Overseers
should do what they could for the procuring of a minister
and what they did or procured to be done herein the town
would rest satisfied ; and so left it wholly to their disposing.

Per. me Joseph Bayly, Re[r]

[Copied in the Revision in the year 1873, from the original
in No. 2, p. 16.]

(*Town Meetings, Vol.* 1,*p.* 45 *and Court Rec., p.* 186.)

---

## [DEED.  RICHARD BRYAN TO WALTER NOAKS.]

[1673, April 22.]

The Records of y[e] Land & medow: ot Walter Noaks,
know all men by these p[r]sents y[t] I Richard Brien of
milford, merchant have from me my heirs Executors,
Administrators & assignes: Bargoned sould and made over.
And doe by these p[r]sents Bargan sell & make over unto
Walter Noaks of Huntington upon Long Island, in Yorkshire. Tayler: All my Right Title and Intrust in and to

my allotment or accommendation: Sittuat and lying in huntington afore sd. The lot ot Thomas Brush on y^e west side: The Reare to y^e Lot of John Sammoys; part of y^e east side with y^e lot of Epenetus platt: frunting to y^e highway: Together with all lands priveledgs, profets and revenews: As also a certain parcell of medow lying on y^e south side of y^e Island: Containing foure acres be it more or less: on two severall necks y^t is to say two acres on a neck called neguntetaug: and y^e two acres be it more or lesse on a neck called y^e east neck: Both being y^e half proportion of a two hundred pound allotment: all which y^e afore sd. Lands and medows I y^e afore sd. Richard Briant doe alinate and estrange from me my heirs execrators administrators and assignes: unto Walter nokes his heirs executors administrators and assignes: all and singuler y^e afore sd. Lot hous, orchyard Lands divided and undevided medow afore specified: except a part of commonadge which I doe Resarve, becaus I will not be a trespesser unto y^e town of huntington els all lands I doe estrange as afore sd. To have and to hold for ever and I doe Ingadge my selfe my heirs and assignes to save harmlesse and indamnefied y^e fore sd. Walter Noaks his heirs & assignes: from any person or persons who may or shall Lay any clayme to y^e fore sd. Lands medows or any part or parcell threof: to y^e indamnefying y^e fore sd. Noaks or his succesors in his or either of their quiat possession. In witnesse whereof I have here unto set my hand this 22 of Aprill in y^e 28 year of his Maj^ts Rain and in y^e year of our Lord 1673, by y^e order of Mr Richard Bryant

Signed and delivered in          JOSEPH BAYLY
y^e presents of THOMAS SCUDDER.
The Mark of ALES × BALY.

This is a true coppy of y^e originell by mee John Corey Reco^r Novembr 22, 1682.

(*Deeds, Vol. 1, p. 121.*)

## [COURT RECORDS.  WALTER NOAKS vs. LOUIS MOTT.]

[1673, July 9.]

July the 9th 1673.

At a towne Court held by ye constable and overseers, constable Isack platt Overseers James chichester, epenetus platt, Tho: weeks.

Walter nooks plaintive against Louice Mott of Hemstead in an action of the case for keeping from the plant his horse in a false and fradelent manner to his great loss and dammag and for seeking to apropriatt the said hors to him self in a false maner.

upon the plea made both by the plaintive and defendant and the evidences prduced and formerly considered.

We find for the plaintife that the defendant shall pay to the pllf. for detaining ye plff horse a month or there about £1 : 10s and for as much as it hath bene fuly evidenced yt the defendant have in devered to cheatt the plff. out of his horse we adjuge the defendant to pay as a fine to ye contey twentie shillings and to pay to the plf. all just charges to gether with cost of sutte.*

(*Court Rec., p.* 273.)

---

## [DEED.  JONATHAN ROGERS AND THOMAS WICKS TO THOMAS MARTIN.]

(1673, August 4.]

Know all men by those prsents that wee Jonathan Rogers

---

[*Louis Mott evidently had a narrow escape from being convicted of horse stealing, the penalty for which crime was then severe.  "Stealers of horses, hogs, boats and canoes" were sentenced to have one of their ears cut off.—C. R. S.]

and Thomas wickes both of huntington uppon Long Eiland have bargened sould and made over from us our heiares execut$^{rs}$ administrators and assignes unto Thomas martin of huntington uppon long eiland afore said husbanman his heirs executors administrators & assignes all our Right title and intrest that wee have or ought to have in part of a farme that Lyeth on Crabmedow necke the lower most farme next to the gutt which parte is a fower hundred pound Rite either of us a too hundred pound Rite, Which is som what more then the third of a farme. The whole farme Containes eleven hundred pounds Rite. Wee saye all our Rite title and intrests unto our part as Is before spesified both upland and meddow wee have estranged from us our heires & assines unto Thomas Martin his heires and assignes too have and too hould forever and doe promis to free it unto this said martin as witnes our hands this fouerth Daye of agust in the yeare of our lord 1673.

JONATHAN RODGERS
THOMAS WICKES

Witnes the marke of
X
MARY BAYLY
JOSEPH BAYLY

This is a true Coppy of the orrigenall p me Tho: Powell Rec$^r$.

*(Court Rec. p. 303.)*

---

## [ORDER OF GOVERNOR TO SEIZE THE ESTATE OF DANIEL "LAM," &c.]

[1673, Nov. 2.]

Mr. Isaac Platt:

Capt$^n$ Knyf hath acquainted his hom$^r$ the Govern$^r$ of y$^e$

Letter, whom did give order that y^e, acct, should be satisfyed, be pleased therefore to appoint some person to receive
it for y^e acct.;

The desired Instructions are sent here enclosed, and
Concerning the Warrants, It is not Customary by the dutch,
to insert the name of any authority in their Warrants, but
receive their authority from the Magestrates by whom they
are signed ;   The oath for yo^r superior officers you may
form yo^r selves, only Inserting the Clause to be true &
faithful to the present Government & the Magestrates in
time being.   Now inclosed is a Letter and order for the
Magestrates of seatalkett wherin they are required to seize
uppon and secure the estate of danel Lam and returne an
acct. therof to his hon^r the Govern^r, to the end yo^r selves
and other true Credetors may come to their due,   Not. else
at present but that from

    [Crest]              Yo^r friend
[Seal] WILLIAM BENDRICK        W. BAYARD.
      20 November 1673
     (*File No.* 43.)

---

## [THE LIST OF TAXPAYERS.]

[1673.]

| A Contie Ratte made in y^e yeer 1673. | £ | s | d |
|---|---|---|---|
| Captt ffleette. | 1 | 4 | 3 |
| Steph. Jarvice | 0 | 13 | 8 |
| Rob: Cranfeild | 0 | 13 | 6 |
| Tho Scudder | 0 | 17 | 5 |
| (2^s 2^d to be added to this after Rate.) | | | |
| James Chichester, Sen^r | 0 | 16 | 8 |
| Na. ffoster | 0 | 11 | 4 |
| John ffinch Senier | 0 | 09 | 8 |
| Captt Baily | 0 | 10 | 2 |
| Tho: Whissen | 0 | 12 | 6 |
| John weeks | 0 | 12 | 6 |

|  | £ | s | d |
|---|---|---|---|
| John wood | o | o6 | 6 |
| Isaac Platt | o | 18 | 4 |
| Joseph Wood | o | 11 | 2 |
| Tho: Powell | 1 | oc | 4 |
| Sam wood | o | 18 | 3 |
| Calleb wood | o | 11 | 6 |
| John michall | o | o3 | 10 |
| Jonathan miller | o | o4 | 5 |
| Jona: Harnet | o | o7 | 10 |
| Tho: weeks | o | 12 | 10 |
| John mathewes | o | o3 | 2 |
| John Core | o | o8 | 2 |
| Epe: Platt | o | 17 | 3 |
| Walter noakes | o | o5 | 7 |
| John Brush | o | o6 | 10 |
| John Page | o | o6 | 8 |
| William Broderton | o | o7 | 8 |
| Phillip Udell | o | o8 | 4 |
| Thos: Skidmore | o | 17 | 4 |
| John Gollding | o | o6 | 9 |
| Jeremiah Smith | o | o6 | o |
| John Adams* | o | o2 | 6 |
| Rich: ward | o | o2 | 6 |
| John Green | o | o8 | 7 |
| Sam griffin | o | o1 | 6 |
| Jams Smith | o | o4 | 4 |
| Joseph wood, cooper | o | o1 | 6 |
| Johanas Race | o | o2 | 6 |
| John Scudder, (John Scudder paid to old John Conklin.) | o | o8 | 11 |
| Rodger guint | o | o1 | 6 |
| James Chichester Junor | o | o4 | o |
| Joseph miller (3ˢ due.) | o | o1 | 9 |
| Rich: williams | o | 12 | 7 |
| Edward Kicham (these 2 to pay) | o | o4 | 2 |
| John Kicham (due to John Kicham 2ˢ : 2ᵈ.) | o | o6 | 4 |
| John Ted | o | 7 | 6 |

[*This is supposed to be a son of the John Adams who came in the "Fortune" from London to New England, in 1621. He was granted a mill privilege in Cold Spring.—C. R. S.]

Tim Conklin
John Ted
John Jones
Rich: Williams
Rob Arter†
Sargant tittus
Sam Kicham
Joseph Whittman
Jonas wood, junor.
Rich. brush
Walter noakes
John brush
Widder Joans
    These all to pay to widder Joans‡

an account of what was paid in my hands of yᵉ Counte.

| Ratte | £ | s. | d. |
|---|---|---|---|
| Calleb wood . . . . . . . | o | 11 | 6 |
| Gerg: Balldin . . . . . . . | o | o6 | 6 |
| Phillip udell . . . . . . . | o | o8 | 4 |
| Cranfield to pay for 1 a. 1¹ᵇ 3ˢ . . . . | o | 13 | 6 |
| My own Ratte . . . . . . . | o | 18 | 4 |

John Samons & timothy Conklin and Sam Kicham are
to Receve 5ˢ each: out of John Kichams woolfe.
        (*File No.* 2.)

---

[† Robert Arthur was probably a son of John Arthur, of Salem,
Mass., who married the daughter of John Gardiner. After the
death of John Arthur, the widow lived at Nantucket, aud is
believed to have moved from there to Huntington, bringing
her son Robert. The "widow Arter" is often mentioned in
the records of the first settlement. Robert married a daughter of Thomas Scudder.—C. R. S.]

[‡ The "widder Joans," here mentioned, was in her maiden
name Catherine Este, daughter of Jeffrey Este, afterwards wife
of Henry Scudder, and later "widow wife," as she called her-
self. of Thomas Jones. It was a novel thing for a woman to
collect the taxes, but the records of the period show that she
was a woman of more than ordinary ability, and for convenience her neighbors paid their taxes in to her. She lived on
East Neck, probably about where Mr. Thurston now resides.—
C. R. S.]

## [TOWN MEETING. THE MILL AT COW-HARBOR.]

[1674, June 30.]

Jun. 30 1674.

At a town-meeting it [was] voted and agreed by the major part of the town that men should go to Cowharbor to view and try the stream and place on the North side of Epenetus ground, whether it were capable of having a mill there, and if it were found suitable for such a purpose that then they would have a mill there.

It was also agreed at the same meeting that the charge of building such a mill should be according to hundreds.

At the same meeting above said it was agreed that all sufficient laboring men that shall labor at the mill work, shall have per day 2 shillings and six pence; and every man and his sufficient team shall have per day 6 shillings and six pence; and that Mr Wood and Epenetus Platt, Jonathan Rogers, John Samwaye shall be overseers of the mill-work to appoint men there [to] worke and to call them out.*

---

[*Up to this time Little Cow Harbor (the name was changed to Centreport about 1836 on the petition of Shallum B. Street, father of the writer) was open, and navigation unobstructed as far south as the tide flowed. The location was considered favorable for a tide mill, something that had become a pressing necessity since the old mill of Mark Meggs, near the "town spot" had been discontinued, and the people at once commenced the work by constructing a dam and the erection of a mill there. I am uncertain as to its exact location. This mill property continued to be owned by the town for many years and millers occupied it under agreements with the town until, as we shall see later on, it passed into private ownership. The large mill building, now probably lower down the harbor, was built at a much later period, but it is possible that some of the millstones or irons in it have survived since this early period. —C. R. S.]

It was also voted and agreed that John Green shall have
4 acres of land by Cowharbor foot path at the Ground Nut
Hollow toward his division.

[Copy from the original in Court Records, p.    , copied
in the Revision in 1873.]

(*Town Meetings, Vol.* 1, *p.* 4.)

---

## [MARK MEGGS, "GROWING ANCIENT," MAKES A DEED TO JACOB WALKER.]

[1674, July 13.]

know all men to whom these presents shall come y^t I
mark megges formerly of huntington on long Island, now
of Stratford in y^e County of fairfield In y^e Collony of
Coneeticutt : growing Ancient and being desirous to passe
the Remainder of my time quietly and without wordly
incumbrances doe there fore make over all y^t estate god
hath given mee and all y^e particulers there of unto my
loveing friend Jacob Walker of stratford and his heirs and
asignes for ever, and doe hereby Impower him and them
to act in and about y^e premises as fully and amply as I my
self could at any time have done, to soe far Recover Re-
caive & posses any sum or sums of mony, goods Chatels
hereditaments or other estate.  also to sell barter alinate
and exchange any part or the whole of housing and lands
or eny other estate formerly belonging unto mee y^e sd.
mark megges at his own pleasure, for his own be hoofe and
proper account acknowledging it to be his own proper
estate by these presents that this is my act and deed is
witnessed by my subscribing this 13 of July 1674

Testis JONAS SMITH          the mark of MARK ✕ MEGGES
       JOHN HAIKIT                                     mark

This is a true coppy compared with the origenall by
mee John Corey Reco$^r$
July 10, 1681.
(*Court Rec., p. 255*)

---

[THE CLAIM OF SMITHTOWN CONCERNING
THE BOUNDARY.]

[No date—1674 probably.]

Richard Smyth plf    } the heads of y$^e$ dec-
Huntington men defts { laration.

first   the defts, did at both tryalls, in both Courts p$^r$duce
a false bill of sale in Asserokin name as may appear.

2$^{ly}$   The defts prodused severall false witnesses wherby
the Jurry & Court were misled, but y$^e$ plff. submite
to y$^e$ Courts gudgment.

3$^{ly}$   The land in question did never pertain to Asserokin,
y$^e$ matinacoc sachem, but Nassetscomset, the sachem
of neesaquauk, was the true proprietor thereof.

4$^{ly}$   That Nassetscomset sold y$^e$ plf y$^e$ sd, land by oraer
of Mr Winthrop & Harford Commisioners, under
which sale y$^e$ plf possessed the same peaceably 7 or
8 years to all purposes til y$^e$ defts. disturbed him.

5$^{ly}$   y$^e$ defts. have taken a vyolent posession, contrary to
law, & after farwarning & have committed many
rioteous abuses, to y$^e$ plffs. great p$^r$iudice.

6$^{ly}$   The plf. presented many petitions to Go$^{vr}$ Lovelacel
who with severall Courts did make severall orders
for y$^e$ plfs. relief if * * were * * * * protested against, by y$^e$ defts. by a accomplishment of
which orders, being hinderd by y$^e$ late change.

7$^{ly}$   The plf. prsented many petitions to y$^e$ Late dutch
Gover$^{nr}$ who in persuance of y$^e$ presedent order did

appoint 2 severall arbitrations, att y$^e$ plf. charge which were by y$^e$ defts, protested against, whose judgment declares y$^e$ plf. right to y$^e$ land in question.

8$^{ly}$  Gover$^{nr}$ Calbert upon y$^e$ plf$^s$ petition granted a hearing in equity & did give sentence & order y$^e$ ffiscal, to give y$^e$ plf. possesion of y$^e$ Land in question, with all charg * * * * * * * which execution was by Mr Smith omitted personally requireing Mr Udell to serv it as may appear.

9$^{ly}$  The Land in question is bounded east by neesaquack river & west by Whitmans Hollow & y$^e$ fresh pond. He did charge y$^e$ plf. to have produced a false order at Court which was y$^e$ cause y$^e$ dutch Court did deferr the case so long.

The deft. hath not settled y$^e$ land according to Gover$^{nr}$ Lovlace direction.

(*File No.* 62.)

---

## [HUNTINGTON'S PROTEST TO Mr. SMITH, CONCERNING THE BOUNDARY.]

[1674, July 17.]

Neighbor Smith, of Hogpaguag: by this yea may understand that what you left a paper for, at yea say the towne, in the hands of Joseph Whittman, written in an unknown tongue, to us, from whence it came or what it is, we know not, nether what you intend by it, we know not, but this we know, y$^t$ we shall take no notice of it, nether can we, and if you would have us to know your mind you must speake and write in a knowne language to us; like wise take notice y$^t$ we heare, and intend to know more fully, shortly y$^t$ yoe or yours have ackted the part of theaves or robbers by ussurping with impudent and shamles bouldnes to com upon our ground and to seize upon our peace for your owne use on unheard of practice and never practiced by honest men, therefor we doe by thes p,sents p.test against your course and wee resolved first to defend our selves & our estates from the hands of violent usurpers, w$^{th}$,s no more than the law of nature and nations allowed. secondly, when the season comes, yoe may expect to have and except the due defeat of such demeritts:

from Huntington, July 17 : 74.

(*File, No.* 63.)

---

[COURT RECORD. THE TESTIMONY OF JONA-

THAN ROGERS.]

[No Date.]

The depotion of Jonathan roggers.

this deponent deposed sayth. wee war going a long the way 3 or 4 of us and met goodman higbe and frances coming up from the Dock and frances cam before and goodman higbe came after him with a stick and comanded him to goe in to y$^e$ gate and he sayd he would not go in so he toke him by the arme and drawd him toward y$^e$ gate and Thomas scuder seing him toke hould of goodman higbe and made him let him goe and bid him goe home to his house that is to say franck and he would beare him out in it and then Tho. Scuder take hould of goodman higbe by y$^e$ shoulder by his wescote and bent his fist at goodman higbee and higbe having a stick in his hand they both sayde strike, and Tho. scuder towld goodman higbe if he had him in place wher he would bring his long sids to thegr ound: and furder sayth not.

(*Court Rec.*, *Vol.* 1, *p.* 24)

## [TOWN MEETING.  THE NEW MILL.]

[1675, April 6.]

1675.

At a towne meeting John Bird (Bud) desired a lot in the town, he being a blacksmith, the town did agree that the said Bird should have a lott in the towne provided he would supply the town with his work.*

[Copied from the original in the Court Records, p, , in the Revision of the Reocrds in the year 1873.]

April 6th, 1675

At a towne meeting it was voted by the inhabitants that inasmuch as they could not make pay to Goodman Webb [of Norwalk] for his work about the mill, it was agreed that they would pay him next Michaelmas togethen with all legal damages.

[Copied from the original recorded in Court Records p. , in the Revision in the year 1873.]

(*Town Meetings, Vol.* 1, *p.* 49, *and Court Rec. p.* 317.)

---

## [COURT RECORD.   FINAL DECREE SETTLING THE BOUNDARY WITH SMITHTOWN.]

[1675, Sept. 24.]

In the case between the Plt. and Defendts the Court after

---

[*According to "Hotten's" lists John Bud, Sr., came from London in th: "America" in 1636.  He was at New Haven in 1639, and his name appears among the first settlers of Southold, about 1640.  He is said to have been tried at New Haven, in 1661, for harboring Quakers.  He left children John, Joseph and Judith.  Whether it was the elder John, or the son, who is referred to above, is uncertain.—C. R. S.]

mature deliberacon, doth finde in equity for the Plt. and the proceedings of the Dutch Court in this case to bee legall and judiciall, and therefore give judgment for the Plt. That the lands in question between Nassaquake River westward and Whitman's Hollow, and so to the fresh ponds, doth of right belong unto him (Richard Smith) and he is to be put in possession of the same, if not otherwise delivered up. The present inhabitts. therefore by the Plts. consent to have leave to stay there until the first day of May next, and also to have liberty to take off the produce of any corne that at or before this tryall was in the ground. However The said Land to bee within the jurisdiction of Huntington, as within their patent, though the Property adjudged to the Plaintiffe. The Deft. to pay the costs of this Cort, but for what hath been formerly each pty. to beare their owne charge.

The bounds* of the land recovered from Huntington by Richard Smith, Senr. and layd out by Thomas Weekes in obedience to the ordr. of the Court of Assizes, he being imployed by the Courts of Huntington to give possession

---

[*The new boundary seems to have been a compromise, neither town getting all that it claimed. Huntington claimed eastward to Smithtown River, and Smithtown claimed westward to Cow Harbor. A middle line was chosen at Fresh Pond and Whitman's Hollow. The exact location of this line was the subject of controversy among the adjoining land-owners, whose titles were bounded by the town line, for more than two hundred years after the date of the above order, until 1884, when, at the urgent request of some of the land-owners, Moses Smith, Supervisor of Smithtown, and Charles R. Street, Supervisor of Huntington, took proceedings for having it definitely fixed pursuant to the law applicable to such cases. After testimony had been taken by a committee appointed for the purpose, the Board of Supervisors passed a resolution establishing the boundary, commencing at Long Island Sound on the north and running to Babylon and Islip towns on the south. A survey and map of the line, made by Scudder V. Whitney, C. E., was filed, and marble monuments were erected at all appropriate points on this line.—C. R. S.]

of the same, is declared to be as followeth, vizt. From
the west most part of Joseph Whitman's hollow & the west
side of the Leading hollow to the fresh pond Unthemamuck, & the West side of this pond at high water marke
(to the River eastward) as it is supposed.

This is attested by Thomas Weekes undr. his hand Sept.
24th 1675.

Possession given by Turfe & Twigge.

---

## [DEED.  CONTENT TITUS TO JOHN KETCHAM.]

[1675, Dec. 1.]

Know all men By These p'sents yᵗ I Content Tittus of newtowne upon Long eiland in yorke shire husbanman have
from mce my heires executoʳ administraʳ & assignes bargened sold and made over unto John Ketcham of huntington
upon Long Island in yorkeshire afore sd. Carpenter all my
Right & intrust in or to a Comendations sittuatte and lying
in huntington afore sd. in yᵉ west end of yᵉ towne bounded
one yᵉ east side with yᵉ high way goeing to hempsteed one
yᵉ north side with yᵉ high way goeing to oysterbay yᵉ south
& west with yᵉ woods in Common ; I say all my Right,
title and Intrest in & to yᵉ same with all houseing out
nousing, orchards, gardens, out lands meadows, pasturs
mines or minerals all and singular every part & parcell
there of yᵗ doth belong to yᵉ said accomodation or any part
or parcell there of or hereafter shall belong to yᵉ p'rmeses
it being by denomination a two Hundred pound lott, as
alsoe eight acars of medow lying and being one yᵉ south
side of yᵉ Iland, six acars bee it more or less one yᵉ west
necke, & yᵉ other proportion a necke called yᵉ little neck
it being yᵉ p potion of a two Hundred pound lott, all &
singular all yᵉ afore sd, Lands and meadows & every part

& parcell there of I y<sup>e</sup> afore said Content Titus have estranged from mee my heirs executors adm<sup>s</sup> & assignes, unto y<sup>e</sup> afor<sup>sd</sup> Jn<sup>o</sup> Ketcham his heires, exe<sup>c</sup>, adm<sup>es</sup>, & assigne to have & to hold for ever, & I doe hereby ingage my selfe my heires & assignes to save harmless & indemnified y<sup>e</sup> s<sup>d</sup> John Ketcham his heires & assignes from any parson or persons who shall or may lay any Clame or title to y<sup>e</sup> afore sd. lands medows or any part or parcell there of to y<sup>e</sup> indemnifieng by y<sup>e</sup> sd. John Ketcham his heirs and assignes in his or theire quiet possession in wittnes whereof I y<sup>e</sup> afore sd. Content Tittus have here unto sett my hand and seale the first Day of December in y<sup>e</sup> twenty seventh year of his ma<sup>ties</sup> Raign & in y<sup>e</sup> year of our lord one thousand six hundred seventy five.　　　　CONTENT TITTAS.
sealed signed and
Ddl. in y<sup>e</sup> p'sents of
　JONATHAN SCUDDER
　THOMAS BRUSH
This is a true Coppy of y<sup>e</sup> orriginall deed, extracted by
　　　　　　　　　　　　　Thomas Powell,
　　　　　　　　　　　　　　　　Recorder.
　　(*Court Rec., p. 292.*)

---

### [TOWN MEETINGS.]

[1675, Dec. 7.]

December the 7<sup>th</sup> 1675.

At a town meeting it was voted and agreed by the major part of the town that every farmer that is turned from their farm and hath no land in the town shall have a lot in the town together with other privileges ; but inasmuch as the town have no meadow to give out at present, it is agreed that when the town can buy meadow of the Indians that then they shall have liberty to take up with the rest of the town according to the hundreds they take up, paying proportionably.*

At the same town meeting it was agreed that James Smith shall have three acres of land for a home lot in the swamp by Thos. Wickes ; to be laid [out] by the layers out as they shall see meet, and he to maintain convenient styles for the path.

It was also agreed that Edward Ketcham shall have a lot at the rear of Joseph Whitmans', and Sam¹ Ketcham's lot to bear the denomination of a two hundred pound lot.

It is also agreed that Rich⁴ White shall have a lot at the hollow westward of Meggs' lot, bearing the denomination of a hundred pound lotment to be cleared or built on in yᵉ space of one year.

It is also agreed that John Samway shall have eight acres of land near the cove in the West Neck, near John Tid's field toward [his] division.

It is also agreed that Benj. Jones shall have 6 acres of and by John Tid's field toward his division.

[Copied in the Revision in the year 1873.]

(*Town Meetings, Vol.* I, *p.* 51 *and Court Rec., p.* 277.)

------

## [DEED.   SAMUEL MESSENGER TO BENJAMIN JONES.]

[1676, Jan. 11.]

To all Christian People unto whome these p'rsents shall come greeting : Know yea that I samuell messenger of Huntington in yᵉ Countie of yourke within yᵉ Jurisdicktion

------

[*As the Court of Assizes had awarded all that part of the terɪitory between Fresh Pond and the Smithtown River to Smithtown, those farmers or colonists who had gone from Huntington and settled there were unsuccessful.  Hence this order that they might have lands elsewhere.—C. R. S.]

of his Royall hiness in Americai for divers good causes & considerations mee heer unto moving But more especially &c of the sum of twentie fowr pound ten shillings of curant Pay of yᵉ afore sd. Countie to mee in hand paid or secured to bee paid by Benjamin Joens of the same place & countie : Haven granted barganed and sould &c and do by these presents give &c unto yᵉ sd, benjamine Joens and his heairs all that too hundred pound allottment yᵗ was formerly Richard wattleses only the share of yᵉ farmes exseptted which tow hundred pound Lottment sittuate lying and beeing att Huntington in yᵉ afore sd. Countie and is bound with yᵉ land of John Teds upon yᵉ north side to gether with what house or housing orchard or orchards and all other ediffeses buildings timber wood trees, springs and all other profitts, commodities and advantages what soever their on beeing or their unto in any wayes belonging or apertaining to have and to hould the sd. prebarganed Land & premises to him yᵉ sd Benjimin Joens and his heairs for ever. In wittness wheare of the afore sd. Samuell messingar doth sett his hand the eleventh day of Januare Anno: dommone, 167⅝

signed and delivered in yᵉ presents of us witnesses

SAMUELL MESSENGAR.

HENRY ╳ SOOPER
his
mark

ELIZABETH ╳ WATTLES
her
mark

(*Deeds, Vol.* 1, *p.* 280.)

[DEED.  JOHN COREY TO RICHARD WHITE.]

[1676, Jan. 16.]

Jan. 16ᵗʰ 1676.

John Corry hàth sold To Richard White all his right in

the old mill pond for a valuable consideration and yᵉ said
white to pay each yeare Rent to marke megg from this
day untill the towne fee expired.

Thomas powell Recʳ

(*Court Record p.* 187.)

---

## [TOWN MEETING.  MR. JONES CALLED AS PASTOR.  A MILLER WANTED.]

[1676, Jan. 16.]

Janeruary 16ᵗʰ 1676.
at a town meeting of the inhabitants of huntington
this present day it was ordered by the said towne
fore. sd. that the Constable and overseers shall with
as much speed as possible send to southhamton to a
man that is a mill-wright to see if hee will bee willing
to com to this town to agree with the town about
our mill to the end wee may obtaine our expectation
of having good mele,

2ˡʸ  It was ordered the same daye that John Sammes
shall have 3 Rode squeare right over against his
house on the west side of the hieway not to impaire
or hinder the highway or to bee any other-wyes in-
convenent to the towne at the judgment of yᵉ men
appointed for that purpose.

this one above entered Book A. page 47.

3ˡʸ  It was this day also ordered by major parte of the
towne that the Constable and overseers together
with goodman Conklin Isaaik plat & Jonas wood
senʳ shall in the townes behalf seriously give Mr
Jones an invitation and fully to manifest their desires for his continuing to despense the word of god
and what more is dutie in the ministeriall offise
amongst us of huntington and what further may bee

requisite for incorragment to the aforesaid end.

4$^{ly}$ It is ordered by the major part of the towne that Mr Jones* shall have for himself and his, for his encorragment four ever twenty acers of upland, to bee his and remaine his for ever, where hee shall think best, not infrenging highways watering plases according to the towne true intent.

5$^{ly}$ It is likewise ordered by ye major vote of the towne ye same day y$^t$ besides the chosen layers out of land to witt: Cp$^t$ bayley & Tho. powell, Rich. williams Samuell Tithus shall be added Cap$^t$ fleet & Jonathan Rogers, then these 6 men shall devide the old mill pond equaly into 4 quarters and the Constable and overseer shall devid the severall hundreds awarding to ye towne method or waye into 4 parts equaly and then ye 4 quarters of hundreds shall cast lotts for y$^e$ 4 quarters of ye mill pond soe divided by these 6 aforesaid men equally both for quantity and quality.

these two below entered Book A. page 47

6$^{ly}$ It was ordered ye same day that Nathaniell ffoster have 2 acres of land more or less as the place will aford on the north side his own land in ye little necke.

7$^{ly}$ It was agreed ye same day y$^t$ John Ketcham should have about 3 Rod of each sid his homlott added more to it.

---

[*Rev. Eliphelet Jones was the son of Rev. John Jones, who came to Charlestown, Mass,. in 1635 and subsequently settled at Fairfield, Conn. Eliphelet was born at Concord in 1641 and in 1669 was a missionary at Greenwich, Conn., from which place he came to Huntington about 1673, so that he had preached here, more or less, after Mr. Leverich. left, down to the time the call was given him, as above stated. He remained in Huntington until his death in 1731, being the pastor of this church fifty-five years. He died at the age of ninety years and had no children. The church building erected on Meeting House Brook about 1665 was long the place of Mr. Jones's preaching.—C. R. S.]

8$^{ly}$ It was ordered ye same day that John ff'ench Se$^n$ should have 4 acres of land upon ye east neck lying betwixt his own lott and Tho. Scudder it is to run along by the watters side.

the above entered New Book A. page 47

9$^{ly}$ it was ordered the same day yt Joseph Whitman should have liberty to take up his division of land where hee shall see it convenient not hindering home lotts, highways or wattering places for catle.

10$^{ly}$ It was ordered the same day y$^t$ Jonathan Miller should have 3 acres of land lying southward of John birds betwixt ye hill and ye path if it may bee Conveniently had in y$^e$ before mentioned place.

(*Town Meetings, Vol.* 1, *pp.* 56-57.)

(see originall of the above line in Town Meetings April, 1, 1679)

---

## [CONVEYANCE OF MILL POND RIGHT.]

[1676, Jan. 19.]

Jan 19$^{th}$ 1676

Nathanell ffoster hath sold to Richard white all his right of the old mill pond for a valuable consideration and y$^e$ said white to pay each years payment to marke meggs untill the terme bee expired.

Thomas Powell, Rec$^r$

(*Court Rec., p.* 187.)

---

## [CONVEYANCE OF MILL POND RIGHT.]

[1676, Feb. 2.]

ffeb$^r$ 2$^d$ 1676.

Jonathan Rogers hath sold to Richard White all his

right & title of y<sup>e</sup> old mille pond which is 500 & ½ right
Thomas Powell. Rec<sup>r</sup>

(*Court Rec.*, *p.* 187.)

---

## [DEED. JOHN BRUSH TO JOHN MITCHELL; THENCE TO ROBERT KELLUM.]

### [1676, March 5.]

Know all men by these presents y<sup>t</sup> I John Brush of
Huntington upon long Island in yorksheeir husbandman
have barganed sold and made over all my Right title &
intrust in a commondation or allotment situate & being in
Huntington afore sd. The Reere of Jonas wood senr and
Richard Brush lots on y<sup>e</sup> north side: ffrunting towards y<sup>e</sup>
high way goeing towards the south; all and singular y<sup>e</sup>
afore sd. home lot housing, gardins fences, with all & other
priveledges y<sup>t</sup> doe or may here after belong there unto I
have sold & made over unto John michell of Huntington
afore sd. carpinter his heirs executors, adminstrators &
asignes for a considerable sum in hand payd the sd. accommondation was given to John holmes weaver by y<sup>e</sup> town
since astranged unto John Brush with all its appurtenences
and I doe hereby these presents estrange and make over
from me my heirs & asignes all my right title and intrust
unto all y<sup>e</sup> fore mentioned premises unto John Michell his
heirs and assignes to have and to hold forever in witnesse
where of I have heere unto set my hand this fifth day of
March in y<sup>e</sup> 28<sup>th</sup> year of his maj<sup>st</sup> Raigne and in y<sup>e</sup> year of
our Lord 1676.

JOHN BRUSH

Signed and delivered in
y<sup>e</sup> presence of.
The marke of
ROGER X GUINT
JOSEPH BALY

Know all men whom this may conserne That I John Michell do by thes presents make over & give and grant and assure full and quiet possesion of y^e full intents of this bill of sale: from me my heirs or asignes unto Robart kellam him his heirs executors or asignes for ever, promising quiat possession febury y^e 28, 1680.

JOHN MICHELL

Witnes
BENJAMEN CORNISH
JAMES SMITH

The above said sale and assignment is as true a coppy as I could take out of y^e broken and Solleyed originall; by meee John Corey Clark desem^r 22. 1684.

(*Court Rec., p.* 192.)

---

## (TOWN MEETING.)

(1676, April 2.)

1676.
Aprill y^e 2^d it was agreed by y^e major part of y^e towne that Thomas Crump shall have a lott against Jona Harnet's & Joseph Woods lott it being one the west side of the swamp. it was also ordered by y^e Constable and overseers that Thomas Crumps lott should bear the denomination of a two hundred pound alottment.

(*Town Meetings, Vol.* 1, *p.* 55.)

---

## (TOWN MEETING.)

(1676, April 27.)

April 27 1676
It was voted and agreed that Jeremy Smith should have

a home lott in the swamp northwest of James Smith's lot, and a piece of dry land on that side of the brook that Capt. Baylis' house [is] for him to set a house on and for yard room so much as the layers out should see fit, and he to maintain convenient styles for the foot path.

[Copied from the original, recorded in Court Records, p.  , in the Revision in the year 1873.]
(*Town Meetings, Vol.* 1, p. 59.)

## (TOWN MEETINGS.)

### (1676, June 5.)

1676 June the 5$^{th}$ it was ordered y$^t$ James Chichester jun$^r$ shall have a lott one the southeast side of Isacke plat's lot which joyne to Samuell Woods lotts.

2. It was alsoe agreed by y$^e$ major part of y$^e$ towne that Steven Jarvis jun$^r$ shall have a lott by y$^e$ side of The: Wickes lott y$^t$ was noah Rogers, soe much as should bee judged fitt by y$^e$ layers out and it to bear the denomination of one hundred pound lotment.

3. It was alsoe agreed by y$^c$ major part of y$^c$ towne y$^t$ garrat Cloud shall have a lot near y$^e$ brickill in y$^e$ west necke 1676 Dec. [all above entered New Book A. p. 46.]

1. it was agreed by y$^e$ major part of y$^e$ towne that Thomas Lawranse shall have a lot between Joseph Bayley and James Cheshesters Sen.

2. it was agreed by y$^e$ major part of the towne that Mr. Jones shall have a lott between John wickes swamp pasture and James Smiths lott.

3. it was alsoe agreed by y$^e$ major par. of y$^e$ towne that M$^r$ Jones shall have the 2 acre of meaddow at y$^e$ harbor which Steven Jarvis & Tho. Whison hath provided upon y$^e$ south of y$^e$ rowade it bee found cleare from them

4. It was alsoe agreed by y$^e$ major part of y$^e$ towne that
   William brotherton shall have the towns right to about
   2 acere of swampy land one freshpond necke by his
   land.
   these below entered New Book A. Page 47.
   (*Town Meetings, Vol. 1, p. 55.*)

---

## [POWER OF ATTORNEY BY SIMON LOBDALE PURSUING A RUNAWAY.]

[1676, July 29.]

Know all men by these p'sents, that I Simon Lobdell of
Harford upon Conecticatt in New England have nominated & Impowered and by these p$^r$sents doe nominatt ordaine
Constitut & Impower my loveing friend M$^r$ Ralph Warner
of Brookland black smith to beé my true & lawfull attorney
for me & in my name place & stead & to my only use &
behooufe to persue over take & by all lawfull ways &
meanes what soever to seiz upon and secure the person of
Rich: foscue who being the bond Sarvant of me the sd.
Simon Lobden & othere ways Indebted unto hath unlaw-
fully departed from my service & the body of the sd. Rich:
foscoe haveing seized to use all lawfull wayes & meanes to
return or cause to bee returned sent & delivered to mee
the sd. simon lobden at Hartford aforenamed or any of the
Estate of the said Rich: foscoe to attach wrest or othere
wayes to suz & condemne for settisfaction of the sd. service
unfullfilld & payment of y$^e$ sd. Debt & that in full & Effec-
tuall maner according to lawes & Custome used in such
cases in the place or places where the sd. Rich: foscue or
his Estate may beé found, Hereby further giveing unto my
s$^d$ attorney full power & authority to make such agreement
or composission with the sd ffoscue as to my s$^d$ attourney
shall seem good for sattisfaction of his debt & time of ser-

vice unfullfilled and upon receipt of such payment or othere sattisfaction fully & for ever discharge & accquit the sd. foscue of & from the sd. service & Debt for ever ffurthere- more I doe by these p^rsents give unto my said attorney full power to make Constitute an attourney or attourneyes under him with the like or limitte power, & what soever my sd. attorney shall doe or cause to bee done in or about the p^rmises I doe by these p^rsents rattifie & Confirm the same in wittness where of I have here unto sett my hand & seale this twenty ninth of July 1676.*

SIMON LOBDELL.

Signed delivered in
presents of us
    ZACHARIAH SANDFORD
    JOHN KESLLIS

Simon lobdell personally appeared this 29th July 1676 and acknowledged that the above written letter of attourney was his act & deed before mee John Allen, asist.

(*Court Rec., p. 300.*)

---

[COURT RECORDS.    SIMON LANE vs. HENRY
SOPER AND WIFE.]

[1676, Sept. 11.]

Att a Court held in Huntington by his ma^tles authority

---

[*This seems to be in the nature of a proceeding to recover a fugitive slave or bound servant. At this distance of time it is difficult to determine which is most outraged in this kidnap- ping, Richard Foster's rights, or the English language. How- ever, when we turn to the law of the period, we find that when a servant ran away or was suspected to be a runaway, the con- stable was to press men into the service of the town by "rais- ing a hew and cry," and pursue and bring him back. It was also required that all laborers and servants shall work in their callings when thereunto required, the whole day, their master or dame allowing them convenient time for food and rest. This was before the eight hour law was invented, or the Knights of Labor organized.—C. R. S.]

the 11<sup>th</sup> of Sept. 1676 by the constable & overseers of the same towne they being James Chetchester Const.

Joseph Whitman ⎫
Samuell Tittus    ⎬ over-
Jonas Wood        ⎪ seers.
Tho. Powell,      ⎭

Simon lane Plant. against
Henry Soper and his wife Def<sup>ts</sup>
the plant declares that the defendents have confest that they did fetch away fruit from the orchard of Jacob Walker and would fetch away more, and told the said lane hee had and would fetch away more in spite of his teeth and when I demanded of them why they stole my apples they replyed they had as much right to them as I and would fetch them away in spit of my teeth for they were common this being the 10th of this Instant.

the depossission of John Rogers aged 36 years
this deponent testifieth that hee was in the orchard* and Hen soapers boy was a top of the peach tree without the fence soe Mr. lane said to the boy Sarra will you never leave of yo<sup>r</sup> theefing trickes then soaper hee replied who doe you call theef, lane replied you I call theef that has taken away my fruit daly & howerly, soaper replied you roge I have as much to doe here as thou hast. upon that lane fetched a stick and bid soaper goe off his ground or else he would make him goe of, soaper replied it was comon and hee would stay there in spit of his teeth. then soapers wife com and said lane what hast thou to doe here more than wee, yea lowsey Roge pay mee what thou owest mee, you sone of a whore pay mee what thou owest mee,

---

[*The Court of Assizes at this period, made whipping the penalty for robbing orchards or gardens, or stealing clothes hung out, the number of stripes corresponding with the magnitude of the offence. The punishment for burglary was : first offence, branded on the forehead ; second offence, branded as before and severely whipped ; third offence, put to death.—C. R. S.]

lane said to soaper sarra if I catch the here to marrow morning I will shout thee, soaper replied I have a goun as well as thee and Ill meet thee here to marrow and sarah soaper said to lane hee was a falce forsworne Roage.

(*Court Rec., p.* 278.)

## [ORDER OF CONSTABLE AND OVERSEERS.]

### [1676, Sept.]

1676—Sep$^t$ it was ordered by the Constable & overseere that John birds (Bud) lot should bare the Denomination of a two hundred pound lottment.

it was ordered by the Constable and overseers that John Everretts lott should barr the denomination of one hundred pound alottment his hom lott being 4 accars granted by the towne.

(*Court Rec., p.* 206 )

## [AGREEMENT BETWEEN THE TOWN AND JEREMIAH SMITH ABOUT THE MILL AT COW HARBOR.]

### [1677, Feb. 26.]

This Writing Witnesseth A Covenant and an Agreement Between Jeremiah Smith of the one part and the Inhabitants of the Towne of Huntington one Long Island in York sheire one the other Part first the Inhabitants of the Town afore said Doth alienate and Make over to the said Jeremiah all their Right and Interest in and to their Mill Lying and Being at Cow harbour, together with A home Lott Lying by the mill, containing six or eight acares and that the Lott shall Bear the Denomination of A two Hundred pound A Lottment, and also A. cove of Creek thatch which the mill Brook runs into. in Consideration of the Premisses, the said Jeremiah Doth bind him self his heirs and assigns to supply the afore said Town with sufficient good meal as Good as they can have in any other place, and so to supply them from time to time, as often as the Inhabitants shall Bring him Corn, and for his tolle he shall have the twelveth of Indian Corn and the sixteenth of english grain, and the said Jeremiah Doth allso engage to keep the mill in good repair Constantly so that the town may have a full supply and if it should so happen that the mill, through all endeavours will not suit the end, and that to the convenience of the Generality of men, then the said Jeremiah shall return all the Iron work and the stones together with all other things which may be usefull for A mill; and the said Jeremiah shall enjoy all other grants for himself and his heirs forever; and the afore said Jeremiah Doth further Bind himself, his heirs, and assigns, for ever that if he or they shall at any time, and that upon Conviction take more of any of the Inhabitants Corn that is Brought to him to Grind then the twelveth of Indian and the sixteenth of English Grain, he or they shall forfit the mill to the town again, and in case the sd Jeremiah Do through any Discontent, not withstanding the mill be found Competent, yet shall see cause to alienate the said mill from him self to some other, yet this obligation to stand firm And sure, truly and honestly to be observed by whomsoever it is that possess it.

in Witness hereof we have set to our hands this 26th of February 1677.

Signed sealed and
Delivered In the Presence
of JONAS WOOD
  EPENETUS PLATT
  JONATHAN SCUDEER

JEREMIAH SMITH,   Constable

SAMUEL TITUS
ISAAC PLATT
JOHN CORE        and
JOSEPH WHITMAN  Overseers
THOS. POWELL

*(File No. 23 and Court Rec., p. 304.)*

## [MR. JONES CHOSEN MINISTER.]

[1677, June 10.]

The tenth of June 1677
Being a Training daye apoynted and Consented unto By
ye whole Companie Mr. Jones, Being Caled unto this
towne to preach the Gospell By the Mager pt. of the Inhabitants : not withstanding himselfe Desired to see how
the Inhabitants were asserted Boath to himselfe and that
more, he Desired to have the Company Drawne up in order,
which Don Mr Jones spake to the Company after this manner. that whereas the providence of god had Brought
him Amongst us in order to the worke of the Minnesetrie
for which hee Desired that hee might see their willingness
I thinking that Mr Jones spake soe low that the whole
Company could not heare what was saide, after silence was
Commanded I spake after this manner follow. Solders
seing it hath pleased ye Lord to send Mr Jones amongst
us you may doe well to manifest your Desires for his Con-
tinuance Amongst us and his affisciating in the worke of
the minnestre By your usuall signe of ye houlding up your
hands to which ye whole Company heald up all thaire
hands But only on man for the Contrary partie was Desired to hould up their hands to the contrary but that man
held up his hand to the truth hereof I have subscribed my
name this 10 day.

Joseph Baylye.

Further that Day Mr Jones Desired that hee might have
a Roome Built for a studdy of about 15 or 16. foot square
Because hee had not Roome to put his Books But only
in that Roome hee made use of, which was not convenient
the company tould him that they were willing to Doe it
But harvest was soo neare it would not bee don suddenly
Mr Jones Replyed hee desired not p'sent Because of their
axertions, But Between this and the next spring to which

all the Company but one man gave their Consent it should
Bee don according to his Desire unto the truth of Booth I
have subscribed

Joseph Baylye.

(*Town Meetings, Vol.* 1, *p.* 63.)

-------

## [SETTLEMENT OF THE ESTATE OF JOHN

## BRUSH.]

[1677, June 11.]

This written Testifieth that whereas Tho: Brush of
Huntington sonn of Tho: Brush deceased did receive a
letter of administration from yᵉ Powers of this govermᵗ of
yorkeshire, to administer on yᵉ deseaseds estate and to act
& doe according as in yᵉ law exprest

These may certifie any whom it may Concerne yᵗ I Rebecka brush daughter of yᵉ said Tho: deceased, have received of my brother Thomas administrateʳ one oure fathers estate my full propottion of yᵗ estate to Content it being to yᵉ value of fifty pounds & thirteen shillins & fower
pence in wittness whereof I have sett to my hand this 11ᵗʰ
of yᵉ 6ᵗʰ mo. 1677.

Witness,                                    her marke

JONAS WOOD                      REBECKA ✕ BRUSH
JOSEPH WHITMAN

These further wittnesseth yᵗ I John brush Sonn to yᵉ above
sd. Tho. deseased have received of my brother Tho: ad-
ministrator one our fathers estate my full proporttion of yᵗ
estat to Content it being the value of fifty pounds thirteen

shillins & fower pence as wittness my hand this 11<sup>th</sup> of y<sup>e</sup>
6<sup>th</sup> mo 1677.*
Witt JONAS WOOD                                    JOHN BRUSH
    JOSEPH WHITTMAN.
    ( *Court Records, p.* 291.)

---

## [EXCHANGE OF LAND BY THOMAS SCUDDER
## AND JACOB WALKER.]

[1667, Sept. 19.]

To any whome it may Concerne these may Signifie, that
wee Thomas Scudder and Jacob Walker have agreed and
bargained, that Thomas Scudder shall have six accers of
Land which formerly pertained to mark meggs lying one
the east neck next to the said Scudders land for and In consideration whereof Thomas Scudder doth promise to pay
the sd. Jacob walker for all y<sup>e</sup> fence of or about the said land
except 15 Rod which y<sup>e</sup> sd. Scudder sett up and the s<sup>d</sup>.
Scudder is to allow unto y<sup>e</sup> sd. Walker six acars of his
devidend of land att Crabmeadow that this our mutuall
agreement is wittnessed by our subscribeing this 19 of Sep<sup>t</sup>
1677.

---

[*At this period upon the death of a person it was the duty
of the constable " to repair to the house and inquire after the
manner of death and of his will. " If a will was found the
constable was to read it in the presence of the widow, children
and relatives, and make inquiry of the estate and report to a
magistrate. Administration was granted to the children or
widow; appraisers were appointcd by the court, and if necessary to raise money to pay debts, the estate was sold at an
"out-cry." Wills were to be recorded within thirty days by
the Clerk of the Court of Sessions and the latter was to certify
it at the Recorder's office in New York.

The usual practice was for the father in his will to give his
sons each a farm, and his daughters each a heifer, but there
are some notable exceptions.—C. R. S ]

Testes.                           THOMAS SCUDDER
  NATHANIELL FFOSTER              JACOB WALKER.
  JOHN PAGGE.
          This is a true Coppy of the orriginall extracted
by Thomas Powell
          Recorder.
      (*Court Records, p.* 283.)

---

## [DEED.  BENJAMIN JONES TO JOSEPH WOOD
## AND SUBSEQUENT CONVEYANCES.]

[1677, Oct. 20.]

Know all men by these present that I Benjamin Jones of
huntington one long Island in the East Riding of new
yorkshire husbandman have barganed sold and made over
from me my heirs and assignes: unto Joseph wood of. huntington afore sd. his heirs & assignes all my Right title and
intrest in and to seaven elevenths of a farm which I had of
Joseph Whitman  and Samuell kecham, except  four lev-
enths of twelve accars of land which was laid out to Samuell  kecham as also all Rights and previledge that doe or
ever may belong to the afore sd. part of farme all which I
the said Benjamin doe by these presents sell alinate and
make over from me my  heirs and  assignes to  the said
Joseph wood his heirs and assignes to have and to hold
forever.
and also it is agreed that what soever the Indeans must have
for the soyle Right of that part of farme I the said Benjemin doe ingage to satisfie the one half in witnesse where
of I have set to my hand and fixed my seale this 20ᵗʰ of the
10ᵗʰ mo. 1677                         BENJEMIN JONES.
signed and sealed and delivered in the presents of us JOHN
BRUSH, THO. WHITSON.

this presents witnesseth that I Joseph wood above said
doe assigne and make over and have sold from me my
heirs and assignes to Jonathon harnitt his heirs, executors
administrators and assignes all my Right title and intrust
in and to this bill of sale above said to have and to hold
for ever as witnesse my hand this 16 of y$^e$ 11$^{mo}$ 16$\frac{77}{78}$

JOSEPH WOOD.

signed and delivered in the presence of us JOHN FINCH,
THO. WHITSON.

these presents witnesse that I Jonathon harnutt of huntington do assigne and make over and have sold from me my
heirs and assignes to John green his heirs executors and
asings all my Right title and intrust in and to this bill
of sall above said to have and to hold from me and all
men for ever as witnesse my hand this 11 day of febury
16$\frac{77}{8}$.

THOS. MARTIN                               JONATHAN HARNETT
THOMAS IRELAND.

This is a true copie Compared with the Originall by me John Corey,

Recor.

(*Court Records, p.* 248.)

---

[TOWN MEETING.]

[1677, Dec. 27.]

Dec. 27, 1677.

At a town meeting it was agreed by the major part
of the inhabitants of the town that, whereas Tho. Powell
had a grant of six acres of land on Tredwell's Plain, he
shall take up six acres of land between the Town and the
east field in the lieu of that on Tredwel's Plain.

It was agreed by the major part of the town that

Tho. Whison and Tho. Powell shall take in an addition to their land at Cow harbor so far as may not be prejudicial to highways.

It was voted and granted by the major part of the town that Jeremiah Smith shall have about three acres of land on the north side of the mill, leaving a sufficient highway to the farmers between the mill and the forementioned land. The forementioned land is bounded on the north with a run of water; on the west with the cove joining to it which was formerly given him in his covenant concerning the mill; on the south with the forementioned highway; and on the east with the woods in commonage. As Epenetus Platt & Saml Titus saith that it was so granted.

[Copied in the Revision in 1873 from the original in No. 2, p. 30.]

*(Town Meetings, Vol. 1, p, 65 and Court Records, p. 198.)*

———————

### [TOWN MEETING.]

[1678, January 3.]

Jan. 3. 1678.

It was agreed and granted by the major part of the town that Rob^t Arthurs lot shall bear the denomination of one hundred pound lottment, and to take up division of land according to the denomination in what division shall be granted after his grant for his lottment.

[Copied in the Revision in the year 1873, from the original in No. 2, p. 29;]

*(Town Meetings, Vol. 1, p. 65 b. and Court Rec., p. 197.)*

## [DEED. JOHN GREEN TO JONATHAN HARNETT.]

[1678, Feb. 11.]

These may certefie whome it may conserne that I John green of hunting upon long Island in york shire husband man have and doe·by these presents assigne unto Jonathen harnut of hunting afore sd his heires and assiges this deed of sale to all intents & purposses from me my heirs and assignes for ever except my medow, as witnesse my hand this 11 day of febuery in yᵉ year of our Lord 1678 signed in yᵉ          the mark of
presence of THOMAS         JOHN X GREEN
IRLAND. THOMAS MARTIN.

This is a true coppy of yᵉ origenall by me John Corey Recʳ.

(*Deeds, Vol.* 1, *p.* 108.)

---

## [TOWN MEETINGS.]

[1678, April 1.]

April 1. 1678.

At a town meeting it was voted and granted by the major part that Thomas Higbee should have that part of the swamp that lieth between Goodman Chichester's home lot and Jacob Walter's swamp; and also the upland joining to it as shall be bounded by the layers out; if he clear it in one year's time after the day above written and keep it clear according to law or else to forfeit to the town again.

By me John Corey, Recᵈ.

[Copied in the Revision in the year 1873, from the original in No. 2, p. 31.

(*Town Meetings, Vol.* 1, *p.* 67, *and Court Rec., p.* 199, *and Deeds Vol.* 1, *p.* 155.)

## [SHEEP MARKS.]

[1678, May 28.]

1678    Jonathan Scudders ear marke hee markes his
May y⁰ 28 Creatures with is a hollow Crop one y⁰ near ear
& a slit one each side y⁰ off ear which makes a
flowered edge.

Joseph Woods marke hee gives his creatures
is a half peny under the off eare & a nick under
the neare eare.

Thomas Whison his marke he gives his crea-
turs is one halfe peny one y⁰ uper sid each eare.

Edward Ketcham his marke hee gives his
Creatures is a Crop one y⁰ near ear & a halfe
peny under side y⁰ same eare and a slit down y⁰
off eare.*

(*Court Rec., p. 228.*)

---

## [TOWN MEETING.]

[1678, June 3.]

June 3. 1678.

At a town meeting it was agreed by the major part of
the town that Thomas Higbie should have a piece of land
added to his piece of swamp which land lieth on the south
side of the old mill path between Capt. Bayley's lot and

---

[*These are specimens taken from hundreds of similar entries in the records. The book of ear-marks has drawings of
the form of the ear after mutilation. Every farmer had a special ear-mark and recorded it in the town book as the law required, and therefore ear-carving became one of the fine arts.
C. R. S.]

Tho. Lawrence's, and his lot to bear the denomination of a hundred pound alotment and to have meadow (when purchased) equivalent as other hundreds shall have out of the meadow he paying for his proportion as other men : it is to be understood a hundred pound lottment of all divisions that is to be laid out after this grant.

[Copied in the Revision in the year 1873 from the original, No. 2, p. 31.]

*(Town Meetings, Vol. 1, p. 69, and Court Records, p. 199.)*

---

[DEED. JOHN EVERETT TO THOMAS POWELL.]

[1678, Oct. 28.]

octob$^r$ the 28$^{th}$ 1678 Sold by John Everit all his wright and intrest in and to a hundred pound alottment, I say I y$^e$ said John have bargained sold and made over from mee my heirs executors and assignes unto Thomas powell of Huntington his heires execato$^{rs}$ & assignes all my Right title & Intrest to all y$^t$ ever did or ever shall belong to my hundred pound alotment except y$^t$ 4 accars I sold to Samuell Ketcham, To have and to hold for ever for which I have received satisfaction already in hand.

Witt.                                                                     JOHN EAVARAT
   THOMAS WHITSON
   JOHN MITCHEL.
    *(Court Rec , p. 306.)*

---

[DEED.  JOHN  EVERETT  TO  SAMUEL
KETCHAM.]

[No date.]

Sold by John Everit his home Lott being foar accars barganed Sold & made over from y^e said John his heires and assignes to Samuell Ketcham his heirs & assignes all his Right & Intrust in and to y^e 4 accars of land being his hom lott haveing received full satisfaction already in hand. I say I have sold & estranged from mee my heires & assignes to y^e said Samuell his heirs & assignes To have and to Hold for ever.

Recorded by order of John Everit By mee

Thomas Powell, Rec^r

(*Court Rec.*, *p.* 306.)

---

## [REGULATIONS CONCERNING KILLING WOLVES*, &c.]

[1679, Jan. 3.]

Some matters recomended from the Governer and Counsell to the late Courts of sessions of the North and west Ridings with their returns there upon and the Governers approbation thereof.

Concerning payment for wolves, and the great anuall abate^mt thereby out of the County Rate.

The same being taken into consideration, it was thought Reasonable that every towne should pay for the wolves killed within their one precinct, and that each towne is enjoyned to keepe two wolfepitts att least in good repare

---

[*The Duke's Laws provided that any Christian or Indian who should bring the head of a wolf or whelp to a constable should be paid twenty shillings. The rule was at first to produce the ears, but as the Indians passed off dogs' ears for genuine wolf's ears, the law was changed to require the production of the whole head with the ears on, and on payment of the bounty the ears were cut off and destroyed. The Court of Assizes required every town to maintain wolf-pits.—C. R. S.]

at the townes charge unless any private person or persons
will undertake to doe the same which if thay shall doe then
the towne to be excused, but the wolves that shall be taken
by such private person or persons are to be payd for by
the towne as the law directs, the which to be observed,
under such penaltie for neglect as the Court of sessions
shall thinke fitt to Impose.

It being likewise recomended to the
Courts to Ascertaine the prices of
Corne provision &c. to be received
for the Countey votes according to a
former Regulation.

It is proposed as ffolloweth (viz)

Porke at . . . . . . . 3$^{d}$: p.: lib-
Beefe at . . . . . . . . 2 : p : lib:
Winter wheat . . . . . at 4$^{sh}$ p Bushell
Summer wheat . . . . . at 3 S p. Bushell
Indian Corne at . . . . . at 2: 3 p. Bushell
Rye . . . . . . . at 2: 6: p. Bushell
Oyle . . . . . . . at 1$^{£}$ 10$^{sh}$ p Barrell
New Yorke January
3: 1679:

The afore mentioned
payment for wolves and
ascertaneing of y$^{e}$ Rates
approved of by the Gov$^{r}$
Matthias Nicholls. sccr.

A true Coppy p. Joseph L Lepherrt.

(*File No.* 21.)

---

[DEED. JOHN MITCHELL TO ROBERT
KELLUM.]

[1679. Jan. 13.]

hunting
Jeneuary 13$^{th}$ 1679 know all whom it may consarn that

whare as John michell of nesaquak in the East Riding of
new york sheer, hath sold his lot that lyeth in huntington
to Robart Kellam of Setoket of the East Riding of New
york sheer, and the sd. Robart kellem doth not find the
lot in such Condision as was mentioned in bargin, in lack-
ing of apell trees and fencing, therefore the above sd. John
Mitchell doth alow eight pound and four shillings out of
the last payment that the above sd. Robart is to pay to
John michell in their bargin of a hous that John Michell is
to build for the sd. Robart kellem.

As. Witnesse                    by me John Core.
my hand.                                Record[r]
    JOHN MICHELL
      (*Court Rec., p.* 290.)

---

## [TOWN MEETING.]

### [1679, April 1.]

April 1. 1679.

At a town meeting it was ordered as followeth: That
this present smith Samuel Griffen and all others that shall
or may desire land in this town shall be bound to build
and fence their lots given them and diligently follow their
particular trades for the benefit of the town in general and
every particular [person] thereof for the term of seven
years at the least and not to make any sale or alienation
thereof during the said term of seven years; and the smith
shall be bound to place a man of the same trade in his
stead in case he see cause to leave the town, or else to
return it into the town's hands again they paying to him
his full charges; and all such as have land given them
under any denomination of hundred or hundreds shall
have land according to what the town shall lay out, but
not according to what the town have already laid out.

The day above written it was voted and granted that Sam¹ Griffen should have a lot in the town upon the fore-mentioned conditions.

The forementioned Sam¹ Griffen doth make choice of a piece of land at the harbor ; but he hath changed with Steven Jarvis Junʳ for that land lying on the south side of the lot that was formerly in the tenour or occupation of Noah Rogers and now Thos. Weeks, it being about 3 acres.

[Copied in the Revision in the year 1873, from the original in the Old Book, No. 2, p. 45 or 59.]

(*Town Mee ings, Vol. 1, p. 71.*)

---

## [TOWN MEETING.]

[1679, April 1.]

Timithy Conklings Land Recʳ

Aprill yᵉ ist, 1679  Voated and granted by yᵉ major part of yᵉ Town unto Timothy Conkling : three or foure Acres of land and swamp towards his divition it lying in yᵉ west neck on yᵉ north side ot yᵉ cove swamp And to be layd out as yᵉ layers out shall see cause

(*Deeds, Vol. 1, p. 143.*)

---

## [TOWN MEETING.]

[1679, April 1.]

April 1. 1679.

At a town meeting it was voted and granted that Joseph Wood, Cooper, shall have a lot on the North side of Joseph Baly's home lot.  The above said lot is bounded on the east and north with the king's highway, and the rear toward the old mill pond; and the above said lot to bear the denomination of hundred pound alotments. Granted by the major part of the town.

By me John Corey Recorder.

[Copied in the Revision in the year 1873 from the original in]

(*Town Meetings, Vol.* 1, *p.* 73.)

---

## [TOWN MEETING.]

[1679, Apr. 1.]

At Town meeting.

Aprill the first 1679 it was voated and agreed by the major part of the towne that the Constable and overseers should make choyse of 3 : 4 or 5 of the neighbors such as they shall think fit and the Constable and overseers together with those that they shall chuse shall lay such rat of tax up on the hundreds as they shall think best for the good of the town.

At a town meeting Aprill the first 1679 it was voated and granted that Jonathan miller should have one hundred pound comonage

The day above written it was voated and granted by voate Jonathan harnit that he shall have fifty pound commonage added to his lot.

Same day above written it voated and granted that Josiah Jones should have a lot lying on the south side of hempsted path and one hundred pound commonage.

these two below Entered in New Book A page 48.

April 1<sup>st</sup> 1679 Isaac Platt, chosen Constable.
Richard willams & Jonathan Rogers overseers
John Core chosen Clerke or Recorder.

now whereas it may seem strange that som of the town
acts that were done in the year 1677 and 1678 and : are
recorded by John Core : these may sattisfie those who it
may Consern that John Core was Chossen overseer in the
year 1677 and by the Constables order at town meeting
when the town Recorder was absent did writ meny of the
town acts and they remained in his hand and when the
time of his being overseer was expired he was chosen Recorder for this town of huntington.

[Copied from Court Records 1681-4 p. 31. or p.      , in
the Revision of the Records in 1873.]

(*Town Meetings, Vol.* 1, *pp.* 75-6-7.)

---

## [REPORT OF ARBITRATORS BETWEEN
## JONATHAN ROGERS AND JONA-
## THAN SCUDDER.

[1679, May 30.]

know all men who it may consern that whereas A difference did arise between Jonathan Rogers & Jonathan
Scudder both of huntington in the east Riding of new york
I say a difference did arise between them about a sertain
parsell of land lying in the old west field and the above
said Jonathon Rogers & Jonathan Scudder made choyce
of Thomas Townsend of oysterbay & John Core of huntington to put an end to their difference and impowered
their 2 arbetraters in case they could not agree to make
choys of a third man who should have equall powr with
them in puting A finall end to their difference and the said

Jonathan Rogers, and Jonathen Scudder bound them selves In A bond of twenty pound in passable pay to stand to the Judgment of their 2 or 3 arbetraters ; and if either parties did desent from the verdit of their arbetraiters he should pay the 20 pounds to the other thus the above said Jonathen Rogers & Jonathan Scudder joyntly consented to each other.

Thomas Townsend & John Core cannot agree about the difference depending between Jonathin Rogers & Jonathan scudder have joyntly consented and made choyce of Joseph Whitman of huntington to be the umpier wee beneath subscribed haveing well wayed and examened the difference depending between Jonathen Rogers and Jonathan Scudder doe determin that Jonathan Rogers shall peacably possesse and injoye the lott of land that he bought or exchanged with william osborne lying within the old west field delivering unto the coustedy of and possession of Jonathan Scudder three akers of land of that which is next to thomas benedicks in the same feild and paying to Jonathan scudder or his order in good marchantable paye in the consideration of the exchange of the afore said lots of land and charges expended in the prosecution of the difference between them ; two pound eight shillings, and each to satisfie their arbetrators for their trouble and lose of time. witnesse our hands in huntington this 30$^{th}$ day of may 1679.

by me John Core Re$^{cr}$

THOMAS TOWNSEND ⎫ memorandem that the formentioned
JOSEPH WHITMAN  ⎬ or fore sd. Jonathan Rogers and Jon-
JOHN CORE       ⎭ athan Scudder did consent to Rest
satisffie with the determenation of their above named Arbytrators by me

John Core. Rec$^r$

(*Court Records, pp.* 285-6.)

## [GOV. ANDROSS'S ORDER TO SEIZE A VESSEL.]

[1679, June 11.]

By the Govern[r]
Whereas I am credibly informed that one Richard Betts hath with a sloope severall times traded in your parts and carried away Goods & Passengers contrary to acts of Parliament as well as Law & custome of these parts, & is now in yo[u] Harbo[ur]
These are in his Ma[ties] name to require you to secure the said sloop & take order that shee bee safely brought to this place where said Richard Betts to answer the above or what shall bee alleaged against him in that behalfe, and that also you give notice to Joseph Whitman late Constable of yo[r] Towne and Henry Disbroue that they likewise appeare here at the same time, upon the same account.

Given under my hand & seale, in New Yorke the 11[th] day of June 1679.

ANDROSS.

To the Constable of
Huntington or his deputy

Examined by mee
Mathias Nicolls, Sec[r]
(*Court Records, p.* 343.)

---

## [COURT RECORD. ELIPHELET JONES vs. JOHN FINCH.]

[1679, July 28.]

At A town Coort held In hunting by his magests authority July 28. 1679. where Isaack platt, constable, Abiell Titus: John Sammons Richart williams: Jonathan Rog-

ers, over seers. the same day above written Mr Eliphelet
Jons plaintive against John finch senior deffendent In an
action of debt upon a bill of 9 pounds ten shillings that
John finch past to Mr Jons In the year 1667. the court finds
for the plentive that the defent. shall pay to the plentive
the Remaining part of the bill which is £2 10[s] in good
marchintable pay at price curant.
and 2 pound dammage with cost of court.

      by me
        John Core Rec[r]
(*Court Record, p. 284.*)

---

## [ISAAC NICHOLS TO JOHN FINCH. SALE OF BEACH AND "DRIFT WHALES."]

[No date.]

    No date orig :
Know all men by these prsent That I Isack Nickalls of
Stratford have and doe by these prsents make over unto
John finch of huntington all y[e] same Rite of beach and all
drift whales y[t] comes ashore upon y[t] Marsapage beach y[t]
I had of Mr. John Rigbell of mamaranock as witnesse my
hand ISACK NICCOLS
Witnesse STEVEN JARVIS, ELIASAPH PRESTON.

           by me John Corey, Rec[r]
  (*Court Record, p. 395.*)

---

## [EXCHANGE OF LAND BETWEEN STEPHEN JARVIS AND SAMUEL GRIFFIN.]

[1679, Aug. 20.]

The Records of y[e] Land of Stephen Jarvis, J[unr] taken out
of y[e] old Book Jun[th] 10: 1682

Know all men by these presents: or who it may concerne y$^t$ where as Steeven Jarvis Junr. had a lot formerly granted to him by y$^e$ town and to bare y$^e$ denomination of a hundred pound alotment and y$^e$ sd hous Lott lying on y$^e$ south side of y$^e$ lott y$^t$ was formerly in possession of Noah Rogers. This writing testefieth to all who it may concerne y$^t$ Samuel Griffin: And Steeven Jarvuis $^{senr}$ both of huntington have agreed and consented to ech other to exchang their house lots: Samuell Griffin to have y$^e$ lot y$^t$ was Steeven Jarvisses y$^t$ lyeth on y$^e$ south side of y$^e$ lot y$^t$ was formerly in y$^e$ possession of Noah Rogers: and Steeven Jarvis to have y$^e$ lot y$^t$ was Samuell Griffens y$^t$ lyeth at y$^e$ harbour by y$^e$ grat hollow or graving place: and is layed out by Joseph Bayly and Thomas powell: men chosen by y$^e$ town for such purpos who have bounded it as y$^e$ place would aforde from y$^e$ hie way to low watter marke, August 20: 1679.

by me John Corey, Record.

(Deeds, Vol. 1, p. 109.)

---

[DEED. JOHN GREEN TO ISAAC PLATT.]

[1679, Sept. 2.]
Know all men by these presents that John green of Crab medow within the bounds of huntington upon long Iland in the east Riding of yorksheere husbandman. have barganed sold and made over from me my heirs executers, adminesters and assings, all my right titell and intrust: unto A sertine parsell of medow land lying and being on the south side of this eiland: on A necke of medow commonly caled by the name of the greate neck: within the bounds of huntington: bounded as heere specified. one the east side with the medow of Tho$^s$: powell: Common meddow and on part with the medow of Isack platt, the west Mr Wood in part and Jonathan Rogers from the Iland down

to the sound. it being the half proportion of A three hundred pound alotment in its first Devision : William Rogers
deseased : thence estranged unto Andrew messinger and
to Samuell messenger from thence to John green : all
which hath three hundred pound preportion of medow
land I have made over unto Isaac platt of huntington
his heirs executors administrators and asigns : for A reasonable consideration in hand paide before the sealling and
delivery heere of for which consideration I have and by
these presents doe alenate and estrange all my Right title
and Intrest of medow land and every part and parcell :
from me my heirs executors administrators and assigns :
unto Isack platt his heirs executors administrators and
assigns ; too have and too hold for ever, and further I the
said John green doth Ingadge my self my heirs executors administrators and assigns to save harmlesse and undamnefied
isack plat his heirs executors administrators and assigns
from any person or person that shall or may by any way
or means whatsoever lay any clame or title to the said
medow land or any part or parcell thereof as witness my
hand and seal this 2' day of september, in the one and thirty yeare of his magesties Rainge and in the year of our
lord one thousand six hundred seventy and nine
signed & sealed and                         the ✕ mark of
delivered In presence of us              JOHN GREEN
JONAS WOOD
JONATHAN HARNET.
    (*Deeds, Vol. 1, p.* 64.)

----

[DEED.  JOHN ROGERS TO JOHN MATHEWS JR.]

[1679, Sept. 24.]

This Writing Certifieth that I John Rogers of hemsteed
uppon Long eiland in the north Riding of Yorkesheare

Brickmaker have ffreely and vollentaryly given and made over ffrom mee my heires executors administrators and assignes all my Rite title and intrest unto a lotment formerly in the tenor or occupation of John Broton given to him by the towne and By order Recorded and Bought of him By mee which Lot with all its privilidges I Doe by these presents make over unto John Mathews Jur. son of John Mathews of huntington in the east Riding of yorkesheare vicktular and to his assignes to have and to hould for ever in witness whereof I have heare unto set my hand this 24<sup>th</sup> of september in the 31<sup>st</sup> yeare of his ma<sup>tis</sup> Raine and in the yeare of our Lord 1679.

Witnes

JOSEPH BAYLY.

(*File No. 72.*)

the marke of

JOHN × ROGERS.

---

[DEED. DANIEL PHILLIPS TO JOSEPH WOOD.]

[1679, October 6.]

Know all men by these presents that I daniell phillips of newtown upon long Iland in the west Riding of york sheer have for and in consideration of the sum of thirteen pound sterling paid unto me the said daniell phillips before the in sealing of these p<sup>r</sup>sents well and truly contented satisfied and paid by Joseph wood coper of Huntington in the este Riding of york sheer on long Iland : where of and where with I the said daniell phillips doe acknowledg my self fully satisfied contented and payed and the said Joseph wood his heyers executors administrators and evry of them doe fully clearly and absolutly acquit and discharge for ever by these presents : know y<sup>e</sup> therefore that I daniell phillips have fully clearly and absolutely barganed and sold and do by these p<sup>r</sup>sents fully clearly and absolutely bargain sell unto the above named Joseph wood his heirs

executors and assinges A frame of a hous newly sett up in
the said town of huntington on a pece of land which joyns
to the north side of Captaine balys lott it is bounded on the
north est side with the street; which goes down to the
harbor to have and injoy the sayd frame to the only use
and proper behalfe of the sayd Joseph wood : his heirs and
assinges for ever : and further the sd. daniell doth covenant
and grant for his heires executors and adminstrators to &
with the sd. Joseph his haires & assings by these presents
that he the said daniell is the true and proper owner of and
singler the p'misses afore bargained and sold and that he
hath full power and lawfull authority in his own right to
bargaine sell, give, grant, convey and assure the same, and
every part and parsell thereof to the said Joseph and I the
sd daniell phillips doe warrant my self good in law free
from any former bargaines and sales or any just claime o
any p'son. or p'sons what-so-ever to the confarmation of the
prmises I the sd. daniell phillips have here unto sett my
hand and seale this sixth day of october in the yeare of our
lord god 1679.

Witness                         DANIELL PHILLIPS.
  JANES SMITH          This is a true copie compared
  BENJAMEN CORNISH        with the originall per mee
                                John Corey
                                    Rec^r.

        (*Court Rec.*, p. 326.)

---

[DEED.  JOHN JONES TO EDWARD BUNCE.]

  [1679, Oct. 27.]

know all men by these present that I John Jons of huntington in the east Riding of New York sheer husband
man : I say I have sold all my Right of a two hundred
pound alotment at Crabmedow farme To Edward bunce of

the same town for a Reasonable Consideration In hand
alredy Received I the above said John Jons have bargoned
sold and estranged from me my heirs executors adminestrators and asings unto Edward bunce of huntington above
sd. husband man and to his heirs executors administers or
asings to have and to hold for ever all my Right unto the
above mentioned tow hundred pound allotment as witnesse my hand this 27 of October 1679

JOHN JONS.

(*Court Rec., p.* 287.)

---

[DEED.  ABIAL TITUS TO EDWARD BUNCE.]

[1679, Oct. 27.]

know all men by these presents that I abiell titus of huntington in the east Ridding in york sheer husband man
have bargoned sold and made over all my Right and title
unto a one hundred pound alotment at Crabmedow farmes
unto Edward bunce of the above sd. town husband man
for A reasonable consideration agreed on: I say I the
above sd. Abiell titus have bargoned sold and estranged
from me my heirs executors administrators and asings
unto Edward bunce his heirs executors administrators and
asings all my right and title that doth or heer after may
belong unto the above sd. one hundred pound alotment at
Crabmedow farme in witnesse where of I the above sd.
abiell titus have here unto sett my hand this 27 of october
1679.

ABIELL TITUS.

John Core, Recorder.
(*Court Rec., p.* 287.)

## [LEASE.  JOHN SCUDDER TO GEORGE BALDING.]

[1679, Nov. 15.]

Know all men whome it may consern that I John Scudder liveing in huntington in y^e East Riding of new york sheire have set and let for y^e terme of four years from y^e date hereof unto gorge Bolding of y^o same town both upland & medow with y^e housing & all priveledges there unto belonging as also y^e sd. John doe let y^e sd. gorge Bolding 2 oxen: 2 heiffers y^t come, 2 yere old apeece & four boxes & 4 hoops for wheeles, one sheare one colter one chain: 2 pair. of yoke irons and clevis & a spade & one wedge and for y^e use of and hire of y^e above mentioned Estate; I y^e above sd. gorge Bolding doe Ingadge to pay or caus to be payed to John Scudder or his heires or assignes y^e full and just sum of five pounds In good and currant merchantable pay yearly during y^e terme of four years above specefied which severall payment is in y^e whole will amount to twenty pounds.

also I y^e above sd. gorge Bolding doe Ingadge; to leave a suficent five Raile fence about y^e sd. land now taken in at y^e end of y^e fower years and to clear & brake fower acres of land with in y^e fore sd. fence before y^e fower yeares be expired and doe Ingadge to leave three loads of good hay, And to deliver y^e fore sd. John Scudder or his assignes y^e fore sd. Cattell and tackling & tooles in as good condition as I now Receive them.  The oxen then to come Eleven years old. and y^e heifers 6 yeares of adge.  Where unto we enterchangably set to our hands this 15^th of November 1679.

JOHN SCUDDER.
the mark of
GEORGE X BALDING

Witnesse
  THOMAS SKIDMOR
  SAMUELL GRIFFEN
    This is a true copie compared with y^e originall by me
                                        John Corey. Rec'r
    *(Court Rec., p. 374.)*

---

[THOMAS SCIDMORE IN DFEAULT.]

[1679, Dec. 8.]

                              december the 8. 1679.
Thomas Skidmore
we are to acquaint you of tow orders we have as you cannot
be ignorant of from the Governor the first is, that charges
you accasioned us to expend at yorke at James Mathews
w^ch is £1 as allso for our tow mans time and other expenc-
es £2. 18s. that at yorke you know was to have been paid
long before this time in p'visions w^ch we expect you to
bring us a discharge for in fourthteene dayes and that y^t
is to be paid heare by the same time, if you faile you may
be asured we will not faile to fetch all the mony due by
stress w^ch will increace the sum.

the 2^nd is that order from the Governer in which order
you are injoyned to doe that with the Indians w^ch you yet
have not done nether for the matter of it nor for the manner of doing therefor we signifie to you yt if you doe not
com within foretene dayes and give us a satisfing account
of your fullfilling in all poynts that order you may be as-
sured we shall render an accountt to the governer who it
is that is still in that matter.

                              this A true Copie by
                              me John Core. Rec^r
*(Court Record, p. 345.)*

## [THE TURK'S RATE.]

[1679, Dec. 8.]

### Turk Rat

| | |
|---|---|
| Samuell Wood | 12 adde 18 maks 30 |
| Richard Willans | 8 adde 12 maks 20 |
| Walter noks | 8 adds 12 maks 20 |
| John golden | 8 adds 12 maks 20 |
| Steven Jarvis | 8 adds 12 maks 20 |
| Captt Joseph bayly | 20 adds 30 maks 50 |
| John brush | 14 maks 10 |

and Thos. brush falling short 4 pound of pork in the former payment it is now 10
The sum of $y^e$ porke is a. $170^{lb}$

Whare as formerly a Rate was made for the payment as of a debt deu at york for the discharge of which debt the towns men added by Rate made upon the hundreds : that every hundred was to pay 4 pound of pork, the which pay was made by most of the town yet not withstanding some have been neglegent have not payd to this : therefore this day it was ordered by the Constables and overseers that those men that have not payd and find them the cause of A. greate deale of damage that is com upon us by their default, they order these men shall pay all the Remainder of what is still deue : to gether with all insedantall charges that may arise either by gathering or transporting.—
this above written sums is to be payd in pork or to be converted into whale bone or butter.

desem. 8$^{th}$ 1679

ISAAC PLATT
RICHARD WILLIAMS
ABIEL TITUS
JOHN SAMMIS
JONATHAN ROGERS

Thomas Brush & John Brush hath payd 2ˢ to Sam Titus, since this order and think so cleered : as S. T. told me

John Corey

for which 2ˢ yᵉ sd. Titus
owneth himself debter
(*File No.* 16.)

---

## [TOWN MEETING.]

[1679, Dec. 9,]

desember th. 9. 1679.
it was agred and voated by the constable and overseers that those men that did not pay their full som to the turks Rate when they ware Required shall now pay the Remainder with all the nesessary charges that shall arise there upon through their neglect.

(*Court Rec.*, *p.* 241.)

---

## [STEPHEN JARVIS'S LANDS.]

[1679, Dec. 22.]

The Records of the lands & medows of Steven Jarvis his hous lott situatt and being In huntington : the hous lot of Thos : fleet on the north side and the hous lot of Robᵗ Cranfeild on the south side and frunting to the street west ward and the Reare to the woods in Comon East ward : as also the medow belonging to the said lot : lying & being on the south side of the Iland on A neck comonly callcd Josias neck namely 8 acars more or less the medow of Jonathon harnit on the east side : the medow of James Chitchester on the west sid : the Reare to the sea & the front to the woods : as also a part of it lying in a parsell of Com-

mon : medow on the same neck his planting land four acars
and a halfe on the east neck the land of James Chitchester
on the westeren side the land of Robert Cranfeild on the
easteren sid of it : and bounded with the beach on the
northern end and the south with the woods in comon as
also seaven acars and a halte of land on the same neck
towards the poynt the land of thomas powell on the west
sid : the land of Robert Cranfeild on the east sid the Rear
to the cleft Northward the front towards the hie way : and
another parcell of land lying on the east neck containing
three acars the land of John finch lying by it given in by
steven Jarvis Junʳ by order from his father in my heareing.

                              By me John Core Recorder.
Desember 22 : 1679.
    (*Deeds*, *Vol.* 1, *p.* 42.)

------

## [DEED.  JACOB WALKER TO JOHN BETTS.]

[1680, Jan. 26.]

know all men by these presents that I Jacob walker of
strattford in the colony of Connecticutt in new ingland for
& in consideration of the summe of one hundred pounds in
curant pay of this collony to me alredy in hand payed by
John betts of weathers feild in the Collony afore named
and for divers other good causes and considerations : me
moving and exciting here unto have sold allinated asigned,
set over given granted and confirmed and doe by these
presents fully frely wholely cleerly and absolutely sell allinate and assign set over give grant and confirm unto him
the sd. John Betts all and every part and parsell of that
housing and lands which was assigned and made over unto
me the sd. Jacob walker by mark meggs and Avis his wife
or either of them sittuate and beeing in the township of
huntington on long Island as it stands Recorded to the said

mark meggs or unto me the sd. Jacob walker; or did or doth appertaine unto him the sd. marke meggs or unto me the sd. Jacob walker together with all the profits commodityes benifits previledges apurtenances and adwantages what soever thence arising or to the same or eny part or parcell thereoff; in any wise belonging or appertaining for him the sd. John betts heirs executors administrators or assignes to have and to hold use occupie possesse and In joy from the day of the date of these presents for ever: with out any evaition, ejecion trouble incumbrance or mollestation what soever from or by mee the sd. Jacob walker or from or by any person or persons what soever claiming or that shall or may claime the same or any part there of from for or by or under me: by vertue or collour of any Right or title any way derived from me warranting and assuring by these presents that I the sd. Jacob walker at and before the ensealling and delivery of these presents have good Right and lawfull title in and unto the same. to sell and confirme the same as in and by these presents I have done and that it is wholely free and cleir accquitted and discharged of and from all other and former sales, grants, gifts, morgages and alinations what so ever. hereby granting full power and authority unto him the sd. John betts his heirs executors administrators or assignes to record or caus to be Recorded the fore mentioned estate unto him and them for ever in the publique Records of the fore named town of huntington or eny other publique Records in the Teritores of new york whare it may or ought to be Recorded and I doe hereby oblydge my self to make and give unto the sd. John betts any further writting or assurance for confirming the same to him and his heires executors administrators or assignes for ever which he the sd. John Betts or his counsell learned in the law shall Resonably desire provided I be not put to travell above ten miles from my dwelling place to accompish the same. for the full conformation and perfict establishment of

all which I have to these presents : put my hand and seale
this 26 of Jeneuary 1680.          JACOB WALKER.
signed sealed and
delivered in the presents
of us.   JOSEPH WALKER
          EDWARD HIGBEE

                Jacob walker personally apered before
                me the 24 of november 1681. and ack-
                nowledged the above written instru-
                ment to be his act and deed.
                        John Corey Clark.

Mr Jacob walker personally appered before mee the 26
of Jeneuary 1680 and acknowledged the above written
instrument to be his act and deed.
                    WILLIAM CURTIS
                       Comisioner
this is a true  Copie extracted out of the originall by mee
                    John Corey  Clark.
    (*Court Rec., p.* 301 )

---

## [RECEIPT FOR MILL-RATE.]

[1680, March 20.]

Recaived of the Constable of  huntington five pounds In
full satisfaction for the mill Rate due to me from the town
for the yeare 1676   I say Received p$^r$ mee.
March 20$^{th}$ 16$\frac{7\ 9}{8\ 0}$.          JACOB WALKER.
    (*Court Rec., p.* 288.)

---

## [TOWN MEETING.]

[1680, April 2.]

  April 2. 1680.
At a town meeting legally  warned by the Constable the

day above written, it was voted and granted by the major part of the town that Rob$^t$ Kellum shall have 4 acres of land, lying on the south side of Isaac Platt's lot which lyeth on the south side of Sam$^l$ Wood's lot ; and the north side of Robert Kellums bounds shall begin eight rods from Isaac Platt's lot, whereof two rods is reserved for Isaac Platt as belonging to his lot, the other six rods is to be a highway between the above said Isaac and Robert and the above mentioned four acres of land is toward his proportion of land. And also a highway to be ten rods wide between Jonathan Millers his lot and Bird's lot and the above said Robt. Kellum's four acre lot above named.

2$^{ly}$ The same day voted and granted by the major part of the town that John Mathews shall have his division of land on the north side of Setauket Path near John Finche's wolf-pit on the east side of a pond of water.

3$^{ly}$ The same day it was voted and granted by the major part of the town that David Scudder shall have about eleven acres of land lying on that north side of Horse Neck path and frunting against the new field.

4$^{ly.}$ It was voted and granted by the major part of the town the same day that Jonathan Scudder shall have the boggy meadow that lyeth northward from the west field by the harbor, and four acres of land joining to the said boggy meadow.

5$^{ly.}$ The same day it was voted and granted that Epenetus Platt shall take in some land at the south end of his lot at Cowharbor, so much as shall be found convenient and not prejudicial to the highway.

6$^{ly}$ The same day it was voted and granted by the major part of the town that John Samons take in about 2 acres of land and a watering place for his cattle, which land and water lyeth at the north end of his field which is on the hill above his house as the layers out shall see cause.

By me John Carey, Red$^r$

April 2 1680.

The same day it was voted and granted by the major part of the town that Mr Eliphalet Jones shall have a piece of land at the head of the meeting house brook; about an acre more or less, provided it be not prejudicial to the highway nor watering places, only to take in a little water for his cattle is granted.

[Copied in the Revision in the year 1873 ; see original recorded in Old Book, No. 2. p. 41 or 55 back.]
(*Town Meetings, pp. 79 and 81, and Court Rec., p.* 244.)

---

### [TITUS FAMILY RECORD.]

[1680, April 27.]

The Record of y^e Children of Samuel titus of hunting.

Hanah titus daughter of Samuell titus was borne y^e 14^th of Aprill in y^e yeer 1669.

Rebecka titus daughter of Samuell titus was borne y^e 28^th of ocktobar 1675.

Patience titus daughter of Samuell titus was borne y^e 27^th of Aprill in y^e yeer 1677.

Exsperience titus daughter of Samuell titus was borne y^e 27^th of Aprill in y^e yeer 1680.
(*Surveys, p.* 162.)

---

### [DEED.   MOSES SCUDDER TO JONATHAN ROGERS.]

[1680, May 24.]

This Indenture made the twenty fourth of may in the

yere of our lord 1680 between Moses Scudder of the town
of huntinton in the East Riding of york sheeir on long
Iland on the one party and Jonathon Rogers on the other
part witneseth that the said Moses Scudder, for and In
consideration of full satisfacion Recaived in hand : hath
granted, aliend barganed sold, Confirmed and by these
presents doth fully, clerly and absolutly grant alien bar
gain, sell and confirm unto the said Jonathon Rogers, three
Acers of land lying in the west neck : and joyning to the
land of Jonathon Rogers on the East and to the woods in
Common on the nort and south : and to the land of Abiell
titus on the west, and now in the tenur or occupation of
moses Scudder above said, and the above said moses scudder dou grant alien bargain & sell from him selfe his heirs
executors administrators or asines unto Jonathan Rogers
his hairs, executors, adminastiators or asines, the above sd.
three Akers of land to have and to hold in quiat possesion,
for ever. and the above said Moses Scudder dou grant by
these presents that at the time of the sale of the above sd.
3 akers of land I am the sole and law full owner there of
and am lawfully seased of and in the same, And doe free
and Cler and Clerely aquit and discharge of and from all
and all maner of former grants, giftes bargains sale Leaces,
morgages or titles : In witnesse where of I the above said
moses Scudder have set my hand,

In presents of            MOSES SCUDDER.

    JOHN CORE.
    JOHN JONES,
       (*Court Rec., p.* 184.)

---

## [DELINQUENT TAXES.]

[1680, June 3d.]

An Note of what Lotts that have lyen wast and are Behind in A Reares ffor Rates as followeth.

Imp^r the Lott formerly in the tennor of trestoram
Hogges.

|      |                                                                 |    |    |    |
|------|-----------------------------------------------------------------|----|----|----|
|      | H for charge in the Manedgment of the towne Rits                 | oo | 16 | o6 |
| 1665 | H towards Bilding y^e Meeting house                              | oo | 03 | oo |
|      | H towards nails for y^e Meeting house                            | oo | oo | o8 |
|      | H for town charge.*                                             | oo | o1 | oo |
| 1666 | H for towne Charges for patten and Recording of the towne Deeds | oo | 04 | oo |

I   05   2

this writting witneseth
that John finch : sen^r hath paid the full som of money
which he did owe to the town for the lott that he bought
of the town : which lot was formerly in the teniur or oco-
pation of trustram hoges and sould to the above sd. finch
at a vandue : by the town : he hath payd the mony by the
Constables orders to Isaac platt which som was foure
pound & one shiling, and Isaac platt Recaives it as mony
dew to him from the town for Rattes or on the Account of
town Rats.

June 3-1680                          by mee John Core, Rec^r
    (*Court Rec., p. 197.*)

[*There are several items in the town records which point to
1665 as the year in which a meeting-house was built, and probably it was the first one erected, but no full account of its
erection is found.  It seems that it was located on what, at that
and a later period, was called " Meeting House Brook ", now
Prime Avenue, in the village of Huntington.  The house
built for " entertaining the ministry " in Mr Leverich's time,
and the " studdy " built for Rev. Mr. Jones were undoubtedly
in the same locality, and Mr. Jones was also given a house lot
about the head of the brook referred to, containing one acre.
The road leading from the south down to Meeting House Brook
was in early time called in the records " Sabbath Day Path."
This meeting house, built about 1665, was erected in obedience
to the " Duke's Laws", first put in force in 1664, which made it
compulsory on all the towns to erect houses for public worship.
This meeting house remained in use until about 1711, when,
after a long and bitter controversy, the old church was demol-
ished and a new one built on the site of the present meeting
house of the First Presbyterian Church.—C. R. S.]

## [DEED. THOMAS BRUSH TO GEORGE BALDWIN.]

[1680, June 26.]

This Indenture made the twenty sixt of June and in the two and thirtieth year of the Range of our Sover,d. lord Charles the second by the grace of god King of Ingland, Scotland france and Ierland defender of the faith: and in the year of our lord Christ 1680 between thomas brush of the town of Huntington in the East Riding of new yorksheere on long Island husbandman, on the one part; and George beldin of the same town and Riding above sd. on the other part: Witnesseth that the said thomas Brush for and in consideration of the sum of fifty pounds to him at and before the Ensealing and delivering of these presents, well and truly in hand payed by the sd. george beldin : whereof and were with he the sd. Thomas Brush doth acknowledge himself fully satisfied contented and payed : hath granted eliened Barganed sold and Confirmed and by these presents: doth fully Cleerly and absolutly grant elien bargan sell and Confirme unto the above said george Beldin all that messuage of tenement or plantation situate or being in huntington on Crabmedow neck, now in the tenure or occupation of the sd. thomas Brush, or his assignes : of six acers of land be it more or lesse bounded as followeth to the land of Edward Bunc on the north and to the land ot Jonethen Scudder on the west. and to the woods in Common on the south and to the Kings hie way on the East as also A certain parsell of medow Containing six acars be it more or lesse lying in two peices one lying next to the beach and joyning to the medow of Thomas Martin on the East the other lying above the Bridge, to gather with half the hous and all the fences: with all woods underwoods commons Commons of pasturs even the whole Right and previledg that doth or ever hereafter

shall be long to the Right of a five hundred pound Alotment Comonly called Crabmedow farm To have And to
hold all the above granted premises to the same belonging
and Apertaining unto the said george beldin his heirs executors administrators and asignes for ever I the above said
Thomas Brush have barganed sold and astranged from
my self and from my heirs executors or assignes : all the
fore mentioned premises, unto gorg beldin his heirs executors administrators and asinges and may by vertue of
these above written premises from time to time and at all
times for ever here after lawfull ly peascebly and quiatly
Injoy for ever in witnesse where of I have set my hand
    and seal                              THOMAS BRUSH
in presence of
JOHN CORE,

> The above mentioned five hundred pound
> alotment is to be understood that as
> eleven hundreds made one whole farme
> so five hundreds is neer halfe A farme
> and as A whole farme goeth under the
> denomination of A three hundred pounds
> lot so this lacketh half a hundred to make
> it bare the denomination of a hundred
> and half pound lot.   This is a true Coppie
> extracted out of the originall by me.
>                              John Core, Rec[r]

        desember th. 9. 1680.
And further I the above sd. gorg Boldin: doe Ingadge
and bind myself my heirs executors administers or assingns
from barganing selling or any way allinating any part or
parsell of the land bought of Tho[s] Brush but doe bind it
over every part and parsell thereof mentioned in my bill
of sale, from me my heirs executors administrators or as-
singens unto Tho[s] Brush above sd. his heirs executors administrators or assings for the security of the payment

of the fore mentioned fitty pounds which if it be not payed according to the true intent this to stand in full force. this is A true copie compared with the originall by mee.

John Core
Recorder.

Aprill y<sup>e</sup> second 1683. George Beldin afore mentioned came before me and declared to me that he had Resighned up y<sup>e</sup> originall of this above said record and that he claimed no more Right to it neither nor for any of his after him, p me John Corey, Clerk.

(*Court Record, pp.* 246-7.)

Six acres of Land layd out to Gorge Bolding as part of his farme y<sup>t</sup> he bought of Thomas Brush and lyeth in y<sup>e</sup> hollow at y<sup>e</sup> head of y<sup>e</sup> Boggey medow : And joyneth to y<sup>e</sup> sd boggey medow which belongeth to y<sup>e</sup> sd. Gorge Bolding & Jonathan Scudder.

John Corey Clerk.

further more all y<sup>e</sup> above said as well as all y<sup>e</sup> afore said is made a null y<sup>e</sup> day above mentioned by y<sup>e</sup> afore said Gorge Bolding from him his heirs executors or asinges.

p. me John Corey Clerk.

(*Court Rec. p.* 247.)

---

## [DEED. BENJAMIN JONES TO JOHN SAMMIS.]

[1680, June 28.]

Know all men who it may it may consarne that I Benjemine Jones of Huntington in the east Ridding of new yorksheer on long eiland husband man : have for a valuable Consideration all Redy Received in hand being there with fully sattisfied contented and payed have bargoned sold and made over all my Right titell and Intrust to all that

part of a farme that formerly I had of John Samons ———
I say: I the fore sd. Benjemen Jones have bargoned sold
an estranged all the fore mentioned farme both upland
& medow being at Crabmedow neck: from me my heires
executors administrators and assignes unto John Samons
of the above sd town & Riding his heires executors administrators & assignes quiatly and peacably to Injoy for ever.
As witnesse my hand this 28 of June 1680.

BENJAMEN JONES

Witness
    JOHN CORE,
        Recorder.
        (*Court Rec., p. 325.*)

---

## [DEED.  CATHERINE JONES TO JONATHAN SCUDDER.]

[1680, Aug. 22.]

Know all men by these presents that I Katherine Jones
of huntington on long Island in new yorkshire in new England formerly wife to henry Scudder deceased doe by these
ppresents assigne and make over unto my sons Jonathan
Scudder all my Right title and intrest in and to that accom-
mandaction which was formerly my husbands henry Scudder it being for and in consideration of an accomnandation
formerly given to the said Jonathan by his Grandfather
which my son david Scudder hath in his possession therefore I doe by these presents asigne and make over from
mee my heirs & assignes to the said Jonathan his heirs and
assignes all and singuler my right title and intrest in the
above sd. accomandtions that is to say all housing except
my life time in the old hous which my husband Hen. Scud-

der built as alsoe a home lot out lands medow orchyard and all Rights and previledges that at present doth or ever shall belong to the said accomandations to have and to hold for ever I say I doe as fully and amply assigne and make it over to the said Jonathan as can be don by any deed or convaience so that he and his heirs shall peacebly enjoy it without any molestation from me my heirs or assinges for ever: as witnesse my hand & seale this 22<sup>th</sup> 8<sup>mo</sup> 1680

the mark of

Test                                             KATHERINE X JONES
   THOMAS POWELL
   JOHN CORE.

this is A true Copie of the origenell by mee John Core

Reco<sup>rd</sup>

Katherine Jones made whole and sole executrixe by her former husband Henry Scudder upon record on the old Book.

      Another Record over leaf.

John Corey Rec<sup>r</sup>

   *(Deeds, Vol. 1, p. 33.)*

---

## [INGERSOLL FAMILY RECORD.]

[1680, Sept. 13.]

John Ingersole The son of John Ingersole of Huntington on Longisland was borne y<sup>e</sup> eleventh of may 1674.

   Jane Ingersole y<sup>e</sup> daughter of Jn<sup>e</sup> Ingersole was borne y<sup>e</sup> 9<sup>th</sup> of June 1676.

   Simon Ingersole y<sup>e</sup> son of John Ingersole was born y<sup>e</sup> 31 of August 1678.

   daniel Ingersole y<sup>e</sup> son of John Ingersole was born y<sup>e</sup> 13<sup>th</sup> of September 1680:

by me John Corey, Clerke.

   *(Court Rec., p. 191.)*

## [TOWN MEETING.]

[1680, Sept. 20.]

September the 20 at a town meeting it was granted that
John Davis brick maker of setaket, in the East Ridding
of new York sheer should have the lot that was formerly
given to garrett geould, on Condition he the afore sd. John
Davis doe supply the town with good bricks as long as he
liveth.

By me John Corey Recorder.
(*Town Meetings, Vol.* 1, *p.* 58.)

---

## [TOWN MEETING.]

[1680, Sept. 27.]

September 27, 1680.
The town gave Mr Eliphalet Jones 20 acres of land where
he should think best.
[Copied from the original in the Court Records p                    ,
in the Revision in the year 1873.]
(*Town Meetings, Vol.* 1, *p.* 83.)

---

## [RECORD OF ELIPHELET JONES'S LAND.]

[1680, Sept. 27.]

Sept. 27 : 1680.
where as yᵉ town hath formerly given unto Mr Eliphelet
Jones twenty acres of upland whare he shall think best and
he hath made choyce of a piece of Land joyning the hether
end of yᵉ new feild in yᵉ west neck on yᵉ north sid of hors
neck path; where he hath taken his twenty acres except

three acres joyning to part of his hous lot being layd out
eighteen Rods broad and thirty Rods in length.

March 12. 168⅘                      John Corey Clerk.

(*Court Rec., p.* 282 *and Town Meetings, Vol.* 1, *p.* 58.)

[DEED. JOHN MATHEWS TO JOHN KETCHAM.]

[1680, Oct. 15.]

Know all men whom it may Consern that I John Mathis
of the town of huntington in the East Riding of york shire
on long Island, victuler. have for a Reasonable Consideration allredy Receved in hand where of and where with I
the afore sd John Martis doe acknowledg my self fully
satisfied and payed have barganed sold and made over all
my Right title and intrust in and to a parcell of medow
lying on the south side of the Island on a neck commly
called Siases neck and bounded as followeth to the medow
of Mr Jonas wood on the north to the medow of Thos
Scudder on the south with a creek on the East and with
the woods in Comonege on the west which afore said
medow Containing fower acars be it more or be it lesse I
the afore sd. John mathis have barganed sold and made
over all my Right, title and intrust in and to the above
mentioned fower acers of medow unto John kecham Carpenter of the above sd. town & riding. I say I have
barganed sold and estranged from my self my heirs executors administrators and assignes unto John kecham above
sd. his heirs executors administrators or assignes to have
and to hold and peacably to injoy from the date here of for
ever and far ther I the afore sd John Mathis doe own my
self at the ensealing and delivery here of to be the sole and
lawfull owner of the fore mentioned four acars of medow
and doe ingage my selfe my heirs executors and assignes
to free the fore sd. medow from any former grant gifts

leases jointers dowries bargans troubls or incumbrances
what soever formerly made by mee or by any means of
mine that the fore said John kecham his heirs executors
administrators or assignes may from time to time and at
all times peacably Injoy and possesse the fore mentioned
fower acars of medow for ever. to the true performence
here of I have here unto set my hand and seal.
Witnesse
   JOHN CORE                    the Mark of ✕ JOHN MATHIS
   ROBERT KELLAM
             October 15$^{th}$ 1680
  This is a true copie of the originall by me
                    John Core Rec$^r$
   (*Court Rec., p.* 252.)

---

## [DEED. JONATHAN SCUDDER TO MOSES SCUDDER.]

[1680, Oct. 22.]

  know all men who it may consarn that I Jonathon
Scudder of huntington in the East Riding of new york
sheir on long Island : doe by these presents make over all
my Right, title and intrust that I have to this within written bill of sale made over from William osbourn of
hempsted in the north Riding of New York shire on long
Island to me my heirs and assingnes I the afore said Jonathan Scudder doe assigne the with in written bill of sale*
unto my brother, moses Scudder of the town of huntington
in East Ridding of yorkshire from mee my heirs executors
administrators and assigne fully and absolutly unto my
brother moses Scudder above sd. his heires executors

---

[*See page 71.]

administrators and assinges to have and to hold and peacably to injoy for ever in witnesse here of I have set to my
hand and seal this twenty second of October in the year
1680

In present's of us )                              JONATHAN SCUDDER
   THOMAS POWELL }
   JOHN CORE          )

                    This is a true coppy extracted out of
the originall by me John Core, Rec<sup>r</sup>
   (*Court Rec., p.* 299.)

---

## [DEED.  JONATHAN SCUDDER TO DAVID
## SCUDDER.]

[1680, Oct. 22.]

Know all men by these presents that I Jonathan Scudder
of the town of huntington in the east Riding of New Yorkshire on Long Island doe make over all my Right title and
intrest that I have in that accomandation and every part
and parcell thereof that was formerly given to mee by my
grand ffather, Jeffery estie for and in consideration of that
accomandacion that was formerly my ffather Henrie Scudder.   I the above said Jonathan Scudder make over all my
Right title and intrest in and to all that forementioned
accomandation that was given me by my grand ffather
above sd. unto my Brother David Scudder of the above sd.
town and Riding from mee my heires executors administrators or assignes unto my  Brother David Scudder his
heirs executors administrators and assignes to have and to
hold and peacably to injoy for ever. in witnesse heere of I

have heere unto seet my hand and seal this twenty second
October in the yeare 1680.

Test.                                    JONATHAN SCUDDER.
    THOMAS POWELL,
    JOHN CORE.
    this is a true Copie extracted out of the origenell by mee
                                    John Core, Recr.

    (*Deeds*, *Vol.* 1, *p.* 24.)

-----

## [TOWN MEETING.   A FORT* AND A MILL.]

### [1680, Oct. 23.]

Huntington October 23 1680 at a towne meeting legally
warned the same day it was voated and granted by the
major part of the town that John Robeson Juynor of oysterbay that he the foresd. Robeson shall have our righ of
the streme at Cold Spring to put up a corn mill and a Saw
mill if he will agree on such conditions as those men chossen
by the town shall make with him and if he do not agree as
above. sd then the stream shall remain the towns as be fore :
These are the names of the men that are chosen to covenant
with John Robinson on the behalf of the town.

| | |
|---|---|
| John Sammis | Jonathan Rogers. |
| Thos. powell | Thoms. weeks, |
| Isaac platt | Richard willams |
| Epenetus platt | John Core Re$^r$. |

The day above written, it was voated and granted by the

-----

[* This is the only reference I remember to have seen in the
records of a Fort in Huntington during this period.  It was
probably a stockade erected at the first settlement to be used in
case of difficulty with the Indians, or the Dutch government,
and it was probably at or near the "Town Spot."   As it had become a ruin, it was given to the Rev. Mr. Jones for firewood.—
C. R. S.]

major part of the town that Mr Jones should have the foort to make fire wood of.

John Corey

(*Town Meetings, Vol.* 1, *p.* 24.)

---

### [TOWN MEETING.]

#### [1680, Oct. 23.]

At a town meeting, held Oct. 23, 1680 it was voted and granted that Robt Arthur shall lay down his lot formerly given him at the West end of the town ; and he shall have his house lot between the highway on the South side of Nathaniel Foster's lott, and the north side of John Finche's lot, and frounting to the street and rear to the woods in common.

By me John Corey, Rec'.

[Copy from the original in Court Records p.  ; copied in the Revision in the year 1873.]

(*Town Meetings, Vol.* 1, *p.* 85 *and Court Rec.,* p. 270,)

---

#### [1680, Nov. 14.]

Jonathan Scudder was married* unto Sarah Brown the fourteneth day of November In the yeare of our Lord : 1680.

(*Court Rec , p.* 289.)

---

[*The law governing the marriage relation at this remote period is interesting to consider. Persons desiring marriage were required to have their names publicly read three successive Lord's days in the meeting house which they attended, or obtain license from the governor ; then to be married by a minister or a Justice of the Peace, provided they purge themselves by oath before the minister or justice, and the penalty for bigamy was "He shall be bored through the tongue with a hot iron."

## [LAND DIVISIONS IN NEGUNTETAGUE.]

[1680, Dec. 12.]

Where as there hath been A diference between Epenetus platt and M$^r$ Jacob Walker Richard Brush and Walter nokes, conserning their medow lying at y$^e$ south on A neck called necuntetaug; their bound marks being down which caused the difference, they doe now agree that their medow shall be layd out again and have chosen Joseph Whitman and John Core to lay out ech mans dewe proportion that belongeth to him in y$^t$ place : and ech mans lot to ly in the place it did.  And doe bind our selves and sucsesers to Remain  satisfied as our fore mentioned layers out shall Bound our proportions and also that it shall be Recorded and so to Remain as a full determanation to us and our heirs for ever and ech man to bare his equall share of y$^e$ charge as witnesse our hands this 12 of desember 1680.

Witness                                JACOB WALKER

    JOHN COREY            EHENETUS PLATT
       Rec$^r$                     the mark of $\times$
                               RICHARD BRUSH
                               WALTER NOKES.

(*Court Records, p. 313.*)

Augost the 17 ; 1681.

                We who are above named layers out have vewed : layed out and bounded the four lots of medow

---

Five years absence' by sea or land with no knowledge of where-abouts of the absent party was presumption of death, and the other was free to marry, "but if he or she has been detained or hindered from giving information by the Turks or heathen then he or she may demand wife or husband."   Any minister or jus-tice who married " any daughter, maid, or servant without the consent of her father, master or dame, or without publishing the bans, was subject to pay a penalty of £20, and a forfeiture of his office."   There was a severe penalty against "harboring wives."—C. R. S.]

acording to our understanding, as equally as we could As witnesse our hands.

JOSEPH WHETMAN
JOHN COREY, Rec<sup>rd</sup>

(*Court Records, p.* 313.)

## [SARAH DAVIS BOUND OUT AS A SERVANT.]

### [1680, Dec. 14.]

The evidence of John Core desember 14. 1680 I being desired by Return devis and Abigell Samons to heere their say conserning bindin Serah devis to Abigall Samons which was as followeth, first John davis doth bind his daughter Sarah to Abigell Samons for one whole year and the abov said Abigall is to keep the above said Sarah davis in sickness and health only finding her suficent meat, drink, washing and lodging for such an aprintis and also to teach the sd. Sarah to read to her best indevoer can do it in her own hous and to knit stockins and further the sd. abigell is to give the sd. Sarah one pair of new shews one pair of new stockins one new jersy spun pety coat: one new home made or spun pety coat one new cersoway wascoat, one hom spun apron and also the sd. Sarah hath a new suit for holy days which the said abigell is to return again in as good condition as they were exdepting the oreinary ware of holy days for the fore sd. time or providentiall loss or destrawin the new suit above mentioned is only a silk hood and scarf and pety coat and wascoat of sarge and further the above sd. John devis doth comand his sd. daughter to obey al her said dames lawfull comands all her fore mentioned time. furthermore John Samons promised to me that he would stand to what bargin his wife made with the sd. davis, for his daughter.

desember 14. 1680 by me John Core Recorder.
(*Town Meetings, Vol.* 1. *p.* 1.)

## [JOHN BRUSH'S HOME LOT.]

[1681, Jan. 7.]

January th 7 1681   The hous and home lot of John Brush,
containing be it more or lesse and Bounded on yᵉ street
end south ward and on yᵉ northwest with yᵉ lot of walter
noks on yᵉ north with yᵉ lot of John Samons on yᵉ west
with yᵉ lot of Thomas Brush and half yᵉ Barn and yᵉ
ground that it stands on.   And also a certain parsell of
medow lying and being on yᵉ south side of yᵉ Island on a
neck of medow called by yᵉ name of necundetaug.  Bounded
on yᵉ south with yᵉ sound and on yᵉ west with yᵉ medow of
Thomas Brush on yᵉ east with yᵉ woods in common on yᵉ
north with yᵉ Town lot.

(*Deeds*, *Vol.* 1, *p.* 89.)

## [DEED.   BENJAMIN JONES TO JOHN INGERSOLL.]

[1681, Jan. 13.]

The Record of John hinkersons land, ─────────
──────────────────────────the second.
Witnesseth these pʳsents.  That I Benjemen Jones of yᵉ
Town of huntington upon Long Island with in yᵉ Collony
of his Roycll highnesse James duke of york in America :
husband man have and by these pʳsents doe allinate sell,
assigne and make over all my Right Title intrast & claime
in & to my hous land and accomandation, lying & being in
huntington above sd. vists : my home lott which contains
five acers more or lesse : with seaven acres & a half to be
taken up according to yᵉ priveledg of an hundred pound
lottment : with all other priveledge and Immunities what-

soever there unto belonging and appertaing or shall hereafter belong or appertain : from me my heirs, executors
administrators & assignes to John hingersoule of huntington above sd. husbandman his heirs executors, Administrators and assignes for ever to have & to hold as fully largely
and amply as may or can be made or done by any deed
grant convayence or any instrument of writing what soever : And ffor & in consideration of y⁰ above mentioned
pᵣmesis yᵉ above sd. John hingersolve is to pay yᵉ said
Benjemen one pair of oxen in hand, alredy a cow with
calf or a calf by her side on may day ensewing yᵉ date and
3 cowes fair with calf or calves by their sides yᵉ next may
day after will be in Anno : 1683, And for performence there
of the sd. John hingersolve doth bind him self his heirs &
asignes firmly by these pᵣsents The sd. cows not to be under
four nor exceeding seven years old : In witnesse whereof
wee yᵉ above mentioned doe here unto subscribe our names
this 13ᵗʰ day of Jen in yᵈ year of our Lord god 1681.

BENJEMEN JONES
the mark of × JOHN HINGERSOALE.

In pᵣsents of SYMON LANE.
the mark of × JOHN GREEN

> This is a true coppy of yᵉ originall
> compared by me John Corey Recoᵣ
> Jun : 20ᵗʰ 1682.

I, yᵉ above said Benjamen Jones doe acknowledg my selfe
to be fully sattisfied contented & payed yᵉ whole debt above
sd. for yᵉ Land above said as witness my hand this 20ᵗʰ day
of June 1682.   BENJAMEN JONES.

Witnesse                        JOHN COREY RECᵣ
JOHN COREY. RECᵣ
   (*Deeds Vol.* 1, *p.* 113.)

## [RECORD OF LANDS OF THOMAS BRUSH.]

[1681, January—.]

The Record of the Lands & medows of Thomas Brush, January, 1681.

The hous and home lot of Thomas brush situate and being in huntington, bounded on y^e south & west with y^e stret and lane; and on y^e north with y^e lot of John Samons; on y^e east with y^e lot of John Brush; and also halfe y^e Barn with y^e ground it stands on and the yard or ground y^e whole length of y^e barn to y^e street. and also a certain parsell of medow lying and being on y^e south sid of y^e Island; on a neck called & known by y^e name of necundetaug and Bounded as followeth. The South to y^e sound; and y^e west to y^e medow of abiell Titus; the north to y^e woods in commons; y^t east to y^e medow of John Brush: Containing eight acres be it more or leese, As also a parcell of Land containing three acres of Land be it more or lesse, lying in a hollow being about two mile from y^e town in y^e woods south ward from y^e town not fur from y^e east side of y^e south path.

as also another parcel of Land Lying in ye^e west neck foure acres be it more or Lesse, bounded on y^e South with y^e high way; & on y^e north with y^e Lot of John Brush and y^e East with y^e woods in Common and on y^e south with y^e Lot of James Chichester ^senr

(*Deeds Vol.* 1, *p.* 99.)

---

## [MORTGAGE. THOMAS SCIDMORE TO JOHN JONES.]

[1681, January 14.]

Tho. Skidmore sen^r. doth by way of morgege bind over

unto Mr. John Juons of new york march $^{nxt}$ his medow lying at Crab medow Containing six acres and is fenced in
with a fine Raile fence : being at ye head of y$^e$ creek over
adjoining William brothertons: for ye payment of y$^e$ Bal-
lance of s$^d$ M. Jnones his acco : according as y$^e$ s$^d$ Jnions
shall make appere : he agreed with y$^e$ s$^d$ skidmore to be
paid at or before y$^e$ first day of Jen$^r$ next insewing y$^e$ date
here of said delivered at y$^e$ town of huntington together
with the Intrest at the rat of 6 p cent p annum.

January 14, 1681.

John Corey Rec$^r$.

(*Town Meetings, Vol.* 1, *p.* 102.)

---

## [LEASE. THOMAS SCIDMORE TO JOSEPH WHITMAN.]

[1681. Jan. 20.)

Witneseth these presents y$^t$ I Thomas skidmor of huntington Black Smith ; with in y$^e$ collonye of his Royall
highness Jeames Duke of yorke uppon Long Island in
America have & by these doe let and to farme let my farme
at y$^e$ fresh pon : with y$^e$ housing & all y$^o$ enclosed Plow or
evalable land lying with in fence or w$^{ch}$ hath been formerly fenced or occupied by me : The sd. thomas skidmore also
my medow which lyeth within fence next unto william
Brotherton, with y$^o$ comonadge of pasture ; Timber or
otherwise : with all other freedoms & Imunities there unto
belonging, or appertaining unto Joseph Whitmer of huntington above s$^d$ husbandman for y$^e$ full terme & time of
three years, to comence & begin at y$^e$ sixteenth of Aprill
next ensewing y$^e$ date here of : not hindering y$^e$ sd Thomas from plowing or sowing winter Corne att michallmas
before : ffor the annall or yearly Rent of nine pounds, p

annum to be payed in marchantable pay as it goeth to yᵉ
marchant and at yᵉ end or expiration of yᵉ time or terme
yᵉ sd Joseph is to leave a good sufficient ffence about yᵉ
out side of yᵉ sd land or pasture.   And if yᵉ sd. Joseph doth
clear yᵉ said pasture & brake it up : he yᵉ sd is to have 3
crops of what he clears : also to keep & leave yᵉ housing
in good Repair causalty of fire excepted : Also yᵉ sd thomas doth engadge yᵗ at yᵉ expiration of yᵉ sd terme he is not
to hire out yᵉ sd land to any other person if he comes not
to live on it himself : At yᵉ Rent of ten pounds p. anum for
what years yᵉ sd. Joseph shall injoy yᵉ sd. farme with  conditions as afore sd. all yᵉ sd. Rent or rents are to be  payed
or delivered unto yᵉ fore sd. Thomas Skidmor at or  before
yᵉ last of march at yᵉ town of huntington to him or his  as-
sins yᵉ first paymenf to begin in yᵉ year 83 and  so  yearly
during yᵉ term or terms in witnesse whereof we  have here
unto set our hands this 20ᵗʰ of Jen. 1681 In huntington afore
sd.

THOMAS   *   *   *   *
JOSEPH   *   *   *   *

In witnesse of
SIMON LANE
ye mark of
JOHN × SKIDMORE Jr.

This is a true Copie  compared
with the originall by me  John
Corey, Rec.

(*Court Rec. p. 383.*)

---

## [RECORD  OF  THE  LANDS  OF  SAMUEL KETCHAM.]

[1681]

1681 The Records of yᵉ land & medows of Samuell Kecham.

The hous & home Lot of y⁰ above sd. Samuell keckam ;
situate and being in huntington Bounded on y⁰ East with
y⁰ land of Joseph Whitman & on y⁰ west with y⁰ lot of
Richard Williams ; y⁰ frunt to y⁰ streets y⁰ Reer to y⁰ woods
in Common ; it being six acars more or leese : As also four
acres of land called the hollow lying on y⁰ west side of y⁰
south path about 3 miles from town ; as also four acres of
land on y⁰ west neck on y⁰ north side of hors neck path
bounded on y⁰ north with y⁰ common and on y⁰ west with
y⁰ land of Rich. brush and the land of david Scudder east ;
y⁰ south to y⁰ path ; as also foure acars of land lying at y⁰
cove on y⁰ west neck and joyning to y⁰ south end or side
of John Samons land. As also medow lying on y⁰ south
side of y⁰ Island ; one parsell lying about the midell of y⁰
half neck Bounded on y⁰ west side with y⁰ medow of Content Titus, and on y⁰ East with yᵗ medow of abiell Titus ;
the south to y⁰ sound y⁰ north to y⁰ woods.
another parsell of medow lying neere y⁰ east sid of y⁰ fore
sd. neck bounded on y⁰ east and y⁰ north with y⁰ medow of
Jonathan Scudder and david Scudder, y⁰ south to y⁰ sound :
The west with y⁰ medow of Content Titus ; another parsell
of medow lying on y⁰ littell neck bounded one west side
with y⁰ medow of Content Titus and one y⁰ east with y,
medow of Samuell Titus the Rear to Copias Creek the
frunt to y⁰ woods.

(*Deeds Vol. p1, . 91.*)

[DEED. JOSEPH BAILY TO ROBERT KELLUM.]

[1681, Jan. 24.]

The Record of (Robart Kellams) medow at Santepaug.

Know all men whom these may consern yᵗ I Joseph
Bayly of huntington in y⁰ east Riding of yorksheir on long
Island have Barganed sold and made over : from me my

heirs executors admines. and asignes unto Robart kellam, Cordwinder of y$^e$ above sd. town & Riding a parsell of medow lying and being on y$^e$ south side of y$^e$ Island on a neck Commonly and called by y$^e$ name of santepaug: y$^e$ fore sd. parsell of medow is called y$^e$ Island. It is Bounded with y$^e$ medow of John wicks on y$^e$ norwest: on y$^e$ south with y$^e$ sound y$^e$ north east & south east surrounded with y$^e$ Creek and pond: except between y$^e$ pond and y$^e$ sound which is parted from my medow with stakes strait from y$^e$ south east side of y$^e$ sound: all which fore sd. Island of medow I y$^e$ fore sd. Joseph Bayly have for a reasonable consideration alredy Recaived in hand: where of and where with I am fully satisfied contented and payed: I y$^e$ fore sd. Joseph Baly have Barganed sould estranged & made over from me my heirs executors, administrators and assignes unto Robart kellam: his heirs executors adminis-trators and assignes y$^e$ fore sd. Island ot medow: To have and to hold use occupie, possesse and peacably to Injoy for ever: And further I y$^e$ fore sd. Joseph Bayly doe bind my self my heirs, executors, adminis. and assignes to save harmlesse and undamnefied The fore sd. Robart Kellam his heirs executors, admi$^{rs}$ and assignes from evry person or persons y$^t$ shall lay any just and lawfull claim to y$^e$ fore sd. medow or any part of it.

And further I y$^e$ fore sd. Joseph Bayly doe grant and allow y$^e$ fore sd. Robart kellam: his heirs executors administra-tors and assigns to have a cart way throw my medow to his Island of medow for ever without any molestation and this above written Instrument I doe own to be my act and deed by my subscribing to y$^e$ same this 24$^{th}$ of Janeuary in y$^e$ year 1681. signed sealled and delivered in y$^e$ presents of

the mark of ✕                              JOSEPH BAYLY
  JOHN DAVIS
  JOHN COREY        This is a true Copie compared with y$^e$ original by me John Corey Record.
      (*Deeds, Vol.* 1, *p.* 103.)

# [DEED. ROBERT KELLUM TO JOHN GOULD.]

[1681, Feb. 3.]

### The Land of John Gould Recorded.

know all men by these p'sents : y' I Robart Kellam of huntington in y° east Riding of york shire on Long Island ; Cordwinder, for divers good causes & considerations we hereunto moving, as also for & in consideration of a valuable sume of mony alredy by me in hand Receaived doe allinate Bargan make over and sell, and by the p'sents have Allinated bargained & made over, from me & mine for ever ffirmely sould unto John Gould now Resident of South hampton in Com', p,ddict ;) all that my Land situat Lying and being in huntington above sd., being six acres of Land be y° same more or lesse as it is bounded : North y° Rear of Jonas Woods hous Lott : And y° Rear of Rich. Brushes : And y° Reare of Joseph Whitmans : West by y° Lean Commonly called Joseph Whittmans Lanne : And South & East by y° Commons, together with a ffifty pound Commonage throw out all y° bounds of huntington and all priveleges appurtenances and Commodityes what soever unto y° sd. Lott of Land and ffifty pound Commonage is or doth unto y° same any way Belong unto him y° sd. John Gould his heirs Executors—administrators & assignes for ever here after To have and to hold y° sd. Lott of Land and y° sd. fifty pound Commonege as his or their own free Land for ever : Without y° Least lett trouble, hindrence or mollestation of me y° sd. Robart Kallam my heirs, executors, administrators or assignes : or any other p'son or p'sons what soever by, from or under me Claiming or Laying any manner of title or Clayme : unto y° sd. lott of Land or any part or parcell of y° same or any thing or things what so ever is or now doth unto y° same in any way or manner doth belong, or unto y° sd. fifty pound Commonage in y° bounds of huntington : above sd. Also at any time or

so often as I shall be there unto Required : to signe, seale
and deliver any further or better deed or bill of sale for yᵉ
same, as he yᵉ sd. John Gould his heirs or assignes shall by
their Learned Counsell in yᵉ law get drawne : And soe
bering to one to signe seal and deliver I hereby warranting & avouching yᵗ I have full power & authoryty so to
dispose and sell yᵉ sd. lott & commonage in witness whereof I have here unto set my hand & seale in Southampton
this 3ᵈ of febuary Annod 168$\frac{1}{2}$

ROBART KELLAM

Signed sealed & delivered
in presence of,
HENERY PEIRSON
JOHN LAUGHTON.
This is compared a true coppy with yᵉ originall by me
John Corey Septr. 19 : 1682.

These may signefie That wee John Gould and Robart
kellam doe with joynt consent make yᵉ within Recorded
bill of sale of none affect, as witnes our hands this 14ᵗʰ of
novembr 1682.

the mark of ✕ JOHN GOULD
ROBERT KELLAM

Witness JOHN COREY, Recr.
(Deeds, Vol. 1, p. 117.)

---

## [RECORD OF LANDS OF THOMAS SCUDDER.]

[1681, Feb. 4.]

The Record of Thomas Scudders farme containing sixty
acars of land which is by denominaton a farm & half with
yᵉ medow belonging thereto : lying and being at Crab
medow on yᵉ east side of yᵉ bogey medow yᵗ lyeth east
ward of george beldings hous lot, and also joyning on yᵉ
north to one part of yᵉ medow which doth belong to it wᵗ

the east & south to y<sup>e</sup> comons. y<sup>e</sup> other parcell of medow is joyning to y<sup>e</sup> medow of William Brothertn as also commonege for cattell according to y<sup>e</sup> above sd. denominaton

The home lot of John Scudder being given him by ye town is bounded as followeth with ye kings hiewaye on y<sup>e</sup> west to y<sup>e</sup> lot of Capt. Thos. fleet on y<sup>e</sup> south to ye woods on y<sup>e</sup> east to y<sup>e</sup> lot of James Chichester Jnr. on y<sup>e</sup> north y<sup>e</sup> above<sup>sd</sup> lot to bare y<sup>e</sup> denominaton of one hundred pound allotment of what land is hear after to be taken up

feber. 4<sup>th</sup> 1681                            John Corey, rec<sup>r</sup>.

(*Deeds, Vol. 1, p. 13.*)

---

[A SHEEP LAW.]

[1681, Feb. 23.]

Huntington ffeb<sup>r</sup> 23, 1681.

The Constable and overseers of huntington haveing taken into their Consideration, the grate nesessety of increasing and presarving of sheep: having had long experience to our grate lose and dammage, of letting y<sup>e</sup> Rames Run constently with y<sup>e</sup> sheep which by so doing y<sup>e</sup> lambs falling in winter menny of them die; In consideration whereof they do order that about one acre of land or acre and half be fenced in with a good and sufficeant seaven Raile fence, where they shall think fit to make a pasture to put y<sup>e</sup> Rams into And every one y<sup>t</sup> have sheep shall fenc proporsionably to y<sup>e</sup> number of sheep y<sup>t</sup> they have And whosoever have not set up his fence at or before y<sup>e</sup> last of may next ensewing the date here of shall pay five shillings for each Rod And all y<sup>t</sup> have Rames shall put them in to y<sup>e</sup> pasture the first of August and there to Remaine till y<sup>e</sup> first of November; And if any person or persons shall neglect to observe this order of putting their Rams into y<sup>e</sup> above s<sup>d</sup> pauster at y<sup>e</sup> time

appoynted : And theire Rames be found Runing with
yᵉ sheep Contarary to this order it shall be lawfull for any
person to kill any such Ram And keepe one halfe thereof
to him selfe and Return yᵉ other half to yᵉ owners.
And any yᵗ shall heere after have sheep yᵗ yet have not
shall observe this order.  And also shall give som Reasonable alowence towards yᵉ fensing yᵉ fore sᵈ pasture.

And to yᵉ end yᵗ this order may stand in force ; our
desire is yᵗ this Court would be pleased to grant a conformation of it.

JONATHAN ROGERS, const.

THOMAS POWELL ⎫
THOMAS WICKES ⎪ Over-
THOMAS WHITSON ⎬ seers.
SAMUELL KETCHAM ⎭

To the Worshipfull Court of  .
Sessions now sitting at Southampton
march th. first. 1681.

The aforesaid order is aproved and Confirmed by
this Courte of sessions held at Southampton March
the second &c. 168½
p, order of Court p. John Howell, Clerk.
(*Court Rec., p.* 361.)

[THE LAW AGAINST GEESE.]

[1681, Feb. 23.]

Huntington febuar. ᵗʰ 23 : 1681
Whereas Complaint hath been made unto the Constable &
overseers of huntington of yᵉ grate hurt done on our Common pasture and in our brooks : of watter by geese which
some particular persons doe keepe : which is and is like to
be very prejeditiall to yᵉ Towne ; Becaus yᵉ sheep as hath
been observed doe not keep in yᵉ streets as formerly, but

Run into y^e woods whereby they are y^e more exposed to be devowered by wolves; becaus they cannot abide to feed where y^e geese doe keep: which is in y^e cheife places both for watter & common pasture in our Towne. And also meny people of this town doe take of y^e watter of y^e brook for their familie use And also in times of drought meny y^t have wells, doe fech of y^e watter of y^e brooks some with their teams & sume with horses for theire use, And also our horses & other Cattell cannot abide to drink where y^e geese do keepe.

The Constable and overseers haveing taken into their consideration the hurtfullnesse and noysomenesse of geese and ducks doe order y^t no person nor persons shall keep any geese or ducks upon y^e commons after y^e first day of Aprill next ensewing y^e day above sd. And if any geese or ducks be found upon y^e Commons after y^e day above s^d it shall be lawfull for any person or persons to kill any such geese or ducks upon y^e commons & convaie them to y^e owners. It is to be understood y^t this order shall not hinder any person or persons from keeping of gecse on their own Inclosed ground, nor any farmer who live so Remote y^t such creatures will be troublesome to none but their owners.

To y^e end this order may stand in full force our desire is y^t this Court would be pleased to Confirme y^e same.

JONATHAN ROGERS, Constable
THOMAS POWELL ⎤
THOMAS WICKES ⎟ Over
THOMAS WHISEN ⎟ seers
SAMUELL KETCHAM ⎦

To y^e wor,full: Court of sessions now sitting at Southhampton; march ^th first: 1681.

This order is Likewise Confirmed by the said Court.
As atest John Howell Clark to sd. courte:
(*Court Rec., p.* 361)

At A Court of sessions held by his mag^{st} authority at
South hampton y^e 1. 2. 3. days 168½ : was presented by Mr
Joseph Loe deputy shrieffe the within written orders to be
by this Court Confirmed which y^e Court having considered
y^e same ; doe at y^e Request of y^e Cons^t and overseers subscribe, allowe, approve off and also Ratefie & Confirme
both y^e orders with in written to all intents & purposes.
Atest John Howell J^r Clarke to y^e sessions for y^e east
Riding of yorkshire &c.

> A true Coppy from y^e backside of this order by me
> John Corey, Clark.
> (*Court Rec.*, *p.* 361.)

---

## [DEED. JOHN TEED TO ROBERT KELLUM.]

[1681, March 1.]

huntington March the first 16⁸⁰⁄₈₁

Know all men whome thees may consarne that I John
Teed of Huntington in the East Riding of new Yorkshire
on long Island husbandman have barganed sold and made
over all my Right title and intrest in and to all my medow
and three polls in breadth of upland Joyning to the above
sd. medow so far as my land and the fore said medow doth
frunt one against the other, all the fore mentioned medow
and the three Rods breadth of upland joyning to it, is
lying and being at the Cove in the west neck, for which
land & medow above sd. I the above said John Tedd do
own and acknowledge my self fully satisfied contented and
payed I say I the above sd John Teed have Barganed sold
and estranged from my self and from my heirs, executors
administrators and asingnes unto Robart kellam shoe
maker of the above sd Town and Riding and heirs executors administrators and asingnes all my Right title and

intrust that I have in and to the above sd. medow and three Rods breadth of upland joyning to it, to have and to hold ffor ever and peacably to injoy for ever & further more I the above sd. John Ted doe bind my self and my heirs to bare harmlesse and undamnefied the above said Robart kellem & his heirs from any person or persons what so ever that shall lay eny just & lawfull Claim to the above said land and medow as witnesse my hand and seal the day above written

Witnesse                           JOHN TEED.
     RICHARD WHITE
     JOHN COREY
              A true Coppy by me
                       John Corey, Rec$^r$

(*Court Records, p.* 204.)

---

### [DEED. JOHN TEED TO JOHN SAMMIS.]

[1681, March 20.]

This writing witneseth to all whom it may consern that I John Teed huntington in the east Riding of new york-shire on long Island husbandman have Barganed sold and made over unto John Samous of the above sd. town and Riding, A parcel of medow lying and being on the west neck at the cove Bounded as foloweth. To the medow of Robart kellam on the north : with the cove on the East, and the Broke on the south : and to the land of John Samous on the west for which medow I the above sd. John Teed doe acknowledg and own my self fully satisfied, contented and payed and have Barganed sold and estranged the above sd. medow and all my Right Title and Intrust There to from me my heirs executors administrators and asinnes. To have and to hold and peacably to Injoy for ever as

witnesse my hand and seal this 20 of march in the
year 16⅘
In presence of
  JOHN COREY
  the mark of ✕ ROGER MONEY
    this A true Copie Compared with the Originall by
    mee John Corey, Rec<sup>r</sup>
    (*Court Rec.*, *p.* 241.)

---

## [DEED. JOHN FINCH TO GEORGE BALDWIN AND THENCE TO ROBERT ARTHUR.]

[1681, March 25.]

March 25, 1681
This writing witnesseth that John finch Sen<sup>r</sup> of huntington in the east Riding of Yorksheer on Long Island : have
sold unto gorge boldin of the above said town A small
parsell of land that lyeth on the north sid of my lot y<sup>t</sup> now
I dweleth on and is without my fence and joyning to my
lot I say I y<sup>e</sup> above sd. John finch have sould from me my
heirs, executors administrators or assignes unto the above
sd. gorge boldin his heires executors or assignes all my
right, title and intrust and to the above sd. land. haveing
Recaived full satisfaction allredy for the same.
                           by me John Corey
                                        Recorder.
I the above sd. gorge boldin doe assigne all my right, title
and intrust that I have in & to the above sd. land that I
bought of John finch : unto Robart Arther his heirs executors administra. or asigns.
I say I the above sd. gorge boldin doe assigne and make
over from me my heirs or asignes unto Robart Arthur his
heirs Executors, adminis. or assignes all my Right title

and intrust that I have in and to the above sd. land to have
and to hold and pessably to injoye for ever.

May 23. 1681.                              by me John Corey

Reco[r]

*(Court Rec., p. 296.)*

---

## [BOND OF RICHARD BETTS FOR HIS APPEARANCE.]

[1681, March 30.]

Know all men by these presents that I Richard bets of
Eatons neck in the east Riding of new york shire on long
Island doe make over my slope called by the name of the
Incresse being about the burthen of 7 or 8 tons unto Rich-
ard White of huntington an his heirs, for my apearnc at
the next court to be held at Southhold the first tuesday in
Jun next ensuing the date here of then & there to answer
Mr John oynen & Capt Thos. ffleet and if I the above sd.
Richard bets do not apere as above sd : then the sloop to
Remaine and be Rich. whits : but if the above sd. Rich.
bets doe appeare at the Court of sesions as afore sd. then
this bond to be voyd and of noe affect as witnesse my hand
and seal this 30 of march 1681.

further more I the above sd. Rich. bets doe Ingage to bring
my sloop into huntington harbor at or before the last of
may next after the date here of other wise this bond to be
of full force and virtue.

signed, sealed and delivered                    RICH. BETS.
in presence of.                      This is a true Copie compared
   JOHN CORE                    with the originall by mee
   HENRY DESBROU.                       John Core. Recr.

*(Court Rec., p. 225.)*

## [TOWN MEETING.]

[1681, April 1.]

April the first 1681 at a town meeting it was voated and granted by the major part of the Town that Jeremiah Smith should have their Right of seven or eight acers of land, which is mowable land A grat part there of and some of it was formerly plowed by Jonathon Rogers and Joseph Whitman, it is lying between the head of fresh pond hollow and Joseph whitmans hollow.

(*Court Rec., p.* 198.)

## [TOWN MEETING.]

[1681, ———.]

huntington ᵗʰ23 1681 the same day it was voated & granted by yᵉ major part of yᵉ town yᵗ Thomas Skidmor senⁱʳ shall have A littel peece of land yᵗ joyneth to Epenetus plats lot Runing from the west end of Samuell griffens shoop down to the brook for him to set a shop & a hous upon and gardin and yard if he doe except there of and continue amongst us and doe our Smith work for us, and upon his Removeall or decase it shall Return to the town again they paying him for his full charge & labour : unless he shall set one of the same Trade upon it. such A one as the town shall like that will doe as aforesd. and when soever it shall be left without A Smith as afore sd. it shall belong to and be the towns again they paying for the full value of it as above said :

But if the town Refuse so to doe : then it shall be lawfull for him to sell or dispose of it as he shall see caus.

And the above sd. peece of land is to com no neerer the Cart way than the layers out shall see caus and when layd out then to be Recorded both the length & bredth of it by mee John Corey Recorder.

(*Court Rec., p.* 44.)

---

## [DEED. BENJAMIN JONES TO JAMES CHICHESTER.]

[1681, May 1.]

Know all men whom these may conserne that I Benjamin Jones of huntington in  *  *  *  *  of new yorksheer on long Island husbandmon: have for a competent sume of good merchantable pay of the country already Receaived in hand where with I doe acknowledge  *  *  *  *  fully satisfied, contented and payed: before the enselling and delivery hereof  *  *  *  *  *  sertain parsell of land & medow: unto James Chichester Junᵣ of the above sd. town  *  *  Riding: and do by thes presents to and with the consent of my wife Johana: bargen, sell, alinate and estrange from my selfe my heirs executors administrators & assignes in  *  *  *  *  James Chichester above. sd. his heirs executors, administrators and assignes, all my right title & intrest that I have in and to a one hundred pound alot-ment of land and medow lying in the town and bounds of huntington: which accommodations did formerly belong to Richard wattells, alinated thence to Samuell messenger, thence to Ben. Jones, and now to James chichester above sd. that is to say eight acars of land be it more or be it lesse lyin in this town and bounded on the south with the hous lot of moses Scudder: on the west with yᵉ wood  *  *  *   *  *  *  *  *  on the north with the lot of John Teed, with the kings hie way on the east, with the orchards and all fences that doth belong to the same, it is to be understood that all the fence  *  *  *  *  is on the north side

of the above sd. lot is to be made and mentained by James
Chitchester and his successours for ever, besides his other
legall Rights of fences: as also three parsells of medow
lying and being on the south side of this Island on a neck
commonly called the west neck and known by that name:
the first parsell of medow is * * * * the Endian
path: the second parsell is lying about the midell of the
neck: bounded on the east with the medow of Timothy
Conklin: with the medow of John Jones on y^e west; with
the woods on the front: the Rear to the sound: the third
parcell of medow is lying on the west side of the neck:
bounded on the south with the medow of John Teed: on
the west with agrat Creek & with the woods on the east:
and with the medow * * * * on the north. with all
woods and common of pasturs what soever that now doth
or hereafter shall belong to the above sd:, one hundred
pound alotment, both of land and medow, with all Rights
and priveledges whatsoever that now doth or at any time
shall belong to it the Right of the farme excepted y^t did
belong to the above sd. allotment Commonly called Crabmedow farmes, being formerly elinated and estranged from
the above sd alotment and is not intended in this sale but
all other the above written primeses: I the above sd. Ben.
Jones for my selfe my heirs, executors, administrators and
assigns: doe covenant, promise and grant by these presents
y^t at y^e time of the enseating hereof I am the sole and lawfull owner of all the fore bargained premises & am lawfully
seased of & in y^e same: and in every part & parsell thereof
in my own Right & y^e above sd. James Chit^r his heirs,
executors administrators and assigns shall and may by
force and vertue of these presents from time to time and
at all time forever here after: lawfully peacably and quiatly
have hold use occupie possess & injoy y^e above granted
premises with all their appurtenences free and clear and
cleerly aquited & discharged of and from all and all maner
of former or other gifts, grants lenes, morgages, joynters,

dowers or titles of dowres judgments, executions or in tales troubles or incombrances what so ever and further I the above sd. Ben. Jones doe ingadge my self & my heirs and asignes to bare harmlesse and undemnefied the above sd. James Chic$^r$ his heirs executors administrators or assignes from any person or persons what soe ever y$^t$ shall lay any just and lawfull claime to any part or parcell of the above sd. premises as witnesse my hand and seal the firs of May in the yeare 1681.

Signed, seled and        BENJAMIN JONES
delivered in presents of        the
    JOHN COREY        JOHANA X JONES
    STEVEN JARVES        mark of

       This is a true copie of the origenell
       by me John ———
                    Clerk.

(*Deeds, Vol. 1, p. 65.*)

---

## [THOMAS HIGBIE'S AGREEMENT WITH THE INDIANS ABOUT KILLING WHALES.]

[1681, May 15.]

This writing Ingadeth us whose names are under written, four being Indians : unto thomas higbe of hunting upon long Island in the East Ridding of York sheer To be Reddie at that season of the yeer which men goe to kill whales : and to goe with him at what time he gives us notise and to use our best indevours therein according to derections given and we doe heere by ingadge our selves, joyntly and severally by these presents not to depart or leve the voiage untill it be wholy Compleated where by the sd. higbee and his asosiats may be any wayes damnefied In witnesse where of wee have joyntly and severly set too our marks for the

Conformation thereof the 15 day of may in the year of our
lord 168-. GEORG his mark
In presence of X
JOHN CORE the mark of X PERROAL
THOS. SHIDMORE the mark of PETOWNK X
the mark of X HANAS CUT
the mark of X JOHN REVEMO
the mark of NAHANCUTTORO X
the mark of X TARRUMPIN
the mark of X SORANORT
the mark of X MACHAT HART

(*Court Records, p* 43 )

---

## [TOWN MEETING.]

[1681, May 23.]

May 23 1681 the same day it was agreed with Thos. higbe
and Joseph wood coper should make and mentain a good
and sufficient foot and hors way over the water th. runs
threw the old mill dam : and to mentain it for evere them
and their heirs for ever and in consideration thereof they
and their heirs are freed from mending or being at any
charge at making or mending any other hie way be longing
to the town.

the day above writen it was voted and granted by the
major part of the town that those men that have taken upland on the east neck should run their fenc from Thos.
Scudders lot and run to the out side of the bogey medowe
that Thos. weeks sen bought of the town to y^e sea not in-
fringing of hie way but maintaining bars or a gate to pass
to ye sea through.

the day above writen it was voated and granted that John
kecham and John Samous shall have ech of them 6 acars of
land lying between the new feild that lyeth at mil ston

brook and Timothe Conklings land lying on the north side of the cart way.

the day above writen it was voated and granted by y^e major part of the towne that Joseph wood husband man should run his fence in to the harbour from his land that lyeth at the mouth of the little neck : that is from the norwest corner and the southwest side in to the harbour. [A copy given of this]

The day above written it was voated and granted that Cpt. Tho. fleet shall have liberty to take up the remaining part of his division of land to y^e eastward or northward of y^e Cove at Cowharbour & hee to satisfie y^e Indians for y^e soile right, y^t y^e towne may bee freed from any Indian demands about it, but in Case y^e towne shall at any time purchase the said land, then ye said land y^t Capt fleet shall take up shall bee Comprehended with their purshase : soe y^t. hee may not pay for it twise.

the next above sd. land is in y^e book dated 1680.

may ^th 23 1681 the same day it was voated and agreed by the major part of the towne that Isack plat shall have 5 achars of land towards his devsion it lying on the south sid of the east feild path and joyning to his lot that lyeth in the east feild

also it was voated and granted that Thomas Weeks should have 5 achars of land towards his devision it lying on the north sid of the east feild path and joyning to his land in the feild.

the day above writen it was voated and granted that John Corey should have about 2 acars of the long swamp the hassackey part of it : neere this end of it the swamp lying eastward of Richarde Brush hollow he to take it as part of his division and also to fence it before the first of May next ensueing the date here of or else the same to be forfit to the towne again.

the day above writen it was granted by the major part of
the town that Richard White shall have Liberty to take
up 4 acars of land joneing to yᵉ new west feild.

it was voted and granted the day abov. writen that John
Ted shall have about 8 acars of land at the Cove and joyning to his land that now he hath : six of it next to John
Samous and the other 2 ackars on the south sid of it, provided not predetiall to hie ways or watering places nor to
be any farme settled there

the day above written it was voated and granted that
Robert Kellum should have about 6 achars of land lying
at the harbor mouth on the poynt of the west neck and
joyning to the cove on the north called hors neck cove
provided there be no farme lot nor watering places or hie
ways hindered . it being division land.

John Corey

(*Town Meetings, Vol.* 1, *pp.* 90-91.)

The 23 of may 1681 it was voated and granted yᵗ Capᵗⁿ
Thomas ffleet shall have liberty to take up yᵉ Remaining
part of his devition of Land at yᵉ east ward or north ward
of yᵉ Cove at Crabmedow.

The above sd. land to yᵉ number of 27 acres is layed out
neere yᵉ head of yᵉ hollow yᵗ Leadeth south ward from
Willam Brothertons hous.

(*Deeds, Vol.* 1. *p.* 105.),

---

## [DEED. JAMES CHICHESTER, Sᴇɴ., TO JAMES CHICHESTER, Jʀ.]

[1681, June 20.]

The Record of James Chichester Junʳ

Know all whom it may consern that I James Chichester
Senr. of huntington in the East Riding of yorkshier on long
Island have as well for & in consideration of yᵉ naturall

love and affection which I have & bare to my well beloved
son James Chichester : as also tor divers other good causes
& considerations me at this present especially moving, have
given granted and by these presents doe give grant and
confirm unto my above sd. son James. a sertain parcell of
land lying and being in y⁼ west feild on the west neck, Containing about fower acars be it more or be it lesse runing
southward & northward to y⁼ woods in Common bounded
on the east with the lot of Jonas wood ˢᵉⁿʳ and on the west
with the lot of Thoms Brush : I say I the above sd. James
Chichester senr have given granted and made over from
me my heirs, executors, administrators and assignes : unto
my son James above sd. all my Right title and in yᵗ I have
in and to the above sd. fower acres of land to him & his
heirs executors, administrators and assigns : peaceably to
possess and to In Joy for ever as witnese my this 20 of
June 1681

JAMES CHICHESTER

John Corey Recorder.

The Record of the hous lot of James Chichester Junʳ
given to him by the Town : it lying at the harbour it beeing two acrees bee it more or be it lesse, bounded on the
north and west : with y⁼ hie way on the Reare with the
woods in Common and on the south with y⁼ lot of John
Scudder. as also one hundred pound to Commonege and
land that shall here after be layd out in devition 1681

By me John Corey, Recʳ

*(Deeds, Vol. 1, p. 67.)*

---

## [CONVEYANCE BY CATHERINE JONES OF RIGHTS IN OLD MILL POND.]

[1681, June 20.]

huntington Jun. 20, 1681
This writing testefieth to any whom it may Consern that

I keterine Jones of huntington in the East Riding of york
shire on long Island haveing bought of abiell Titus A thre
hundred pound Right of the old mill pond and also I have
bought of John Teed A two hundred pound Right of the
old mill pond : these above said Rights I doe devide and
give to my 3 sons : to my son Jonathan A two hundred
pound Right which being aded to that which he hath belonging to his accomondation, maketh his Right in the old
mill pond A fower hundred pound Right.

Also I give to my son moses Scudder one hundred pound
Right in the old mill pond : it being aded to y$^t$ he alredy
posseseth maketh his Right to be fowre hundred pound in
the old mill pond.

also I give to my son david Scudder a tow hundred pound
Right in the old mill pond. it being aded to y$^t$ he hath
alredy in possesion maketh his Right to be 4 hundred pound
Right in the old mill pond.

by me John Corey<br>Rec$^r$

(*Court Rec., p.* 250.)

---

## [RECORD OF THE LANDS OF THOMAS BRUSH.]

[1681, June 30.]

Jun. 30 : 1681.

Recorded.                    Thomas Brush.

The medows of Thom$^s$ brush lying on the east neck :
next eastward to santepaug the first parsell is on y$^e$ west
side of y$^e$ above said east neck in y$^e$ sault marsh it being
ten Rods broad, and bounded on y$^e$ south with the lot of
Richard Brush and on y$^e$ north with the lot of Walter
Nokes : with the Creek on y$^e$ west and thence Runing
through sault and fresh to the midel of y$^e$ neck eastward.

The second parse.l is also on y<sup>e</sup> west side of the neck it being six Rods Broad and bounded on y<sup>e</sup> south with the lot of Richard Brush and on the north with the lot of John Samous and with y<sup>e</sup> creek on the west and Runing east ward to y<sup>e</sup> midel of the neck as also a small parsell of medow given as amendment to Thos. brush & Richard it lyeth on the norh sid of Edward ketchams north lot.——the Creek on y<sup>e</sup> west the woods on the east the Endian path on y<sup>e</sup> north also a third parsell is lying on y<sup>e</sup> east side of the same neck it is ten Rods broad and bounded on the south side with y<sup>e</sup> lot of Walter Noaks and on the north side with the lot of John brush withe Creeke on y<sup>e</sup> east and Runing west ward to the midel of y<sup>e</sup> neck. The fourth parsell is also on the east side of the same neck it being bounded with the grate creek on the east and a littell creeke south ward and west ward Joseph whtmens lot west it is further to be understood that the fore sd medow lyeth by the grate hammok of Clam shells—as also a right to a parsell of medow at the lower end of the same neck.

By me John Corey, Recor,

*(Deeds, Vol. 1, p. 87.)*

[THE DIVISION OF EAST NECK, SOUTH.]

[1681, June 30.]

Jun 30. 1681.                    Town Lott medow.

The Records of the Town lott ; medows lying on y<sup>e</sup> east neck one parcell lying on y<sup>e</sup> west side of y<sup>e</sup> neck part thereof of it salt marsh it being five Rods broad : and bounded with y<sup>e</sup> creke on y<sup>e</sup> west : Runing to y<sup>e</sup> midell of y<sup>e</sup> neck east ward and with y<sup>e</sup> medow of Epenetus platt on y<sup>e</sup> south : with y<sup>e</sup> medow of Joseph whitman on y<sup>e</sup> north.

also another parcell of medow lying on ye same side ot y⁰
neck it being all fresh : bounded on yᵉ east and west as before said with the medow of Jonas Wood on the south side
and the medow of Epenetus platt : on yᵉ north side it being
six Rods Broad.   Also another parcell of medow lying on
yᵉ est sid of y⁰ same neck it being five Rods Broad : and
bounded on y⁰ east with the Creeke and Running west
ward to yᵉ midel of the neck : bounded on y⁰ south with
yᵉ lot of John Bats : and on y⁰ north with the lot of Joseph
Whitman, Another parcell Runing est and west as before
on the same side of yᵉ neck it lying next the Endian feild
and joyning the lot of Joseph Whitman on the south : the
Town hath yet som Right in the lower part of the neck
which is not yet devided.

by mee John Corey, Clerk

Know all men whom these may concerne That all those
men yᵗ have medow at yᵉ east neck next to Santepaug :
have layd out their medow : this 30ᵗʰ of June 1681. And
when they were about it : after a vew of it : they Resolve
mutually to lay out their lots acrose yᵉ neck : and doe agree
yᵗ their Cart ways shall goe throu every mans medow as
their need shall Require without being counted any trespasse to any man. provided yᵗ they soe keepe to their
severall cart ways and as need Require to mend them.
And not to spoyle any mans medow by making divers ways
throu it : which shall be counted a trespasse if don : after
warning given to yᵉ contrary : by yᵉ party wronged this
they agree on in the behalfe of them selves & their suc-
cessers :

This being agreed as afore said. They lay out their
medow accordingly and cast lots for their shares as shall
be found on Record in this Book : By me John Corey Recorded, who being one of yᵉ afore sd : in the behalfe of
Epenetus platt

(*Deeds, Vol.* 1, *p.* 69.)

# [JOHN BATES'S LANDS—EAST NECK, SOUTH.]

[1681, June 30.]

Jun. 30. 1681. John Bats

The Record of the medow of John Bats lying on y<sup>e</sup> south sid of y<sup>e</sup> Island on A neck comonly called the east neck: and joyning next to Santapaug est side: the parcels layd out are four. The firs devition: is on the west side of the neck and also called the first lot of the first devition: begining at y<sup>e</sup> north end of the salt marsh it being ten Rods broad and bounded with the lot of John brush on the south: the lot of Richard Brush on y<sup>e</sup> North the Creek on the west and Runing to the midell of the middell of the neck east ward. The second devision is also on y<sup>e</sup> same side of y<sup>e</sup> neck and is five Rods broad & bounded with the lot of John Samous on the south and the lot of walter nokes on the north, the Creeke on the west and Runing to the midell of the neck east ward.

The first devision on the est side of y<sup>e</sup> neck which is the third parcell is bounded on the south with the lot of John Sammons and on the North with y<sup>e</sup> lot of y<sup>e</sup> town.

The fourth parcell is also on the east side of y<sup>o</sup> neck: bound with the lot of Walter noks on the south, and the lot of John Brush the north and is six Rods broad and is bounded on the East with the Creek and Runing west ward to the middell of the neck: The fore mentioned third parsell is eight Rods broad and Runeth from the East Creeke or fore mentioned Creeke to the middell of the neck west ward.– – –, Also a certain parcell of medow at the lower end of the neck not yet devided where in the fore said John bats hath a right according to proportion: All the fore mentioned medow doth belong to the lot that was formerly Mark Megges: by me

John Corey Rec<sup>or</sup>

(*Deeds, Vol. 1, p. 71.*)

# [RICHARD BRUSH'S LANDS—EAST NECK, SOUTH.]

[1681, June 30.]

Jun 30: 1681.  Richard Brush

The Record of yᵉ medows of Richard Brush lying and on yᵉ south sid of yᵉ Island one part of his medow lyeth on yᵉ east neck next joyning to Santepaug it being in five parsels : The first devision is on the west side of yᵉ neck it being, eight Rods and a half Broad and bounded as followeth on the south with a litell creek that cometh out of yᵉ great Creek neer the mould holes. and on the north with yᵉ lot of Thomas Brush : on the west with the grate creeke and Runing to the midell of the Neck east ward. The second parsell is also on the west side of the neck it being foure Rods Broad : it being bound on the south with yᵉ lot of John Bats : and on the north with the lot of Thomas Brush with yᵉ Creek on the west : and Runing East ward to yᵉ middell of yᵉ neck.

third parsell lying on the same side of yᵉ neck which is allowed by the compeny to Richard Brush : And Thomas brush to mend their west side lots and is Bounded on the south with Joseph whitmans north lot : and then Runing north ward to the Endian : old foot path : with the creeke on the west and the woods on the east : As also the fourth parsell lying on the est side of the neck which is six rods wide : bounded with the lot of Jonas wood on the south : withe yᵉ lot of Epenetus plat on the north with the Creek on the est and Runing to the middill of yᵉ neck west ward : And the fift parcel is bounded with the lot of Jonas wood on the south and the lot of Joseph whitman on the north : with the creek on the est and Runing to the middell of the neck westward it being eight Rods broad it being also on yᵉ est side of the neck : Note that the lower end of the neck is not yet devided where in the said R- Brush hath a Right also.                    by me John Corey, Rec[r]

(*Deeds, Vol.* 1, *p.* 73.)

---

## [LANDS OF JONAS WOOD—EAST NECK, SOUTH.]

[1681, June 30.]

The Records of Jonas Woods J[unr] medow on east neck.

the medow belonging to Jonas wood J[ur] which lyeth on the east neck which neck is next to Santepaug on the east side : The fore mentioned medow is layd out in four parsels and Bounded as followeth : the first parsell is on y[e] west side of y[e] neck in y[e] salt marsh it being nine Rods broad : y[e] lot of John Brush on y[e] north : the lot of John Sammons on y[e] south side and the creek on y[e] west and Runing east ward to y[e] middell of the neck. The second parsell is also on y[e] west side of y[e] neck it being six Rods Broad and bounded on y[e] north with the Town lot : and on the south w[t] y[e] lot of Walter Noks and with the Creek on y[e] west and Runing to the middel of the neck east ward : The third parsell is lying on the east side of the same neck in y[e] lower devition and Bounded on the south with the lot of John Brush : on y[e] north with y[e] lot of Richard Brush on y[e] east with the Creek and Runing to y[e] middell of y[e] neck west ward it being nine Rods broad :—The fourth parsell is also on y[e] east side of y[e] same neck and toward the woods. it being seaven rods Broad and bounded on y[e] south with the lot of John Brush : and on the north with y[e] lot of Richard Brush and with the Creek on y[e] east and Runing west ward to y[e] middel of y[e] neck. The lower end of all y[e] neck not yet devided, where in the said Jonas hath also A Right acording to proportion : Jun [th] 30, 1681 by mee

                                        John Corey Rec[r]

(*Deeds, Vol.* 1, *p.* 79.)

## [LANDS OF JOHN BRUSH—EAST NECK, SOUTH.]

[1681, June 30.]

Jun 30: 1681.   Recorded—John Brush.

The medow that belongeth to John brush lying on yᵉ east neck next east ward joyning to Santepaug: The first parsell lying on yᵉ west side of yᵉ above sd. East Neck in yᵉ sault marsh and bounded on the south with lot of Jonas wood and on the north with the lot of John bats, with yᵉ creek on the west and Runing eastward in sault and fresh to yᵉ middell of the neck: it being seaven Rods broad: The second parsell is also on yᵉ same neck on the west side, it being foure Rods broad and Bounded on the south with yᵉ lot of Epenetus platt, on the north with yᵉ lot of Edward kecham: with the Creek on the west, and Runing east ward to the woods or midell of the neck; The third parsell is lying on the east side of yᵉ neck: the above sd. east neck, it being six Rods and a halfe broad bounded on yᵉ south with the lot of Thomas Brush and on the north with the lot of Jonas Wood: The Creek on yᵉ east and Runing west ward to the middell of the neck –

The fourth lot or parsell is lying on the same side of the above sd. east neck it being five Rods broad and bounded with the lot of John Bats on yᵉ south side and on the North side with yᵉ lot of Jonas wood: The Creek on yᵉ east and Runing west ward to yᵉ middell of the neck: As also a Right in a parsell of medow at the lower end of the same neck not yet devided

by me John Corey, Recᵒʳ

(Deeds, Vol. 1, p. 89.)

[LANDS OF EPENETUS PLATT—EAST NECK,

SOUTH.]

[1681, June 30.]

The 30 of Jun. 1681. Epenetus Platt.
The Record of y$^e$ medow belonging Epenetus platt and lying on y$^e$ south side of the Island : on a neck called the est neck next to Santepaug estward. the fore mentioned medow is layd out in fower parcels the first is on the west side of y$^o$ neck in y$^e$ south marsh it being ; nine ; Rods Broad and Bounded with the town lot on the north and with the lot of walter noks on the south side : with the creek on the west and Runing estward to the middell of the neck : The second parsell is also on the west side of y$^e$ neck bounded on the south with the Town Lott : and on y$^e$ north with the lott of John Brush : it being six Rods Broad Bounded with y$^e$ creek on the west and Runing to the middill of y$^e$ neck est ward : The third parsell is on the est side of the neck it being nine Rods and a halfe Broad and bounded on the south with y$^e$ lot of Richard Brush and on the north with the lot of John Sammous with the creek on the est. and Runing to the middell of the neck westward. The fourth parsell is also on the est side of the neck ; it Being five Rods and a halfe Broad and Bounded on the south with y$^e$ lot of John Samous : on the north with y$^e$ lot of walter noks with the creeke on the est and Runing to the middell of the neck west ward.
As also haveing a Right of pro. to the lower end of the neck not yet devided.

By me John Corey, Reco$^r$

(*Deeds, Vol.* 1, p. 75.)

## [LANDS OF JOSEPH WHITMAN, EAST NECK, SOUTH.]

[1681.]

1681. The Record of Joseph Whitmans medow.
The medow belonging to Joseph whitman lying on the
east neck on y<sup>e</sup> south sid of y<sup>e</sup> Island on y<sup>e</sup> east sid oft he
Creeck : The first parsell is on the east sid of y<sup>e</sup> neck it being eight Rods broad and bounded on y<sup>e</sup> south with the
Town lot and on the north with the lot of John Sammous
and on y<sup>e</sup> east with y<sup>e</sup> medow of Thos. Brush and a littel
creek the second parsell is also on y<sup>e</sup> same side of y<sup>e</sup> neck
and bounded on the south with Richard brush : and on y<sup>e</sup>
north with the Town lot : with the Creek on y<sup>e</sup> east and
Runing west ward to the middell ot y<sup>e</sup> neck it being eleven
rods broad as also a Right in the lower end of y<sup>e</sup> neck not
yet devided.

by me John Corey Reco<sup>r</sup>

(*Deeds, Vol.* 1, *p.* 85.)

---

## [THE MINISTER'S RATES WHICH THOMAS POWELL REFUSED TO PAY.]

[1681.]

thomas powell* debter to y<sup>e</sup> minister Rates as appears by
y<sup>e</sup> accounts following :

|  | £ | s. | d. |
|---|---|---|---|
| In y<sup>e</sup> yeare 1676 . . . . . . | 1 | 15 | 00 |
| In y<sup>e</sup> yeare 1677 dewe . . . . | 1 | 13 | 03 |
| In y<sup>e</sup> yeare 1678 dewe . . . . . | 1 | 09 | 06 |
| In y<sup>e</sup> yeare 1679 dew . . . . . | 1 | 10 | 09 |
| In y<sup>e</sup> yeare 1680 dew , . . . . | 1 | 02 | 05 |
| in y<sup>e</sup> yeare 1681 dew . . . . . | 1 | 04 | 11 |
|  | 8 | 15 | 10 |

(*Court Rec., p.* 414.)

---

[*Elsewhere we noted the fact that Thomas Powell was a
Quaker, and as such he refused to pay the tax annually levied

## [SETTLEMENT OF THE ESTATE OF ADAM
## WHITEHEAD.]

[1681, July 12.]

Whare as Adam Whithead late ot Huntington deceased, $y^e$ last end of augost 1681 and left some small estate behind him. The then present Constable as law did direct take an Inventory there of and an Aprisement also which did amount to £12 : 07s : od : And did with all set up proclemation that who so ever $y^e$ deceased were in debted to should bring in their just debt to $y^e$ Constable the which being don his debts appers to be £2 10s. 1d. : and that his just debts may be payed and $y^e$ Remainder Rightly disposed of to the next In Relation : The present Conste. & overseers doe order, as followeth that John Inckison father-in-law to $y^e$ dessesed shall administer of $y^e$ Estate, and pay out of $y^e$ estate first all Just debts : And $y^t$ he shall pay to Thomas whithead 3£ : and to $y^e$ 2 sisters £2 15s. each sister and $y^e$ Remainder being £1 6s. 11d. : The said John Inckison to have for his pains and trouble provided that $y^e$ said John Inckison give his bond to $y^e$ Constable and over seers for the true parformance here of according to the true Intendment of $y^e$ Con$^{ste}$. & over seers And that the sd John Inckison shall pay the sums to Thos. whithead brother to the

---

for the support of a Puritan minister. As has been already stated, the Duke's Laws compelled the people of the towns to build churches and support the ministry, and at a later period the Court of Assize made an order that the ministers' rates should be paid by those whose property was assessed for taxation, whether they believed in the particular form of worship maintained or not. It is evident from the purport of several records that there was a bitter feeling here against Thomas Powell on account of his refusal to pay the church rates. I think some of his property was finally sold to meet the charge. It may be here mentioned that, under the Duke's Laws, to explicitly "deny the true God" was punishable by death.—C. R. S.]

deseassed and Jemima and Elizabeth Whithead sisters to
the deceased, when he coms to the eage of 21 years and to
the sisters at eighteen years or at the day of their marriage.

Constable JONATHAN ROGERS

Huntington          Overseers {  THOS. WICKS
    July 12ᵗʰ 1681.               THOS. WHITSON
                                 THOS. POWELL
this is a true Copie of the originall Compared by me
                            John Corey, Clerk.

*(Court Rec., p. 256.)*

Bee it known to all whome it may conserne that I Jonathan Lewis of huntington doe acknowledg to have Received full satisfaction for that part of yᵉ estate which Adam
whithead deceased left to Jemimah whithead his sd. sister
who now being yᵉ wife of me Jonathan Lewis I doe owne
yᵉ above sd. as witnesse my hand.

                            JONATHAN LEWES
p John Corey, Clark, december 31. 1683
    *(Court Rec., p. 416.)*

---

[DEED.   JOHN FINCH TO NICHOLAS ELLIS.]

[1681, July 15.]

The Record of Nicholas Elles        This deed of gift is
                                    made voyd all but
                                    yᵉ medow owned by
                                    John finch and Nic-
                                    olas Elles to me John
                                    Corey Recorᵈ

To all Cssian, peopell to whome this pʳsent writing shall
come I John finch: of huntington upon long Island in yᵉ
est Riding of yorkshire husbandman : have of my owne
vollentary and free will given and granted being in my

power so to doe. unto Nicolas Elles of huntington upon long Island in y$^e$ est Riding of yorkshire afore sd. husband man : part of my home lot : sittuate and lying in huntington afore. sd. the lot of Thom$^s$ whitson on the east side y$^u$ frunt to y$^e$ hieway or street the nort or noreweast my lot the Reare the woods in commondge the length sisty seaven Rods the Breadth nine Rod and half with what fruit trees is with in that Compas, I say all my Right title and Intrust in that part of my home lott ; with a hundred pound Right of Comonadge. and four acres of medow or my halfe part of medow lying and being on the south side of y$^e$ Island on A neck of medow called by the name of y$^e$ littell east neck I say all y$^e$ fore mentioned lands, medows and pastures : and every part and parcell there of I the afore named John finch $^{senir}$ : have alinated and estranged from me my heirs executors administrators and assignes unto the sd. Nicolas Elles his heirs executors administrators and assignes for ever to have hould use occopie and injoy without any fraud trouble or molestation : of any person or persons what soever together with all previledgs proffits or Reveneus there to belonging or ever here after shall belong : by any way or means what so-ever, only I the said John finch doth Resarve libarty to live in the hous with Nicollas Elles and mary his wife : after he have built on, for the terme of my life : if the sd. Nicolas and mary his wife chance so long to live : and stay or live in huntington : but if the said Nicollas elles chanch to leave huntington and should sel the fore mentioned premises or any part or parcell, there of that then I the sd John finch $^{senr}$ or my son John finch J$^{nr}$ or either of our assignes shall have the first Refusall : of such sale so tendered at an other mans price in witnesse whereof I have here unto sot my hand and seale in the 15 day of July : In y$^e$ 33 yeare of his Maties Raine and in y$^e$ yeare of our lord 1681.

JOHN FINCH

signed sealed and in y$^e$
presents of the mark of
ALES × BAYLYE
JOSEPH BAYLYE.

                    This is A true copie extracted of the
                    originall by.
                                    mee John Corey Rec$^r$

    (*Deeds, Vol.* 1, *p.* 77.)

---

## [DEED. ABIAL TITUS TO RICHARD BRUSH.]

[1681, July 18.]

This writing witnesseth y$^t$ I abiall Titus of huntington in
y$^e$ est Riding of yorkshier on long Island : have for a Reasonable consideration alredy Received in hand sould a
Cartain parsell of medow lying on y$^e$ south side of y$^e$
Island unto Richard Brush it being bounded as followeth :
it being y$^e$ south est corner of my medow containing about
halfe an acre be it more or be it lesse : it is neere or alto-
gether compessed with a littel creek from all the Rest of
my medow : on y$^e$ est side with y$^e$ lot of Thom$^s$ Brush :
with y$^e$ Sound on y$^e$ south : I the above sd. abiall Titus
have barganed sould estranged and made over from me
my heires executors, administrators and assignes all my
Right title and intrest that I have in & to the medow
above mentioned unto Richard Brush his heires executors,
administrators and asignes to have and to hold and peacably to Injoy for ever as witnesse 18 of July 1681. as witnesse
my hand

                                    ABIEL TITUS

  JOHN CORE Recor$^{dr}$ witnes.
    (*Deeds, Vol.* 1, *p.* 73.)

[DEED. BENJAMIN JONES TO THOMAS FLEET.]

[1681, July 27.]

July 27. 1681. Thomas ffleetts, Record of half neck medow.

This writing witnesseth to whom it may consern y$^t$ I Benjemen Jones: of huntington in y$^e$ East Riding of york shire on long Island husband man: have for a reasonable consideration alredy Recaived in hand, whare of and where with I am fully satisfied and payed: sould all my Right title & intrust that I have in a one hundred pound Right of medow: unto Cap$^{tn}$ Thomas ffleett of y$^e$ above sd. towne and Riding. The above sd. medow is lying on y$^e$ south sid of y$^e$ Island: on the west side of y$^e$ halfe neck and bounded with the lot of Moses Scuder, on the south: and with the Creek on y$^e$ west.

I the above sd. benjemen Jones have sould  *  *  *  * me my heirs executors administrators or asignes: Unto the above sd. Cap$^{tn}$ Thomas ffleett his heirs Executors administrators or assignes all my Right title and intrust that I have in y$^e$ above said medow: all the Right that I have on that neck: and y$^e$ above sd. Jones doe bind myselfe, my heirs executors administrators or assigns from molesting troubling or hindering him y$^e$ above sd ffleett or his heires or successors   And by vertue of these he may have use occopie and injoy the above said medow for ever: to the premises above written I have set to my hand In the presents of.

JOHN CORE, Reco$^r$        BENJAMIN JONES.
(*Deeds, Vol.* 1, *p.* 81.)

## [DEED. JOSEPH WHITMAN TO EDWARD KETCHAM.]

[1681, Aug. 2.]

### The Record of Edward kecham

This writing testefieth to whome it may consern that I Joseph Whitman of huntington in y⁰ east Riding of york sheir on long Island have sold unto Edward Kecham of the above sd. town and Riding tow parsels of medow lying on the south side of y⁰ Island on A neck called y⁰ east neck next to santepaug. The firs parsell is in the sault marsh it being eight Rods broad : and Bounded with the Town lot on y⁰ south : and the lot of John Samons on y⁰ North and with y⁰ Creek on the west and Runing to y⁰ middell of the neck east ward : boath sault and fresh : The second parsell is also eight Rods Broad and bounded with y⁰ woods on the north side and also one parsell of medow belonging to Thomas B. and Richard Brush lying on one part of the fore sd. north side : bounded also on the east with the woods in Comonege : and with lot of John Brush on y⁰ south side : and with the Creek on the west end.

The tow : fore mentioned parsels of medow I the above sd. Joseph witman have bargaed sould alienated and es-tranged : for a reasonable consideration alredy Receaived in hand where of and where with I doe acknowledge my self fully satisfied, contented and payed : from me my heires executors administrators and assignes unto Edward Kecham his heirs—executors administrators and assignes to have hold nse ocupie posses and peacably to Injoy for ever : to witnesse the truth of the above written premises I have here unto set my hand this 2 day of august 1681.

It is to be under stood the two
parsels of medow above mentioned
are boath lying on y⁰ west side

of the east neck, fower words
scratched out ; in y[e] fift line [be]-
fore the signing here of witnesse
John Core Reco[r]

JOSEPH WHITMAN

(*Deeds, Vol.* 1, *p.* 83.)

---

[TOWN MEETING.]

[1681, Sept. 24.]

Sept. 24, 1681.

At a town meeting, legally warned, it was voted to make
choice of one or two men to be deputies to act in the town's
behalf with the Assembly that in this place shall meet to
consider of such things as shall be thought good for the
publick.

The day first above written Capt. Thomas Fleet and
Isaac Platt are chosen deputies for this town.*

[Copy from an original recorded at p. 48 of the Court
Records. Copied and inserted in the revision in the year
1873.]

(*Town Meetings, Vol.* 1, *p.* 93 *and Court Rec., p.* 48.)

---

[*There was at this period discontent and hostility in all the
towns growing out of the arbitrary and tyrannical conduct of
the then Colonial Governor, Sir Edmund Andross. The people had little voice in public affairs, and to protest against this
state of things, assemblies of the people met to discuss public
matters. It was such an assembly that was now called to meet
in Huntington, and to which Thomas Fleet and Isaac Platt
were chosen deputies. The calling of this assembly was a bold
move, for in April previous, Isaac Platt, Epenetus Platt, Samuel
Titus, Jonas Wood and Thomas Weeks, all of Huntington, were
arrested and put in prison in New York without trial, on a
charge of having attended meetings for the purpose of devis-
ing means for redressing public grievances. The recall of
Andross to England prevented further aggressive measures.—
C. R. S.]

## [DEED.  JONATHAN SCUDDER TO JONAS WOOD, Jr.]

[1681, Oct. 3.]

This writing witnesseth to whom it may conserne that I Jonathan Scudder of huntington in y^e east Riding of new york on long Island have sould a certain parsell of land lying and being in y^e east feild unto Jonas Wood ^Junr of y^e sd. town & Riding for a reasonable consideration alredy Receved in hand whare of and where with I doe acknouledg my self fully satisfied, contented and payed, I say I have Barganed sold and made over frome me my heirs executors admi^s and assignes unto Jonas Wood afore sd. his heirs executors administrators and asignes y^e fore sd. land foure acres be it more or be it less  bounded  as followeth y^e south with y^e cart way : y^e west with y^e lot of Cap^tn Joseph bayly y^e noth to y^e woods in Common, y^e east with y^e lot of Jonathan harnet and further I the fore sd. Jonathan Scudder doe ingadge my self my heirs executors, admin^r and assignes to bare harmelesee and undemnefied the fore sd. Jonas wood his heirs, executors administrators and asignes from any person or persons y^t shall lay any just or lawfull claime to y^e fore sd. land y^t he y^e sd, Jonas wood and his may hold it in quiat posession for ever, as witness my hand this 3 of october 1681.

JONATHAN SCUDDER.

John Corey Rec^r
   (*Deeds, Vol.* 1, *p.* 79.)

---

## [TROUBLE WITH THE INDIANS.]

[1681, Oct, 10.]

huntington Could Spring ^th 10 of october 1681 John Robison being about y^e age of 27 years saith upon oath y^t on y^e

7 day of this present month at night. An Indean named pauwas, demanded his gun of me and I Refused and Tom y$^e$ endian in y$^e$ mean time stole a gun from me which was in poun for debt or took it from me and hide, y$^e$ sd. gun; and came & helped pauwas against mee and y$^e$ sd. Tom had pauwas fetch y$^e$ pail & he would fill it with Rum, and so when they had drank y$^t$ they would have more and when they had drunk y$^t$ they came and broke open y$^e$ dore and Roulled out y$^e$ Barrill of Rum, while they did it two other Indians named memicksieys and Ahunshin they garded me with their guns coked threatening to shoot mee if I Resisted Ahunshing bad me bring out my tobackah and my venison which accordingly I did; not daring to Refuse further more whilest they were drinking out y$^e$ paile of Rum I hid an Anker of Rum abroad : which they found y$^e$ sd Anker of Rum ; and ware seen the next morning by another Indean named whatnews a drinking the Rum, and the Rum and anker be gone from me, but in y$^e$ night afore sd. I be in afraide of our lives my wife with me shut our selves in y$^e$ inward Rome the Indians Broake open the dower upon us ; and took what they pleased and went forth to drinking in the mean while we locked our cheasts or boxes, and fleed privetly at a back dore to huntington in y$^e$ night for Relief, they also broke my windows it is to understood that they broke in to the Rome twice before Wee fleed thretned to abuse my wife and thrust her against y$^e$ wall and threw about a peck of salt upon my child in y$^e$ bead and when they went out I bared the dore and fleede as afore sd. privetly while wee ware gone they broke open the windowes and dore and tooke what they pleased ; and spoyled our linen with treading in y$^e$ durt and with grapes they stayned them, but to give a perticuler acount of our loss and damege I cannot yet doe.

(*Court Records, p. 356.*)

[1681, Oct. 10.]

huntington Cold spring, october 10 : 1681. Jane Robison

being about y$^e$ age of 27 yers saith upon [oath] that upon
y$^e$ 7 day of this present month that indens named Tom &
pauwas desired to see a gun that we had in keeping that
they might shew their friend how it was broke and was to
be stocked by John Robison my husband. which gun was
to ly in paun; for debt which gun as soon as Recaived Endian Tom Run away with; and after the departure of david
scudder which was then present the indian named pauwas
asked me for his gun pretending as if he would goe away.
I told him there was his gun he might take it and he toke
it up and went into y$^e$ inward Rome and said he must have
another gun and tooke my husbands gun: but my husband
Refused to let him have his gun, pauwas said he would
have it my husband striving to keep his own gun then in
came Tom and memipeys and they toke his gun from him
by force and gave them to memipeys to keep and he keept
the 3 guns and when we ware disarmed one said to y$^e$
other fetch y$^e$ pail I fearing they would draw Rum I put
out y$^e$ light, and fasned the dore; but memipeys secured
my husband notwith standing he y$^e$ sd. Tom broke up y$^e$
dore and drew about a paile full of Rum and spilt agreat
quantiety besides this don they went into y$^e$ bushies with
y$^e$ Rum but presently turned again and sd. they would
make us yeld to them for they would drink by the fire like
men. and as they did drink they macked us saying com
and drink with us and why doe you not shout us, or com
and shout us, when as they had our gun, so we shut ourselves in y$^e$ inward Rome and bared the dore; we haveing
an anker of Rum: formerly drawn out my husband caryed
it ot a back dore and hide in y$^e$ bushesh. then we locked
our things and lay down on y$^e$ bead when they had disposed of y$^e$ Rum by drinking or other they came and
staved at the dore with their guns and I held y$^e$ dore with
an yorn crow with all my might in y$^e$ meene time my husband looking throw a crives of the clabords to see how
they did act: they presed hard at y$^e$ dore and thretned to

shout us my husband said to me for gods sake open y<sup>e</sup> dore
or they[1] shout us, so I left y<sup>e</sup> dore and they broke it open
and came in ; and my husband came out of y<sup>e</sup> bead Rome
to perswade them to forbare and I stept into y<sup>e</sup> bead Rom
thinking to preserve my child and to save the Rum that
was left in y<sup>e</sup> barrell and pauwas broke in upon me and
the other 3 endians keept my husband from helping me ;
and I striving to save my child and the Rum, they hunched
me and thrust mee against y<sup>e</sup> wall and shelf and barrell
which caused me to cry murther : my husband prayed
me to com out if I could so I got out and beged he would
not kill my child, but he took up a salt box of about a pecke
of salt in it and threw it upon my child ; but y<sup>e</sup> pillows
preserved it, it was but little hurt : then they Rouled out
y<sup>e</sup> barill of Rum then I took up my child to ascape and I
heard them say they would have more things yet and
heard them also command my husband to bring them his
venison, my husband stop to the back dore to me and told
me wee must fly to huntington to save our lives for they
did cok their guns at me and he would make fast the dores,
so wee went to huntington in y<sup>e</sup> night for Releife and I
came home again the next morning. I finding my hous Ran-
sacked my things spoyled that they left my child bed linen
spoiled and trod in y<sup>e</sup> durt my bed tumbled up and thrown
about but to give a just acount of our losses as yet I cannot
wee have lost a considerable quantety of mony, in wam-
pom and silver, 2 blankits and a coat that we now know
wanting.

the anker of Rum is now found in the time of the writing
of this saide, wanting about a gallon of Rum out of it ; it
was removed from y<sup>e</sup> place that my husband set it ; and
was hide in y<sup>e</sup> swamp and further saith not.

(*Court Records, pp. 357-8.*)

[COURT RECORD.  RICHARD WHITE vs.
RICHARD BETTS.]

[1681, Oct. 17.]

October
17-1681

At Acourt held in huntington in y$^e$ Est-Riding of
New York by his Mag$^{ts}$ authoryty The members
where of are Mr Jonas Wood Jus$^{ts}$ of y$^e$ peace.
Mr Wood Refused to sit.

JONATHAN ROGERS, Constable.

THOMAS POWELL ⎫
THOMAS WICKS ⎬ over seers.
THOS. WHISSEN ⎭

Richard Whitte plen$^{te}$ against Richard Botts,
de$^{fnd}$ in an accion of the case.

Richard White pleads y$^t$ where as he formerly was
bound for Richard Bots aperanc at y$^e$ session Court in
South hold : y$^e$ sd Richard White find his securety not
suffitient where upon there is Charge arrisen by his ob-
taining suficent security.

The Court finds for y$^e$ plent$^f$ that y$^e$ defendant shall pay
unto y$^e$ plen$^t$ 9$^s$ with cost of sute.

The Charges.

| | £ | | |
|---|---|---|---|
| for y$^e$ halfe of 2 days expended about giveing in bond . . . . . . . | o | o2 | o6 |
| for 1$^s$ payd y$^e$ Recorder for Recording y$^e$ bond | o | o1 | oo |
| for 1$^s$ 6$^d$ y$^e$ Constable for attaching y$^e$ sloope for better security . . . . | o | o1 | o6 |
| for 1 day expended about y$^e$ above sd . . | o | o2 | o6 |
| for 1$^s$ 6$^d$ for somoning Ric$^d$ Bots to town Court | o | o1 | o6 |

(*Court. Rec., p.* 258.)

[TOWN MEETING.]

[1681, Oct. 31.]

October the 31. 1681

At a town meeting it was voated and granted that

Thomas Powell should take up sixteen acres of land between y^e land of Samuell woods lot and y^e east feild.

the same first above writen: it was also voated and granted y^t Thomas Wicks shall take up foure acres and a half of land adjoyning to Thomas powells land affore said.

the same day it was voated and granted y^t Samuell Wood shall take up ten acars of land adjoining to Tho^s powells land afore sd.

the day above sd. it was voat and granted: y^t Jonathan Miller shall take up six acars of land joyning to Samuell's land afore sd.

the same day it was voated and granted y^t Thomas Whitson shall take up ten acares of land by Jonathan Miller and Samuell Woods land aforesaid.

the same day it was voated and granted y^t Robert Canfield shall take up six acres of land by Richard Whites land in the west neck

The day afore said it was voated and granted that Robr^t Arther shall take up six acars of land next to Robert Canfeilds land afore sd.

The day above said it was voated and granted that Mr Jonas Wood sen^r shall take up ten acars of land towards his division it lying on y^e south side of stony brook path on the East side of y^e town.

Book A.- 74—.

the day above sd. it was voated and granted y^t Isac plat shall take up sixteen or eighteen acres of land towards his division it lying on boath sides of Jonathan harnets grown up hollow: on y^e north side of Stony brook path.

the day above written it was voated and granted that Joseph Baylye shall take up six acres of land towards his division it lying at stony brook joyning to his land there.

it is to bee understood that all y^e severall parsells of land is land of division above written

by me John Corey Record.

October 31. 1681.

at a town meeting the day above said it was voated and granted that James Chichester senior shall take up foure acres of land towards his devision it lying on yᵉ west side of yᵉ head of yᵉ Cove on yᵉ East Neck

The day above written it was voated and granted that Steven Jarvis Junʳ shall take up six acres of land towards his division it lying about yᵉ midell of yᵉ east Neck by abriery swamp.

The same day it was voated and granted yᵗ Robert Cranfeild shall tak up three acres of land towards his division it lying on yᵉ east neck and joyning to the land of Steven Jarvis afore said.

The day above sd. it was voated and granted that Jonathan Rogers shall take up 16 or eighteen acres of land towards his division it lying on yᵉ west neck on yᵉ south side of yᵉ Cove over against John Teeds land which lyeth on yᵉ north sid of yᵉ cove.

the day above said it was voated and granted yᵗ Edward kecham shall tak up three acres of land towards his division it lying at ye East end of wigwam swamp if not prejidditiall to yᵉ town.

The same day it was voated and granted that Samuell kecham shall take up 4 acres of land at yᵉ cove joyning to John Sammous land. yᵉ south end or sid of it: part of it is swamp. The sd four acres of land is towards his division.

Entered New Book A page 75.

(*Town Meetings, Vol.* 1, *pp.* 95–6.)

---

[1681, Nov. 1.]

Thomas ffleetts mark yᵗ he gives his Creatures is A crop on yᵉ neere ear and 2 slits in yᵉ crop.

Thomas ffleet son of Capᵗⁿ Thomas ffleet was maried to Esther parat the first of november in yᵉ yeare 1681.

(*Deeds, Vol.* 1, *p.* 81.)

## [DEED. JOHN FINCH, Sen., TO NICHOLAS ELLIS.]

[1681, Nov. 13.]

Nicalos Elles.

To all Cptian peopell to whome these psents shall com. I John Finch senʳ of huntington upon long Island in yᵉ est Riding of yorkshier Mariner have of my owne vollentary & free will given and granted being in my own power so to doe unto my son in law Nicollas Elles of huntington upon long Island in yᵉ east Riding of york sheir afore said husband man all my Right title and intrust in my hous and home lott yᵗ I now live in formerly in yᵉ tenor or occopation of Trustrum hedges & purchased of me of yᵉ town of hunting : at avandue I say all my Right title and intrust in yᵗ. hous and home lot yᵗ is with in my fence from yᵗ place whare yᵉ petition fence Runs between yᵉ lot yᵗ was formerly in yᵉ tenor or occupation of caleb wood : and so to yᵉ hie way yᵗ leadeth to yᵉ harbour & so to yᵗ lot or land of Robart arthers yᵗ I sold to gorge Belding togather with all Rights and tittels of Comonage there unto be longing or ever after shall be long to yᵉ sd. pr–mises : or any part or parsell there of except what I sould unto gorge Bolding yᵗ he elinated to yᵉ fore sd. arther, but all yᵉ Rest : viz : My hous garding home lot and Comonadge theree unto belonging Which is a two hundred pound Right by denomination I yᵉ fore sd. John finch ˢᵉⁿʳ. have alinated by these presents all my Right title and intrust from me my heirs executors administrators and assignes with foure acres of medow be it more or lesse : or yᵉ half preportion of medow yᵗ I have on a necke of medow on yᵉ south side of yᵉ Island comonly called by yᵉ name of yᵉ littel est neck unto Nicolas Elles his heirs, executors administrators and assignesse : To have and to hold for Ever without any hinderance of him yᵉ sd. John finch sen. or any Claiming from by or under him in consideration where of y⁰ fore sd. Nicolas, doe promis and ingage at y⁰ sealing & delivery here of to Resigne up unto y⁰ fore mentioned John finch ser. yᵗ part of lot with its hundred pound Right of comonadge : with its former deed of gift to be in his own power and disposell : and I y⁰ fore sd John finch senr y⁰ giver of y⁰ fore mentioned premises doe Reserve liberty if he see cause to live in y⁰ hous with Nicollas Elles and mary his wife as long as they or either of them live in huntington : for y⁰ true performence of y⁰ afore mentioned, I have here unto sot my hand and seal this 13ᵗʰ of novemher : in y⁰ 33 yeare of his maᵗⁱᵉˢ Reign and in y⁰ yeare of our lord 1681 : According to y⁰ Computation of The Curch of England.

JOHN FINCH

the mark of

ROGER × GUINT
JOSEPH BAYLY.

This deed of gift was owned by John finch seʳ above sd. to me to be his act and deed before y⁰ Recording of it
    John Corey Recʳ

This is a true copie compered with y⁰ originall by me John Corey, Record. The fore sd. nicolles Elles did own to me yᵗ he Resined up the deed formerly made all but y⁰ medow which is also given in this and is y⁰ true intent.

John Core Record

(*Deeds, Vol.* 1, *p.* 93.)

---

## [THE BROTHERTON FAMILY RECORD.]

[1681, Nov. 17.]

William Broderton sonn of william broderton was Borne y⁰ 17ᵗʰ of may in y⁰ yeer 1678.
John Broderton sonn of william broderton was borne the first day ol may in y⁰ yeer 1686.

Mary Broderton was borne y$^e$ 17$^{th}$ of november in y$^e$ yeer of our lord 1681.

(*Surveys, p.* 160.)

---

## [COURT CHARGES.]

[1681, Nov. 21.]

Nov. 21. 1681.

Thomas Higbie against Sarah Griffin

The charges of y$^e$ cort afore sd. anseth as followeth.

|  | £ | s. | d. |
|---|---|---|---|
| for y$^e$ Constable and 3 overseers | o | 07 | o6 |
| for the entry y$^e$ accion and judgment | o | 05 | o6 |
| for entry of 7 testimonys | o | 04 | o6 |
| for y$^e$ entry of y$^e$ accounts andcharges | o | 03 | oo |
| for y$^e$ constable summoning Thomas higbe & Samuell Griffin to court | o | 03 | oo |
| for supeny for witnes | o | oo | o6 |
| for entring a venere | o | o1 | oo |
| for y$^e$ Constable Troubels in taking bond | o | o1 | o6 |

(*Court Rec, p.* 381.)

---

## [DEED. JONN FINCH, Sen., TO JOHN FINCH, Jr., THENCE TO EDWARD HIGBEE.]

[1681, Nov. 30.]

A Record of y$^e$ deed of gift to John ffinch Ju$^r$.

To all Cspian peopell to whome these p$^r$sents shall com I John ffinch of huntington in y$^e$ east Riding of yorkshire Marriner: did by mine indever purches an acomandation or a tow hundred pound alotment of one Samuell davis,

then of faire feild Within y^e Colony of Conyticott with all
its Rits and previlledges boath of upland and medow also
on more a lotment of y^e town of huntington at a vandue
formerly in y^e tenor or ocupation of one trustrum hodges,
with all its Rights and previledges both of upland and
medow which rite of upland both hous and home lot with
all its Rights and previledge y^t doth or ever here after may
there to belong : with half my Rite of medow on a neck of
medow on y^e south side of y^e Island called by y^e name of
y^e litel east neck formerly belonging to y^t Alotment purchased of Samuell davis : afore sd : I have past away by
deed of gift unto my son in law Nicolas Elles : And what
so ever y^t I John finch sen^r have not past away as afore sd :
I doe by this deed of gift pas over by this deed of gift unto
my dugtyfull son John ffinch Jun^r after my deseas ; his
heirs and sucsessers for ever that is to say my home lot &
orchyard, situat & lying in huntington adjoyningt o y^e lot
of Thomas Whitson with all its Rits and priveledge of lands
devided & undevided : as also eight acars of medow lying
on y^e south side of y^e Island on aneck called by y^e name of
santepaug which is a tow hundred Rite of medow formerly
belonging to y^e lot of trustum hedgges : with my other
half share or hundred pound Rite of medow on a neck of
medow called by y^e name of y^e litle east neck, always belonging to y^t purchesed of Samuell davis afore mentioned :
I say all my Rite titel and intrust in my two hundred
pounds Rite of upland : with home lot & orchyard with y^e
fore mentioned three hundred pound Rite of medow land,
I have past as afore sd to my well beloved and dutyfull son
John ffinch Jun^r he his heirs executors administrators and
assignes. To have and to hold forever. and doe by these
p^rsents according to y^e custom of y^e law of England before
y^e sealing & deliverying : deliver unto my beloved son on
iron pottadg putt in lew of y^e fore mentioned p^rmoses in
witnesse whereof I have here unto set my hand & seal : the
last day of november in y^e 33 yeare of his mag^tie Raine :

And in yᵉ year of our lord ; according to yᵉ Church of England 1681.

signed, sealed and delivered }    JOHN FFINCH ˢᵉⁿʳ
in pʳsents of us whose names }
are here subscribed.

the mark of
ROGER ✕ GUINT
JOSEPH BAYLY.

A. true copie of yᵉ orıgınall compared by me John Corey Recoʳ: and owned by John finch senʳ to be his act and deed.

(*Deeds, Vol.* 1, *p.* 101.)

---

Know all men by these pʳsents yᵗ I John finch Junʳ of Huntington on Long Island in yᵉ east Riding of new york. shire doe for my self my heirs executors, administrators & assignes fully & absolutly by thes presents allinate and asigne set over & confirme unto Edward higby of Huntington all my Right title & intrust in yᵉ within written deed gift of accomunondations all yᵉ pʳveleedges and apertenances there unto belonging from me John finch afore sd. for him yᵉ sd. Edward Higby his heirs, executors, administrators and assignes to have and to hold possesse improve injoye from yᵉ day of yᵉ date here of for ever peasfull and free and ample maner in all Respects what so ever as I yᵉ sd. John finch ever was to doe by vertue of this within written deed of gift affirming yᵉ sd. Edward Higby That yᵉ sd. accommondation is free from gifts grants morgdges or assignments made by me and here assigned by me yᵉ sd. John finch and made over from me my heirs executors and assignes or any other person Laying claime from by or under yᵉ sd. John ffinch, And for confirmation here of I have here unto set my hand & seale this 6ᵗʰ of October

in yᵉ yeare 1683, signed, sealed delivered in presents of us
witnesses IERENUS ADAMS, RICHARD WHITE.

JOHN FFINCH

the above sd is Recorded The 17ᵗʰ of January 1683 p.

John Corey<br>Clerk.

(*Deeds, Vol.*, 1, *p.* 102.)

---

## [DEED. JOHN EVERETT TO SAMUEL KETCHAM.]

[1681, November.]

Sold by John Everrit: his hom lot being four acres, barganed sold and made over from yᵉ said John his heirs &
assignes, to Samuell kecham his heirs and assignes all his
Right & Intrust in & to yᵉ 4 acres of land being his hom
lott: haveing Receaved full satisfaction alredy in hand I
say I have sold and estranged from me my heirs & assignes
to yᵉ said Samuell his heirs & assignes To have And to
hold ffor ever.  This a true copie extracted out of yᵉ originall by me John Corey Recʳ
november 1681.

Recorded by order of John Everrit<br>by me Thomas powell, Recʳ

it is to be under stood that yᵉ above said lot is joyning to
yᵉ west side of Richard Whites home lot. yᵉ north to yᵉ
hie way yᵉ south & west to yᵉ woods in common by me
John Corey, Recʳ

(*Deeds, Vol.* 1, *p.* 91 )

---

[1681, Dec. 15.]

Joseph Wood, husbandman, was married to Euenice Jarves the 15ᵗʰ day of December 1681.

(*Court Records, p.* 350.)

## [RECORD OF LANDS OF PHILIP UDALE.]

[1681, Dec. 16.]

The Record of Phillip Udale, Land and medow.

To all Cristin people to whome these presents shall com : Whereas there was a marage sollemnised between phillip udele, son of phillip udele of flushen in y$^e$ west Riding of york. of y$^e$ on party & mary baly daughter of Joseph Bayly of huntington in y$^e$ east Riding of york shire afore sd of y$^e$ other party : know y$^e$ y$^t$ I y$^e$ afore sd. Joseph Bayly have given and granted and made over unto y$^u$ fore sd. Phillip udel and mary his wife her heirs, executors, administrators and asignes half my farme lying and being with in y$^e$ Bounds of huntington above said at a place called and known by y$^e$ name of y$^o$ fresh pond : bounded on y$^e$ east side with y$^e$ hassokie meddow or swamp at y$^e$ head of y$^e$ sd. pond : on y$^e$ south & west with y$^e$ woods in comonnage : on y$^e$ north with a litel hollow and y$^e$ land of y$^e$ fore sd. Baly : also y$^e$ south part or halfe of my medow : lying on y$^e$ east side of Crabmedow : Bounded with y$^e$ woods y$^e$ east end : and y$^e$ south side with y$^e$ medow belonging to thomas Skidmor or Willam Broterton together with all Rites and priveledges as doth or ever here after may belong to the afore sd. half farme : I say all my Right title and Intrust I have made over and estranged as afore sd. provided y$^e$ sd. phillip udel and mary his wife doe not give grant nor estrange y$^e$ fore mentioned promises nor any part nor parsell there of. But after y$^e$ deseas of y$^e$ afore mentioned phillip and mary his wife : to Remaine and falle to mary udele daugter of y$^e$ afore sd. phillip and mary : But if y$^e$ sd. mary chance to die unposessed of y$^e$ fore sd. land and medow : then to fale to y$^e$ next suckseesfull heire of y$^e$ fore named mary udele and if y$^e$ sd: phillip udele chance to die before mary his wife : the heirs of y$^e$ said phillip and mary, Shall not claime any part there in, untill

after y<sup>e</sup> desease of y<sup>e</sup> sd. mary : And then to Remaine and
be in y<sup>e</sup> powre & possesion of y<sup>e</sup> sd. mary udele daughter
of y<sup>e</sup> fore mentioned mary udele or her heirs if any or to
y<sup>e</sup> next sucksesfull heir : for which end I have estranged
y<sup>e</sup> fore mentioned p<sup>r</sup>mises and every part and parcell there
of with all its Rites and priveleges unto phillip udele and
mary his wife. their heirs or heirs as aforesaid. to have and
to hold forever. In witnesse whereof I have here unto set
my hand & seale <sup>th</sup> 16 of december ; in y<sup>e</sup> 33 of his ma<sup>ties</sup>
Rain : and in y<sup>e</sup> yeare of our lord according to y<sup>e</sup> computation of y<sup>e</sup> curch of England 1681.

JOSEPH BAYLY
the mark of
ALES × BAYLY

signed sealed and delivered.
In y<sup>e</sup> preasants of y<sup>e</sup> mark of
NICOLLES × ELLES
MARIA ELLES

> A true copie of y<sup>e</sup> originall Com-
> pared by me John Corey Record-
> And owned by Joseph Baly to be
> his act and : deed before y<sup>e</sup> entry
> hereof.
> Jenuery th 10: 168½.

(*Deeds, Vol.* 1, *p.* 97.)

---

## [JONATHAN LEWIS TO THOMAS SCIDMORE.]

[1682, Jan. 11.]

Know all men by these p<sup>r</sup>sents y<sup>t</sup> I Jonathan Lewis of
y<sup>e</sup> Town of westberly In y<sup>e</sup> Colony of Road Island in new
England doe bind myself my heires executors administra-
tors or assinges to pay or cause to be payed unto thomas
skidmor Jun<sup>r</sup> of Huntington In y<sup>e</sup> East Riding of york

shire on long Iland husbandman him his heires executors administrators or assignes y$^e$ full & just sume of three score and twelve pounds : In good and merchantable beife porke winter wheat sumer wheat and Indeau corne In somes and maner following : That is to say 12$^{1b}$ p year for six years going untill y$^e$ whole three score and twelve pounds be payed viz : The firs £12 is to be payed in y$^e$ year 1684 at or before y$^e$ 10$^{th}$ of march : The second payment is to be payed at or before y$^e$ 10 of march in y$^e$ year 1685. The third payment to be made and payed at or before y$^e$ 10$^{th}$ of march in y$^e$ year 1686. The forth payment to be payed at or before 10$^{th}$ of March in y$^e$ year 1687. The 5$^{th}$ payment to be payed at or before y$^e$ 10$^{th}$ of march in y$^e$ year 1688. the 6$^{th}$ and Last payment to be made y$^e$ 10$^{th}$ of March in y$^e$ year 1689 or before y$^e$ 10$^{th}$ of March next above sd. and all y$^e$ above s$^d$ payments to be payed and delivered at any one house in Huntington where y$^e$ above s$^d$ Thomas skidmore or his successors shall from yeare to yeare give order. And y$^e$ above sd. Thomas skidmore shall provid a team on his own charge to draw all y$^e$ sd. payments to Huntington, all which pay is for and in consideration of a halfe farme sould unto y$^e$ above Bounden Jonathan Lewis with all its Rights and priveledges mentioned at large in y$^e$ bill of sale all which I y$^e$ above said Jonathan Lewis doe assigne and make over y$^e$ above sd. Thomas skidmore his heires executors administrators and assignes untill y$^e$ fore sd. three score and twelve pounds be fully answered and payed the yearly payment in beife at 2$^d$ per pound Round, porke at 3$^d$ per pound winter wheat at 5$^s$ p bushell sumer wheat 4$^s$ 6$^d$ per bushell Indian corn at 2$^s$ 6$^d$ pr bushell And further if y$^e$ above sd. farme be forfit for want of y$^e$ full performence of y$^e$ above $^{sd}$ payments Then it shall be Lawfull by vartue of these for y$^e$ above sd. Thomas skidmore his heires executors administrators or assinges if he or either of them shall see cause to take all y$^e$ afore sd. Lands again from y$^e$ sd. Jonathan Lewes or his successors and y$^e$ said Jonathan

Lewis shall allow £4 10s. per yer as Rent. And yᵉ sd. Thomas shall Returne yᵉ over plush if any In such as he did Receive And pay it to any hous in huntington where yᵉ sd. Lewes or his successors shall order and to yᵉ true performance here of I have here unto set my hand and seale this eleventh of Jenueary 1682.

Witness                                   JONETHEN LEWIS
 JOHN COREY
 SAMUELL GRIFFEN

      This is a true coppy taken by
      me John Corey Clerk

            1682

decembr yᵉ 29. 1688. Thomas skidmore came before mee and did acknowledge hee had Received the full contents of the bill of Jonathan lewises above written as witnesse my hand. Isaac Platt

    Recʳ                    the mark of ✕ THOMAS
           SKIDMORE.

(*Court Rec., pp.* 403-4.)

---

## [FINED FOR TRAVELING ON SUNDAY.]

[1682. Jan. 29.]

huntington Jan yᵉ 29ᵗʰ 1682.

Return Davis aged about 45 yeres testfieth yᵗ upon a Lords day not long since, towards night I in my hous heard yᵉ sound of a hors troting. I Looked out and saw Robart kellam on hors back coming from oyster bay haveing a bag under him which had yᵉ like of 6 pecks in it as I thought & I supposed it was meal And I asked him why he set out from oyster bay on yᵉ lords day to come home he said it was not lords day for it was night I said look yonder, I think yᵉ sun is half an hour hie and I belive you came out of oyster bay about yᵉ begining of yᵉ afternoon meeting and I told him I thought he wold be taken notis of. I also asked him whethcr he had got his meal now he said yes he could not have it soon anouf to com hom yester day and further saith not.

In y^e absence of y^c justis sworne before me p. Isack Platt.

Thomas weeks being sworn saith y^t he was at John kecham hous on a lords day towards night and I saw Robart kellem coming from oyster on hors back with a bag under him and further saith not.

the action is entred on y^c back side of y^e 23 page or 24.

(*Court Rec., p.* 373.)


At a town court held in huntington Jan. 29, 1682 by his magist authoryty. The member where of are Mr Jonas wood Justis of y^e peace.

Isack plat Constable
Samuell ketcham
Thomas whitson
Epenetus platt, overseers.
James Smith

The evidence are Tho: wicks & Return Davis entred on y^e first page.

a complaint entered against Robart kellem for braking y^e sabath by traviling and caring of a burdin and the Court finding it Leagely proved.

The court sentence is that y^e sd. Robart kellam shall pay twenty shilling or make such an acknowledgment as y^e Court shall except of and pay what is dew to y^e court.

| The court Charges | - | - | - | - | 0 | 12 | 06 |
| The Constables fees | - | - | - | - | 0 | 05 | 00 |
| The Clerks fees | - | - | - | - | 0 | 03 | 11 |

(*Court Rec., p.* 394.)

## [TOWN MEETING. THE IMPRISONED MEN TO HAVE AN ALLOWANCE.]

[1682, April 1.]

Apr. 1. 1682.

At a town meeting legally warned it was voted and granted by the major part of the town that John Adams shall have the town's right of the stream commonly called and known by the name of Cold Spring to set up a good sufficient grist-mill and saw-mill upon it the said John Adams would take it upon such conditions as the constable and overseers (with so many of the neighbors as they shall chose) shall make with him in behalf of the town.

[These are the names of those that are to make the above said covenant.]

Isaac Platt, Constable  
Tho. Whitson ⎤  
Sam¹ Kecham ⎰ Over  
Epen. Platt ⎱ seers  
Jas. Smith ⎦

Them of the neighbors that they have [chosen] are.  
⎡ Mr Jonas Wood, Senʳ  
⎪ James Chichester Senʳ  
⎪ Saml Titus  
⎪ Rich. Brush  
⎪ John Kecham  
⎣ John Corey

(*Court Records*, 1681–4, *p.* 1.)

Tho. Powell was chosen constable but he refuseth to serve having scruples of swearing as the law directs. The day above said Epenetus Platt & James Smith [were chosen] overseers.

The day above said it was put to vote whether or no the town would pay the five men that were forced to New York and suffered imprisonment together with their charges & loss of time, viz: Isaac Platt, Epenetus Platt, Saml. Titus, Jonas Wood & Thomas Wicks; it being voted

and granted that they should have allowence out of the
next town rate, it then being put in.
(*Court Records*, 1681-4, *p.* 10.)

Aprill the first 1682.
At a town meeting legally warned Isac platt chosen Constable.  Epenetus platt James Smith overseers.

the day first above written it was voated and granted that
John Wicks shall take up ten acres of land : towards his
division : it lying above ye head of ye hollow y$^t$ goeth to
the old East feild on y$^e$ south side of ye path.

The day above sd it was voated and granted y$^t$ Richard
Brush, Timothy Conkling, Thomas Brush & John Brush
shall take up esh man eight acres of land towards his
division : It lying on the West neck, between the mill ston
brook and John Samous feild y$^t$ lyeth at y$^e$ cove.  (the two
above grants entered Book A. page 75).

The day above sd. it was voated & granted y$^t$ Thomas
Scudder shall take up six acres of land towards his division
if so much found Convenient lying on y$^e$ west or nor west
side of his land lying by y$^e$ harbour on y$^e$ east neck Running between John finches land & y$^e$ sd. Tho$^s$ Scudders
land home to y$^e$ west poynt.

It was voated and granted y$^e$ day above sd. y$^t$ Henry
Soper shall take up eight acres of land towards his division.  It lying on y$^e$ south side of y$^e$ hors neck path over
against y$^e$ new feild y$^t$ lyeth on y$^e$ west neck.

The day above sd.  It was voated and granted y$^t$ Steven
Jarvis sen$^r$ shall take up ten or twelve acers of land towards
his division where hee shall thinke best except found pre-
jedetiall by y$^e$ estimation of y$^e$ surveyors & when layed
out : to be recorded where it lyeth with ye bounds
thereof                                    John Corey Recde.
(the 3 above Entered Book A. 76 page)

The day first above written it was voted and granted
that Epenetus Platt shall take up 16 acres or 18 of land, it
lying on the south side of the old east feild next the Reed
Pond

The day above said it was voted & granted that Nicollas
Ellise shall have ten acres of land towards his division in
the east neck where the surveyors shall see cause; and
then the place and bounds to be recorded.

The day above said it was voted and granted that Rich^d
Williams should have nine acres of land towards his division, it lying at the new field near Horse Neck path, and
bounded on the east by the land ot Edw. Kecham and on
the west with land of Rich^d Whit[man.]

The same day above said it was allowed & granted that
John Corey shall take in so much upland with his piece at
Long Swamp as the surveyors shall see cause.

John Corey, Recorder.

[Copied from Court Records for 1681–4, at the pages
indicated in connection with the several parts, this last
being from p. 15 of the old number, p.     of new, in the
year 1873.]

(Town Meetings, Vol. 1, pp. 97, 99, 101 and 103.)

Aprill y^e ist. 1682. It was granted untoo Thomas brush
That he should have eight acars of land in y^e west neck:

It now being layd out and is eighty Rods in Length and
sixteen in breadth Runing East ward and west ward to y^e
Commons And joyning to y^e land of Richard Brush on y^e
north And to y^e Land of John brush on y^e south it being
towards his divition.

(Deeds, Vol. 1, p. 87.)

Aprille y^e ist: 1682 granted unto John Brush eight acars
of Land towards his diavtion; by y^e major voat of y^e Town:
The sd. land lying on y^e west neck: between Jn^o Sammis
cove lot & y^e mill ston brok: The sd. land is laid out it

Runing eastward and westward to yᵉ commons: being
eighty Rods in Leangth and sixteen in breadth and joyning
to yᵉ Land of Thomas brush on yᵉ * * and to yᵉ Comons
on yᵉ * * *
(*Deeds, Vol.* 1, *p.* 89.)

[1682, April 1.]

Richard Brush Land Recd:
one parcell of Land granted unto Richard Brush Containing foure acres and lying in yᵉ west neck  Bounded on yᵉ
front with yᵉ high way on yᵉ northwest with yᵉ land of
Edward kecham: And on yᵉ south east with yᵉ land of
Samuel kecham.

Aprill yᵉ ist 1682, granted unto Richard Brush Eight
acres of Land towards his division  It lying on yᵉ west
neck being eighty Rods in Length and sixteen in breadth,
Runing East and west to yᵉ Commons And Joyning to yᵉ
Land of Timothy Conkling on yᵉ north and to yᵉ land of
Thomas Brush on yᵉ South.
(*Deeds, Vol.* 1, *p.* 115.)

Aprill yᵉ ist 1682  It was voated and granted by yᵉ
major part of yᵉ Town, That Timothy Conkling shall have
eight acres of land towards his devition lying on yᵉ west
neck: The sd Land is now Layd out being eighty rods
long and Runing East and weast to yᵉ Comons and joyning to yᵉ land of Richard Brush on yᵉ * * * and to
ye * * * * *
(*Deeds, Vol.* 1, *p.* 143.)

[DEED. THOMAS BRUSH TO JOHN SAMMIS.]

[1682, June 12.]

The Records of yᵉ Land of John Sammis
know all men by these pʳsents yᵗ I Thomas Brush of hun-

tington in y$^e$ east Riding of yorkshire on Long Island have barganed & sould eight acres of land unto John Sammis of y above sd. Town and Riding for a reasonable considera- tion alredy Receaived in hand where of & where with I am fully satisfied contented & payed ; The above sd. eaight acres of Land is lying on y$^e$ hill above y$^e$ hous lot of y$^e$ afore sd. John Sammis and bounded with y$^e$ land of samuel titus & Jonathan Scudder on y$^e$ west : on y$^e$ north with y$^e$ land of y$^e$ above sd. Joh Sammis on y$^e$ east & south with y$^u$ commons I say I y$^e$ above sd. Thomas Brush have bar- ganed sould and made over all my Rite titele and intrust y$^t$ I have in & to y$^e$ above sd. eight acres of Land and by these prsents doe bargan sell and make over from me my heirs executors administrators & assignes all my Right title and intrust y$^t$ I have in & to y$^e$ above sd. eight acres of land unto John Sammis his heirs, executors, administra- tors and assignes to have hold use and quiatly posesse for ever without any let or molestation by me or by any means of mine as witnesse my hand this 12$^{th}$ of June 1682

Witnesse                                    THOMAS BRUSH
JOHN COREY        )
JONAS WOOD Junr. ) This is A true coppy compared with
                y$^e$ originalle by me John Corey, Rec$^r$
    (*Deeds, Vol.* 1, *p.* 111.)

---

[TOWN MEETING. SALE BY BURNING AN
INCH OF CANDLE. EPENETUS PLATT
SENT TO YORK WITH A PETITION.]

[1682. June 26.]

June the 26$^{th}$ 1682.

It was voted and agreed by the major part of the town that the Hassokey swamp over against Jonathan Rogers and joyning to James Chichester Sen[rs] home lot shall be sold at a vandue by the burning of an inch of candle : and so many improve for some public use for the town as the Constable and Overseers shall see cause. And the said swamp to be sold for good and merchantable pay of this country at merchantable price, and to be payed at or before the first of May next [after] the date hereof. And he that buyeth the said swamp shall pay as aforesaid ; and, if the whole sum be not paid at the day appointed, shall forfeit five shillings per week for every week till the whole debt be paid as aforesaid. And the said forfeit shall also be for the town's use.

It is to be understood that a highway against the swamp shall be 4 rods wide between Jonathan Roger's [and] Henry Soper's lots and the said swamp, to butt against John Bet's swamp on the south and run towards the trench only one rod broad to be kept on the south side of the tren[ch] towards the highway.

This day aforesaid, at the vendue James Chester Jun[r] bade the last and greatest sum which amounted to twenty four pounds eight shillings.

It being doubted by some whether James Chichester or Robt. Arthur [bid the highest sum, it is decided that] Rob. bad 24 lb. 7s. Testified by Jonas Wood Jun. who was eye witness ; as well as Jonathan Scudder, James Smith and John Adams as ear witnesses, that James Chichester Jun[r] bad the last and bad twenty-four pound 8s.*
Possession granted to James Chichester Jun[r] : John Corey, Clerk.

---

[*This mode of sale by the burning of an inch of candle pre-vailed during all the period of the early history of the town. After the auctioneer had lit the piece of candle an inch long, the bidding was continued until the candle was consumed and the last flicker of flame was visible, the last bid taking the property independent of the auctioneer.—C. R. S.]

The day above said it is voted that Epenetus Platt shall go to York or where the assembly shall meet if Mr. Wood will not go to carry a pe[ti]tion, and to spake to it when occasion shall be.†

[Court Records of 1681-4 p. 12 being p.        of present numbers.]

The 26 of June 1682, voted and granted by the major part of the town that Jonas Wood Jun<sup>r</sup> shall take up 4 or 5 acres of land lying on the east side of the south path on this side of the hollow pond between the town & the hollow pond ; viz: the western south path.

The day above said it was voted and granted by the major part of the town that Jonathan Lewese shall have a lot westward of Josiah Jones' house-lot sold unto him upon such a price & pay and day as the Constable and Overseers shall agree with him ; and the money to be for some public use for the town, as the Constable and Overseers shall think fit. And the said lot to contain so much as the Constable and Overseers shall see cause to lay out or allow to be laid out : And the said [lot] to bear the denomination of one hundred pound allotment, and when laid out to record the guaranty and the bounds as also the price.

J. HINGERSON (?)

It was also voted and granted by the major part of the town the day above said that John Hinkerson shall have four acres of land towards his division if the place will afford it without hinderance to hie ways or watering. The

---

[†The principal grievance of the people which Epenetus Platt was to lay before the Governor was that they had no voice in making the laws or levying the taxes. Similar protests went from other towns and the discontent was so great that Gov. Andross was called back to England. Thomas Dongan, who succeeded him the next year, called a General Assembly, which met in New York City Oct. 17, 1683.—C. R. S.]

place mentioned is on the south side of the west neck path, and joining to Sam¹ Kecham's everet pasture, the west side of the said pasture.

Per mee, John Corey, Clerk.

[Copied from the original in Court Records 1681–4, p. 23 of the old paging, being p.    of the present paging, in the Revision in the year of our Lord, 1873.]

(*Town Meetings, Vol.* 1, *pp.* 105–9.)

---

[DEED. NICHOLAS ELLIS TO THOMAS FLEET.]

[1682, July 7.]

The Record of yᵉ medow of Capᵗⁿ ffleet

Witneseth these pʳsents yᵗ I nicolas Ellas of yᵉ Town of huntington upon Long Island within yᵉ Collony of his Royall Highness James duke of york have and by these pʳsents do sell asigne and make over all Right titlle Intrust and Claym in and of a parcell of land or medow Lying, situate and being in and upon a certan neck called by yᵉ name of Anusbymonica lying and being on yᵉ south side of Long Island being bounded on yᵉ East by a Creke: on yᵉ south by yᵉ medow of Capᵗⁿ Thomas ffleet on yᵉ west by Samuell wood on yᵉ north to John finch unto Capᵗⁿ Thomas ffleet of yᵉ Town above sd. his heirs executors administrators and assignes for ever to him yᵉ sd. Thomas from me yᵉ sd. nicollas my hairs administrators and assignes for ever to have and to hold with out any let, trouble eviction or molestation of any person or persons what soever as fully largely and amply as may or can be don by any deed grant instrument of writing Convaience or town order what soever:

he yᵉ sd. Thomas ffleet haveing satisfied mee yᵉ fore sd. Nicollas Elise to my content haveing payd me yᵉ full and

just sume of twelve pounds which I acknowledge in full
satisfaction of yᵉ above sd. p'rmeses for and in consideration
where of I oblege me yᵉ sd. Nicolas to deliver yᵉ sd medow
layd out according to on hundred pound lot ment In witness where of I have subscribed this 7ᵗʰ of July in yᵉ year
of our lord God 1682

signed, sealed                             MARY ELLIS
delivered In yᵉ                      the mark of
presence of                      NICOLAS X ELLIS
     THOMAS SKIDMORE
     WILLIAM BROTHERTON

                  This is A true Copy of yᵉ Originall
                  Compared by me John Corey Clerke
                  this 16ᵗʰ of Feb. 1682.
     (*Deeds, Vol.* 1, *p.* 135.)

---

## [CONTRACT TO BUILD A HOUSE.]

     [1682, July 28.]

     This writing witneseth a bargan and an agreement made
between John Corey and Jonathon Lewes both of huntington in yᵉ East Riding of york shire on Long Island where
in they doe bind them selves their heirs exectors administrators & asignes to performe & doe for & to each other
as followeth, first yᵗ yᵉ sd. Lewes shall doe all yᵉ diging
work of a seller 5 feet within ground and git good stones
and make a good and sufficeant stone wall laying yᵉ foundation stones a little way be neathe yᵉ bothem of yᵉ seller
so deep as is need full and to make yᵉ stoon wall six foot
from yᵉ bothem of yᵉ seller to yᵉ top of yᵉ stone worke and
in bignesse fit for ahous as about 14 & 16 foot in breadth
& length and yᵉ insides of yᵉ wall to be square up with yᵉ
in sides of yᵉ seeles of yᵉ hous.
     And also to git good sound timber 9 or 10 inches thick

when well squared and frame it well to gather at y^e top &
y^e bothem and make it 3 foot wide within y^e same and not
more y^e lengthe to be y^e depth of y^e wall and to set it upon
y^e wall; and also to git good sound timber of 7 inches
thick and 12 inches brood or more y^e in sides and uper sids
to be well hewed and to be laid upon y^e wall y^e length of
y^e hous: And six sleepers of good and sound timber well
hewed to six inches square to ly y^e breadth of hous upon
y^e 2 afore mentioned seels, for flower to ly upon And further more y^e sd Lewes shall pull offe all y^e clabords from
y^e Roofe and y^e 2 sides and one end to y^e plats & beame of
y^e sd. hous and to save all y^e nailes y^t he can by drawing
them for y^e sd. Corey And to git good lathes well hewed
one inch & half thick so meny in number as are sufficant
for y^e well Laying of 4 foot & half shingles and also y^e sd.
Lewes shall git good shingles and Claboards of a sufficent
thicknesse and well dressed and lay them in posse forthwith and shall shingell y^e whole Roofe: The 2 sides & one
end to be Claborded from y^e bothem of y^e seels to y^c top of
y^e plates & beame of y^e sd hous all to be good & sufficent
worke well done at or before y^e 28^th of october next and to
y^e intent it it should be so don y^e sd Lewes is to make it
his constent imployment till he have finished it.

Now for and in consideration of y^e work afore sd. being
well and truly performed as is promised by y^e said Lewes.
The said Corey shall give y^e sd lewes his diat all y^c time
y^t he was at work for him both lords days and Rainey days
in y^e fore sd worke And to allow him his teame and tackling, namely his 2 oxen & hors for y^e fore sd. Lewes to Cart
all ye fore mentioned stones And timber with all And to
give him That brown 3 yeer old heifer yt he had of Epenetus platt if sound and well to out ward vew, And if otherwise then another that shall be Judge as good by some yt
know her. And also one of y^e beest cowes y^t y^e sd. Corey
shall then have and both y^e sd cattell to be delivered at or
before y^e 28 of octobar next y^e this date if y^e fore sd. worke

be don as is said further more what time y^e sd. Lewis wasteth needlessly or if by sicknesse or y^e like then y.^e sd. Lewes is to pay for his keeping all such time so much as shall be judged Reasonable further more y^e sd. Lewes shall not hinder y^e sd Core of his teame & tacklin when he is to stock his hay.

And after y^e shingles & clabourds are dreassed and layed in presse then y^e sd. Corey shall not hinder y^e sd. lewes from giting so much hay as shall be needfull for his own cattell and not otherwise.

memorandom if y^e sd. Corey have not procured nailes for y^e sd. work that nothing be wanting but what shall be by that neglect then y^e sd Lewes when y^e nailes are goten and he have 6 or 8 days notis there of, shall goe and finish or caus to be finished fore sd work according as promised, Then notwithstanding y^e cattell shall be delivered as afore sd.

And to y^e intent y^t alle promises afore said shall stand in force they have set to their hands. this 28^th of July 1682.

In presence of                    JONATHAN LEWIS
  EPENETUS PLATT                   JOHN COREY.
  JOSHUA SNELL

> The Bargan above sd. is per-
> formed by boath parties to our
> satisfaction : so fare That with
> both our consent we cros the
> same as witnes our hands, JOHN
> COREY JONATHAN LEWES

(*Court Rec., pp.* 45–6.)

---

## [PLATT FAMILY RECORD.]

[1682, Sept. 29.]

Elizebeth platt y^e daughter of Isaack platt of huntington was borne y^e 15^th of Sept^r 1665.

Jonas platt y$^e$ son of Isack platt was born y$^e$ 10$^{th}$ of august In y$^e$ year 1667.

John platt y$^e$ son of Isack platt was borne y$^e$ 29$^{th}$ of June 1669.

Mary platt y$^e$ daughter of Isack platt was born y$^e$ 26 of octob 1674.

Joseph platt y$^e$ son of Isack plat was born y$^e$ 8$^{th}$ of Septr 1677.

Jacob platt y$^e$ son of Isack platt was borne y$^e$ 29 of Sep$^{tr}$ 1682.

(*Court Rec*, *p.* 289.)

## [BRUSH FAMILY RECORD.]

[1682, Oct. 20.]

Esther Brush daughter of Richard Brush was borne y$^e$ 2$^d$ of Aprill in y$^e$ yeer 1670

Richard Brush sonn of Richard Brush was borne y$^e$ 28$^{th}$ of september in y$^e$ yeer 1673

Thomas Brush y$^e$ sonn of Richard brush was borne y$^e$ 13$^{th}$ of Januare in y$^e$ yeer 167$\frac{5}{6}$

Mary Brush y$^e$ daughter of Richard Brush was born y$^e$ 31$^{st}$ or Last day of march in y$^e$ yeer 16$\frac{77}{78}$

Robart Brush sonn of Richard Brush was borne y$^e$ 30$^{th}$ or Last of June in y$^e$ yeer 1685.

Benjamine Brush sonn of Richard Brush was borne y$^e$ 20$^{th}$ of octobar in y$^e$ yeer 1682.

(*Surveys, p.* 160.)

## [DEED. JOSEPH BAILEY TO NICHOLAS SMITH.]

[1682, Nov. 10.]

Witneseth these p$^r$sents That I Joseph Baly Yeoman of

y^e Town of huntington upon Long Island within y^e Collony
of his Royall Highnes James Duke of yorke in America
have and by these p^rsents doe sell alinate assigne & make
over all my Right Titel intrust and Claime in and to my
farme of Land Containing twenty Acres of upland; and
six acres of medow, with y^e hous or housing there on which
sd. upland lyeth sittuate neare y^e farme of Thomas skidmor
senior: viz sixteene alredy taken up and most part fenced:
And foure acres not yet taken up: belonging to y^e sd.
farme, the sixteen acres above sd. lyeth bounded on y^e
north & west with y^e land of Thomas Skidmor above sd.
on y^e south with y^e farme of phillip Udall: and, on y^e east
with y^e high way: and fresh pond: The six acres, more or
lesse of medow lyeth at Crab medow. And is bounded with
y^e medow of Thomas Scidmor Junior, on y^e north with y^e
high way; on y^e east with y^e medow of phillip udall on y^e
South: And Crab medow great Creeke on y^e west: And
all p^rveledge of Commonage y^t doth or shall here after belong to y^e land or farme thane sold unto Nicolas Smith
Carpenter of y^e Town of Milford in ye Collony of Connet-
icut in new England from me y^e above ^sd Joseph Baly my
heirs executors, administrators and assignes: To him y^e
above sd. Nicolas Smith his heirs executors administrators
and assignes for ever to have & to hold soe firmly and fully
larglye and amply as may or can bee made by this or any
other deed grant or Instrument of writing whatsoever with
Rights and priveledges: there unto belonging and appertaining or shall or may appertaine hereafter: he y^e above
sd. Nicolas Smith satisfieing and paying in manner and
forme following viz ten pounds pp an num in winter wheat
at five shilling p^er bushell sumer wheat foure shillings and
six pence p^r bushell Rye ffour shillings per bushell, oats
Two shillings p^r bushell, not exceeding ten bushells of oats
in one year.   Indian corn two shillings six p^r bushell, beefe
two pence per pound; porke three pence p^r pound Round:
the said Land to stand securely & for y^e sd. pay.   The first

paiment to be made and begin in march Com twelve month ensucing y⁰ date here of which will be in yᵉ yeare 1683 in witnesse whereof I have here unto sett my hand and seale this tenth day of november in yᵉ yeare of our Lord God 1682.

JOSEPH BAYLY.

signed sealed and deld.
in yᵉ pʳsents of yᵉ marke of
JOHN ✕ INGORSULL
JONATHAN HARNED.

This is a true coppy Compared with yᵉ originall by mee

John Corey, Recʳ

november 15ᵗʰ 1682.

(*Deeds, Vol.* 1, *pp.* 119-120)

Know all whome this may con sern That Joseph Bayly and Nicollas Smith both afore mentioned in yᵉ above sd. Bill of sale: came before me this 7ᵗʰ of november 1685 and yᵉ said Nicolas Smith did surrender ———— up all his Right title and Intrust that he hath or ever had, to the farme afore mentioned from him his heirs, executors administrators or assignes unto Joseph Bally afore named him his heirs executors administrators and esignes for ever And all yᵉ afore mentioned Records to be anull between yᵉ sd partys at witnes his hand,

yᵉ mark of

hɪs

by me John Corey
Clerk,

(*Deeds, Vol.* 1, *p.* 120.)

NICOLLAS ✕ SMITH

mark

---

## [BOND TO PAY IN PRODUCE AND BUILD A CIDER MILL.]

[1682, Nov. 13.]

Know all men by these pʳsents yᵗ I nicolas smith of mil-

ford within y^e colony of coniticutt carpenter doe bind my
selfe my heires executors administrators and assignes to
pay or caus to be payd unto Joseph Bayly of Huntington
upon long Island in y^e east Riding of yorkshire husbandman y^e full and just some of four score & ten pounds in
good marchantable Beif poorke, winter wheat sumer
wheat, Rie Indian corn, & oats in manner & forme following viz, ten pounds p yeare for nine years The first ten
pounds to be payed at or before y^e tenth of march in y^t
yeare 1683.   The second payment y^e tenth of march 1684:
and so ten pounds p yeare yearely untill ninetye pounds
be fully satisfied and payed : which pay is for and in consideration of a farme sould unto y^e above Bounden Nicolas Smith which sd. farme with all its Rits and priviledges:
I y^e sd. nicolas smith doth by these presents assigne over
unto Joseph Bayly afore sd. his heires and assignes : untill
y^e fore sd. ninetie pounds be fully answered and payed
unto y^e above s^d Joseph bayley his heires executors administrators and assignes, And I y^e sd. Joseph Bayly doe promis to allow unto y^e above bounden nicolas smith, twenty shillings which is y^e Indian purchas for y^e whole farme :   The
next paye after the sd. smith have payd it to y^e inproprio-
tors, All y^e Rest of y^e pay is to be paied at winter wheat at
five shilings p bushell, sumer wheat at 4^d and six pence  to
Rie at 4^d Indian corn at 2^d & six pence ots at 2^d p  bushell
not exceeding ten bushells p yeare : beif 2 pence Round
poorke 3 pence The greater part of y^e yearly pay to be
in graine and y^e above Bounden Nicolas Smith doth ingage to make a wheele to grind apples and y^e post to stay
y^e wheele at y^e dweling hous of y^e afore sd. Joseph Bayly
free bee a contract in bargan ;  as witness my hand and
seale this 13 day of november in y^e 34th year of his Mag^st
Raine And in y^e yeare of our lord 1682.

the mark of

NICOLLAS  X  SMITH

signed sealed
and ddl. in y⁰
presents of the
mark of
JOHN X HINGERSOLL
JONATHAN HARNED.

This is a true coppy compared with
yᵉ originall by me John Corey Recʳ.

(*Court Rec., p.* 397.)

---

[DEED. NICHOLAS ELLIS TO JOSEPH BAILEY.]

[1682, Nov. 15.]

The Record of Capᵗⁿ Joseph Baylys Land
know all men by these pʳsents that I Nicolas Elles of
Huntington upon long Island in yᵉ east Riding of York
shire within yᵉ collony of his Royall highnesse James duke
of Yorke in Amarika and Mary my Wife have and by
these pʳsents doe, sell allinate assigne and make over all
our Right title and intrust and claime in and to our hous
and home Lot situate and lying in huntington afore sd.
The Lot of John finch on yᵉ east side. The north wᵗ yᵉ lot
of Robart Arther, the west to yᵉ high way yᵗ leads to yᵉ
harbour togather with all priviledgs of Commondage as
Erbidge out lands, devided or undevided except fifteen
acres of devition Land : which is yᵉ first & second devision
belonging unto yᵗ lot : which is a two hundred pound allotment by denomination which fifteen acars yᵉ above sd.
Nicolas Elles doth Reserve unto mine only use & behoof :
all yᵉ Rest of yᵉ afore sd. housing gardings fruit trees
hom Lot devition lands yᵗ doth or ever shall belong or appertain unto yᵉ sd. pʳmises me yᵉ afore sd. Nicholas Ellas
and Mary my wife, have allinated and astranged from us
our heirs executors, adminstrators for ever for a consider-

able vallue in hand payd by y$^e$ afore sd. Joseph Baylye
unto y$^e$ fore sd. Nicolles Ellise for which caus we y$^e$ afore
sd. Nicolas & Mary my wife, doth assigne over the afore
sd. p$^r$mises unto y$^e$ above sd. Joseph bayly his heirs executors administrators and assignes to have and to hold for
ever: as firmly tully amply and fully as may or can be
made by any deed or Convaience what so ever: this Land
of hous home Lott and all priviledges: was firs in y$^e$ tenour or occupation of Trustram Hedges, estrangned unto
John finch sen$^r$. by a vandue, for divers considerations:
thence unto me y$^e$ sd. Nicollas Elles by deed of gifte from
from my father in Law, John finch sen$^r$. And Estranged by
us from our heirs executors, adminestiators & asignes unto
y$^e$ above said Joseph bayly his heirs executors administrators & assignes as witnesse our hands & seals this 15th day
of november in y$^e$ 34th year of his Mag$^{ts}$ Rayne and in y$^e$
year of our Lord 1682,

Signed, sealed and
delivered in y$^e$ pres-
ents of y$^e$ Mark of
RICHARD $\times$ FLOYD
STEVEN JARVIS Sen$^r$

the mark of

NICOLAS $\times$ ELLES
MARY ELLES

This is a true coppy, Compared w$^{th}$ y$^e$ originall by me
John Corey Rec$^r$

(*Deeds, Vol.* 1, *pp.* 123, 124.)

---

## [DEED. JEREMIAH SMITH TO JAMES SMITH.]

[1682, Dec. 10.]

This Indenture made y$^e$ tenth day of desember, in y$^e$
14$^{th}$ year of y$^e$ Raigne of our sov$^{rn}$ Lord Charles y$^e$ sec$^{en}$
king of Grat Brittan france & Ireland defender of y$^e$ faith
etc. And in y$^e$ year of our Lord 1682. Between Jeremiah
within y$^e$ bounds of Huntington upon Long Island in y$^e$

County of Suffolk in y$^e$ province of New York in Amerika Cooper of y$^e$ one party : And James Smith of y$^e$ afore sd.: town County and province of y$^e$ other party cooper : Witness that y$^e$ Jeremiah Smith for divers good causes me there unto mowving : But Especially for and in y$^e$ consideration of y$^e$ summe of ten pounds of good & currant monie of this province : have Barganed, alinated sould & confirmed and by these p$^r$sents from mee my heirs executors, administrators & assignes : doe alinate Bargan sell and confirme unto y$^e$ afore sd. James Smith All That my home Lot Land situate Lying & being in y$^e$ town of Huntington afore sd. & is bounded on y$^e$ north with y$^e$ land of Joseph Baily : on y$^e$ West with y$^e$ land of Thomas Wicks and Jn$^o$ Wicks on y$^e$ south west with y$^e$ Land of M$^r$ Eliphelet Jones, on y$^e$ east with y$^e$ Land of James Smith on y$^e$ North east with y$^e$ common: Together with all grants Rights, priveledgs & appurtanences unto y$^e$ same belonging or in any wise appurtaining together also with all ways waterings fences hedges diches watter courses commons commons of pasture turfing woods & under woods unto y$^e$ same belonging or in any appurtaining to have and to hold y$^e$ sd. granted Bargand p$^r$mises & appurtanences unto y$^e$ sd. James Smith his heirs executors administrators and assignes for ever yelding & paying here by his annuall & yearly proportion of what may belong to y$^e$ Government of this province And I y$^e$ sd. Jerimiah Smith fer him selfe his heirs executors administrators and assignes doe covenent promis & grant to and with y$^e$ sd. James Smith afore said : that y$^e$ sd. Jeremiah Smith now is and stands firmly sceasd of a good & sure & perfitt estat in Law of y$^e$ sd. Lot of Land with its appurtanences & hath good Right & lawfull authoritye to sell and convaye y$^e$ same and y$^e$ sd. Jeremiah Smith for himself heirs executars administrators and assignes doth further covenent to & with y$^e$ sd. James Smith his heirs executors administrators & asignes : y$^t$ y$^e$ Lot of Land is free from all other former grants Bargans sales

Morgages Leases Judgments executions Convayences
dowries widow Rights or Intrust whatsoever and further
yᵉ said Jeremiah Smith doth for himselfe his heirs executors administrators or assignes doth covenent promis and
grant to & with yᵉ sd. James Smith yᵗ at any time or times
here after upon Request made yᵉ said Jeremiah Smith
shall and will be Redy to give all other & further securities as he or his learned Counsell shall think fitt :   & yᵉ said
Jeremiah Smith his heirs executors administrators & assigns doth covenent promis & grant to & with yᵉ sd. James
Smith his heirs executors administrators or assigns : That
yᵉ sd. Jeremiah Smith togeather with his heirs executors,
administrators or asignes shall and will warrant and defend
yᵉ sd. granted pʳmises with their appurtanences from any
manner of just Right title claime or demand of any person
or persons claiming from by or under me or my heirs or
from any other person or persons what so ever in witness
whereof I have here unto set my hand and seale yᵉ day &
yeare above written.

JEREMIAH SMITH

Signed sealed and delived
in yᵉ presence of
    JOHN MICHELL
    JONATHAN HARNED
    The above sd. Indenture was acknowledged by Jeremiah
Smith to be his act & deed And his Wife Elizabeth Smith
doth volentary and freely consent to yᵉ above said deed :
both acknowledg before me this 12ᵗʰ day of March 168⅘
                    EPENETUS PLATT Justis.
    This is a true Coppy out of yᵉ originall p mee John
Corey Clerk.

March 168⅘

I Jeremiah Smith doe acknowledg my selfe to be fully satisfied Contented and payed for all yᵉ with in mentioned
pʳm sell : before yᵉ sealing and delivery thereof as witnesse
my hand to these pʳsents.

(*Deeds, Vol. 1, pp.* 187-8.)

## [RECORD OF LAND OF EPENETUS PLATT.]

[1682, Dec. 23.]

These may signefie to whom it may concerne : that according to yᵉ grants of devition Land upon Record.

unto Epenetus platt: Wee whose names are subscribed being appoynted for laying out Land for ye east end of yᵉ Town, have layed out for Epenetus platt thirty acres on yᵉ south side of yᵉ east feild. At yᵉ east end of yᵉ feild sixty Rods in length, by yᵉ side of yᵉ swamp or Reed pond : And eighty Rods by yᵉ south sid of yᵉ feild: So yᵗ piece of Land is sixty Rods one way south ward: And eighty Rods in Length east & west: And yᵉ wattering place for Cattell is a small swamp, on yᵉ east sid of yᵉ main swamp, Two Chestnut Trees marked in oppossission on of another which swamp Epenetus platt hath promised to make a small dam to keep yᵉ watter in, if it will be : when he dreeneth yᵉ other :  It is also to be understood that twelve acres of yᵉ fore sd. land is of devition belonging to yᵉ Lot yᵗ was Thomas Skidmors Lott.

desembʳ 23: 1682        JOSEPH BAYLY
by me John Cory       THOMAS POWELL
       Recʳ
*(Deeds, Vol. 1, p. 127.)*

---

## [OVERSEERS' ORDER CONCERNING JOHN FINCH.]

[1683, Jan. 2.]

Huntington : Jeneuary 2ᵗʰ 168¾
A. town Court being then held by his majsᵗ authority

Complaint being then made to yᵉ constable & overseers

conserning John finch sen$^r$ That he is deprived in some measure of his Intuelectals, and y$^t$ he is very subject to swounding fits: And y$^t$ he is very much given to extravegent courses of drinking strong drink where by he is like to come to want And the Town like to be burdened by him. The Constable & overseers haveing taken the same into their serious consideration of the dangerous consequences y$^t$ may follow upon such Impotentcy and extravegency doe order yt all y$^e$ known Estate yt y$^e$ sd. John finch hath in his present possession shall be attached by warrant and secured and presarved and improved as the Constable & overseers shall think best for y$^e$ livelyhood and mantanence of y$^e$ sd. John finch whereby he may not suffer nor the Town be damnefied.

John Corey
Clark.
(*Court Rec.*, *p.* 401.)

ISAAC PLATT.
EPENETUS PLATT
THOMAS WHITSON
JAMES SMITH

---

## [DEED.   THOMAS SCIDMORE JR., TO JONATHAN LEWIS.]

[1683, Jan. 11.]

Jonathan Lewis Recd.

Know all men by these p$^r$sents y$^t$ I Thomas Scidmor Junr. of ffresh pond in y$^e$ p$^r$smgs of Huntington In y$^e$ East Riding of yorkshire on Long Island husbandman have for & in consideration of y$^e$ fulle of seaventy twoo pounds: well and truly payed in hand before y$^t$ ensealling and delivery here of: where with I doe acknowledge myselfe fully satisfied contented & payed, Barganed sold alinated, estranged and made over And by these p$^r$sents doe bargan, sell alinate,

estrange and make over from me my heirs executors, ad
ministrators and asignes unto Jonathan Lewis of yᵉ town
of westerly in yᵉ Colony of Road Island his heirs executors, administrators and assignes all my Right title and
Intrust yᵗ I have in & to halfe A farme by denomination
one hundred & fifty pound allotment which was given to
me : by my father Thomas Skidmore : it lying and being in
fresh pond neck, that is to say my hous and home lot Containing two acres & ahalfe, bounded on yᵉ north with yᵉ
land of Thomas Skidmore senʳ. The high between : And
on yᵉ east with yᵉ hie way, on yᵉ west with yᵉ woods in
common : As also another parsell of Land Containing
seaventeen acres & a halfe be it more or lesse And lying on
yᵉ south sd. of yᵉ above sd. hous lott. The high way of
about fower Rods wide Runing between, As also six acres
of medow lying & being in Crabmedow and bounded on yᵉ
South witn the medow of Joseph Baly : on yᵉ north and
west with yᵉ medow of John golding, on yᵉ East with yᵉ
woods in common : Together with all priveledgs & Rights
of garding orchyards, fences Commons pasturs all Lands,
devided or undevided that now doth or here after shall any
way belong unto yᵉ above sd. accommondations : And
further yᵉ above sd. Thomas Scidmore Junʳ doe Ingadge
my self my heirs executors administrators and asignes to
save harmlesse and Indamnefied the fore sd. Jonathan Lewis
his heirs executors, administrators and assignes, And to defend him & them for ever from any person or persons yᵗ
shall or may Lay any just or lawfull claim to yᵉ above sd.
Land or any part or parcell there of : And also to free and
cleere yᵉ sd. Lands from all devos debts Rate or in Cum-
brancesse from yᵉ begining of yᵉ world to yᵉ date hereof,
except what yᵉ Indeans shall demand for their soyle Right :
Which yᵉ above sd. Jonathan shall pay and cleere him selfe :
And also shall subscribe to yᵉ covenent made between yᵉ
town & yᵉ farmers.

further more I yᵉ above sd. Thomas Skedmore Junʳ doe by

These p'sents Bind my selfe my heirs and sucksessers to Ratefie and Confirme all y° above sd accomondation and every part and parsell y' now doth or here after may belong to y° same, Lying and being in fresh pond neck and Crabmedow, In y° p'sings of Huntington afore sd. Unto Jonothon Lewis his heirs, executors (other wise successors) And every of them for his and their proper Right use and be hoofe: to have and to hold use and quiatly to possesse for ever And for y° Confirmation of y° p'omises above written I have here unto set my hand and seall this ii of Janeuery 168¾

The mark of THOMAS ✕ SKIDMORE Jun'

In p' of
  JOHN COREY
  SAMUEL GUFFEN

These may satisfie any whome it may Conserne That I Thomas Skidmor senr doe by these p'sents Confirme and consent to what my son Thomas Skidmor hath don by y° above sd. writting be tween him and Jonathon Lewis as witnesse my hand this 12 of Jeneuary 1682.

THOMAS SKIDMOR.

In p'sents of
  JOHN SAMIS
  ABIGALL SAMIS

This is a true Coppy of y° originall by me John Corey, Rec' Jan, 15 168¾

    *(Deeds, Vol. 1, pp. 129-130.)*

---

## [DEED. ROBERT KELLUM TO WILLIAM MOORE.]

[1683, Jan. 14.]

The Record of William Moores Land.

Be it known to all whom these may concarn that I Robart kellam of Huntington in Suffolk on long IsLand have

Barganed sold and made over all my Rite, title and Intrust in and to a hous Lott, Lying and being in Huntington,
joyning to y^e Reare of Richard Brush his and Jonas
Woods, jun^r hous Lots. The South and East to y^e wood
in Common. The frunt to y^e south path : formerly belonging to John holms weaver by y^e towns grant being in y^e
denomination of six acres and thence allinated to Jn° Brush
thence to Jn° Michell, thence to Robart kellam all and
every part and parcell of y^e fore sd. Lott with all priveledges That now doth or here after may belong to it. togather with fifty pound Commondege I y^e afore sd. Robart kellam doe Bargan sell estrange and make over from
me my heirs executors, admistrators and assignes unto
William more of pencilveny Luck Smith, him his heirs
executors Admynstrators and asignes to have and to hold
for ever And further more I y^e above sd. Robart Kellam
doe by these p^rsents Bind my self my heirs Executors, Administrators and asignes to save harmlesse and Indamnefied
the fore sd. William more him his heirs Executors administrators and asignes from any person or persons y^t shall
lay any just or Lawfull Clame to any part or parcell thereof giveing y^e sd. William afore sd. and all his successors
quiat possesion to use occupye And quiatly to Injoy for
ever as witnesse my hand and seale this 14th of Janury
1683, further I y^e above sd. Robart doe acknowledg y^t I
have Received full satisfaction for all y^e above sd. Lands
and priviledgs.

Witnesse                   ROBART KELLAM

       his
BENJEMEN X SCIEVINER
     mark

JOHN COREY Clerk,

                This is a true Coppy of y^e
                origenall p me John Corey
                              Clerk.
                  Januery y^e 25, 1683.

(*Deeds, Vol. 1, p. 141 and File No. 66.*)

## [ESTATE OF MOSES SCUDDER.]

[1683, Jan. 17.]

Huntington Jenuery y$^e$ 17 1683.
An Envintary taken of y$^e$ Estat of Moses Scudder, decased
as followeth:
namely a three hundred pound allotment or accomandation
two oxen two cows 1 two year old steer one yearling hifer
two calves. two small swine two mares two horses one gun
two pistoles an old saddel one oyxon pot one cheast. three
shirts one broad cloath wascoat. two pair sarge breeches
one home spun pair ot breeches one tuffteed holland wascoat. one holland shirt one Camlet coat one Norwester two
pair of stockens one pair of white drawers 6 neck cloaths,
1 caster hatt a bible, a sithe, & sickel.
katheran Jones Widdow and mother to y$^e$ fore sd. moses
Scudder, deceased doth Ingage and promis to keep y$^e$
within sd. estat from Imbayelment untill order from y$^e$
Court also david Scudder Brother to y$^e$ sd. Moses deceased
doth also Ingage with his mother afore sd. for y$^e$ safty of
y$^e$ sd. as witnesse our hands this 17$^{th}$ of Jenuery 1683

the mark of KETHEREN ✕ JONES<br>
the mark of DAVID ✕ SCUDDER.

In presenc of
ISAAC PLATT constable.
ABIEL TITUS ⎱ overseers.
EPENETUS PLAT ⎰

   The above sd is a true Coppy of y$^e$ originall formerly
taken by me John Corey Clerk by y$^e$ Comand of ISACK
PLATT Constable
   March y$^e$ 13 168$\frac{3}{4}$.

   (*Court Records, p.* 260.)

# [TOWN MEETING.]

[1683, Feb. 16.]

Feb, 16. 1683.

At a town meeting John Corey was chosen by the major part of the town, to be one of the committee to sit at Southold to act in the behalf of Huntington on the 20[th] of this instant.

[Copied from the original in Conrt Records 1681-4 p. 32, (being page 111 of the present paging) in the Revision in 1873.]

*(Town Meetings, Vol. 1, p. 111.)*

---

# [TOWN MEETING. "CASK GAGER" CHOSEN.]

[1683, April 2.]

At a towne meeting Legally warned y[e] 2[d] of Aprill 1683. the day a bove sd. abiell tittus was chossen constable. the day a bove written Joseph whittman John Samis and Isac Platt weere legally chossen Comissioners.* the day abov. written Joseph Whitman was chossen leather sealler.†

[*Governor Andross having been called back to England on account of the unpopular character of his administration, Anthony Brockholst exercised the functions of commander-in-chief. On his recommendation the Duke of York had a general assembly of delegates summoned from the towns, and a new governor, Thomas Dongan, was appointed and assumed authority. The division of the province into ridings was abolished and twelve counties were established this year, among them Suffolk. There was also a Town Court established to be held by three commissioners. This court was short-lived, as it did not meet the approval of the people.—C. R. S.]

[†These offices of "leather sealer" and "cask gager" were created this year, but were not continued long here. Hides were tanned and leather was made here probably from the first settlement of the town. Thomas Scudder is the first tanner mentioned in the records, the court records giving the minutes of a trial about his tanning leather. There is reason to believe that his tanning vats were on the east street of Huntington, near the the brook.—C. R. S.]

The day above sd. John Wood was chosen caske gager.
the same day above written Robert kellum did propose to
y^e towne for 20 acrs of land joyning to his land upon the
cow neck upon the west necke frunting east ward to ye
harbor : noe other person to have it from him.

The day above written was granted to Captt. fleet, Mr
wood & Samuell Wood to take up their devision of land 7
acors & a ½ to a hundred, where they shall see cause to doe
it not to hinder hie ways & watering places for cattel, alsoe
y^e same grant is to all y^t have not taken up a cording to y^e
devision mentioned.

the day abov. sd. was granted to Rich. gildersleeve 22 acers
of land 6 or 8 acers of it at y^e hed of claboard hollow and
ye remainder of it betwixt william brodeton and his owne
land facen against Crabmedewe.

the day above written was granted to tho. Scidmor 20
acers of land in bred en chese hollow joining to the north
side of Phillip udels land and 20 acers of land was granted
the same day to Tho. scidmore one the north side of the
hog pond upon Crabmeder necke.

Apr. 2. 1683.

At town meeting held in Huntington, Thomas Whitson
[was] chosen constable ; John Ketcham and Abiel Titus
Overseers.

The day above said it was voted and granted by the
major part of the town that. Walter Nokes shall have the
remaining part of his division of land in the West Neck
and joining to the West end of Rich^d Brush, Thom. Brush,
John Brush and Timothy Conklin's land ; which is 13
acres.

The day above said it was voted and granted that John
Sammis and John Kecham shall take up, each of them, 12
acres lying at the head of Hempstead Hollow on the Northwest side of the path.

The same day it was voted and granted that Joseph Wood Capt, and James Smith shall take up six acres each of them, it lying on the West Neck, lying by David Scudders land.

The day above said it was granted that Jonathan Scudder and Thomas Skidmore Jun' shall have a swamp between them, it lying in Crabmeadow hollow and joining to their land and meadow ; they laying down so much of their proportion if the town shall see cause to demand it.

[Court Rec. 1681-4 p. 42, old paging, p. ——present paging.]

It was voted and granted by the major part of the town that John Bets shall take up 10½ acres of land towards his division lying on the West Neck above Jo[hn] Sammis his field beyond the cove.

[Copied from Court Records 1681-4, p. 43 or ——, in the Revision of the Town Records 1873.]

(*Town Meetings, Vol.* 1, *pp.* 115-117.)

---

## [DEED. THOMAS BRUSH TO THOMAS SCIDMORE, Jr.]

[1683, April 2.]

The Record of y^e Land of Thos. Skidmor, Jun^r

Know all men by these p^rsents y^t I Thomas Brush of Huntington In y^e East Riding of Yorke shiere on Long Island Husbandman have for y^e full and just sume of sixty two pounds & ten shilings well and truly payd in hand before y^e ensealing & delivery heer of, Where of and where with I doe acknowledg my self fully satisfied contented and payed : Bargained sold allinated estranged, confirmed and made over, And doe by these p^rsents Bargan sell alli-

nat Estrange confirme and make over from me my heirs
executors administrators and assignes unto Thomas Skid-
mor J$^{unr}$ of freshpond In y$^e$ p$^r$sincts of Huntington in y$^e$ east
Riding of york shire afore sd. husband man him his heirs
executors, administrators and assignes. All my Right title
and Intrust y$^t$ I have in and to a five hundred pound Right
of a farme, both of upland. and medow. lying & being in
Crabmedow in y$^e$ p$^r$sincts of Huntington afore sd. That
is to say six acres of Land be it more or lese: And
bounded on y$^e$ north with y$^e$ Land of Edward Bunch:
And on y$^e$ west with y$^e$ land of Jonathan Scudder and on
y$^e$ south with y$^e$ woods in common And one y$^e$ east with y$^e$
highway. As also two percels of medow Containing six
acers be it more or be it lesse: one of y$^e$ sd. parcels is lying
next y$^c$ beach. And joyning to y$^e$ medow of Thomas
Martin on y$^e$ East. The other parcell is lying above y$^e$
bridge: Together with all p$^r$iveledgs and Rights of housing gardings, orchyards fences. commons, pastures And all
Lands devided or undevided yt now doth or here after
shall any belong unto y$^e$ same. I say I y$^e$ above sd. Thomas Brush do promis and Ingage my self my heirs executors,
administrators and assignes to save harmlesse and Indamnefied y$^e$ fore sd. Thomas Skidmor J$^{ur}$ his heirs executors,
administrators or assignes and to defend him and them and
every of for ever from any person or persons y$^t$ shall or
may Lay any just or lawfull claim to any part or parcell
there of and also to free and Cleere y$^e$ above sd. accommondation from all dues debts demands Rate or Incum
brances from y$^e$ begining of y$^e$ world to y$^e$ dat here of—
Except what y$^e$ Indeans shall demand for y$^e$ soyle Right
which y$^e$ sd. Thomas Skidmor Jun$^r$ shall pay and cleere
what charge and trouble y$^t$ may arise about y$^e$ same him
selfe and also shall subscribe to y$^e$ covenent which was
made between y$^e$ town and y$^e$ farmers: ffurther more I y$^e$
above sd. Thomas Brush doe by these p$^r$sents bind myselt
my heirs executors administrators and assignes to Ratifie

and Confirme all y$^e$ above sd. accommandation and every part and parcell there of afore mentioned unto Thomas Skidmor Jun$^r$ his heirs executors administrators or assignes for his and their own proper Right use and behoofe To have and to hold use occupie possesse And quiatly to In-joye ffor ever: And for y$^e$ Confirmation of y$^e$ p$^r$mesis above written I have heere unto set my hand and seale this second day of Aprille 1683.

In presents of           }         THOMAS BRUSH
  ABIELL TITUS
  JOSEPH WHITMAN }     This is a true Copy Compared with y$^e$ originall by me John Corey Clerk: Aprill the ii: 1683.

*(Deeds. Vol. 1, pp. 149-152.)*

---

## [LANDS OF JONATHAN ROGERS.]

[No Date.]

Laied out for Jonathan Roggars In y$^e$ bogges at y$^e$ head of y$^e$ mill swamp an Acare & halfe of Low Land three quarters of a Acare of Land bog the mill pond side eight acars betwene y$^e$ ould way going to oyester baye & y$^e$ mill betwene y$^e$ hill & y$^e$ broock the forth parsell Lying upon y$^e$ hill betwene y$^e$ two high wayes going to Could spring being tenn Acars.

bey Mee John Ketcham Clerk,

                SAMUELL TITUS
                JOSEPH WHITMAN
                Apoynted by y$^e$
                towne.

*(Deeds, Vol. 1, p. 114.)*

---

## [DEED. JOHN WICKS TO JONATHAN ROGERS.]

[1683, April 3.]

Know all men whome it may Consern that John wickes

of Huntington In yᵉ east riding of yorke shear on Long
Island husband man have Bargned sould & Made over a
parcell of Hassokey medow lying & being in yᵉ east neck
Containing about six acers be it more or less unto Jonathan
Rogers of yᵉ abovesd Town & Riding & yᵉ a bounded with
the sea on yᵉ north & on yᵉ east with yᵉ Comonds and on
yᵉ west with yᵉ land of Robert Cranfield and John wickes
I say and doe by thes presents bargan sell and make over
yᵉ above sd boggey or hassokey medow from me my heirs
exectours adminᵉˢ & assignes unto Jonathan Rogers him
his heires executors adminᵉˢ or assignes for a valliable consideration all ready Reseaved In hand whereof and where-
with I am fully satesfyed contented and paid I Doe Ingage
my selfe & my heires to bare him yᵉ sd. Jonathan Rogers
his heires & assignes harmeless from anie person or persons
who may or shall lay anie lawfull and just claime to ye
above sd medow or anie part or parcell thereof for ever
and by vertue of thes have use ocepye & peacebly to Injoye for ever  It is to be understood yᵗ yᵉ above sd.
Medow did belong to my father Thomas wickes wich he
did by of yᵉ town and thence to me & from me & my heirs
as afore sd. unto Jonathan Rogers & his sucessors as wittness my hand this third Day of Aprill 1683

THOMAS WICKES                    JOHN WICKES
          her
ELIZABETH ✕ KETCHAM
          mark

The afore sd. Is a true Copey taken out of yᵉ Boock of
records by me John Corey Clearke for yᵉ Records in Hun-
tington· May yᵉ 29—1682.

This is alsoe a true Coppey extracted out of yᵉ origenall
Deed by me John Ketcham Clarke

Apeared before me this 17ᵗʰ day of January 170⅞ Justices
John Wickes & doth acknowledge yᵉ within written convaiance to be his free & volentary act & Deed

                              ·Test.  JOHN WICKES

(Deeds, Vol. 1, p. 43.)

## [BRUSH FAMILY RECORD.]

[1683, Apr. 3.]

Rebeck Brush   The daughter of Thomas Brush was born the 3ᵈ of Aprill in the year of our Lord 1681.

Thomas Brush   son of Thomas Brush was born Jeneuary the 16 at the 12 hour or there abouts In yᵉ year of our Lord 168⅔

John Brush yᵉ son of John Brush was born Aprill the 3ᵈ In yᵉ year of our Lord 1683.

(*Court Rec.*, *p.* 259.)

---

## [THOMAS SCIDMORE'S LANDS.]

[1683, April.]

Thomas Skidmor Land.

Thomas Skidmor hath Eight Acres of Land Layd out, in Aprill 1683 by yᵉ side of Crabmedow hollow, on yᵉ north side of yᵉ path : not fare from a small Round swamp of watter yᵗ Lyeth nere yᵉ Road to towne in Length thirty nine Rods which Runeth neere East & west the breadth thirty eaight Rods, Layd out by me Joseph Bayly, this is a true copy of yᵉ note from yᵉ survaier ;*
by me John Cary, Clerk.

(*Deeds*, *Vol.* 1, *p.* 131.)

---

[*This, I think, is the first record mentioned where a grant of land was located by an actual survey. The practice seems to have been for the applicant and the town authorities to measure the ground without much regard to accuracy, bounding it by visible monuments, such as trees and stones.—C. R. S.]

## [DEED. NICHOLAS ELLIS TO THOMAS HIGBEE.]

[1683, Apr. 26.]

Know all men by these p^rsents, That I Nicollas Ellise of Huntington in y^e East Riding of york shir on long Island have sold unto Thomas Higby of y^e above sd. Town and Riding, A parcell of land containing ten acres : And doe by these p^rsents Bargan sell and make over all my Right title and intrust that I have in and to y^e above sd. ten acres of land from me my heirs, executors, administrators, or assignes unto, Thomas Higby above sd. him his heirs, executors, administrators and assings, to have and to hold use and Improve and quiatly to possese for ever. And y^e above sd. land is lying and being in y^e great east neck in Hunting bounds in y^e great hollow west ward of stony brook, lying in Leangth north and south In breadth twenty Rods : And in Length eaighty Rods : And for & in consideration of y^e above sd. ten acres of Land I y^e above sd. Nicollas Ellis have Recaived a Reasonable consideration in hand where of and where with I am fully satisfied and payed : furthermore y^e above sd. land was part of my division, which be longed to my hous Lot : And y^e above sd. Instrument I doe Acknowledg to be my act and deed By my setting to my hand and seale this 26^th of Aprill 1683.

Witnesse

JOHN COREY
JOHN KECHAM

the marke of

NICOLLAS X ELLIS

This is a true coppy extracted out of y^e originall p me

John Corey : Clerk

May the 5^th 1683.

(*Deeds, Vol.* 1, *p.* 155.)

---

## [NICHOLAS ELLIS'S LAND.]

[1683, April 26.]

according to y^e towns grant to Nicolas Ellis I have layd

him out ten acars in y$^e$ grat Hollow to y$^e$ west of stony
Brook hollow on y$^e$ east neck, it lyeth in length north and
south : in breadth 20 Rods and in length 80 Rods, with
Rume for a Cart way on boath sides of y$^e$ hollow. The
marked trees on y$^e$ south one a young Chesmut and a white
oke, one y$^e$ north end an old dead oke at each corner :
Aprille y$^e$ 26$^{th}$ 83. JOSEPH BALY.

This is a true copy by me John Corey Clerk aprille 28.
1683.

(*Deeds, Vol.* 1, *p.* 94.)

---

[TOWN MEETING.]

[1683, May 5.]

Att a town meeting it was agreed by y$^e$ major part of y$^e$
Town That Thomas Higby should have a piece of Land
added to his piece of swamp which Land lyeth on y$^e$ south
side of y$^e$ old mill path between Cap$^{tn}$ Baylyes lot &
Thomas Larrances : and his Lott to bare y$^e$ denomination of
a hundred pound alottment And to have medow, (when purchased) equivilent as other Hundreds shall have out of y$^t$
medow he paying for his proportion as other men, it is to
be understood a hundred pound allotment of all devitions
y$^t$ is to be layd out after this grant.

Both y$^e$ above sd. are taken out of y$^e$ old book By me
John Corey

May y$^e$ 5th 1683. Clerk

(*Deeds, Vol.* 1, *p.* 155.)

---

[DEED. JONATHAN HARNET TO ISAAC PLATT.]

[1683, May 15.]

Isacke Platts : Land Record
Huntington May y$^e$ 15$^{th}$: 1683
This writting : witnesseth to all : or any before home

this pʳsents may come That I Jonathan Harned : of Huntington Shomaker have sould barga;ned and made over from me my heirs executors, administrators and asignes for ever fower acres ot wood-land Land now lying in common yᵗ did formerly belong to yᵉ A lotment of Willam Rogers deseased : from him to Andrew messenger from him to John Green and granted and given to John Green by yᵉ town : And from him sould to mee.

The Land lyeth in a place commonly called and known by yᵉ name of grounnut Hollow : Bounded on yᵉ East & west side by Isacke plats land on yᵉ south by yᵉ high way on yᵉ north by yᵉ common : I say & by these pʳsents witnesse that I have sould : unto Isacke platt of Huntington Husbandman yᵉ fore mentioned Land : to him his heirs executors administrators and assignes : to have and to hold for ever : and have alredy Recaived a valiable consideration for yᵉ said Land and have given yᵉ sd. Isack platt full and free possession thereof and further I do Ingage my selfe to free yᵉ sd. Isack plat from all claims or demands And to free yᵉ sd. Isack plat from all Indemnetys of any person or persons what so ever and to yᵉ full and true performance of all above written I doe profixe my hand and seal yᵉ day and year above written

sealed, signed and                          JONATHAN HARNED
delivered in yᵉ pres-
ents of JONAS WOOD Senʳ
            her
ELIZEBETH ✕ WOOD
            mark

   The word : writting : in yᵉ first line was not in yᵉ originall : but my oversight.

This is a true Copy of yᵉ Originall by me John Corey Clerk May yᵉ 18. 1683.

may the first in the yer agty aight Wheras it is sad three acres in the deed & record the word three is mad four with my consent and aprobation as witness my hand.

JONATHAN HARNED.

(*Deeds, Vol.* 1, *p.* 157.)

## [TRAVELING ON THE LORD'S DAY.]

[1683, June 3.]

Where as we whos names are under written have y$^e$ last winter traveled from huntington to hempsted upon y$^e$ Lords day for which we are sori yt we have sinned against god and ofended our neibors for which we desir god to for give us and hope we shal never ofend god nor man in y$^e$ Like maner.

THO: HIGBY
EDWARD HIGBEE
MOSES SCUDDER.

Huntington June 3: 1683   The above sd. owned & subscribed In y$^e$ presents of y$^e$ Constable & overseers p me John Corey, Clerk.

(*Court Rec., p.* 363.)

---

## [DEED.  RICHARD WHITE TO THOMAS FLEET.]

[1683, June 11.]

The Record of Cap$^{tn}$ Thomas ffleets Rite of mill pond swamp.

Know all men whom these may conserne that I Richard White of huntington in y$^e$ east Riding of york sheir on long Island: have Bargened sold and made over all my Right and title yt I have in & to severall shares of y$^e$ old mill pond swamp: unto Cap$^{tn}$ Thomas ffleet of y$^e$ above sd. town & Ridding: for a Reasonable consideration already Received in hand where with I am fully contented and payed: The fore mentioned Rights of swamp I y^e fore sd. white bought of John Corey a two hundred pound Rite: also a two hundred pound Rite of nathaniell ffoster and also five hundred and half of Jonathan Rogers: All which severall shares are Recorded to me y^e above sd. white: And I y^e fore sd. Richard White have Barganed sold & Estranged from me my heirs, executors, administrators and asignes: all my Right title & intrust y^t I have in & to y^e above sd. swamp unto y^e above said Cap^tn Thomas ffleet his heirs, executors administrators and asignes to have and to hold for ever: And for y^e conformation here of I have here unto set to my hand this: 11 of June 1683.

Witness                                    RICHARD WHITE
  ABIEL TITUS
  JOHN KETCHAM.

                                    John Corey Recorder,

  (*Deeds*, Vol. 1, p. 105.)

---

[INDIAN DEED OF MEADOWS, SOUTH SIDE,
BY CAPT. OPASSUM.]*

[1683, Sept. 17.]

Be it known unto all Christian People to whom this my Deed of sale may come or any ways concern know ye that I, Capt. Opasum, alias Osaways, an Indian, and son unto Takapausha, Sachem, formerly of Massapage, and now Inhabitant upon Cow Neck, haveing a Privilege given me by

---

[*Nearly, perhaps quite all the beaches and meadow described in this deed are now in the limits of the town of Oyster Bay, the Marsepague Indians occupying territory farther west than Huntington as well as in Huntington. It was along this shore of the Great South Bay in Oysterbay town, where Capt. John Underhill and his soldiers, about the time of the first settlement attacked and massacred nearly the whole Marsepague tribe and destroyed their villages on slight provocation. | C. R. S.]

my Father, Takapousha, of all the meadow, fresh and salt, lying and being on the south side of Long Island and joyning to the Beach from the Great Gut, commonly called Massapage Gut, west or therabouts to the West gut, commonly called and known by the name of Merreek Gut, have upon good consideration and for a Reasonable Value of money in hand Received, have bargained, sold, alienated and in present Passession Delivered, all the meadow, fresh and salt, lying and joyning to the Beach between the two Guts as above said, and the Hammock or Broken Meadow any where, or in what nature soever lying, being between Oyster bay Meadow and the Beach above said, the Previlege of the Beach Included, to the salt sea, unto Adam wright, Job Wright, John Wright, Thomas Weeks and Thomas Townsend all Inhabitants of Oysterbay, to them, the above said five Persons their heirs, executors Adm$^{ms}$ and asigne forever, to have and to hould Occupy, Passess and enjoy, as all or either of their propper Right, title or Interest that they may now Possess, from me my heirs, ex$^m$ Adm$^n$. or Assigns or any other person English or Indian laying claim to any parcel thereof, forever as firmly unto all Interests and purposes as might or could be written or Drawn by any Deed of sale or conveyance Whatsoever Acording to Law, engage to Defend them or any of them, ther heirs or assigns, in Peaceable Possession & Injoyment of the Premises forever, as Witness my hand & seal, in Oysterbay, the 17$^{th}$ Day of September 1683.
Sealed and delivered In Presence of

JAMES WICK                          Capt OPASSUM, alias
his                                        × ORAWAY mark
JOHN × mark

Signd over to his Son in Law, Thos. Jones, Fort Neck, Paten of Oysterbay, 14 Sept. 17$\frac{13}{14}$.

THOS. TOWNSEND.

then to Frelove Jones, 18 Febry. 17$\frac{13}{14}$

THOS. WEEKS

Inst
SAML SEAMAN.
JOHN CLEMMENT.

Entered 14 July 1715, John Smith Clk.
from Records Queens County Clks. office Lib. E. page 60
& 61

Compard.
Whited Hicks Clk.

(*File No.* 30.)

---

## [TOWN MEETING. DELEGATES ELECTED TO THE SOUTHOLD ASSEMBLY.]

[1683, Sept. 24.]

Sept. 24. 1683.

At a town meeting legally warned the town being ordered by warrant from the high sheriff to make choice of
four men to go to Southold to meet in Assembly for the
choosing of two men for the East Riding to go to New
York Sizes.

The town having made choice of Isaac Platt, James Chichester, Epenetus Platt, Thomas Whitson.

The day above said, it was put to vote whether the town
would build a comfortable house upon the town lot for the
Ministery or exchange with Mr Jones for a lot that the town
formerly gave him lying between Jonas Smith house lot
and Thomas Wicks his pasture; and the major part of the
town's vote was to change with Mr Jones, that he should
have only the town lot; the meadow and other privileges
thereunto belonging to the town lot to remain and be the
town's forever.

[Copied from the original in Court Records 1681-4. p.

28 old paging, p. new paging, in the Revision of the Records in the year 1873.]

*(Town Meetings, Vol. 1, p. 119.)*

---

## [DEED. ROBERT ARTHUR TO JAMES SMITH.]

[1683, Oct. 2.]

The Records of James Smiths Land.

Know all men by these prsents y<sup>t</sup> I Robart Arthur of Huntington up on Long Island in y<sup>e</sup> East Riding of york shire waver, have and doe by these p<sup>r</sup>sents Bargan sell & make over unto James Smith of Huntington upon Long Island in y<sup>e</sup> East Riding of york shire afore sd. coper, a certaine pe<sup>r</sup>sell of Land situate and being in y<sup>e</sup> west neck of y<sup>e</sup> town of Huntington Containing Eaight acres being part of my division Land given me <sup>by</sup> y<sup>e</sup> town of Huntington and Layd out by order there of, which sd. Land Bounded as specified, the Land of Robart Cranfeild on y<sup>e</sup> East, The west side with y<sup>e</sup> woods in commonadg. so is also north and south ends I say all y<sup>t</sup> p<sup>r</sup>sell of Land wit all its fence there to belonging with all division Right or Rights y<sup>t</sup> may or ever here after shall be Long to y<sup>e</sup> afore sd. Land or Lands by divition Right or any other Lawfull way what so ever I have frome me my heirs executors Administrators and assignes Barganed sold and made over unto James Smith his heirs Executors Administrators and asignes, for y<sup>e</sup> sume of twenty one pounds passable pay of this Countrey to be payed in hand off y<sup>e</sup> sealing & delivering here of In Consideration whereof I doe by these p<sup>r</sup>sents sell Elinate, estrange & make over from me my heirs executors administrators and assignes unto James Smith his heirs executors administrators and assignes To have And to hold for Ever and further I doe Ingadge my selfe my heirs & assignes to save harmelesse and indamnefied y^e fore sd. James Smith his heirs executors, administrators and assignes from any person or persons who may or shall lay any Claime or title to y^e sd. Land or fence or any part or parsell thereof to y^e Indamnefing y^e sd Smith or his sucksesrs in his or there quiat possesion in witnesse where of I have heere unto set my hand & seale this 2^d day of October in y^e 35^th year of his mag^ties Reigne And in y^e year of our Lord 1683.

signed, seled and de-
livered in y^e presents of
the mark of
JAMES CHICHESTER          ROBART ✕ ARTHUR
THOMAS WHITSON            the mark of
                         MARY ✕ ARTHUR

This is a true Coppy of y^e originall by me John Corey Clerk, Oct. 20. 1683.

The above sd. Robart Arthur came to my house in company with James Smith afore sd. and acknowledged y^e afore sd. Instrument to be his owne volentary act and deed.

John Corey Clerke

(*Deeds, Vol. 1, pp.* 161-2.)

---

## [DEED. JOHN FINCH TO EDWARD HIGBEE.]

[1683, Oct. 6.]

know all men by these p^rsents yt I John ffinch ^senr of Huntington upon Long island In y^e East Riding of New York shire: ffor and in consideration of y^e sume of forty five pounds and ten shillings: In Currant pay of this Collony: to me alredy in hand payed by Edward Higbey of huntington, on long Island afore said for divers other good causes and considerations me heer unto moving And other good consideration Exciting: have sold him y^e sd. Higby all and every part & parcell of y^t accommondation of myne which was formerly Calub wood situated and being in y^e town ship of huntington on long Island and then sold to

Samuel davis and then to me John finch: which is bounded on y$^e$ East side with y$^e$ Lot of Thomas Whitson joyning to Joseph Bayly and frunting to y$^e$ street to gether with twelve acres of medow Lying on y$^e$ south side of y$^e$ IsLand Eaight acres Lying on a neck called by y$^e$ name of Santapauge and being bounded on y$^e$ East side y$^e$ medow of Epenetus plat and on y$^e$ west side with y$^e$ medo of Jonathan Rogers and foure acres of medow more or Lesse lying on a neck called by y$^e$ name of y$^e$ East neck joyning to foure acres of Cap$^{tn}$ fleet I y$^e$ fore sd John ffinch have made over & doe by these p$^r$sents make over from me my heirs Executors administrators & assignes unto Edward Higby his heirs executors Administrators & assignes y$^e$ home Lot orchyard fence gardin out Lands, belonging there unto to have And to hold for Ever and I doe by these p$^r$sents Ingage my selfe my heirs and assignes to save harmeles and indamnefied y$^e$ fore sd. Edward Higby his heirs and assignes from any person or p$^r$sons who may or shall Lay any Claime to y$^e$ fore sd. p$^r$messes or any part or parcel there of In witnesse where of I have heere unto set my hand & seal y$^e$ 6$^{th}$ day of Octobr In y$^e$ 35$^{th}$ of his mag$^{sts}$ Raine And in y$^e$ year of our Lord 1683. Signed sealed & delivered in y$^e$ p$^r$sents of us.

RICHARD WHITE                   JOHN FFINCH
JEREMY ADAMS

this interline I y$^e$ above sd. John finch doe owne to be before y$^e$ signeing and sealing of this bill of sale.

Huntington Aprill 1684

Apered before me this 7$^{th}$ of Aprill Jn$^o$ finch sen$^r$ of y$^e$ town of huntington in y$^e$ County of Suffolk on long Island and owned this within Instrument to be his act and deed.

ISAC ARNOLD. Justis.

y$^e$ above sd. is a true Coppy p. me Jn$^o$ Corey Clerk
Aprill y$^e$ 9$^{th}$ 1684.

(*Deeds, Vol. 1, p. 165.*)

## [COREY FAMILY RECORD-]

[1683, Oct. 28.]

huntington

John Core was maried to Mary Cornish the 15 day of desember 1667.

Mary Core the daughter of John Core was borne october the 20 1668 on the third day of the week in the night about the 10 hour.

Abigall Core the daughter of John Core was born the 13 day of November on the second day of the week about the 9 hour 1670.

Elizebeth Core, the daughter of John Core was born Jeneuary the 9 in the year 1672 on th 5 day of th week in the afternoon.

John Core the son of John Core was borne the 3 day of febery in the yere 1674 on the 4 day of the week in the after noon.

Martha Core the daughter of John Core was born the 17 day of febuary in the yeer 1677 the 7 day at evening.

Elnathan Core the son of John Core was born the first day of June in the yeare of our lord 1679 on the first day of the week in the morning before the sun was up.

Thomas Corey, the son of John Corey was born the 21 of September in y$^e$ year of our lord 1681 one y$^e$ fourth day of y$^e$ week called wednesday about noon.

Abraham Corey* was borne y$^e$ 28$^{th}$ of October 1683 on y$^u$ first day of y$^e$ week in y$^e$ night about y$^e$ 12 hour.

(*Court Rec., p.* 350.)

---

[*Considering how large a family John Corey left, it is singular that the name has entirely disappeared from the town of Huntington.—C. R. S.]

## [TOWN MEETING.]

[1683, Dec. 24.]

Dec. 24, 1683.

At a town meeting it was put to vote how many men they would send in order to the warrent sent the town. The vote is they would send one and impower two. John Sammis is chosen, and Epenetus Platt impowered. with him in order to the warrant.

[Copied from the original in Court Records 1681-4, p. 32 old paging, p.——new paging, in the Revision of the Records in the year 1873.]

(*Town Meetings, Vol.* 1, *p.* 121.)

---

## [WARRANT OF COMMISSIONERS FOR COUNTY ASSESSMENT.]

[1683, Dec. 27.]

Y$^e$ are to bring in, fayrely written the Certificate of the Names and y$^r$ names of all and every p.son & p.sons dweling & Residing within the bounds o$^r$ Limits of y$^r$ townes: and also of the substance and valllieu of every of them in Lands, Moneys & all other visible estate with out Concealement Lour * * * dread o$^r$ Mallis in order to the payment of the free gift or p$^r$sent which our Represuntatives gave as a grattuity to o$^r$ honorable governer,* being

[*The governor here referred to was His Excellency, Thomas Dongan, who had but recently landed, and who had promised great things in the way of a liberal government, but whose word, as afterward appeared, was of no more value than that of an Indian. He was, like the latter, always wanting a present. He subsequently seized the charter and title papers of Huntington and held them until he received a "present" as an inducement for their return.—C. R. S.]

one peny for every pounds vallue of all the Reall, personall & visible estate of all & every the free houlders & inhabitants of y<sup>r</sup> towne & limitts as also to choose & p<sup>r</sup>sent
to us the name of some Meete p<sup>r</sup>son in y<sup>r</sup> town to be Collector of sayd Money : this to be brought in to us at the
house of Mr Joseph fordham in South Hampton upon the
16 day of January Next: tis to bee under stood that all yo<sup>r</sup>
vallueables are to be as Money soe are the payments to be
also.

27<sup>th</sup> Decemb<sup>r</sup> 1683.

for the p<sup>r</sup>sentus or assessors of Huntington these.

J Sloss Hobart
Joseph fordham
Thomas Mapes
Epenetus Platt
} Comisioners.

(*File No.* 15.)

## [WOOD FAMILY RECORD.]

[1684, Jan. 6.]

Eliphelet Wood son of John wood was born the 14 day of
febuery in the yeer 1677.
John Wood the son of John Wood was born Aprill the
sixt 1680;
Martha Wood y<sup>e</sup> daughter of John wood was born y<sup>e</sup> sixt
of Jenuery In y<sup>e</sup> year of our Lord 168¾.
(*Court Rec., p.* 289.)

## [DEED. JOHN GOLDING TO NICHOLAS SMITH.]

[1684, Jan. 28.]

Nicolas Smith Land Rec<sup>r</sup>
This Indenture made y<sup>e</sup> 28<sup>th</sup> day of Jenuary in y<sup>e</sup> 36<sup>th</sup>

year of y$^e$ Raigne of our Sov$^e$ Lord Charles y$^e$ second by y$^e$ Grace of God of England Scotland, france & Ireland, king defender of y$^e$ faith etc. And in y$^e$ year of our Lord according to y$^e$ Computation of y$^e$ Church of England 1684 Between John Golding of fresh pond with in y$^e$ bounds of Huntington upon Long Island and in y$^e$ County of Suffolk in America of y$^e$ one party planter. And Nicollas Smith of y$^e$ same place & county afore sd. Carpenter of y$^e$ other party, Witnesseth : That y$^e$ sd. John Golding : for divers good causes mee moving, but especialy for and in Consideration of y$^e$ sume of twenty six pounds in hand payed before y$^e$ sealing and delivery of these p$^r$sents by y$^e$ sd. Nicollas Smith where with y$^e$ said John Golding doth acknowledg him selfe fully satisfied, contented and payed: Hath granted allinated bargened sold and confirmed and by these presents doth fully cleerly and absolutly grant alinat : bargan sell and confirme unto y$^e$ afore said Nicolas Smith his hous, orchyard home lot lying and being in y$^e$ town of Huntington in y$^e$ tener or occupation of y$^e$ fore said John Golding y$^e$ lot Containing three acres be it more or lesse ; With all housing Barnes, stables, gardens, Buildings fences or other herid-nts to y$^e$ same be longing or appartaining to y$^e$ sd. hous or tenements formerly Injoyed by John Lum : thence estranged to John Mathis thence to Jeffrey Lake again Recaived by John Mathis thence to John Golding Buting & bounding as specified y$^u$ land of Tho$^s$ Wicks on y$^e$ east end : The land of John Corey on y$^e$ south side : y$^e$ west & north to y$^e$ kings high way to gether with all Woods under Woods Commons of pasture what soever doth to y$^e$ same belong. To have And to hold y$^e$ said housing garding, orchard home lott with all y$^e$ fore mentioned p$^r$meses with all their Rights & priveledges y$^t$ now doth or ever here after may or shall be long or appertain unto y$^e$ same, unto y$^e$ above sd. Nicollas Smith his heirs, executors administrators and asignes : And to y$^e$ only use and behoofe of y$^e$ afore sd. Nicollas Smith his heirs

executors, administrators & assigns for ever. And y^e above
said John Golding for him selfe his heirs executors administrators and asignes doe Covenent p^romise and grant
by these p^rsents y^t at y^e time of y^e sealing and delivery here of he then was y^e sole and Lawfull
owner of all y^e afore mentioned p^rmeses and am
lawfuly seased of and in y^e same and in every part and
parcell there of in my own Right And y^e said Nicollas
Smith his heirs executors, administrators and assignes shall
and may by force and vertue of these p^rsents from time to
time and at all times here after Lawfully peacably and
quiatly have hold use occupy and injoy the afore mentioned
ed primeses with all their appurtinences free and cleer and
cleerly acquited and discharged of and from all and all
maner of fines gifts grants, Leases morgageses joynters
dowers titles of dower judgments executions entailleings
and of and from all other titles troubles and incumbrances
what so ever had made, committed witingly or willingly
suffered or don by y^e sd. John Golding or by any other
person or persons whatsoever Lawfuly claiming from by
or under him y^e sd. John Golding: or by his meanes or
assent or privet procurment And y^e sd. John Golding his
heirs and assignes and all and every person and persons
what soever lawfuly claiming in from or under him shall
and will warrant and for ever defend: by these p^rsents y^e
fore mentioned premices only what intrast belongs to his
Royal highnesse y^e Duke of Yorke: In Witnesse where of
I have here unto set my hand and seale y^e day & year
above written.

signed sealed and                    ye marke of
delivered in y^e p^rsents of        JOHN ✕ GOLDING.
JOHN COREY, JOSEPH BALY.

    this above sd. deed was acknowledged before me this 29
of January 168⅘ EPENETUS justis of y^e peace.

    Memorandam I Grace Golding wife of John Golding
doe acknowledge, condesend, consent and agree to and

confirme as much as in me lyeth to all and every of y^e
within mentioned bargan sale and alination of all and every
of y^e within mentioned p^rmeses as my hand and seale
doth testefie y^e marke of GRACE × GOLDING signed sealed &
delivered in y^e p^rsents of JOSEPH BALY, JOHN COREY. This
above sd. acknowledgment was owned by y^e woman to be
volentery and freely don before me EPENETUS PLATT justis
of y^e peace.

This Bill of sale is a true coppy compared with y^e originall by me John Corey Clerk. Feb. 27, 168⅘.

(*Deeds, Vol.* 1, *pp.* 185-6.)

---

## [DEED. THOMAS MARTIN TO THOMAS SCIDMORE.]

[1684, Feb. 12.]

This Indenture Made y^e twelfe day of febraware in y^e
thirtie six yeer of y^e Raine of our sov^r Lord Charls the second & in y^e yeer of our Lord one thousand six hundred
eaightie fowr five Between Thomas martin of Crabmedow
neck w^th in y^e bounds of huntington upon long Island in y^e
Counte of Suffoke and provaince of new yourke in Americae husbandman of y^e one partie & Thomas Scidmore of y^e
same place in y^e counte and p^rovince a fore said of y^e other
Partie Wittneseth that for divers good considerations moving mee their unto have barganed sould asighned & made
over and doe by these p^rsents Bargaine allinate estrange
and make over from mee my heirs exseceters Administrators and Asighnes all my Right tittle & intrest in and too A
sertaine p'sell of medoe land containing three quarters of
an acker or neer there abouts. Butting and bounding as
speecified Bounded one y^e east side w^th A small Creeke on
y^e north or norewest w^th y^e hieway, high way w^th A small
slow where y^e tide coms up : on y^e south side wth A small

Creeke I say this Parcell of meddow Land w<sup>th</sup> all it Rights
and Priveleges acording to its denomination bee it more or
lesse for & in consideration of y<sup>e</sup> sum of twentie five shillings in hand Paid before the ensealling & delivering heer
of wherein and where of I y<sup>e</sup> sd. Thomas marten doe Ac.
knowledge my self too bee fully satisfied, contented and
Paid by y<sup>e</sup> afore sd Thomas Scidmore, for which I the said
Thomas martin have granted sould Alinated and Confirmed
& by these p<sup>r</sup>sents, doe confirm from mee my heirs exseketers administrators & asignes unto Thomas Scidmore his
heiars exsecketers administrators and Asighens to have and
to hold for ever y<sup>e</sup> afore sd. p<sup>r</sup>mises and y<sup>e</sup> sd Thomas
martin for him self his heairs & a sighns doth warant my
self to bee y<sup>e</sup> Lawfull owner of y<sup>e</sup> afore mentioned p<sup>r</sup>mises.
And y<sup>e</sup> said Thomas Scidmore his heairs exseckters Adminestraters or Asighns shall or may by force & vertue of
these presents from time to time & att all time for ever
Lawfully Peacably & quietly have hold use ocupie posses
aud enjoe y<sup>e</sup> same cleerly Aquitted and discharged of and
from all gifts, grants Leasses morgages, jointurs dowreis,
tittles of dowreis judgments exsecutions, entaills and from
all other tittles, troubles and incombrances what soe ever
had made or committed by y<sup>e</sup> said Thomas martin or by any
other Person or persons whatsoever Lawfully Claiming
from or under him y<sup>e</sup> said Thomas martin or by his means
assent or procurement and doe warant to defend for ever
y<sup>e</sup> a fore sd. pmeses onely Reserving the in trest of his
Ryall heiness y<sup>e</sup> Duke of yorke in witnesse whereof I have
hereunto set my hand and seale the day & yeer first above
written.

| Witnese | The mark of ✗ |
|---|---|
| JEREMIAH WOOD | THOMAS MARTIN |
| his ✗ marke | The mark of ✗ |
| JAMES SMITH | MARY MARTIN |
| May y<sup>e</sup> 6<sup>th</sup> 1686 | |

This above written oblygation was acknowleged before mee this ii of Aprill 1686

EPENETUS PLATT

Justice of peace

(*Deeds, Vol.* 1, *p.* 131.)

Recorded.

The Bill of salle on y^e other side Relatting to Thomas martin and Thomas scidmore is a true Coppy Comparied with y^e origanall p mee Isaac Platt

Rec^r

(*Deeds, Vol.* 1, *p.* 132.)

---

## [NOKES FAMILY RECORD.]

[1684, Feb. 15.]

John nocks sunn of walter noakes was borne the 23 of Aprill 1672. Thomas nocks was borne 15^th of march 16$\frac{74}{75}$. Walter nocks was borne y^e 26^th of septembar in y^e yeer of our lord 1676.

Isaac noacks was borne 15^th of september 1678. sara nocks daughter of walter nocks was borne the 12^th of Aprill in y^e yeer 1681 Rachell nocks borne y^e 15^th of feburwary in y^e yeer 16$\frac{83}{84}$.

(*Surveys, p.* 150.)

---

## [THE TURK'S RATE.*]

[1684, Feb. 16.]

The Turks Ratte.

Agreed apone: by us hos names ar underritten that

---

[*The "Turks Rate" was a term used to denote a tax levied by the British Government to provide funds for ransoming prisoners taken by Algierian pirates in the Mediterranean Sea and other waters.—C. R. S.]

thos men how war bee hind of the payment of the : turkes
mony : ar now to pay the remaindar in Speshy and prise
foll being that is to say :
good  marchantabell : wintar  whet at : 4 p bus : ll.
good  marchantabell  somar  whet at : 3 : 6 :  per  bus : ll
good  merchantabell Indian Corne at ; 2 : p. bus : ll.
good  merchantabell pork at 2ᵈ : p pound——
good long whall bone at : 6ᵈ : p pound——

<table>
<tr><td>febeuary 16ᵗʰ</td><td>ISAAC PLATT</td></tr>
<tr><td>168¾</td><td>EPENETUS PLATT</td></tr>
<tr><td></td><td>JAMES SMITH</td></tr>
<tr><td></td><td>ABIEL TITUS</td></tr>
</table>

The names of thos men yᵗ are behind of the turks Ratte :
it com to 2d upon yᵉ hundred to be paid as within  written

|                 |     | hundred |
| --------------- | --- | ------- |
| Sam. Wood       |     | :3      |
| Rich. Williams  |     | :2      |
| Walter Noack    |     | :2      |
| John Go ldin    |     | :3      |
| Captt. Baily    |     | :5      |
| John Brush      |     | :2      |

      (*File No.* 10.)

---

## [ACCOUNT OF WOLVES KILLED.]

   [1684.]

Suffolk
      Dr to Huntington

| | | | | |
| --- | --- | --- | --- | --- |
| To eleven wolves and fower Indian wolves | . | 18 | 06 | o |
| To John Weeks for a Jernne to Hum sted | . | oo | 07 | o |
| To Joseph Whittmen | . | o1 | 11 | o |
| To Epenettus Platt for expencs | . | oo | o6 | 9 |
| To Jonathan Scudder for friet | . | oo | o9 | o |
| To James Wood as Committee | . | o2 | o9 | o |
| To yᵉ warrant to Jonas Wood | . | oo | o2 | 6 |
| To yᵉ treseur for collecting the summe | . | o2 | o6 | 6 |
| | | 25 | 17 | 9 |

An Anount arisen in Huntington in yᵉ County of Suffolk.
1 wolfe killed by Thomas Higby yᵉ 18ᵗʰ of november 1684.
1 (one) wolfe killed by Richard Soopper and Edward Higby: yᵉ 2ᵈ of desʳ 1684
5 (five) wolves killed by Edward Higby; at desemʳ yᵉ 3ᵈ
one; January yᵉ 21 three, septembʳ yᵉ 19 one 1685.
2 (two) wolves killed by timothy Conkling and brought to
me yᵉ 22ᵈ of desembr 1684 and yᵉ 24ᵗʰ of March, after.
1 Richard Sopper killed one Wolfe and brought yᵉ head,
feb. yᵉ 20ᵗʰ 168⅘
2 Jeremiah Smith one wolfe yᵉ 19ᵗʰ of Sep. 1685: the other
was a yong wolf killed by an Indian.
2 John Wicks two young wolves killed, Indeans, Jan.: 30:
and oct yᵉ 5ᵗʰ
1 James Smith one young wolf, killed by an Indean: called
Amphery, october 21: 1685.
for John wicks going to hempsted to pylot a man which
had Letters for yᵉ Govenour Sept. yᵉ 7ᵗʰ 8ᵗʰ for which he
demands 0; 7: 0:
for going to Setalket to carry our voats for chusing esem-
bly men upon ye 18ᵗʰ of Sept. 1685.
for Joseph Whitman Grand Juriman for ye towne of Huntington at South hempsted Court Last yᵉ march.
The valuation of yᵉ estates of Huntington is 6298ˡᵇ 16ˢ 8ᵈ
Huntington Novembr yᵉ 7ᵗʰ 1685; by order of ye town of
Huntington.
                                    John Corey Clerke.
for ye Comitty now sitting at South hold for yᵉ County of
Suffolk.
    (*File No. 7.*)

---

[SAMMIS FAMILY RECORD.]

[1684, March 14.]

John Samis sonn of John Samis was borne yᵉ 13ᵗʰ of septembar in yᵉ yeer 1673,

Silus samis sonn of John Samis was borne y$^e$ 2$^d$ of novembar in y$^e$ yeer 1676

deberah Samis daughter of John Samis was borne y$^e$ 13$^{th}$ of Novembar 1678.

david Samis sonn of John Samis was borne y$^e$ 4$^{th}$ of ocktobar in y$^e$ yeer 1681.

Isaac Samis sonn of John Samis was borne y$^e$ 14$^{th}$ day of March 16$\frac{83}{84}$

(*Surveys, p.* 162.)

---

### [MARY SIMPSON TO SARAH SOPER.]

[1684, March 15.]

know all whome it may concerne y$^t$ I mary simson do acknowledg y$^t$ in y$^e$ time of my widdowhood in huntington when I had knowledge y$^t$ I had a rite in Crabmedow farmes in huntington bounds I went to my daughter Sarah Soper and bequathed all my Right in y$^e$ sd. farme to her to keep for her son Richard soper when he come of age.

Huntington

March y$^e$ 15$^{th}$ 168$\frac{3}{4}$

witnes

J$^{no}$ COREY

RICHARD BOTT.

ye marke of

MARY $\times$ SIMSON

This is a true Coppy of y$^e$ originall p me John Corey.

Clerk

March y$^e$ 15. 168$\frac{3}{4}$

(*Court Records, p.* 400.)

---

### [COURT RECORD.]

[1684, March 21.]

Whereas Katrine Jones of Huntington did peticion this

Court of sessions now sitting this 21$^{st}$ of march 168$\frac{3}{4}$ at South hampton : y$^t$ she may Injoy the Estate of Moses Scudder deceased, for her Comfortable subsistance y$^e$ Court haveing Considered y$^e$ same doe order & determin y$^t$ y$^e$ sd. Widow Jones shall quiatly Injoy all y$^e$ Estate In her possession, or y$^t$ y$^e$ said Moses Scudder with his said mother died possessed of to In joy as afore sd. dureing her life & at her decease ; to Returne to y$^e$ heires according to Law : unlesse y$^e$ children can agree with her upon other termes to her satisfaction, which granted, giveing in securety to Law

p order of Court p John howell ; Junr : Clarke.

y$^e$ Charge arising in refference to y$^o$ premises is fifteen shillings in mony. J. H.

This is a true Coppy of y$^e$ originall Compared by me John Corey, Clarke.

(*Court Records, p.* 367.)

----

## [COURT RECORD. A GRAND JURY CHOSEN.]

[1684, March 22.]

Itt is ordered by this Courte of sessions* holden for y$^e$ County of Suffolk now sitting in Southampton this 22$^{th}$ day of March 168$\frac{3}{4}$ as followeth, that there shall bee a grand Jury Chosen (viz$^{st}$) three substantiall faitfull men In each Respective towne in this County to be Chosen by the Majority of y$^e$ free holders of every towne to make a true presentment acording to Law of all missdemeaners that shall be Committed in there townes Respectively

----

[*At the Assembly held the previous October, (1683) the division of the province into ridings was . abolished and twelve counties were established, among them Suffolk. This was, I think, the first court held in this County under the new order of things.—C. R. S.]

Dureing there office of grand Jurymen (viz^{st}) swareing
profanes, Sabeth Breaking, Drunkeness, fornication Adul-
tery and all such abomniable sins and the said jurymen
be sworne to there office by the next Justice off the Peace.

By the Courte,

John Howell, Clarke.

To y^e grand Jurymen of y^e
towne of Huntington
   (*Court Rec. p.* 369.)

---

[DEED.   JOHN BETTS TO EDWARD HIGBEE.]

[1684, March 29.]

To all Expian peopel to whome these p^rsents writing
shall come I John Beets of huntington upon long Island
within y^e County of Sufolk husband and abigal my wife
have for divers good causes & considerations as these
p^rsent witnesseth know y^e y^t we John Beets & abigall my
wife doth for and in consideration of a marriage y^t have
been made and sollomnized between Edward higby of y^e
one party & abigal adams of y^e other part my daughter in
Law have given granted and doe by these p^rsents give and
grant and make over from us our heirs executors, administrators & asignes unto our son in Law Edward Higby of
huntington on Long Island within y^e County of Suffolk
afore sd. husband man The south west end of my home
situat and lying in huntington afore sd. Containing two
acres be it more or lesse now in y^e possesion of y^e sd. higby bounded on y^e east side with y^e high way y^t was formerly a mill pond and y^e south west end y^e hiway y^e west
or norwest y^e highway y^t Leads to y^e west feild or harbour y^e north end with my home lot we say all & singluer
y^e sd. land and fence before specefied we doe by these
p^rsents elinate and estrange from us our heirs, executors,

administrators & asignes unto Edward higby his heirs executors admynistrators and assignes to have and to hold
for ever in witnesse where of wee have here unto sot our
hand & seal this 29<sup>th</sup> of March in y<sup>e</sup> 36 year of his maj<sup>sts</sup>
Raine and in y<sup>e</sup> yeare of our Lord 1684.
signed sealed & dd.                          JOHN BEETS.
in y<sup>e</sup> p<sup>r</sup>sents of
    JOHN COREY
    EPENETUS PLATT

huntington Suffolke, appeared before me this 7<sup>th</sup> of Aprill
1684 Jn° beets and acknowledged y<sup>e</sup> above Instrument to
be his act and deed.                         ISACK ARNOLD
                                                  Justes.

    a true Coppy by me John Corey, Clark
        Aprill 9, 1684.
        (*Deeds, Vol.* 1, *p.* 167.)

---

## [TOWN MEETING.]

[1684, April 7,]

at a town meeting Legally warned and being so met this
7<sup>th</sup> of Aprill 1684. The day afore said Mr Epenetus platt
chosen tresurer.

The day above said Jonathan Scudder chosen collecter
for this present year. Also it was voated by y<sup>e</sup> major part
of y<sup>e</sup> town Capt. thomas fleet, Thomas powell, Thomas
Whitson, for Comiciners for this present year.*

further more y<sup>e</sup> day above said abiell titus was chosen
Constable for this present year.

---

[*A Town Court had been created which was to be held by
three commissioners. These men refused to take the oath as
such commissioners. This office was short lived, as it did not
meet with public approval.—C. R. S.]

Upon consideration that y⁰ said Thomas fleet and thomas powel : and thomas Whitson are not willing to take y⁰ oath according to Law. therefor y⁰ town have preseeded y⁰ day above sd. to a new choyce and by y⁰ major part of y⁰ voate

Isaac plat  
Epenetus plat  } Comisioners  
and John Corey

the day above sd. it was voated by y⁰ major part of y⁰ voats that Joseph Whitman, thomas wicks and James Smith shall sarve as grand jury men for this present year.

(*Town Meetings, Vol.* 1, *p.*126.)

---

## [JOHN FINCH TO EDWARD HIGBEE.]

[1684, April 18.]

At y⁰ Request of Edward Higby this Eighteenth of Aprill 1684 thomas whitson and Martha his wife, doth declare yᵗ John finch senʳ did som time in October last goe into his lot then sold unto Edward higby : and gave y⁰ sd. Edward higby possession by braking a twig and diging a turfe : and delivering y⁰ turfe and twig* to y⁰ sd. higby and sd. by vartue of this I give you possion of this my lot and all yᵗ medow and out Land belonging to it.

John Corey, Clerk.

(*Deeds, Vol.* 1, *p.* 166.)

---

[*The delivery of land upon a sale "by turfe and twig" was a a custom derived from England, where it had prevailed from a very remote period, and before written records of conveyances were made. The mode of delivery is in this conveyance very plainly stated.—C. R. S.]

## [DEED. THOMAS FLEET Sen. TO JOHN SAMMIS.]

[1684, May 20.]

John Samis.

Where as there is a certain parcell of swawp or bogey medow lying in this town of huntington comonly caled and known by yᵉ name of yᵉ old mill pond where in most of yᵉ freeholders had formerly a Rite therin and did agree to lay it out into four quarters so yᵗ every of yᵉ proprietors had knowledg in which of yᵉ quarters his proportion lay & yᵉ said swamp or bogey medow is layed out in to foure quarters to Run East and west so yᵗ yᵉ quarteʳ next yᵉ mill dam may be call yᵉ first quarter and yᵗ quarter which lyeth next to Epenetus plats hous lots & Tho wicks his pastuer may be called yᵉ fourth & last quarter—Wherefore know all whom these may consern that I Thomas fleet senʳ having a four hundred pound Rite there in by vartue of my accommondation, in yᵉ fore sd. bogey medow and have also made lawfull purchas of severall persons shares there in namly of Samuel wood his three hundred pound Rite of Thomas powell his three hundred pound Right: of Thomas Whitson his two hundred pound Rite: of John finch senʳ his fower hundred pound Rite: also of Richard White severall shars which he purched: namely of John Corey his two hundred pound Rite: of Joseph wood his two hundred pound Rite: of Jonathan Rogers his five hundred & fifty pound Rite: all which Rite & shares are lying in yᵉ second quarter except yᵗ four hundred bought of John finch afore sd. which lyeth in yᵉ first quarter of yᵉ afore sd. bogey medow; which first quarter lyeth next yᵉ mil dam afore said   This writing further witneseth to all whom it may consern yᵗ I Thomas fleet senʳ of huntington in yᵉ county of Suffolk Merchant have bargamed sold & made over unto John Sammis of yᵉ above sd. town &

county all my Right title & intrust y$^t$ I have in all and
every of y$^e$ fore sd. Rite & shares of old mil pond swamp
or bogey medow for a Reasonable consideration alredy,
Receaived in hand where of & where with I am fully contented & payed : And doe by these p$^r$sents bargan sell
estrange and make over all my Rite title and intrust y$^t$ I
have in and to all & every part & parcell' of my Rights and
shares afore mentioned in y$^e$ fore sd. old mill pond swamp
or bogey medow from me my heirs executors, administrators & assignes unto John Sammis afore sd. him his heirs
executors administrators & assignes To have and to hold
to use & improve and peacably to injoy without lett or
mollestation for ever. And further I y$^e$ afore said Thomas
fleet sen$^r$ doe Ingage my selfe my heirs executors administrators & asignes to save harmlesse & indemnefied y$^e$ fore
sd. John Sammis his heirs executors administrators and
assignes from any person or persons who may or shall lay
at any time any Just & lawfull claim to any part or parcell
of y$^e$ fore mentioned Rites or shares of y$^e$ fore sd. old mill
pond swamp or bogey medow And for y$^e$ performence and
confirmation of all & every of y$^e$ perticulers afore sd. I
have here unto set my hand & seal this twentyeth of may
In y$^e$ year of our Lord 1684 THOMAS FLEET, signed sealed
and delivered in y$^e$ p$^r$sents of JOHN COREY :

And y$^e$ marke of WALTER×NOAKS

This is a true Coppy Compared with y$^e$ originall p me
John Corey clark.

May y$^e$ twenty ninth 1684.

(*Deeds*, Vol. 1, p. 169.)

---

## [TOWN MEETING. THE INDIANS TO PAY RENT.]

[1684, June 23.]

At a town meeting legaly warned by y$^e$ constable y$^e$ 23$^{rd}$

of June and y° meeting held y° 26th of June abov. sd. 1684. The first thing that was voted y° day abov sd was publak Red the second thing was voated y° day abov sd. was that there should be a collector to gather all Rates that is to say y° County Rate ye ministers fifty pound a year and all towne Rats : for this present year ensewing the third thing was voated y° day above said Jonathan Scudder was chosen by y° major voat to be Collector for this ensewing year.

The fourth thing y^t was voted y° day above sd : Mr Wood, Isack platt Thomas powell & John Corey to discourse with y° Indians about their setling on our Land : And to give them order to Remove or give some smalle Rent as acknowledgment as y° shall (see) fit for so Long time as you shall allow him provided y^t hee take up no more Land.

y° fifth thing y° day above sd it was voted and granted y^t Jonathan Scudder shall take up six acres of Land towards his division it lying not fare from y° wigwam swamp and fronting towards y° claft. if it do not prejudish highways or watering places.

y° sixth thing voted it was voated y° day abov. sd. that Benjamin Scrivenir shall have three acres of Land for a home Lot. And Liberty for his Cattell on ye Commons provided y^t he live ten years in y° town and follow ye trade of weveing for y° inhabitants of huntington y° sd. Land is lying on y° north sid of y° Cart way Leading to hempsted at y° discression of y° layers out.

But in case he Remove out of ye town before y° ten years abov. sd be expired then this to belong to y° town again but if he did inhabit in this town before y° ten years bee expired then y° above sd Land and priveledge shall belong to his heirs forever.

(*Town Meetings, Vol. 1, p. 129.*)

## [QUIT CLAIM.   THOMAS SMITH AND OTHERS
## TO THOMAS BRUSH.]

[1684, June 25.]

Whereas our ffather William Smith now deceased, formerly of Huntington did sell allenate & make over his hous &
lands with all preveledges & apurtnences there unto belonging unto Thomas Brush of yᵉ sd. place & Receaved pay
for it of yᵉ sd Thomas Brush : we yᵉ natural born children
of yᵉ said William Smith doe bind & ingage & for our
selves & assignes covenent & promise not to molest or des-
turb yᵉ fore sd. Thomas Brush his heirs or assignes in yᵉ
quiat & peacable possession of yᵉ said lands bought by
Thomas Brush of our deseased father as afore sd.   That is
our act we testifie by our subscribing our hands this 25ᵗʰ
day of June Ano domini 1684.

his mark<br>
THOMAS ✕ SMITH<br>
JOSEPH SMITH<br>
NEHEMIAH SMITH<br>
WAIT SMITH.

subscribed before us
DANᴸᴸ DENTON
JOSEPH SMITH Juᵉʳ

this is a true coppey of ye original yᵉ 27 of June
1684.

John Corey Clarke.

(*Deeds, Vol.* 1, *p.* 99.)

---

## [TOWN MEETING.]

[1684, June 26.]

June yᵉ 26ᵗʰ 1684, att a town meetting it was granted yᵗ
Thomas Brush should have six ackars of land in yᵉ west

neck att A deep hollow neer his other land formerly granted: y⁰ wch. Land was Laid out by Samuell titus servaer fortie fowr Rods one way and twentie too Rods y⁰ other way.

p mee Isaac Platt<br>Clarke.

(*Deeds, Vol.* 1, *p.* 87.)

## [SCRIVENER FAMILY RECORD.]

[1684, June.]

Benjmin Scrifner sonn of Benjiman Scrifner of huntington was borne y⁰ 12ᵗʰ of may in y⁰ yeer of our Lord 1682

John Scrifner sonn of Benjamin scrifner was borne The tenth of June in y⁰ yeer 1684.

(*Surveys, p.* 164.)

## [DEED. BENJAMIN SMITH TO JOHN BRUSH.]

[1684, June 28.]

The Records of y⁰ Lands & medows of John Brush.

This deed Bearing date this 28ᵗʰ day of June in y⁰ year of our Lord Christ 1684 in y⁰ 36ᵗʰ yeare of y⁰ Reighn of our sovereigne Lord Charles the second by y⁰ grace of god of England, Scotland france and Ireland, King defender of y⁰ faith &c. Witneseth yᵗ I Benjamen Smith, of milford in y⁰ County of new haven in y⁰ Collony of Conecticut in new England, ffor and in consideration of full sattisfaction in hand alredy Receaived have given granted Bargaed and sould And By these presents, doe give grant bargan and sell unto John Brush of Huntington in y⁰ County of Suffolk upon Long Island a cartaine accomondation of Land, being a two hundred pound alotment Lying in y⁰

afore sd. town of Huntington, and formerly in y$^e$ possession
and belonging to me and now in y$^e$ possession of y$^e$ afore
sd. J$^{no}$ Brush. The home lot containing about four acres of
Land be it more or less : Being bounded with y$^e$ street or
high way south : Jo$^n$ Samons his lot north Walter Nokes
his Lot East and Tho. brush his Land west And one percell
of medow upon a neck called Naguntatoge containing four
acres be it more or less bounded east with y$^e$ passonage
medow and west with y$^e$ medow of Thomas brush and y$^e$
wood land north and y$^e$ sound south also four acres of
medow more or less on y$^e$ east neck all which fore mentioned Land and medow together with y$^e$ priveledges and
Appurtinances thene unto belonging with all divitions of
land y$^t$ formerly hath doth or here after may belong to y$^e$
sd. accommondations y$^e$ sd. John brush is to have and to
hold to him his heirs and assignes for ever and further I
y$^e$ sd. Benjamen Smith doe for me my heirs executors &
administrators covenent to & with y$^e$ sd. John Brush his
heirs & asignes y$^t$ he y$^e$ sd. Jn$^o$ Brush his heirs execut. administrators & asignes shall quiatly & peacably possess
hold and Injoy all & singular y$^e$ fore sd. accomondations
with all y$^e$ divisions priviledges and appurtenances, there
unto belonging for ever with out any Let or molestation
from any person or persons what so ever y$^t$ shall Lay any
Leagal Claime there unto or any part there of In witnesse
where of I have here unto set my hand and seal y$^e$ day &
yeare first above written.

signed, sealed And                    BENJAMIN SMITH
dellivered In y$^e$ p$^r$sents of us.

JOHN BEARD
SAM$^{ll}$ EELLS.

The a bove written deed of sale was acknowledged by
y$^e$ above sd Benjamin Smith to be his act & deed And
Sarah Smith y$^e$ wife of y$^e$ sd Benjamin Smith did freely
with out Either treating or flattery given her free and full

consent there unto & set her hand here unto this 28ᵗʰ of June 1684.                                    SARAH SMITH.

before me JOHN BEARD, Comm, in Milford

yᵉ above said is a true Coppy of yᵉ Originall by me John Corey Clerk.

July yᵉ 17 1684.

(*Deeds, Vol. 1, p. 173.*)

---

## [LANDS OF JONATHAN SCUDDER.]

[No Date.]

The Records of yᵉ lands of Jonathan Scudder.

six acars of land at Crab medow joyning to Edward Bunch on yᵉ north. The land of Thomas Brush on yᵉ east and six acars more joyning to yᵉ south side and west end of his fore mentioned land.

(*Deeds, Vol. 1, p. 95.*)

---

## [GREEN FAMILY RECORD.]

[1684.   Aug. 24.]

John Green son of John Green was borne yᵉ 30ᵗʰ of June in yᵖ yeer 1675.

Elizabeth green was borne yᵉ 15 of august 1677.

Thomas Green was borne yᵉ 16ᵗʰ of february 167$\frac{8}{9}$

William Green was borne yᵉ 1ˢᵗ of march in yᵉ yeer 16$\frac{81}{82}$.

Ame Green daughter of John Green was borne yᵉ 24ᵗʰ of August in yᵉ yeer 1684.

(*Survey, p. 150.*)

# [DEED.   JOSIAH JONES TO BENJAMIN
## SCRIVENER.]

[1684, Aug. 29.]

Benjamen Scriveners Record of Land.

Know all men whom these p^rsents may consern: y^t I Josiah Jones of Huntington in y^e county of Suffolk on  Long
Island in New York shire, have for a  valuable  consideration bargan and sold and made over unto Benjamen Scrivener wever of y^e above sd. town & County my hous &  lot
lying and being in huntington afore sd. being formerly  by
y^e town granted unto me to gether with  y^e  denomination
of one hundred pound commondege and Right  of  upland
even all y^e Rights and priveledges granted & given me by
y^e town of huntington for all which I  have  Received  full
satisfaction in hand where of & where with I am fully  satisfied contented and  payed  I say I  y^e above sd.  Josiah
Jones do by the p^rsents bargan sell estrange &  make  over
from me my heirs executors administrators or asignes my
hous Lot afore said Liying on y^e south sid  of  hempsted
path & joyning to y^e west side of y^e Lot formerly granted
to Johanas Rase which now belongeth to y^e  town  againe
together with all Rits & p^ryeledge y^t now doth  or hereafter may or shall any way there unto be  long,  unto  Benjaman Scrivener above said him his heirs executors, administrators or assignes to have and to hold to use and improve
and quiatly to possesse and Injoy ffor ever:  with  out  any
Let or molestation by me or any meanes of myne And further I y^e above sd. Josiah Jones doe  Ingadge  in behalf of
my selfe my heirs executors administrators and assigns  to
bare harmlesse and indamnefie y^e fore sd. Benjaman Scrivener him  his  heirs  executors administrators  and assigns
from any person or persons who shall or may Lay and just
or Lawfull claime to any part or p^rsell of y^e afore sd. Lands

or p$^r$veledgs : as witnesse my hand and seal this 29$^{th}$ of
Augcst and in y$^e$ year of our Lord 1684

JOSIAH JONES.

signed, sealed and delivered
in y$^e$ p$^r$sents of
   y$^e$ mark of
HENRY X SOPER
JOHN COREY ; Clerk.

    This is a true Coppy of y$^e$ originall by me John Corey,
      Sept. 16 1684.                 Clerk.
     *(Deeds, Vol. 1, p. 175.)*

---

## [ESTABLISHING THE BOUNDARY WITH OYSTER BAY.]

[1684, Oct. 4.]

    October y$^e$ 4: 1684
Whereas we have Received some lines under hand from
Cap$^t$ Thomas Townsend of Oyster Bay to send men to Run
y$^e$ line between Huntington & Oysterbay y$^e$ 9$^{th}$ of y$^e$ above
s$^d$. Accordingly the Commsioners Namely Isack plat-
Epenetus p!at and John Corey have In y$^e$ town of Hun
tingtons behalfe made Choyse of Thomas powel and abiel
titus to run y$^e$ Line : with them y$^e$ 9$^{th}$ of the abov `sd

                      John Corey, Clerk.
The Comis.r choyce of those 2 men above s$^d$ namely
thomas powell and abiel titus to run y$^e$ line abov. sd. they
are excepted of and confirmed by cleer voat in town meeting october 28, 1684 J. Corey Clerk.

Thes may sertefie to all people who are any wise conserned
y$^t$ whereas Thomas Townsen Nathinel Cobles & John
wilks : being appointed by y$^e$ town of oyster bay for to run
y$^e$ line of division between oysterbay & huntington. And

yᵉ fore sᵈ inhabitants of huntington have Chosen to run yᵉ
fore sᵈ line of division betwixt them & oyster bay and have
chosen & empowered Thomas powel & abiel Titus in yᵉ
behalf of ye fore sd town to run yᵉ fore sᵈ line. viz wee the
above sd. do agree to begin at yᵉ head of yᵉ Cold Spring
river at a white oake tree with H. marked on one side and
O. on yᵉ other side : And from thence to a white oake on
yᵉ same side of huntington cart path unto yᵉ plains which
is on yᵉ west side of yᵉ flow of water yᵗ ye fore sd cart path
goes threw & so runs south as neere as we could marking
trees with O & H. untill we come  *   *   *   unto yᵉ middel of ye Island as neere as we could perseive or understand and this afore sd. line Run by these men as inhabitants of boath towns being fully impowered by yᵉ a fore sᵈ
towns for a perpetuall line of division to Remain ˙so to
them and their heirs for ever : this line run yᵉ ninth of
Augoust 1684. and upon ye 29ᵗʰ of october ensewing as
witness our hands. THOMAS TOWNSEND. NATHANIELL
COBLES, JOHN WICKES : for oysterbay.
THOMAS POWELL, ABIEL TITUS for Huntington.*

                                        p John Corey, Recʳ
     (*File No. —. Town Meetings, Vol. 1, p. 130.)*

                    [TOWN MEETING.]

          [1684, Oct, 28.]

    The 28ᵗʰ of October 1684 it was voated & Granted unto
Nathaniell ffoster that he should have twelve acars of Land

----

[*The original paper with the signatures of the commissioners thereon is in the Town Clerk's office.  As will be noticed,
it only covers that part of the line of division beginning at the
head of Cold Spring Harbor and running southerly to about
the middle of the Island.  This line was the subject of further
dispute in after years.  The last time it was settled by a survey
made under authority of the State Engineer, in 1860, and monuments were then erected entirely across the Island.—C. R. S.]

by y⁰ cart path side yᵗ gooth from yᵉ harbour to y⁰ east feild on ye north side of yᵉ path : And layed out by Joseph Baly & Thomas powell forty eight Rod in Leangth west and be. north and west & be. South forty Rods Broad : south and be west and north west : The description of yᵉ bounds given by yᵉ above sd Layers out and was Layd out yᵉ 22 of November 1684

John Corey, Clerk.

(*Deeds, Vol.* 1, *p.* 7.)

---

[DEED. ANDREW GIBB TO JOHN SCID-

MORE, JR.]

[1684, Nov. 1.]

This Indenture made at Huntingtowne in yᵉ County of Suffolk upon long Island on yᵉ first day of November in yᵉ 36ᵗʰ year of yᵉ Raighne of our Soveraigne Lord Charles yᵉ Second by yᵉ grace of God : of great Brittaine france & Ireland King defender of yᵉ faith &c. & in yᵉ year of our Lord God 1684. Between Andrew Gibb of Brookhaven in y⁰ County afore sd. Marchant of yᵉ one party and John Skidmor Junʳ of Crabmedow within yᵉ town ship of Huntington afore sd. yoeman of yᵉ other party witnesseth yᵗ whereas by vertue of a letter of atturney from George fforman Merchant, dated yᵉ 7ᵗʰ day of Septembʳ 1682 Wherein are severall powers granted unto yᵉ sd. andrew Gibb : And yᵉ said Andrew Gibb haveing Recovered possession of a tract of meadow which belonged to Thomas skidmor, deseased, lying and being at Crab medow afore sd. for yᵉ use of yᵉ sd. George foreman : Now know yᵉ yᵗ for a valluable consideration secured to be payd to yᵉ sd George fforeman

by yᵉ sd. John Scidmore Junʳ: yᵉ said Andrew Gibb hath
Given granted Bargened & sold allinatted, asigned and
set over and doth by these pʳsents freely Cleerly & absolutly Give grant Bargain & sell allenat Asigne and set over
unto yᵉ sd. John skidmor all yᵉ fore sd. tract of medow
lying at Crabmedow, afore sd. containing six acres more or
lesse being buted and bounded by yᵉ Records of Huntington afore sd. To have And to hold yᵉ fore sd. tract of
march or medow together with all fences or other priveledges or appertenences to yᵉ same belonging or in any
ways appertaining to him yᵈ sd John Skidmor his heirs or
assignes : to his yᵉ sd. John Skidmor his heirs or assignes
their sole & proper use and uses for ever and yᵗ yᵉ sd. John
Skidmor his heirs or asignes may & shall Lawfully occupy
possesse and Injoy yᵉ fore sd. tract of medow with all yᵉ
above barganed premises free & cleere & cleerly freely
acquitted of and from all former and other gifts, grants
Bargans sales Rats Mortgages dowereyes or other titles
or incombrences what so ever. had made or Comitted at
any time or times heeretofore with warranty against yᵉ sd.
Geore fforeman his heirs or assignes or any other pʳson
claiming by from or under him or any of them  In witnesse where of yᵉ affore sd. perties have heere unto set
their hands and seales the day and year first above written,
sealed and delivered in yᵉ presents of ISACK PLATT, JOSIAH
PLATT.

Acknowledged before me yᵉ day and yere above sd.

EPENETUS PLATT. Just.
ANDREW GIBB

The above sd. is a true Coppy, Compared with yᵉ originall by me John Corey Clark

November yᵉ 18ᵗʰ 1684.

Andrew Gibb should be above Epenetus platt.

(*Deeds, Vol.* 1, *pp.* 177-8.)

## [DEED. WILLIAM JONES TO RICHARD BRYAN.
## CONVEYANCE OF EATON'S NECK.]
### [1684, Nov. 13.]

To all Christian People to whome these presents shall come Greeting Know yee and all men hereby that wee William Jones of New Haven in the Collony of Connecticutt in New England Planter and Hannah Jones wife of the said William Jones and Daughter of Theophilus Eaton sometime of new haven aforenamed Esqr Deceassed  well in our own Right as also in the right of Theophilus Eaton the son and heir of the aforenamed Theophilus Eaton deceased passed to us or one of us as more fully may appear by his deed bearing date the twenty eighth day of march in the year of Our Lord one thousand six hundred fifty and nine wee or att least one of us haveing Lawfull right and title in and unto all and every part of the Reall and Personall Estate of or of right belonging unto either the aforenamed Theophilus Eaton Esqr father of the aforenamed Hannah Jones or the aforenamed Theophilus Eaton Esqr Brother of the said Hannah Jones of what nature or kind whatsoever being in New England or elsewhere in America, and not by either of them partickularly disposed of that is to say not partickularly disposed of by Theophilus Eaton the Elder before the fowerth day of July in the yeare of Our Lord one thousand six hundred fifty and nine and not disposed of partickularly by Theophilus Eaton the Younger before the twenty eight day of March in the same year for and in consideracon of the Sume of thirty pounds to us or at least one of us all ready in hand paid and contented or secured to Our full content to be payd and for divers other good Causes and Consideracons us and either of us here unto especially moveing and Exciteing Have sold Alienated Assigned Enfeofed Set over given Granted and confirmed as alsoe Released acquitted and exonerated And Doe by these presents ffully freely wholely clearly and absolutely

Sell Alienate Assigne Enfeoff Sett over Give Grante and
Confirme and allso releas acquitt and Exonerate unto Richard Bryan of Millford in the Collony of Connecticutt
aforenamed Marchant all and every part and parcell of a
certain Island neck or Tract of land Scittuate Lying and
being on Lond Island in the Territory or Province of New
Yorke In America at or near a place called Oyster bay
which sd. Island Neck or Tract of land commonly called
and known by the name of Eaton neck Bounded to the
Midle of the beach Scittuate and being on the Eastward of
Oyster Bay Alias Huntington and thence to all other the
Limmitts Extents and Bounds of the said Island neck or
Tract of land as it belonged or ought to belong to the aforenamed Theophilus Eaton though not particularly in these
presents menconed together with all Buildings Edifices
Courtlages Gardens Orchards Land Meaddows pastures
woods underwoods wasts ways waters water Courses ease-
ments Proffits priviledges and advantadges whatsoever
thereon being thereunto belonging or thence ariseing by
any manner of wayes or means what soever for him the said
Richard Bryan his heirs Executors Administrators or assignes To have and to hold from and after the day of the date
of these presents forever without any Suite lett claime truble
incumbrance eviction ejection or Mollestation whatsoever
ffrom or by us the said William Jones and Hannah Jones
or either of us or any other person or persons whatsoever
claiming or that may or shall at any time or times hereafter
claime the same or any part thereof for from or under us
or either of us by virtue of any Right or title any way
derived from us and Wee do by these presents fully acquitt
and discharge the sd Richard Bryan of and from all Further and future Demands of ours for any rent or other
payment or Allowance for the Use and benefitt of the said
Tracts of Land for the time all ready past and do further
covenant and promiss to and with him the said Richard
Bryan his heirs Executors Administrators and Assignes

that wee and either of us will give any other or ffurther deeds or Assurances unto him or them for the aforesaid Tract of land which shall resonabbly be devised and Desired by him or them provided it be within one twelve month next comeing and att the costs of him or them and that neither of us be putt to travell above twenty miles to accomplish the same In Witnesse whereof and for comfirmation of all which wee have hereunto sett our hands and seals this thirttenth day of Novembr in the year of Our Lord one thousand six hundred Eighty and four and in the six and thirtieth year of the reigne of Our Soveraigne Lord Charles the second King of England Scotland ffrance and Ireland &c. WM. JONES HANNAH JONES.

Signed sealed and Delivered in the presence of Us SAMUEL EELLS Senr THOMAS COLLSY Mr William Jones Esqr and Mrs Hannah Jones psonally appeared in New haven the theirteenth day of November 1684 and Acknowledged the above Written Instrument to be their voluntary act and deed according to Law before me

JOHN NASH Asist'tt

Recorded for Lr John Hutchins

STATE OF NEW YORK
OFFICE OF THE SECRETARY OF STATE, } ss.:

I have compared the preceding copy of patent with the record thereof in this office, in Book Number Nine of Deeds, at page 436, and I do hereby certify the same to be a correct transcript therefrom and of the whole thereof.

WiITNESS my hand and seal of office of the Secretary of State, at the City of Albany, the 19th day of April, one thousand eight hundred and eighty-two.    ANSON S. WOOD,

Deputy Secretary of State.

*(File Eaton's Neck Papers, F.)*

## [LAND OF STEPHEN JARVIS.]

[1684, Nov. 27.]

November yᵉ 27–84. Laide out for Stephen Jarves ˢᵉⁿʳ
twelve acears of Land on yᵉ east side of yᵉ Cart way yᵗ
Leads to yᵉ Lettell east neck 48 Rods in Length north and
south and 40 Rod in bredth east and west, bounded on yᵉ
south end with a great hollow yᵗ Leads in to yᵉ midell of
yᵉ neck and yᵉ north end with a small hollow.

JOSEPH BAILLE
THOMAS POWELL

## [LAND OF JAMES CHICHESTER.]

Layed out for Jeames Chitester ˢᵉⁿʳ, the same Day It was
granted eight acears of Land bounded on yᵉ east by yᵉ cart
way yᵗ goes to yᵉ Lettel east neck on yᵉ north by a hollow
yᵗ Leads to yᵉ harbour side on yᵉ south by a holow yᵗ
Leads to yᵉ harbour side on yᵉ west by yᵉ᾽saveg Clife.

JOSEPH BAILEE
THOMAS POWELL

(Deeds, Vol. 1, p. 74.)

## [JONATHAN SCUDDER AND EDWARD KETCHAM. EXCHANGE OF LAND.]

[1684, Dec. 1.]

This writing signefieth a mutuall agreement made
between Jonathan Scudder and Edward ketcham, cŏnsern-
ing exchanging of a parcell of each of their Land yᵉ sd.
Edward kecham doth give four acres of cleared Land to-

gether with y<sup>e</sup> fence belonging there to unto Jonathan Scudder: being bounded on y<sup>e</sup> west with y<sup>e</sup> land of Na-thanell williams & on y<sup>e</sup> east with y<sup>e</sup> Land of Richard Brush y<sup>e</sup> south to y<sup>e</sup> cart path y<sup>e</sup> north to y<sup>e</sup> woods in common y<sup>e</sup> said four acars of Land be it more or Lesse is lying on y<sup>e</sup> north sid of hors neck path on y<sup>e</sup> west neck: And in con-sideration of y<sup>e</sup> sd. 4 acars of Land y<sup>e</sup> said Jonathan Scud-der doth give unto Edward kecham six acres of wood Land Lying on y<sup>e</sup> south sid of wigwam swamp and bounded on y<sup>e</sup> west upon y<sup>e</sup> edge of y<sup>e</sup> Clieft and otherwise to y<sup>e</sup> woods in Comon being Layd out six acres more or Lesse, and for y<sup>e</sup> Conformation of all y<sup>e</sup> above said we have heere unto seet our hands this first of desember 1684 In presents of

JOHN COREY

Clerk

(*Deeds, Vol.* 1, *p.* 96.)

JONATHAN SCUDDER

EDWARD KETCHAM

---

[DEED. JOHN MATHEWS TO JOHN GOLDING.]

[1684, Dec. 11.]

This indenture made y<sup>e</sup> 11<sup>th</sup> of desemb<sup>r</sup>: And in y<sup>e</sup> 36<sup>th</sup> yeare of y<sup>e</sup> Raigne of our sovrend Lord Charles y<sup>e</sup> second: by y<sup>e</sup> grace of God king of England Scotland france and Ireland, defender of y<sup>e</sup> faith And in y<sup>e</sup> year of our Lord Christ 1684. Between John Mathis of y<sup>e</sup> town of Hun-tington in y<sup>e</sup> County of Suffolk in new york shire on Long Island victuler on y<sup>e</sup> on party And John Golding of y<sup>e</sup> above sd. town & county planter on y<sup>e</sup> other party witness-eth y<sup>t</sup> y<sup>e</sup> sd. John Mathis for divers Reasons and good causes wee moving here unto but Especialy for & in con-sideration of y<sup>e</sup> sum of twenty foure pounds & ten shillings to him at & before y<sup>e</sup> Enseling & delivery heer of these p<sup>r</sup>sents well & truly in hand payde by y<sup>e</sup> sd. John Golding where of and where with he y<sup>e</sup> sd. Jn<sup>o</sup> Mathis doth

acknowledg him selfe fully sattisfied, contented & payd hath
granted aliened barganed sold and confirmed & by these
p$^r$sents doth fully cleerly & absolutly grant alien bargan
sell & confirm unto y$^e$ sd. John Golding his home lot lying
and being in Huntington in y$^e$ tenure or occupation of y$^e$
sd. John Mathis of three acres of Land or there abouts be
it more or lesse and all housing barnes, stables, orchyards,
gardens, buildings & all other heriditaments to y$^e$ same belonging or appertaining or with y$^e$ sd. hous or tenements commonly used occupyed, or injoyed buting and bounding as followeth to y$^e$ lot of John Corey on y$^e$ south to y$^e$ land of
thomas wicks on y$^e$ East and on y$^e$ north and west with y$^e$
kings highway with all woods & under woods comons and
common of pasture whatsoever doth to y$^e$ same belong to
have & to hold y$^e$ sd home lot with all other y$^e$ above granted
priveledges with all & every of their Rights, priveledges
and appurtenances y$^t$ now doth belong unto y$^e$ above sd.
hous lot or here after may or shall any way belong or appertain unto y$^e$ same unto y$^e$ above sd. John Golding And
his heirs, executors administrators and asignes to y$^e$ only
proper use and behoof of y$^e$ sd. John Golding and y$^e$ heirs
executors, administrators and asignes of y$^e$ above sd. John
Golding for ever and y$^e$ above sd. John Mathis for himselfe
his heirs executors administrators doe covenent promis &
grant by these presents y$^t$ at y$^e$ time of y$^e$ ensealing here
of I am y$^e$ sole & lawfull owner of all y$^e$ fore bargaoed
p$^r$mises and am lawfully seased of and in y$^e$ same and in
every part and parcell there of in my owne Right and y$^e$
sd John Golding his heirs executors administrators and
asignes shall & may by force and vartue of these presents
from time to time and at all times for ever here after lawfull,
peacably and quiatly have hold use occupy possesse and
injoy y$^e$ above granted primeses with all their appurtenances free and cleer and cleerly aquited and discharged ot
& from all and all maner of former & other gifts grants
leaces Morgages joyntures dowers titles of dowers Judg-

ments executions entailes and of & from all other titles troubles & incumbrences what soever had made commited or willingly suffered or don by yᵉ sd. John Mathis or by any other person or persons what so ever Lawfully claiming from or under him yᵉ sd. Jno. Mathis or by his means assent privetly or * * * * * & yᵉ sd. John Mathis his heirs & asignes & all & every other person & persons what soever Lawfully claiming by from or under him them or any of them shall and will warrant and for ever defend by these prsents only Reserving unto yᵉ duke his intrust and in witnesse of all yᵉ above sd. I yᵉ above sd. John Mathis have here unto set my hand & seale yᵉ day & yeare first above written.

sighned, sealed and
quiat possesion de-
livered in yᵉ presents
of, EDWARD GREY ⎫
    JOHN COREY ⎭

ye marke of

JOHN ✕ MATHIS

The above sd. indenture was owned & acknowledg before me this 11ᵗʰ day of desʳ 1684, EPENETUS PLATT Justise of yᵉ peace.

This is a true coppy of yᵉ originall by me John Corey, Clerk.

desenʳ 22. 1684.

(*Deeds, Vol.* 1, *pp.* 178-9.)

---

[DEED. JOHN SAMMIS TO JOHN INGERSOLL.]

[1684, Dec. 17.]

know all men whom these may concern: That I John Sammis of Huntington in yᵉ County of Suffolk in new york shire on long Island husband man: have bargened sold and made over unto John Ingersole of yᵉ above sd town &

county, husbandman: All my Rite of one third part of a
farme, both upland & medow & lying and being at Crabmedow in yᵉ pʳsints of Huntington above sd: for and in
consideration of yᵉ sume of twenty five pounds in currant
passable pay of this Countery Received of yᵉ afore
sd. John Ingersole: where-of and where with I am fully
sattisfied contented & payed: I say I yᵉ above sd. John
Sammis doe bargan sell & astrange & make over from me
my heirs executors administrators & asignes, unto John Ingersole afore sd. him his heirs executors, Administrators &
asignes all my Rite title & intrust yᵗ I have in & to yᵉ
above sd. one third part of a farme of both upland & medow
together with all Rites and privelegdes yᵗ now doth or
here after shall or may any way belong unto yᵉ above sd.
Rite which is one third part of a farme and sume what
better yᵉ above sd. upland is lying in Crabmedow Neck
And yᵉ fore sd. medow belonging there unto is lying &
being in Crabmedow being bounded with yᵉ highway
which lyeth on yᵉ north side of John Greens land: being
twenty eight Rods wide and on yᵉ east with a little creeke
which Runeth from a peice of boggey medow into yᵉ grate
creeke and one yᵉ north with yᵉ fore. sd. grat Creek: and
on yᵉ west bounded also with yᵉ medow of John Green on
a straight Rang to yᵉ afore sd. grat Creek: all which
Rights of land and medow afore sd. I yᵉ afore sd. John
Sammis doe Ingage my selfe my heirs executors administrators & asignes: to save harmlesse & indamnefied yᵉ fore
said John Ingersole him his heirs executors administrators
& asignes: from any person or persons who shall or may
lay any just & lawfull claim to any part or parcell of yᵉ
afore sd. land or medow and yᵉ fore sd. John Ingersole
him, heirs executors, administrators & asignes, shall & may
by vartue of these take into his & their possession all yᵉ
afore sd. land and medows with their priviledges to Have
And to Hold to use occupye Improve and peacable to Injoy with out let or Molestation for ever, in witnesse where

of I have here unto set my hand and seale this 17<sup>th</sup> of
desem<sup>r</sup> 1684:
Signed sealed and delivered with quiat possession in y<sup>e</sup>
presents of,

JOHN COREY }
SAMUELL GRIFFEN } abigal Samis y<sup>e</sup> wife of John Sammis doth vollentaryly without threatning or fflatery set to
her hand

                                    ABIGAL SAMMIS

Huntington this 17. desem<sup>r</sup> 1684 this above written deed
was owned and assented unto before me

                                    EPENETUS PLATT, Justis.

This if a true Coppy of ye originall by me John Corey
Clerk.

                                    Janna. y<sup>e</sup> 5. 1684.
    (Deeds, Vol. 1, p. 179, b.)

---

## [DEED. ROBERT KELLUM TO JONATHAN JARVIS.]

[1684, Dec. 22.]

This indenture made y<sup>e</sup> 22<sup>th</sup> of desemb<sup>r</sup> and in y<sup>e</sup> 36<sup>th</sup>
year of y<sup>e</sup> Raigne of our sovernd Lord Charles y<sup>e</sup> second
by y<sup>e</sup> grace of God king of England Scotland ffrance &
Ireland, defender of y<sup>e</sup> faith: And in y<sup>e</sup> year of our Christ
1684. Between Robart kallam of y<sup>e</sup> town of Huntington
in y<sup>e</sup> County of soffolk on long Island cordwinder on y<sup>e</sup>
one part And Jonothon Jarvis of y<sup>e</sup> above sd. town & county. planter on y<sup>e</sup> other part. Witnesseth that y<sup>e</sup> sd. Robart
kellam for divers Reasons & good causes mee here unto
moveing: But especially for & in consideration of y<sup>e</sup> sume
of foure pounds & five shillings in passable pay. to him at
& before y<sup>e</sup> ensealling & delivery of these p<sup>r</sup>sents well &

truly in hand payed by y^e above sd. Jonathan Jarvis where
of and where with: he y^e above sd. Robart kellam doth
acknowledg him self fully satisfied contented and payed
hath given granted alined Bargened sold & confirmed and
by these p^rsents doth fully cleerly and absolutly Give
grant alien bargan sell and confirme unto y^e above sd. Jonathan Jarvis all my Right title & Intrust y^t I have in & to
foure acres of Land lying & being in Huntington Bounded
on y^e North with y^e lane: on y^e west with y^e kings high
way that Leadeth to setalket and on y^e south & East with
y^e woods in common And all Barns stables, orchyards,
gardins and buildings y^t doth or may belong to y^e same.
And y^e above sd. Rob^t kellam doe by these p^rsents acknowledg yt at y^e time of y^e ensealing hereof I am y^e sole
and lawfull owner of y^e above sd. four acres of land, being
granted unto me towards my devision by y^e town as may
be seen upon Record: And doe by these p^rsents give
grant alien bargan sell and estrange and make over all my
Right title & intrust y^t I have in & to all y^e above sd. four
acres of land from me my heirs executors administrators
and asignes unto Jonathan Jarvis him his heirs executors
administrators and assignes to have and to hold to use And
improve occupy and quiatly to possese with out let or
mollestation for ever only Reserving unto his Royel highness his intrust and further y^e above sd. Robart kellam doe
by these p^rsents ingage & bind him selfe his heirs executors administrators & asignes them & every one of them
from time to time and at all times for ever to warrant &
defend y^e above sd. Jonathan Jarvis him his heirs, executor administrators & asignes them and every one of them
from any person or persons who shall or may lay any just
or lawfull Claim to y^e sd. foure acres of land or any part of
it and to keep it cleer and cleerly aquited of and from all
maner of former gifts grants morgages, troubles or incumbrances what-so-ever in witnesse where of I y^e above
sd. Robart kellam have heire unto set to hand and seale y^e

day & year first above writen, signed sealed & delivered in
y⁴ pʳsents of
EDWARD HIGBY
    yᵉ mark of
JONATHAN × CHICHESTER
Hanah kellam yᵉ wife of yᵉ above sd. Robart kellam hath
without flattery or thratening consented to yᵉ primese
and sale above sd. and set to her hand.
                                ROBART KELLAM
                                HANAH KELLAM
    This is a true coppy by me John Corey Clerk.
            Jene. 13. 1684.
            (*Deeds, Vol. 1, p. 181.*)

---

## [LANDS OF THOMAS SCIDMORE AND JOHN GOLDING.]

[1685, Jan. 13.]

this is my knowledg and yᵉ knowledg of John ffinch senʳ
yᵗ Thomas Skidmor gave unto his Son in Law John Golding sunken medow farme and delivered to him by yᵉ
Custom of our English Nation by turfe and twig without
any Refermation after gaind by Mr. Smith; lost yᵗ farme;
In consideration where of yᵉ town upon yᵉ Request of
Governour Andrews gave this farme yᵗ he now posseseth
unto him which is in Length on yᵉ North side from Crabmedow neere yᵉ sd. Skidmores Spring on yᵉ South East
with yᵉ high hill unto a spring yᵗ is in yᵉ high way: yᵗ
comes from Crab medow to Jonathan lewes: the west side
with yᵉ hill towards Crabmedow: Layd out by my self
and Thomas powell which is forty acres:
January yᵉ 13, 1684, there is belonging to this farme twelve
acars of medow next yᵉ beach bounded with thomas skid-

mors medow on y$^e$ East And y$^e$ west side with y$^e$ medow of Edward Bunch.

This is a true Coppy extracted out of y$^e$ originall by me John Corey Clark;

huntington Jane. y$^e$ 27, 168$\frac{4}{5}$.
   (*Deeds, Vol.* 1, *p.* 178, *b.*)

---

[1685, Jan. 14.]

Samuel Griffen and Elizebeth platt ware maried y$^e$ 14th day of Jeneuary 168$\frac{4}{5}$.
   (*Court Rec. p.* 289.)

---

[BOND OF NICHOLAS SMITH.]

[1685, Jan. 28.]

know all men by these presents y$^t$ I nicolas Smith of fresh pond neck within y$^o$ bounds of Huntington upon Long Island in y$^e$ County of Suffolk in america, carpinter Am bound & firmly ablyged unto John Golding of y$^e$ same place & County planter y$^e$ just and intire sume of Eaighteen pound eleven shillings in good marchantable pay of this Countery viz beefe pork winter wheat sumer wheat or Indean corn, winter wheat at five shillings p bushel : summer wheat at four shillings six pence p. bushell Indean Corn at two shillings six penc p bushell, pork at three pence p pound : beefe at two pence p. pound Round : That is to say seaven pounds eleven shillings at or before y$^e$ first of march which will be in y$^e$ year 1685 And y$^e$ other eleven pounds at or before y$^e$ first day of March which will be in y$^e$ year of our Lord 1686 And for y$^e$ true performance here of I binde my selfe my heirs executors and assighns to pay y$^e$

above sd. pay before specefied unto John Golding afore sd. or his order in witnes where of I have here unto set my hand & seal y⁰ 28ᵗʰ of Jenuary And in y⁰ year of our lord 168⁴⁄₅

In y⁰ presents of

JOSEPH BAYLY
JOHN COREY

the marke of

NICOLLAS X SMITH*

The above sd. is a true Coppy compared with y⁰ origi-
by me

febu. y⁰ 23, 168⁴⁄₅.

(*Court Rec., p.* 251.)

John Corey

Clerk

---

[KETCHAM FAMILY RECORD.]

[1685, Feb. 4.]

A Record of Samuell Kichams Children.

Samuell kicham his eldest sonn was borne y⁰ 5ᵗʰ of may in y⁰ yeer 1672.

Joseph kicham sonn of Samuell Kicham was borne y⁰ 17ᵗʰ of Januare 1674.

Mary kicham daughter of Samuell Kicham was borne ye 4ᵗʰ of June in y⁰ yeer 1677.

Nathaniell kicham sonn of Samuell kicham was borne y⁰ 9ᵗʰ of ocktobar in y⁰ yeer 1679.

Jonathan kicham sonn of Samuell kicham was borne the first of Aprill in y⁰ yeer 1682.

Ephriem kecham sonn of Samuell kicham was borne y⁰ 4ᵗʰ day of febeawary 1685.

(*Surveys, p.* 162.)

---

[*This instrument has no special value now except that it shows the price of various items of farm produce over two hundred years ago.—C. R. S.]

## [DEED. DAVID SCUDDER TO JONATHAN LEWIS.]

[1685, Feb. 14.]

Jonathan Lewis Records.

This Indenture made yᵉ 14ᵗʰ day of febuary in yᵉ 36ᵗʰ year of yᵉ Raigne of our sovr. Lord Charles yᵉ second by yᵉ Grace of God king of grate britan france & Irland defender of ye faith, etc. and in yᵉ year of our Lord 168⅘ betweene David Scudder of huntington upon Long Island in yᵉ county of Suffolk in yᵉ province of new york in America, husbandman and Mary his wife off yᵉ on party: And Jonathan Lewis of fresh pond Neck with in yᵉ same town county & province afore sd. husbandman of yᵉ other pᵗy, Wıtnesseth that yᵉ sd. david Scudder & Mary his wife have divers reasons & good causes us moveing here unto but especially for & in consideration of yᵉ some of eaight pounds five shillings: to them at & before yᵕ ensealing & delivery of these pʳsents well & truly in hand payd by yᵉ sd. Jonathan Lewis where of and where with we yᵉ sd. david scudder & Mary his wife doth acknowledge our selves fully sattisfied contented & payde hath granted alinated Barganed sould and confirmed and by these pʳsents Doth fully clearly & absolutly grant allenate bargan sell & confirme unto yᵉ sd. Jonathan Lewis all his upland & medow Land yᵗ lyeth in & neer Crabmedow which is yᵉ third part of yᵗ part of farme yᵗ lyeth between Jonathan Scudder & david Scudder: now in yᵉ tenor or ocupation of david Scudder with all its Rights & priveledges as commons, medows pasturings woods under woods springs mines or menoralls yᵗ shall or may fall within yᵉ pʳmeses. To have And to hold all and every of yᵉ above granted pʳmeses with all & every of their Rights & priveledgs & appurtenences y$^t$ now doth belong to y$^e$ same or ever here after may or shall belong or appertaine to y$^e$ same unto y$^e$ above sd. Jonathan Lewes his heirs executors, administrators or assignes to y$^e$ only proper use & behoofe of y$^e$ sd. Jonathan Lewis And y$^e$ heirs executors administrators and assignes of y$^e$ above sd. Jonathan Lewis for ever And y$^e$ above sd. David Scudder and Mary his wife for ourselves our heirs executors administrators and assignes Doe Covenant promise & grant by these presents y$^t$ at y$^e$ time of y$^e$ ensealing heare of we was y$^e$ sole and lawfull owner of all y$^e$ afore granted p$^r$mises and am Lawfully seased of and in y$^e$ same and in every part and parcell there of in my own Right: And y$^e$ sd. Jonathan Lewis his heirs executors administrators and assigns shall and may by force and vartue of these p$^r$sessents from time to time & at all times for ever here after Lawfully peacably & quiatly have hold use occupie possesse and Injoy all y$^e$ above granted p$^r$mises with all their appurtenances free and cleer and cleerly aquited and discharged of and from all and all manner of fines and other gifts grants, Leases, morgages joyntures dowries titles of dowries Judgments, executions entailes & of & from all other titles, troubles and encumbrances what soever had made commited or wittingly or willingly suffered or don by y$^e$ sd. David Scudder or Mary his wife or by any other person or persons whatsoever Lawfully claiming Right from or under them or by their means or assent privatly or procurment And y$^e$ said David Scudder and Mary his wife their heirs and assignes and all and every other person or persons whatsoever Lawfully Claiming by from or under them or any of them shall and will warrant and for ever defend these presents only Reserving y$^e$ soyle Right to be satisfied by Jonathon Lewis according to y$^e$ obblygation of y$^e$ town of Huntington and Reserving unto his Royal highnes y$^e$ Duke of York his Intrast In Witnesse where of y$^e$ above sd. David Scudder & Mary his wife have here unto set our hands and seales y$^e$ day & yeare above written.

DAVID SCUDDER ✕ his mark
MARY SCUDDER her ✕ mark

signed sealed and
delivered in prsents of
ABIEL TITUS
SARAH SCUDDER

This deed was owned before me by David Scudder and Mary his Wife y$^e$ day and year above said

EPENETUS PLATT Justis of y$^e$ peace

Memorand 1. David Scudder within mentioned doth Ingdge myselfe to satisfie for y$^r$ Soyle Right of y$^e$ within mentioned p$^r$meses And y$^t$ it shall be free to Jonathan Lewis only y$^e$ Duks intrust as witnesse my hand to these p$^r$sents.

ABIEL TITUS                          DAVID SCUDDER
SARAH SCUDDER                      his ✕ mark
   witnesse

This above sd. Mamorandam was accknowledg by David Scudder this 14$^{th}$ of febury 168$\frac{4}{5}$ before me

EPENETUS PLATT Justis of y$^e$ peace.

this is a true Coppy ol y$^e$ originall Compared by me,

John Corey
Clerk,

(*Deeds*, *Vol.* 1, *pp.* 189-90.)

---

## [TOWN MEETING.]

[1685, Feb. 17.]

a town meeting being warned by order of Mr Isack Arnold Justis of y$^e$ peace : & met together y$^e$ 17 day of febuery 168$\frac{4}{5}$ The acts of y$^e$ late essembly Read and published by y$^e$ sd Justis.

[Cut from Court Records 1681-4, being Old Book No 4, & inserted among Town Meetings in the Revision in the year 1873.]
(*Town Meetings, Vol. 1, p. 131.*)

---

## [LAND OF JONATHAN HARNET.]

[1685, February.]

Layd out for Jonathan Harned, twelve acres of Land according to yᵉ towns grant, lying on yᵉ south side of John wicks & Joseph Woods Land : the leangth sixty Rod, the breadth thirty two Rod yᵉ west end Joyns to Joseph woods Lot : yᵉ north side yᵉ Reare of John wicks Land yᵉ est. end to Thoˢ whitsons Land : Layd out by thomas powel & Joseph Bayly : And this Coppy given by them : John Corey Clark.

febu.: 168⅘,

(*Deeds, Vol. 1, p. 183.*)

---

## [MANORIAL GRANT TO JAMES LLOYD. THE LORDSHIP OF QUEENS VILLAGE.]

[1685, March 18.]

Thomas Dongan Leiut. Governor and vic-admiral of New York and its Dependants under his Maj James the Second by the Grace of God of England Scotland, France and Ireland King Defender of the Faith &c. Sovereign Lord and Proprietor of the Coloneys and Provinces of New York & its Dependants in America &c. To whome this shall come Sendeth Greeting Whereas the Right honᵇˡˡ Col. Richard Nicolls Lieut. & Genl. under his Royal

Highness James Duke of york and Albany and of all his
Terrotories in America did by his certain patent or writing under his hand and seal bearing date the 20. day of
November 1667 and entered on record in the secretaries
office ratify confirm and grant unto Nathaniel Sylvester,
Thomas Hart & Latimer Sampson a certain parcell or tract
of Land in the North Riding of Yorkshire (now Queens
Co.) on Long Island & being in a Neck on the North side
thereof stretching out into the Sound or East River commonly called or known by the name of Horse Neck,
bounded on the West with Oysterbay on the east with
Cow Harbor toward the North with the Sound and toward
the South with a Beach extending to the head of a certain
Creek which parteth or dividith the bounds of the Town
of Huntington & the said Neck which said parcell or tract
of Land had been before that time purchased of the Indian
Proprietors & due satisfaction given for the same & at the
General Meeting held at Hempstead it was adjudged to
John Richbell of the said Riding, Merchant against John
Conklin on the behalf of his wife and some orphans who
laid claim thereunto & also at a General Court of Assizes
held in this City in the Month of Sept 1665 against the inhabitants of the Town of Huntington and afterwards by
means aforesaid conveyed by the said John Richbell unto
the said Nath¹ Sylvester, Thomas Hart and Latimer Sampson Together with a neck of Meadow called the Fort Neck
lying upon the South side of Long Island aforesaid and
belonging to the Township of Oysterbay.   As also all
woods, beaches, Marches, meadows, pastures, Creeks,
waters lakes, fishing, hawking hunting and fouling & all
other Profits comodities & Emoluments to the said tract
or parcell of land annexed or appertaining with their &
every of their appurtanances, To have and to hold the said
Tract or parcell or neck of land & premises with the Neck
of Medow afore mentioned with all & singular the priviledges and appurtenances unto the said Nath. Sylvester

Tho. Hart & Latimer Sampson their Heirs & assignes to the proper use & behoof of the said Nath. Sylvester. Thom. Hart and Latimer Sampson their heirs & assigns forever as free land of inheritance Rendering and paying as a Quit rent for the same the value of Four Bushells of wheat yearly upon the 29th day of September if demanded unto his Royal Highness the Duke of York & his Heirs or such Gov. or Governers as shall be from time to time appointed & set over them as in & by the said writing or pattent relation being thereunto had may more fully & at large appear. And whereas the said Nath. Sylvester by a certain Deed or writing under his hand & seal bearing date the 17 day of Nov. 1668 hath remited released & for ever quit claimed unto the said Thomas Hart and Latimer Sampson parties to the above mentioned grant their Heirs and assigns for ever all his right interest, estate, Title and demand which he ever had of in & to all and singular the afore mentioned Tract or parcell of land & appurtenances by virtue whereof the said Thomas Hart & Latimer Sampson were seized & become the only owners & proprietors of the aforementioned tract of Land commonly called Hors Neck togather with a Neck of meadow called the Fort Neck both lying & situate as above recited as in & by his Deed under his hand & seal Recorded doth now fully & at large appear.

And Whereas the above said Latimer Sampson did by his last Will & Testament bearing date the 16 day of Sept. 1668 Give and bequeath his estate both real & personal upon Long Island, shelter Island or else where in New England unto Grizzell the Eldest daughter of the said Nath. Sylvester as by the said Will now on Record in the Secretaries office may likewise more fully appear. And whereas Robart Strey of this City Merchant & John Brown of Flushing in Long Island substitute attorney unto the said Thomas Hart did convey unto James Lloyd of Boston Merchant all the right Title & interest of him the said

Thomas Hart in & unto the said before mentioned tract, neck or parcell of Land and premises as in and by their Deed under their hands and seals recorded in the Secretaries office may appear And whereas the said Thos. Hart did afterwards release unto the said James Lloyd all his right claim or title unto the premises so conveyed by the said Robart Storey and John Brown as in & by the said release likewise on record may more fully appear. And whereas the said James Lloyd hath intermarried with the said Grizzell, Daughter of the said Nathanill Sylvester as aforesaid & hath made application unto me for a confirmation of the said parcell of land & meadow & premices by pattent under the seale of this province Now know yee That I the said Thomas Dongan for the consideration aforesaid by vertue of the power & Authority from his most sacred Maj. to me devised and in pursuance of the same here Give, Granted, Ratifyed Released and confirm and by these presents Do Give, grant ratify release and confirm unto the said James Lloyd his heirs & assigns All that before recorded Tract Neck or Parcell of land situate, lying and being on the North side of the said Long Island called Horse Neck, butted and bounded as afore said as also all that before mentioned Neck of meadow on the south side of the said Long Island called Fort Neck togather with all the mesuages tenements buildings fencings, orchards, gardens pastures, meadows marshes wood under woods trees timber Rivers runns, Brooks Ponds streams creeks harbors Beaches fishing hauking Hunting & fowling and all other the right members Proffits advantages and appurtenances whatsoever and advantages to the said Neck Parcell or Tract of Land & meadow or any part thereof in any way annexed adjoining belonging or appertaining or adopted reputed taken known or accepted as part parcell or member thereof. And moreover by vertue of the power & authority atore said to me the said Thomas given & in we residing and for the reason & considerations aforesaid I have &

by these presents so make, erect, and constitute the said
tract Neck or parcell of land & meadow together with all
and every the above granted premises with every of their
appurtenances unto one Lordship & Mannor to all intents
and purposes & the same shall from henceforth be called
the Lord ship and Manor of Queens Village and I the said
Thomas Dongan have also given & granted and by these
presents do give & grant unto the said James Lloyd and
unto the heirs & assignes of the said James Lloyd forever
full power & authority at all times for ever hereafter in
the said Lord-ship & Manner on Court Lut to hold & keep
at such time & times & so often yearly as he or they shall
see meet for the tryall of all causes not exceeding the sum
of Five Pounds and also from time to time to award and
issue out the customary writts to be issued and awarded
out of the said Court Lut to be kept by the said James
Lloyd his heirs and assigns forever or his or their steward
deputed & appointed, with full & ample power & authority
to destiain for rent and services payable by reason of the
premises and all other lawfull remedies and means for the
hearing proposing, receving, levying      *      *      *      *
and enjoyning the said premises and every part and parcell
of the same and all and every sum or sums of mony to be
paid as a port fine upon any fine or fines to be levyed of
any lands, tenements or hereditements within the said Lord
ship or Mannor of Queens Village and I the said Thomas
Dongan by virtue of my said power and authority have
given and granted and by these presents do give and grant
unto the said Jams Lloyd his heirs & assignes that all and
singular the tenements of him the said Jams Lloyd within
the said Manner shall and may at all times hereafter meet
together and chuse assessors within the Manor aforesaid
according to such ways rules and methods as are prescribed for Cities Towns or Townships within this goverment by the act of the General Assembly of this Province
for the raising of money to defray the public charge and

all such sums of money so raised to collect & dispose of for
the use aforesaid according as in the said act is set down
and prescribed to have and to hold all and singular the
the said tract parcell or Neck of land and meadow the said
Lordship and Mannor* of Queens Village and all and
singular herebefore granted or mentioned to be granted
premises with there and every of their rights, members
privileges and appertenances unto the said Jams. Lloyd
his heirs and assigns forever to the only proper use benefit
and behoof of him the said James Lloyd his heirs and assigns forever yielding and paying there fore yearly and
every year from henceforth unto our Sovereign Lord king
James the second his heirs, successors & assignes or to such
officer or officers as shall be appointed to receive the same
on the 25 day of March yearly from hence forth. the quit
rent of four bushells of good winter wheat at New York
or the value there of in current money of this province in
full of all rents or former reserved rents services and demands whatever to be holden of his most sacred Majesty
his heirs and successors in free and common socage
according to the tenor of East Greenwich in the County of
Kent in the Kingdom of England given under my hand
and seal with the seal of the said province at Fort Jams in

[*The Patent from Gov. Richard Nicolls to John Richbell of
Lloyd's Neck, dated Dec. 18, 1665, has already been inserted.
Mrs. Charlotte Lloyd Schmidt, in her "Memoranda concerning
Lloyd's Neck," mentions two other colonial confirmation grants
made of the same territory, copies of which are not among the
papers in our Town Clerk's office.   They are, an additional
patent by Gov. Nicholls, Nov. 20, 1667, and still another by
Gov. Andross, 1677.   They contain no very special features not
embraced in the other grants.   The last, given above, created
a Lordship or Manor, and included a method of local government under which justice was administered and civil affairs
carried on independent chiefly of adjoining towns.   This manorial government continued in force down to the Revolutionary
War, nearly one hundred years.   It was then abolished and the
territory annexed for governmental purposes to the town of
Oysterbay.—C. R. S.]

the City of New York the 18 day of March in the year of
our Lord 1685 and the second year of the reign of our said
Soverign Lord Jams the second by the Grace of God, of
England Scotland France and Ireland King defender of
the faith.

THOMAS DONGON [Seal.]

May it please your Hon.

The Attorney Gen<sup>l</sup> hath perused
this pattent and finds nothing contained therein prejudicial to his Majestys interest

JA. GRAHAM

Examined March 17. 1685

Recorded by John Sprague secr. March 18. 1685.

*(File Lloyd's Neck Papers, G.)*

---

## [TOWN MEETING.]

[1685, Apr. 2.]

April 2. 1685. At a Town Meeting it was voted & granted
that John Brush shall have four acres of land towards his
division, lying and joyning partly to the lot formerly
granted to John Holmes.

The day above said, it was voted and granted that Epenetus Platt shall have ten acres of land, towards his division
lying on the east of John Brushes four acres, & Rich
Brushes house-lot or land joyning to his hous lot.

[Copy made in the year 1873 from original in Court
Records, p. —.]

at a town meeting Aprill y<sup>e</sup> second 1685 it was voated and
granted y<sup>t</sup> John davis shall change his land at y<sup>e</sup> brick
kills for a peece of land lying between Edward ketchams

& Benjamin scrivners lots to be layd out at ye discrescion
of ye surveyors.

yᵉ day above sd it was voted and granted that Joseph Whitman shall have fifteen acers of land joyning to yᵉ north sid
of Isake platts land on yᵉ East sid of yᵉ town by stoney
Brook path.

it was voted and granted by yᵉ town that John Wicks
shall have a piece of land in ye East neck about an acare
more or less joyning to his land to be layed out at ye discresion of yᵉ layers out.

The day above said it was voated and granted that Timothy
Conkling shall have six acres of Land towards his division
lying on yᵉ north side of abiel titus & Jonathan Scudders
land upon yᵉ halfe mile hill.

yᵉ day afore sd. it was voated and granted yᵗ Robert Cranfeild shall have towards his division of Land three acres
joyning to James Smiths on yᵉ west neck neer hors neck.

Richard davis has a grant of about 2 acres of Land by ye
major part of yᵉ town yᵉ day above sd. yᵉ Land Lyeth between Edward kecham's hous Lott & Benjamen Scrivners
hous lot and yᵉ sd. two acers of to be Layd out by discression of yᵉ surveyors yᵉ sd. Richard davis is hereby injoyned
to be subject to yᵉ town act conserning trads made.

(*Town Meetings, Vol.* 1, *pp.* 123-5.)

---

# [DEED.  EDWARD KETCHAM TO RICHARD
DAVIS.]

[1685, April 10.]

This Indenture made yᵉ tenth day of aprill and in yᵉ 37ᵗʰ
yeare of yᵉ Raigne of our Soverd. Lord Charles yᵉ Second

by y^e grace of God king of England Scotland ffrance &
Ireland, defender of y^e faith ect. And in y^e year of our lord
Christ 1685. Between Edward kecham tayler of y^e town
of Huntington in y^e County of Suffolk in y^e province of
New york on long Island in America on y^e one part and
Richard Davis of y^e above sd. town & County weaver on
y^e other parte, witnesseth y^t y^e above sd. Edward kecham
for divers Reasons & good Causes, me heere unto moveing,
But especally for and in consideration of y^e sume of thirty
and one pounds in passable pay to him at and before y^e ensealling and delivery of these p^rsents well & truly in hand
payed by y^e sd. Richard Davis whare of and where with he
y^e sd. Edward kecham doth acknowledge him selfe fully
sattisfied Contented & payd hath granted barganed sold &
by these p^rsents doth fully cleerly and absolutly grant
alinate bargain sell and confirme unto y^e sd. Richard Davis
his hous and six acres of his hous lott lying and being in
huntington and all Barnes stables orchyards gardins and
fences togeather with all benifits priveledges & profits of
woods springs of watter mines or munaralls y^t now is or
heere after shall be in or upon y^e above sd. six acres of
Land being butted and Bounded as followeth : To y^e kings
high way on y^e noth to y^e lot of Jn^o Davis on y^e west to y^e
woods on y^e South : to y^e Land of Edward kecham & Richard Williams on y^e East To have And to hold the sd. six
acres of Land with all y^e above mentioned and every one
of y^e above mentioned priveledges unto y^e above said Richard Davis his heirs executors, administrators or assignes :
and to y^e only proper use and behoofe of y^e sd. Richard
Davis him his heirs executors administrators or asignes for
ever : And y^e above sd Edward Ketcham for himself his
heirs executors, administrators or assignes doe Covenent
promis and grant by these p^rsents That at y^e ensealling
hereof, I am y^e sole and Lawfull owner of all y^e fore bargained primeses and am Lawfully seased of & in y^e same in
my own Right And y^e sd. Richard Davis his heirs executors

administrators and assignes shall and may by force and
vartue of these presents from time to time and at all times
for ever here after Lawfully peacably and quiatly hold use
occupy possesse and injoye yᵉ above granted primeses free
and cleere and clerly atquitted and discharged of and from
all manner of former & other gifts, grants, Leaces, mor-
geages joynturs, dowres, titles, titles of dower judgments
executions entailes and of & from all other titles troubles
and incumbrences what so ever had made Committed or
wittingly or willingly suffered or don by the said Edward
Ketcham, or by any other person or persons what so ever
Lawfully Claiming from by or under him yᵉ sd. Edward
ketcham or by his means, esent, privetly or procurment :
and yᵉ sd. Edward ketcham his heirs executors and assignes
& all & every other person and persons what so ever Lawfully claiming from by or under him them or any of them
shall and will warrant & for ever defend only Reserving
unto his Royel highnesse his Intrust in witnesse where of I
yᵉ above sd. Edward Ketcham have here unto set to my
hand fixed my seale yᵉ day and year first above written.
Signed sealed and quiat possesion delivered in yᵉ presents
of

JOHN KETCHAM ⎱ This above sd. indenture was acknowl-
SAMUEL TITUS ⎰ edged by Edward ketcham and his wife
Mary ketcham to be don vollenteryly and freely by them
both this 14ᵗʰ of Aprill 1685 before mee, EPENETUS PLATT
Justis of yᵉ peace.

EDWARD KETCHAM<br>MARY KETCHAM<br>X her mark.

a true coppy of yᵉ originall
by me John Corey       May 12
          Clerk     1685.
   (Deeds, Vol. 1, pp. 193-4.)

[COURT RECORDS. SUIT ABOUT A COAT.]

[1685, June 3.]

At a Court held in huntington by his Maj$^{as}$ authoryty
Jun y$^e$ 3, 1685.
The members where of are
Mr Isack platt
Mr James Chichester
Isack Gray plant. against
Steven Jarvis Jun. defendant
                      Entered.
In an action of debt for a barill of oyle dew  by Covenant
to y$^e$ plentive.
                The Charges of y$^e$ Court.

|                        |    | s  | d |
|------------------------|----|----|---|
| for an acion           |    | 7  | 6 |
| for writin y$^e$ warant |    | 1  | 3 |
| for serving            |    | 0  | 9 |
| for y$^e$ clark        |    | 3  | 9 |
| for y$^e$ cry          |    | 1  | 0 |
| for y$^e$ plen$^t$     |    | 1  | 3 |
| 2 witness              |    | 1  | 0 |
|        1   0   0       |    | 16 | 6 |
|        1   3   0       |    |    | 9 |
|        1               |    |    |   |
|                        |    | 17 | 3 |

Winecha Barnes testefieth y$^t$ steven Jarves Jun$^r$ came to
her hous about y$^e$ latter end of Last March or y$^e$ beginning
of Aprill to have a cote made and he tryed Isace grays
cote on him and said it fit for him, and said Isack gray
said I wish I had 1 barill of oyle for it, steven sd. I will
give you one barrill of (oyle) for it; Isaac said let me take
my gloves & hanckerchief out of y$^e$ pockets and you shall
have it. then steven Jarvis gave him his hand and said he
would deliver him 1 barrill of oyle either at this town or

yorke which he pleased, and further seth not: Aloso Win-
cha Samons testifieth y[e] same with her Mother above.
sworne in open Court. The Court haveing heard y[e] cause
and serious-Ly Considered y[e] same; doe finde for y[e] plen[t]
y[t] y[e] defend. shall according to his bargan pay y[e] plent[t].
one barrill of oyle or for want there of shall pay other pay
aquivelent; together with cost of suit and other ensident-
all charges ensuing there upon*

(*Court Rec., p.* 419.)

---

## [DEED. JOHN MITCHELL TO THOMAS FLEET.]

### [1685, June 12.]

This Indenture mad y[e] twelveth day of June: and in y[e]
first year of our sover,d Lord James y[e] second by y[e] Grace
of god king of England Scotland ffrance & Irland defender
of y[e] faith and in y[e] year of our Lord Christ 1685: Between
John Michell of y[e] town of Huntington in y[e] County of
Suffolk in new yorkshire upon long Island Carpenter on y[e]
one part And thomas ffleet: sen[r] of y[e] above sd. town &
County. Marchant on y[e] other part: Witnesseth y[t] y[e] sd.
John Michell: for divers' Reasons & good Causes him
heere unto moving but especially for & in consideration of
a valuable sum of merchantable goods: to him at & before
y[e] ensealling & delivery of these presents well & truly in
hand payed by y[e] above sd. Thos. ffleet: where of & where
with he y[e] sd Jn[o] Michell doth accknowledg himselfe fully
satisfied contented & payd hath granted aliened Bargened
sold and confirmed And by these p[r]sents doth fully cleerly

---

[* This is only given as a specimen out of a great number of
such suits about small matters, and which fill the greater part
of one book entitled "Court Records." It has not been thought
best to print them, at least until after more important records
have been printed.—C. R. S.]

& absolutly grant alien bargan sell and Confirme unto y$^e$ above sd. Thomas ffleet my hous & home Lott Containing about two acres & three quarters be it more or be it Lesse lying & being in Huntington above sd. and formerly grannted by y$^e$ town unto James Chichester J$^{unr}$, thence allinated unto Jn$^o$ Michell above sd. being bounded on y$^e$ South with y$^d$ Lot y$^t$ did formerly belong to John Scudder: on y$^e$ west & north with y$^e$ kings high way and on y$^e$ east with y$^e$ woods in Common together with all Barnes stables, orchards gardens and buildings, with all fences to y$^e$ same belonging, unto y$^e$ above said Tho$^s$ ffleet him his heirs executors administrators and assignes

To have hold use occupy possesse and peacably to Injoye with out let or mollistation for ever and further y$^e$ above said John Michell doth bind him selfe his heirs executors, administrators and assignes to save harm lesse and indamnefied y$^e$ fore sd. Thomas ffleet sen$^r$ him his heirs executors Administrators and assignes from any person or persons what so ever who may or shall lay any just and lawfull claim to any part or parcel of y$^e$ above granted bargan and by these p$^r$sents shall & will Warrant and defend and for ever defend only Reserving unto his Maj$^{ests}$ his Intrust In witnesse whereof I y$^e$ fore mentioned John Michell have here unto set my hand and seal. The day and year first above written,　　　JOHN MICHELL.

signed sealed and 　　　　　　　　the mark of
quiat possesion 　　　　　　　MARY ✕ MICHELL
delivered in y$^e$ p$^r$sents
of us.

　Witnesse
　　　the mark of
　THOMAS BIGES ✕
　THOMAS HIGBYE.

This is a true Coppy of y$^e$ originall by mee John Corey Clark

　　　　　　　　　　　　July y$^e$ 6$^{th}$ 1685.

　　(Deeds, Vol. 1, pp. 197-8)

## [DEATH OF JOHN FINCH.]

1685, June 19.]

John ffinch, senior: departed this Life June y$^e$ nineteenth in y$^e$ year of our Lord 1685
(*Court Rec., p.* 207.)

---

## [STEPHEN JARVIS ARRESTED FOR DEBT.]

[1685, July 6.]

Huntington July y$^e$ 6$^{th}$ 1685 : to y$^e$ Con$^{st}$ there of.
You are hereby Required in his Maj$^{st}$ name to take y$^e$ body of Steven Jarvis Jun$^r$ or for want there of his estate for y$^e$ Satisfing of Isaac Gray in on barrill of oyle or y$^e$ vallue there of according to y$^e$ judgment of y$^e$ Court : together with cost y$^e$ of Court and other charges there upon incurred being alredy £0 17$^s$ 11$^d$ as followeth.

|                                                                        | £. | s. | d. |
|------------------------------------------------------------------------|----|----|----|
| for y$^e$ tryel of y$^e$ accion                                        | o  | 07 | 06 |
| for y$^e$ warrant                                                      | o  | 01 | 03 |
| for y$^e$ sarving 1$^s$ : 6$^d$ : for y$^e$ cryer 1$^s$  for supening 2 witnes 8$^d$ | o | 03 | 02 |
| for y$^e$ Clerke 3$^s$ 9$^d$ witnes 1                                  | o  | 06 | 6  |
| for y$^e$ plentives time 1$^s$ : 3$^d$                                 |    |    |    |
| for y$^e$ 2 witness time 1 : o                                         |    |    |    |

(*Court Records, p.* 420.)

---

## [DEED.  ROBERT ARTHUR TO JOHN GREEN]

[1685, Aug. 6.]

Witneseth these p$^r$sents y$^t$ I Robart Arther of y$^e$ town of Huntington in y$^e$ County of Suffolk upon long Island And

in y^e Collony of our soverign Lord king James y^e second
&c. on y^e sixt day of augost in y^e first year of his Majesties
Raigne have and by these p^rsents doe upon good Consideration sell alinate and make over my accommondations home
lott orchard with my dweling hous or seller and one hundred pounds Commondage with all y^e priviledges &
Imanities there unto belonging or what shall or may belong
unto y^e sd. p^rmeses from me y^e sd. Robart Arther my heirs,
executors administrators and assignes to John Greene of
Huntington his heirs executors administrators and assignes
for ever: for him y^e sd. John Greene to have And to hold,
to him & his heirs for ever with out Lett trouble hindrence
or molestation of any person or persons what so ever, justly,
or Injustly claiming any Right unto y^e sd. p^rmeses or any
part or parcell there of and as fully Largely and Amply as
may or can be made or granted by any deed, bill of sale or
any other convayence what so ever the above sd. John
Greene satisfing y^e said Robart Arther twenty pounds according to bill And for y^e performence here of I have here
unto set my hand and seal the 6^th of August 1685
sealed and delivered                    ROBART ARTHER
in presents of                              his × mark
    SYMON LANE                       MARY × ARTHER
        1685
    EDWARD KETCHAM.

                            y^e above sd. is a true coppy
                            of y^e originall by me.
                                John Corey, Clark.

        (*Deeds, Vol.* 1, *p.* 199.)

---

[MARRIAGE OF JONATHAN MILLER.]

[1685, Sept. 28.]

Jonathan Miller was maried to Mary Teed sept. 28. 1685.
(*Court Rec., p.* 47.)

## [AGREEMENT. NATHANIEL WILLIAMS AND RICHARD BRUSH.]

[No date.]

Thes p'sants witneseth An agreement betwen Nathanill willams of Huntington In yᵉ County of Suffolk on Long Island In Amaracah weaver of yᵉ one party and Richard Brush of yᵉ same towne and County of yᵉ other party witneseth that yᵉ sd. Nathanill Willams Is to make & maintaine A suficant Cart way over neare yᵉ head of mill ston Broock And yᵉ sd. Nathanill willams Doth bind my selef my heires & exectours Administrators and Assignes to maintaine yᵉ sd. Richard Brush, And his haires A suficent Cart way over yᵉ sd. mill stonn Broock & to maintaine yᵉ sd. Cart way for ever so that yᵉ sd Richard Brush is not to bee Damified for want of yᵉ same.

NATHANILL WILLAMS

A true Copey by mee
John Ketcham Recʳ.
(*Deeds, Vol.* 1, *p.* 198.)

## [PAYMENT OF JUDGE PALMER'S SALARY.]

[1685, Nov. 16.]

November yᵉ 16ᵗʰ, 1685
Then Reseved from Mʳ epenetus Platt yᵉ sume of foure pounds foure shillings and six pense it being for yᵉ prepor. tion of yᵉ towne of huntington towards yᵉ judges sallery due from yᵉ counte of Suffolk I say receved per mee
J. PALLMER.*

[*John Palmer was for a considerable time a member of the Governor's Council and a member of the Court of Chancery, to which appeals were taken. He afterwards made some trouble in this town by procuring a patent of lands about Crabmeadow, founded on an old Indian deed. These papers are on record in the office of the Secretary of State at Albany.—C. R. S.]

A true coppy of y^e origanall Resept given by Judge Palmer himselfe p. mee Isaac Platt Rec^r.

Mr Epenetus Platt after due Respecks, I send to you these lines is to desire you: if your coleckter have payed yo^e Judges Ratte to you acording to his warant and allsoe y^e coleckter of Smithtowne that then you would bee pleased to deliver y^e money to my brother John Howell and his reseipt with this my order shall bee ye^r full discharge as wittnes my hand          EDWARD HOWELL
                              Treserur for y^e countie of Suffolke
Southhamton y^e 26^th of novemb^r 1686
          (*Town Meetings, Vol.* 1, *p.* 151.)

---

## [INVENTORY OF THE GOODS AND CHATTELS OF JOHN "CORE."]

[1686, Jan. 25.]

Huntington y^e 25 of January 168⅚.
An Inventore and aprizment of the Estate of John Core deceased, apprized by James Chichester Sen^r and Joseph Whitemen senour.

| | £. | d. | s. |
|---|---|---|---|
| 6 Cattell and an old horse | 15 | 00 | 00 |
| 8 sheeps | 03 | 00 | 00 |
| 3 small shots | 00 | 15 | 00 |
| for beding of divers sortes | 16 | 00 | 00 |
| all the deseased wareing clothes of all sorts | 06 | 08 | 00 |
| Chestes, boxes, bedsteds, cradell & table | 04 | 06 | 00 |
| potts and kittells and warming pann | 05 | 00 | 00 |
| peuter and spunes | 01 | 10 | 00 |
| by divers books | 02 | 00 | 00 |
| a loume and weavers geer and other lumber | 08 | 00 | 00 |
| by wooden & housell stuff | 07 | 00 | 00 |
| Cart yoak and Cart clevey | 03 | 10 | 00 |

| | | | |
|---|---|---|---|
| axes, howes   *   * | 01 | 01 | 00 |
| for Reeds and weaving geers | 04 | 00 | 00 |
| a bout 20 bushels of corn: and sum<br>more provision for their present use | 03 | 00 | 00 |
| by yarn and wool | 02 | 00 | 00 |
| Total | 82 | 10 | 00 |

In testimony heir of wee, above named have sett too our hands

JAMES CHICHESTER<br>
JOSEPH WHITMAN

(*File No.* 45.)

---

## [ORDER OF THE GOVERNOR CONCERNING EXCISE AND QUIT RENTS.]

[1686, March 4.]

To Epenetus platt Esq one of his majestys Justices of the peace for the County of Suffolk

Huntington

S<sup>r</sup>

This is by order of his Excellency the Gov<sup>r</sup>: and the Councill to acquaint yo:<sup>w</sup> that on the five and twentieth day of this Instant March the excyse of the sevarell Countyes on Long Island either together or each County by it selfe will bee publickly Lett to farme att New York to the highest bidder — you are therefore required to give publick notice thereof within yo<sup>r</sup>: Towne that such persons as may have a minde to farme it may not losse the opportunity that offers: I have not else but that I am,

y<sup>r</sup> friend & serv<sup>t</sup><br>
J. SWINTON.

Newyork March 4<sup>th</sup> 1686.

The Governor likewise ord<sup>rs</sup> yo<sup>u</sup> to acquaint the people of y<sup>r</sup> Town that unless they come speedilly & agree about their qnittrent they will bee every man Exchequered and that if they doe come they may expect all the favo$^r$ & Justice they can desyre in having their pretences confirmed to them & theirs upon reasonable termes.

and as for those people that are settled upon Crabb meadow his intent is not that they shall bee in the least disturbed but enjoy their settlement to them & theirs peacably forever.

ffor his majestys especiall service,
To bee dispatched forward from place to place with all possible expedition.*

(*File No.* 12.)

---

[*Gov. Dongan resorted to every method possible for raising revenue, and his greed in this respect made him very unpopular. In his report to the Committee of Trade in London, dated Feb. 22, 1687, he says :—(*See Doc. Hist., N. Y.*)

"Besides these, my Lords, I finding that many great inconveniences daily hapned in the managemt of his Ma$^{ts}$ particular concerns within this province relating to his Lands, Rents, Rights, Profits @ Revenues by reason of the great distance betwixt the Cursory settled Courts @ of the long delay which thereon consequently ensued besides the great hazard of venturing the matter on country Jurors who over @ above that they are generally ignorant enough @ for the most part linked together by affinity are too much swayed by their particular humors @ interests, I thought fit in Feb. last by @ with y$^e$ advice @ consent of y$^e$ Council to settle and establish a Court which we call the court of Judicature (Exchequer) to bee held before y$^e$ Gov$^r$ @ Council for the time being or before such @ soe many as the Gov$^r$ should for that purpose authorize, commissionat @ appoint on the first Monday in every month at New York, which Court hath full power and authority to hear, try @ determine suits matters @ variances arising betwixt his Ma$^{ty}$ @ y$^e$ Inhabitants of the said Province concerning the said lands, rents, rights, profits @ revenues."

"The first year there was £52 offered for the Excise of Long Island, but I thought it unreasonable it being the best peopled place in this Goverm$^t$ @ wherein theres great consumption of Rumm @ and therefore I gave commission to Mr Nicholls @ Mr Vaughton to gather it with whom I made this agreement that out of it they should have fourty pounds, @ that they should account with Mr Santon for the remainder."—C R. S.]

## [SETTLEMENT OF DISPUTED BOUNDARY WITH LLOYD.]

### [1686, March 10.]

An agreement made 10 day of march 16$\frac{8.5}{8.6}$ between Isaac Platt James Chichester Joseph Whitman townsmen in behalf of themselves & y$^e$ Rest of y$^e$ inhabitants of y$^e$ towne of huntington and James Loayd owner of hors neck for y$^e$ statting & settling of ye bounds of y$^e$ Town of Huntington & y$^e$ said neck Itt is hereby muttually agreed and declaired that y$^e$ bounds between y$^e$ sd. Town & neck shall bee between y$^e$ south Beash of hors neck & y$^e$ upland of Huntington west necke as followeth : vizt : from y$^e$ enterance s$^d$. beach shall bee sixteen Poles or Rods measured by y$^e$ south creek side extending into y$^e$ body of y$^e$ beash or meddowe from y$^e$ upland of west necke : and from y$^e$ next Point of s$^d$ upland northeasterly shall þe extended sixteen Rods into y$^e$ body of y$^e$ sd. meadowe allsoe from y$^e$ third Point or station still north easterly from west neck upland shall bee exstended eighteen Rod into y$^e$ body of y$^e$ medowe, allsoe from y$^e$ fourth Point or station still north eastward from s$^d$. west neck upland shall bee extended into y$^e$ body of s$^d$ meadowe twenty Rods which last point lyeth nigh y$^e$ northest Part of s$^d$ medowe soe y$^t$ y$^e$ Bounds betweene huntington & horse Neck shall bee from extended point to point succesively and from y$^e$ fourth or last y$^e$ line to Run into y$^e$ River northerly sixteen Rod to ye westward of ye upland of y$^e$ blufe point of west neck which lyeth toward the enterance of y$^e$ upland of hors neck soe far as shall include y$^e$ Remainder of s$^d$ meadowe on y$^e$ west neck shore on Huntington side : moreover y$^e$ town & townsmen of huntington aforesaid doe grant unto s$^d$ Loyid his heirs & Asignes and tenants or those y$^t$ may inhabitt on horse neck free egresse and Regrese for them selves cattell and creatures to use of the fresh water or Run w$^h$ Runeth att ye enterence of y$^e$ beach or meadowe att y$^e$ joining of Huntington west neck : not encroching or claiming any Benefitt privelige on any Part of y^e upland on west neck more than liberty of watering att y^e foot thereof and hie way to horse neck : In witness hereof wee have hereunto set our hand & seals and delivered ·in

| the above said agreement was owned and acknowledgd before mee y^e year & day ab. sd.  EPENETUS PLATT Justice of Peace | JAMES LOYD [L. S.]  JAMES CHICHESTER [L. S.]  JOSEPH WHITTMAN [L. S.]  and  ISAAC PLATT [L. S.] |

signed, sealed & delivered in p^sed of us.

JONATHAN SCUDER

JOHN SAMIS

A true coppy compaired with y^e origanall. per mee

Isaac Platt Rece^r.*

*(Town Meetings, Vol. 1, p. 139 )*

[*There is nothing in the records showing the authority of the Huntington men who made this agreement to make the same and bind the town, but it is probable that they were duly authorized. Trustees of the town did not exist until some two years later, when they were appointed under a new charter to the town, so that the authority to make such an agreement must have come from a town meetiug. Probably the records of such a town meeting have been lost, as no mention is made of it. Whatever differences had heretofore existed about the division between Lloyd's Neck and Huntington, all such disputes were supposed to be settled by this agreement, but differences afterwards arose as to the boundary. In 1734 the dispute was referred to William Willis, D. Jones and Richard Woodhull as arbitrators, and they signed a decision fixing the boundary, and monuments were erected on the line. Quit-claims by the respective parties were then executed. Although by the act of the Legislature passed in 1886, Lloyd's Neck has been annexed to Huntington, this old line established in 1734 is yet important, as it continues to be the line of title as to private ownership, and continues to be the boundary through Lloyd's Harbor between the lands under water *owned* by the town and those who *own* the lands under water to the north of the line. So that while the line as a township and county line has been extinguished, it still continues as a line of title.—C. R. S.]

## [TOWN MEETING.  THE PEOPLE UNWILLING
## TO GIVE UP THEIR PATENT.]

[1686, April 2.]

Aprill 2, 1686,

at the same time a voatt past to keep there patten intire and that the towne would not grant M$^r$ Smith his desire.

the towne manifested by an unanannimos voatt ther unwillingness to give up their patten which was by Governer Nicell given and granted to us but to give a coppie thereof if it be legally desired or summoned.

at the same towne meeting it was voated and agreed upon that Thomas powell, John Sammos, John Cheehan, Jeremiah Smith shall treatt with and settell the line and boundes of this town betwixt the Indians and the towne both the south and east lines and what further may be requisitt and what may be expended for the furtherance and incouragment of the Indians to further this desire with moderation the towne doe ingage satiffie.*

the same day it was voated y$^t$ William broderton shall have y$^e$ Refusall of six akers of loe land att y$^e$ head of y$^e$ fresh pond swamp hee to have it for his mony as the town & hee shall agree.

---

[*Granting confirmation patents was one of the sources of revenue of the Colonial Governors, not only on account of the fees exacted, but often in the new patent larger quit-rents or annual dues were made payable to the governor.  Huntington was content with the grant it already held from Gov. Nicholls, made in 1666, but Gov. Dongan wanted the people to surrender it and take out a new one.  They answered that they would give a copy only.  The demand of the governor on them is not in the records, but it was probably accompanied (as was his custom in such cases) with a threat that he would grant the lands not then purchased from the Indians to strangers, if they did not comply ; hence we find the people voting to immediately negotiate with the Indians for further purchases.

April 2, 1686 it was voated and granted y\*t\* Jeremiah Smith shall have six ackers of Land att y\*e\* head of Cow harbor swamp part of it swamp soe far as shall be judged meet.

*(Town Meetings, Vol.* 1, *p.* 133.)

---

## [JARVIS FAMILY RECORD.]

[1686, April 26.]

Stephen Jarvis sonn of Stephen Jarvis Jun\*r\* was borne y\*e\* 2 of June in y\*e\* year 1683.

Abraham Jarvise sonn of Stephen Jarvis was Borne y\*e\* 26\*th\* of Aprill in y\*e\* yeer 16$\frac{85}{86}$

*(Surveys, p.* 160.)

---

## [DEED. JOHN GOLDING TO JOHN SKIDMORE.]

[1686, May 17.]

This indenture made y\*e\* seventeene Day of may in y\*e\* second ycer of The Raine of our sovr. Lord Janes the second King of greate Brittan france and Ireland et cet. and in y\*e\* ycer of our Lord Acording to y\*e\* computation of y\*e\* Church of England one thousand six hundred eaightie six,

---

Gov. Dongan, in his report to the Crown officers in England, in 1687, after complaining of the small quit rents, says:

"These people have renewed their Patents under a greater Quit-Rent as will appear by the list sent herewith most of these patents granted by mee were confirmations alsoe

The methods I took for obliging them to this was finding several tracts of land in their townships not purchased of the Indians and soe at his Maty\*s\* disposal. They were willing rather to submit to a greater Quit Rent than have that un-purchased land disposed of to others than themselves".—

*(See Doc. Hist. N. Y.)*—C. R. S.]

Beetweene John Goulding of fresh pond necke w$^{th}$ in y$^e$
Bounds of huntington upon long Island w$^{th}$ in the Counte
of Suffooke & province of new yorke in America husbanman and grace his wife of y$^e$ one p$^{tie}$ and John Scudimore
Ju$^r$ of the afore sd. town counte and Province husbanman
one y$^e$ other Partie witnesseth that y$^e$ said John golding &
grace his wife for divers good causes and considerations
us thereunto moving butt especially for & in y$^e$ consideration of y$^e$ sum of fortie eaight Pounds of Currant Pay of
this provence in hand secured before ensealling and delivering of these p$^r$sents, Have barganed Allenated sould and
Confirmed and by these presents from us our heirs exseketers administrators assignes : Doe allenate Bargain sell &
confirme unto y$^e$ afore sd. John Scudemore all and singaler
that eaighteen acars of upland sittuate and lying on fresh
pond neck butting & bounding as specified, the east end
neer a spring that Lyeth in Commonedge between this sd.
land and the land of Thomas Scudimore the south side
with y$^e$ buring hill of y$^t$ Place the west end south west w$^{th}$
y$^e$ hie way that leads to Crabmedow as allsoe backe of my
medoe Bounded on the east with y$^e$ medow of Jonathan
Luice situate lying one y$^e$ north eas part of crabmedow,
one y$^e$ south with a Creeke one the west w$^{th}$ y$^e$ medoe of
John betts one y$^e$ north side with the Beach : which whole
proportion of medoe is to bee equally Devided in to too
parts and John Goelding to have y$^e$ first choice the other
part of medow w$^{th}$ y$^e$ Aforesaid mentioned eaighteen Acars
of upland Bee it more or lese to gether w$^{th}$ all Rights &
priveliges that doe or may beelong or in any wise Apertaine to y$^e$ same to together with all wayes, woods, underwoods unto y$^e$ same Belonging or in any wise Appertaining
wee say all our Rights & tittle as it belongeth unto us
deriving from Gov$^r$ Lovelace and a court of asizes or by
deed or grant from y$^e$ town of huntington or from any
other p son or psons as by giuft from Indian or any other
what soever we doe Confirm unto the afore said John Scud-

amore to have and to hold all y⁰ afore said and granted
pʳmises and Apurtinances unto y⁰ sd John Scudimore his
heirs exseketers adminestators and asighnes for ever : only
the said John Scudimore to cleere y⁰ soill Right upon his
own Charge and doe cleer John Goulding of and from the
same and I the said John goulding and grace my wife for
our selves our heirs esecutors administrators and asighnes
doe Covenant promise and grant to and wᵗʰ y⁰ said John
Scudimore afore sd. yt. the said John goulding and grace
my wife is and stand firmly seced of a good sure and perfit
estate in y⁰ law of y⁰ sd. upland and medoe exsept before
exsepted : and yᵗ the afore mentioned premises is free from
all grants bargens sales morgages or convaances what
soever and further the said John goulding and grace my
wife doth for our selves, our heirs an asighnes Covenant
promise and grant to and with y⁰ sd. John Scudimore his
heaires and asighnes yᵗ at any time or times heer after
upon Request made y⁰ said John goulding and grace his
wife shall and will bee Reddy to give all other and further
securitie which hee or his learned Counsel shall thinke fitt.
In Witnesse whearof wee have heerunto set our hands and
seals the day and yeer above written.

signed sealled and delivered   the marke × of
in y⁰ pʳsents of us     JOHN GOULDIN
 JOSEPH BAYLY    the marke of
 THOMAS HIGBE   GRACE × GOULDIN
 May y⁰ 28ᵗʰ 1686

This bille of saille was Acknowledgd this seventeen of
may 1686: before mee EPENETUS PLATT Justice of The
Peace.

This is a True Coppy of y⁰ origanall p mee Isaac Platt.
Recʳ

 Enterlind before  }
 sighned a true Copy }
  (*Deeds, Vol.* 1, *pp.* 203-4.)

## [LAND OF ROBERT KELLUM.]

[1686, May 27.]

the six acars of Land granted to Robart Kellam by yᵉ town
may yᵉ 23ᵈ 1681, upon yᵉ west neck att yᵉ harbors mouth
was Layd out by Samuell Titus survaor, yᵉ 27ᵗʰ of may
1686 fortie Rods in Length and twenty four Rods in bredth
in yᵉ same Place where yᵉ town did grant it.

p mee Isaac Platt, Recoʳ

(*Court Rec., p.* 56.)

---

## [BENJAMIN JOHNSON BOUND TO SERVICE.]

1686, June 10.]

Bee it known to all men by these presents that I Robart
Johnson and mary his wife hath freely given a sonn called
by the name of Benjamin Johnson unto Thomas whisson
and martha his wife till hee come of age and that the said
Thomas whisson shall not dispose of the said child unto
any person without it bee to a good traide and a consien-
sius man and a good Liver and that yᵉ said thomas shall
bring him up to Readding Righting sifering, In wittnes
here of I have heer unto sett to my hand, the above said
prmased I, doe hope to perform as wittnes my hand.

THOMAS WHITSON.

June yᵉ 10ᵗʰ 1686
A true Coppy comparied wᵗʰ the origanall p. mee

Isaac Platt Recʳ.

(*Town Meetings, Vol.* 1, *p.* 141.)

---

## [DEED. DAVID SCUDDER AND WIFE TO THOMAS BRUSH.]

[1686, June 28.—Abstract.]

This Indenture Mad yᵉ twentie eight Day of June 1686

Betwene David Scuder of nesaquage within y$^e$ bounds of broke haven & Mary his wife & Thomas Brush of Huntington, Witnesscth y$^t$ y$^e$ sd David Scuder and Mary his wife for y$^e$ sume of twentie nine pounds tenn shillings of good pasable paie have bargned, alinated, sould, and confirmed unto y$^e$ sd thomas Brush all my Dwelling house orchard Garden, home Lott of land containing six acars be it More or Less together with all fence belonging to y$^e$ same situate within the town of Huntington, Butting & bounding as spesified y$^e$ frunt or east end with y$^e$ streete y$^e$ south side with y$^u$ highway y$^t$ Leadeth to oyester bay y$^e$ Reare or west end with y$^e$ woods in Comans y$^e$ north side with y$^e$ Lot of Jonathan Scuder to have & to hould y$^e$ sd granted & bargned premises unto y$^e$ sd thomas Brush, his heyers, executors &c forever, With full covenant & warranty of title.   Signed & sealed

signed & sealed                                    DAVID SCUDER
In y$^e$ presents of                                his $\times$ Marke
   JOHN KETCHAM                      MARY SCUDER
   NATHANILL WILLAMS                 hur $\times$ Marke
     Acknowledged May 23, 1687.

                     EPENETUS PLATT, jus$^t$

*(Deeds, Vol. 1, p. 422.)*

## [THE WICKS RECORD.]

[1686, July 1.]

John Weeks sonn of John weeks of huntington was Borne y$^e$ 8$^{th}$ of Jully in y$^e$ yeer of our Lord 1674.

Esther wickes daughter of John weicks was borne y$^e$ 11$^{th}$ of ocktobar in y$^e$ yeer 1679.

Nathaniell wickes sonn of John weeks was borne y$^e$ 9$^{th}$ of Septembar in y$^e$ yeer 1683.

Jonathan wickes, sonn of John wickes was Borne the first day of Jully in y^e yeer 1686.

(*Surveys, p.* 164)

---

## [DEED. HENRY SOPER TO JONATHAN ROGERS.]

[1686, July 7.]

To all Xtion People to whome These p^rsents shall come Henry Sooper of huntington In y^e Counte of Suffolke sendeth greetting Know y^e that for divers good causes and Considerations mee there unto moving: & more especially for a valiuable sum to mee In hand Paid by Jonathan Rodgers of y^e same town and County a fore said before y^e ensealing of these p^rsents where with I doe acknowledge my self to bee fully satisfied and paid and from y^e same and every Part thereof doe heerby for my selfe my heires & assignes a quit and fully discharge y^e sd. Jonathan Rodgers, his heirs executors administrators and asignes : have given granted allinated barganed & sold Infeofed and confirmed and doe herby fully freely & absolutly give grant bargen sell enfeefed and Confirm unto y^e sd. Jonathan Rodgers my Right title and Intrest y^t I have In Crabmeadowe neck between Cowharbor brooke and nessaquake River y^t I had of my mother In law y^e widdow wattles and all soe part of my swamp y^t did belong to my home lott adjoyneng to y^e Lott of y^e sd. Jonathan Rodgers by estimation three acars bee it more or less to have and to hold all and singaler the afore demised premises w^th all libarties previliges and apurtenances to y^o same belonging or any way apertaing unto him y^e sd. Jonathan Rodgers his heirs executors administrators or asignes for ever and I doe heer by Ingage to defend his tittle against all & all maner of persons that

shall Lay Clame to yᵉ same or any part or pcell thereof
either by from or under mee my heirs executors administrators or a sigens a vouching my self before yᵉ ensealling
of these pʳsents to have been yᵉ Rightfull owner of yᵉ above
demised premises and for sure confermation of all and singular yᵉ above sd. pʳmises I have heer unto sett my hand
and fixed my sealle this seventh day of Jully In yᵉ second
yeare of yᵉ Reaigne of King James yᵉ second annoye
domine 1686.                                   the marke of

                                 HENRY ⨯ SOOPER-
signed sealed and delivered
In presence of
    JOSIAH HUBART
    PETTER BENSON
Septemʳ yᵉ 11ᵗʰ 1686.
    This deed was acknowledgd yᵉ day a fore sd. by Henry
Soper to bee his act and deed before mee
                    EPENETUS PLATT Justice of the Peace
A True Coppy of yᵉ origanall
deed p. mee Isaac Platt Recoʳ
        (*Deeds, Vol.* 1, *pp.* 207-8.)

[DEED. HENRY SOPER TO JONATHAN
ROGERS.]

[1686, July 8.]

    These psents witteseth an agreement made between
henry soper of huntington upon Long Island In yᵉ Counte
of Suffolke and Jonathan Rodgars of yᵉ other Part In yᵉ
same towne Island County affore said : viz : that yᵉ said
henry soper for and In Consideration of twelve pounds
eleven shillings three penc in Country Pay all Redy Received In hand of yᵉ sd. Jonathan Rodgars have assigned
and made over unto yᵉ sd. Rodgars three acars of medowe

from yᵉ woods to yᵉ Creek bounded with Isaac Platts one
yᵉ south and a peece of fresh meadowe above yᵉ Indian
Path Lying upon a neck called santepauge and I yᵉ saide
henry soper for yᵉ causes above sd. doe by these pʳsents
putt yᵉ sd. Jonathan Rodgars in quiet and Peacable posesion
of all and every part of yᵉ a fore sd. meadowe to have and
to hold all the said p-cels a fore sd to him his heairs or
asigens from mee my heairs or a signes wᵗʰ out any lett or
mollestation : Provided Allsoe that I the said henry soper
doe not wᵗʰ in six yeers from yᵉ day of yᵉ datte heer of pay
or cause to bee paid unto yᵉ said Jonathan Rodgars the
full sum of twelve pounds eleven shillings and three pence
a fore specified that then upon the non payment of yᵉ sum
afore sd. unto yᵉ sd Rodgers or his asigens at or before the
time above mentioned that the said land shall wholy forfite
unto yᵉ sd. Rodgers and allsoe I doe oblige my self upon
failure of paing the money to make and confirme good and
suficent writtings unto yᵉ sd. Rodgars for him his heairs &
asigens quietly and peacably possesing the sd. meadowe for
yᵉ full confirmation of the above demised pʳmises I have
heer unto sett my hand and fixed my seale this eaight day
of Jully In year of our lord 1686

signed sealled
and delivered in
yᵉ pʳsence of
  Thomas wicks
  Petter Benson

the mark of

HENRY ✕ SOPER.

acknowlegd before mee the day
and yeer above mentioned.
  Epenetus Platt
  Justice of Peace

A True Coppy of yᵉ originall morgage p mee
    Isaac Platt Recoʳ Septemʳ yᵉ 11ᵗʰ 1686.

Jaunary the 15ᵗʰ 17³⁴/₃₆ received of William Soper 6 pounds

and Last may I Received 6 pounds of the sd. soper being
in all twelve pounds in full of the within morgage

JONATHAN ROGERS

Recorded by me Epenetus Platt Clerk.
(*Deeds, Vol.* 1, *p.* 209.)

---

## ["A CROP IN YE NEER EARE."]

[1686, July 20.]

Jully yᵉ 20ᵗʰ 1686.

The marke of Joseph Vaille entered and Recorded which
is as followeth, A Crop one yᵉ Left eare or usally called yᵉ
neer eare: and too slits acrose yᵉ under side of yᵉ Right
eare or of eare

p mee Isaac Platt
Recorᵣ.

(*Deeds, Vol.* 1, *p.* 106.)

---

## DEED. JOHN JONES TO JONATHAN WOOD.]

[1686, Aug. 23.]

This Indenture made yᵉ three and twentie day of August
in the second yeer of yᵉ Raine of our Sovᵣ Lord James
King of great brittan france and Irland et,cᵣ and in yᵉ yeer
of our lord acording to the computation of the Church of
England one thousand six hundred eaighty and six Between
John Joens of nessaquage ales smithstowne within yᵉ
bounds of brookhaven ales seatauket in yᵉ countie of Suffolk and province of new yourke in americai hus banman of
the one partie with mary his wife and Jonathan wood of
huntington upon long Island wᵗʰ in the countei and province
afore said weaver of the other partie: wittneseth that the

sd John Joens and mary his wife for divers good causses
and considerations us there unto moving Butt especially
for and in y^e consideration of the sum of twentie five
pounds of good passable pai of this province as it paseseth
from man to man viz winter wheat att five shillings p
bushell and Indian corne at too shillings six pence p. bushell
and other paie equivelent their too, have barganned allinated sould and confirmed and by these presents from us our
heairs executors adminestrators and asignes doe allien
Bargon sell and Confirme unto y^e afore sd Jonathan wood
the north side of my home lott or the north haulfe of my
home lott with my dwelling house from y^e front or east
end with a strait line along y^e midell of my lott as equall
as it can bee devided to y^e west end with y^e woods in comanige and wheras I have sould my orchard and the south
side of my home lott unto abiel tittus it was mutually
agreed by abiell titus and Jonathan wood y^t the partition
fence between them should Run to y^e midel of the well
and that the well shall bee for the use of both parties w^th
out y^e lett or hinderance of each other their heairs and
sucsesers : which part of my lott containeth three ackers
bee it more or les I say the north haulfe of my home lott
with my housing fences trees or fruit trees with in y^t denomination I have estranged from mee my heairs and
asigens for ever unto Jonathan wood his heairs executors
adminestraters and asigens to have and to hold for ever
the sd. granted and barganed premises yielding and paying therefore his anuall and yeerly proportion of what
may bee long to this goverment of this province and wee
y^e sd John Joens and mary his wife for our selves our
heairs exsecutors administrators and asignes doe covenant
promise and grant too and with y^e afore said Jonathan
wood that y^e said John Joens and mary his wife now is and
stands firmly seaized of a good sure and perfit estate in the
lawe of y^e house and haulfe lott of land before mentioned
and hath good Right and lawfull athoritie to sel and con-

vae y⁰ same ; and yᵉ sd John Joens and mary his———— for
our selves our heairs exsecutors administrators and asigns
Doth further covenant promise and grant to and wᵗʰ yᵉ sd
Jonathan wood his heiars executors adminestrators and
asigns that yᵉ afore sd. house and haulfe part of lott and
every of it is free and cleer of and from all other and formar bargains grants sales morgages leases judgements executions convayance or convayences, dowries widdow-
Rights tittles or interest whatsoever and furthermore the
said John Joens and mary his wife for our selves our heairs
executors administrators and asigns doe further covenant
and promis and grant too and with yᵉ sd Jonathan wood
his heairs executors administrators and asigns that yᵉ sd.
John Joens and mary his wife shall and will defend the
same from any manor of just Rights claims or demands of
any person or persons what soe ever as wittnes our hands
and seals the day and yeer above written.

signed sealled JOHN JOENS
and delivered in the mark of
yᵉ presence of us MARY ✕ JOENS
ABIELL TITUS
JOSEPH BAILY

This Indenture was acknowledg before me ye 4ᵗʰ of
octobaʳ 1686
EPENETUS PLATT Justice of yᵉ peace.

A True coppy of yᵉ origanall deed compared yᵉ 26ᵗʰ of
octobaʳ 1686 p mee Isaac Platt Recor.

(*Deeds, Vol.* 1, *pp.* 219-220.)

---

## [GOVERNOR DONGAN'S GRANT OF THE LORD-SHIP AND MANOR OF EATON TO ALEX. BRYAN AND RICHARD BRYAN.]

[1686, August 23.]

Thomas Dongan, Lieutenant Governor and Vice Admirall

of New York, and its Dependencies, under his majesty
James the Second by the Grace of God, of England, Scotland, France, and Ireland, King Defender of the faith and
Supreme Lord and Proprietor of the Colony and Province
of New York, and its Dependencies in America, &c., to all
whom this shall come. Sendeth Greeting, whereas the
Right Honorable Richard Nicoll Esq. Late Governor
Generall under his Royall High[ss] James, Duke of Yorke
and Albany now his Present Majesty of all his Territorys
in America, did by Pattent under his hand and seale bearing date the Twenty Second day of June Anno Dom: one
thousand six hundred sixty six, grant, rattifie and confirme
unto George Baldwin of Huntington on Long Island a
certaine parcell or neck of land comonly called Eatons
Neck, lying and being in the East Rideing of yorkeshire on
Long Island aforesaid on the North side of said Iseland to
the east of Huntington bay, where striking out into the
Sound it is thereby bounded to the North east and south,
and on the west with Huntington Harbour from where it
goes on east to the beach which devides it from Crabb
Meadows the midle of which said beach is the bounds betwixt said Neck and Crabb Meadows which alsoe joyns it
to the Iseland the Neck of land aforesaid, containing by
estimation about one thousand five hundred acres be it more
or less. As by said Pattent remaining upon record in the
Secretarys office, relation being thereto had doth fully and
att large appear; and whereas the said neck or tract of
land was afterwards by meane assurance, conveyed and
transported by the said George Baldwin, unto Alexander
and Richard Bryan both of Milford, merchants, as by the
Indorsement on the back side of said Pattent refference
being thereto likewise had, Doth at large appear. And
whereas the said Richard Bryan did also by certaine writing or deed of gift convey and transport unto his eldest
sonne Alexander Bryan all that his right, title and interest,
to the one moyety or half part of the aforesaid tract or par-

cell of land called Eatons Neck, together with all privelidges
and appurtenances thereunto belonging, as by the said
writeing, relation being thereto had may more fully and att
large appear : and whereas the said Richard Bryan and his
sonne Alexander Bryan have been att charge and expenses
in purchasing the said tract and parcel of land and also in
settling improving the same, and for encouraging the future
settlement the said Richard Bryan and his sonne Alexander
have made application unto mee that they might constitute
and erect the said tract or parcell of land within the bounds
and limitts aforesaid to be a Lordship and Mannor and confirme the same unto them, their heirs and assignes by
pattent under the seal of the Province : Know Yee therefore that I the said Thomas Dongan for the consideration
aforesaid by virtue of the authority to me devised from his
most sacred majesty and the power in mee residing have
given, granted, rattefied, released and confirmed and by
these presents doe give, grant, rattifie, release and confirm
unto the said Richard Bryan and his sonn Alexander Bryan,
their heirs and assigns all that tract and parcel of land lying and being, situate within the limitts and bounds above
recited, together with all the messuages, tenements, buildings, fences, orchards, Gardens, pastures, meadows, woods,
underwoods, trees, timber, quarryes, rivers, rivolettes,
brooks, ponds, lakes, streams, creeks, harbours, beaches,
fishing, laking hawking, hunting, and fowling, mines, minerals (Silver and Gold mines only excepted) and all the
rights, members, libertys, privileges jurisdictions royalties,
hereditaments, proffiitts, advantages and appurtenances
whatsoever to the said tract or parcell of land belonging
or in any ways appurtaining, or accepted, reputed, known
or occupied as part, parcell or member thereof. And moreover by virtue of the comission and authority to me the
said Thomas Dongan given and the power in mee residing
and for the reasons and consideration above recited I have
and by these presents do Erect, make, and constitute the

said tract and tracts of land as in the limitts and bounds
aforementioned together with all and every the above
granted premises with every of their appurtenances into
one Lordship or Manor to all intents and purposes and the
same shall from henceforth be called the lordship and
Mannor of Eaton, and I the said Thomas Dongan have alsoe
given and granted and by these presents doe give and
grant unto the said Richard Bryan and Alexander Bryan
full power and authority att all times forever hereafter in
the said Lordship and mannor, one Courte Leete and one
Conrte Barron to hold and keep att such time and times
and soe often yearly as they shall see meett, and all fines,
issues amercianments att the Courte Leete or Courte Barron to be holden within the said Lordship and Mannor to
bee lett forfeited or imposed and payable or happening at
any time to be payable by any of the inhabitants of or within the said Lordship or Mannor of Eaton or the limitts and
bounds thereof and also all and every the powers aud au-
thoritys herein before mentioned for the holding and
keeping the said Courte Leete and Courtt Barron from
time to time and to award and issue out the customary
writte to be issued and awarded out of said Court Leett
and Courtt Barron to be kept by the said Richard Bryan
and his sonn Alexander Bryan, their heirs and assigns forever or their or any of their Stewards, deputed and appointed with full and ample power and authority to
distraine for the rents, services and other sumes of money
payable by reason of the remisses and all other lawfull
remedies and means for the having, possessing, receiving,
levying and enjoyeing the premisses and every part and
parcell of the same and all wastes, estrayes, wrecks, dro-
dands, goods of fellows, happening and being forfeited
within the said Lordship and Mannor and of all and every
sume and sumes of money to be paid as a Postfine upon
any fine or fines, jobs, levyed of any lands, tenements or
hereditaments within the said Lordship or Mannor of Eaton

together with the advonson and right of patronage and all
and every the church and churches established in the said
Mannor And Lastly the said Thomas Dongan by virtue of
the power and authority aforesaid doe give and grant nnto
the said Richard Bryan and his son Alexander Bryan, their
heirs and assigns — — — — — — — — — Then within the said
Mannor shall and may at all times hereafter meet together
and choose assessors within the said Mannor according to
such rules, ways and methods as are provided for Cittyes
and Townes within the province by the acts of the general
assembly for the defraying of the public charge of each respective Citty, Towne and County and all such sumes of
money soe raised to colect and dispose of for the use aforesaid according as in the said act of Generall Assembly is
established and directed To have and to hold all and singular the said Manor of Eaton and premises with theire
and every of their appurtenances unto the said Richard
Bryan and his sonne Alexander Bryan, their heirs and assigns forever, to the only proper use of them the said
Richard Bryan and Alexander Bryan his sonne, their heirs
and assigns forever to bee holden of his said Majesty, his
heirs, successors and assigns in free and common soccage,
according to the tenure of East Greenwich in the county
of Kent in the Kingdome of England, Yeilding and paying
therefore yearly and every year from henceforth unto our
soveraigne Lord King James the Second, his heirs, successors and assigns or to such officer or officers as shall be
appointed to receive the same on every five and twentieth
day of May the quitt rent of fouer bushells of good winter
wheat at New York or the value thereof in currant money
of this Province in lieu and stead of all services and demands whatsoever—

In Testimony whereof I have caused these presents to
be entered upon record in the Secretaryes office and the
Seals of the Province to be hereunto affixed this 23rd day of

August one thousand six hundred and eighty sixth and in
the second year of his Majestyes Reigne

THOMAS DONGAN [Seal.]

May it .Please Yo<sup>r</sup> Honor—

The Attorney Generall hath granted
this pattent and finds nothing contained therein prejudicial
to his Maj<sup>tys</sup> interest. Exam<sup>d</sup> August 25<sup>mo</sup>

1686                    C. JA. GRAHAM.*

Recorded in the Secretaryes office for the Province of
New Yorke in Lib: No. 1. book of Pattents begun 1684
pages 508–509–510–511–512–513—

G. Sprigge
Secr.

*(File Eaton's Neck Papers, G.)*

---

[DEED. JOHN JONES TO JONATHAN MILLER.]

1686, Aug. 23.]

This Indenture made the twentie third day of August

---

[*We have seen how Theophilus Eaton had procured an Indian deed of Eaton's Neck in 1646; how the title, by various
transfers, had come to George Baldwin and a grant had been
made by Gov. Nichols to Baldwin of all the territory of Eaton's
Neck, similar in terms with grants made at that period, and
how in several litigations, the last in the Court of Assize, Baldwin had maintained his title. Richard and Alexander Bryan
now appear as purchasers from Baldwin, and on their application, Gov. Dongan creates Eaton's Neck into the "Lordship or
Manor of Eaton," with the important powers and privileges
pertaining thereto. Practically, the people of Eaton's Neck
had now an independent municipal government of their own.
Their grant was also as liberal in its terms as any other of the
period, including all rivers, brooks, creeks, harbors, beaches,
fishing, hawking, hunting and fowling. It does not appear,
however, that the Bryants and other settlers on Eaton's Neck
exercised the powers they possessed as to a manorial government. Forty-two years later the title passed to John Sloss and
John Sloss Hobert, who held it until after the Revolutionary
War, and in 1792 it came to the Gardiner family.—C. R. S.]

in y^e second yeer of y^e Raine of our sover Lord: James the
second king of great brittan, france & Ireland et&c: and
in the year of our lord Acording to y^e Computation of y^e
Church of England one thousand six hundred eaightie six
Between John Joens of huntington upon long Island in y^e
Countie of Suffolk in y^e Province of new yourke in Amer-
aicai husbanman of the one Partie and Jonathan millard of
y^e afore sd town Countie and province of y^e other partie
witneseth, That y^o sd. John Joens and mary his wife for
divers good causes and considerations us their unto moving
but especiaily for and in the consideration of y^e sum of
fourteen pounds in good and curant silver coyne payable
in this province as it paseth from man to man have barganed allinated sould and confirmed and by these p^rsents
from us our heairs exseckutors administrators and asignes
doe, Alein Bargan sell and confirme unto y^e afore sd. Jonathon millard A cartaine parcell of medowe land sittuate
lying and being one y^e south side of this Island w^th in y^e
bounds of y^e towne of huntington afore sd. one a neck of
medow comonly called or knowne by y^e name of y^e haulfe
necke lying and beeing in too parts or parcells butting and
bounding as speciefied the eastermost peece Richard williams his meadow one y^e east side: the west side w^th y^e
medow of John Ted The south end with y^e sound the north
end with y^e woods in Comanige the westermost parcell
Jonathan Scuder one y^e east side the medowe of John Ted
one the west side y^e south end to y^e sound y^e north end to
y^e woods in Comonige both parcells containg fowr acers
bee it more or less it being by denomination an hundred
pound Right of medowe acording to y^e Rest of y^e other
Rights as equall as men could devide them I say these too
parcels of medow land w^th all y^e Rights and previliges belonging to it one y^t neck Too have and too hould y^e sd
granted and barganed p'mises unto y^e s^d Jonathan millard
his heairs exsecutors adminestrators and asignes for ever
yeilding and paying therfore his anuall and yeerly propor-

tion of w$^t$ may belong to this government of this province and wee the sd. John Joens and mary my wife for our selves our heairs exsecutors administrators and asignes doe covenant promise and grant too and w$^{th}$ y$^e$ afore sd Jonathan millard that y$^e$ said John Joens and mary my wife now is and stands firmly seized of a good, sure and perfit estate in y$^e$ law of y$^e$ sd too parcels of medow land before mentioned and hath good Right & lawfull authoritie to sell & convae y$^e$ same and y$^e$ sd John Joens and mary his wife for our selves our heairs exsecutors administrars and asigens doth further covenant too and w$^{th}$ y$^e$ sd. Jonathan millard his exsecutors administrators and asignes y$^t$ the sd. medow land and every part and parcel their of is free from all other and former bargans, grants sales morgages leasses judgments exsecutions convance or convances dowries widoe Rights tittels or in trest what soever and furthermore y$^e$ sd John Joens and mary his wife for our selves our heairs exsecutors, administrators and asignes Doe covenant promise and grant too and w$^{th}$ y$^e$ sd. Jonathan millard his heairs and asigens, That the sd. John Joens and mary his wife together w$^{th}$ our heairs executors Admines. trators and asigenes shall and will warrant and defend y$^e$ sd premises from any manor of just Right tittle claime or demand of any person or persons what soe ever In wittnes wheare of I have heer unto set my hand and seale the day and yeer above written.

signed sealed and delivered      JOHN JOENS
in y$^e$ presence of         the mark of
    ABIELL TITUS        MARY × JOENS
    JOSEPH BAILY

This Indenture was acknowledd y$^e$ 4$^{th}$ day of october 1686 before mee EPENETUS PLATT Justice of y$^e$ peace.

A True coppy Compaired w$^{th}$ y$^e$ origanall deed y$^e$ 25$^{th}$ of ocktob$^r$ 1686, p mee
      Isaac Platt Reco$^r$
   (*Deeds, Vol.* 1, *pp.* 217-8.)

# [DEED. JOSEPH BAILEY TO JAMES SMITH.]

[1686, Aug. 24.]

This Indenture made the twentie fourth day of August in the second yeer of y^e Raine of our Sou^r Lord Jams the second King of great Brittan france and Ireland ect^r and in y^e yeer of our Lord acording to the computation of y^e church of england one thousand six hundred eaightie six between Joseph Baily of huntington uppon long Island within y^e Countie of Suffolk & province of new yourke in america of the one partie husbandman and alce his wife and Jams Smith of the same towne Countie & province afore said cooper of the other partie witnesseth that y^e sd. Joseph baiely and alce his wife for diverse good causes and considerations us heer unto moving but especially for and in y^e consideration of the sum of six pounds to bee paid to Mr John Jackson of hemsted, winter wheat at five shillings p. bushell and Indian corne at too shillings six pence p bushell and y^e carting of twentie loads of wood all in hand secured before y^e enseailing and delivery heer of have bargoned alinated sould and confirmed and by these presents from us our heairs executors administrators and asignes doe allen bargon sell and confirme unto y^e afore said Jams Smith a certaine parcell of land sittuate lying and beeing on y^e east side of huntington afore sd. in a field comanly called or knowne by y^e name of y^e east field by estimation three acers bee it more or lesse which was y^e first devision land y^t belonged to y^e lott Joseph baily now liveth in. Butting and bounding as specified the Land of Leuitenant wood on y^e east side y^e land of Thomas Whitson one y^e west side the frunt or south end to a cart waye yt leadeth through ye said field the north to y^e woods in comanige. Too have and to hould the sd. granted p^rmises unto y^e afore sd. Jams smith his heairs executors administrators and asignes for ever yeilding and paying there fore his

anuall and yeerly proportion of what belongs to yᵉ goverment of this province and wee yᵉ said Joseph bayly and
alce his wife for our selves our heairs executors, administrators and asignes covenant promise and grant too and
with yᵉ afore sd. Jams yᵗ wee the sd. Joseph baily and alce
his wife now is and stands firmly seized of a good sure &
perfict estate in yᵉ lawe of the sd land before mentioned
and hath good Right and lawfull authoritie to sell & con-
vay the same, and the sd. Joseph Bayly and alce his wife
for our selves our heires executors administrators and
asignes doth further covenant promise and grant : too and
with the sd James Smith his heaires executors administrators and asignes, that the afore mentioned land is free and
cleer from all former bargans, grants sales, morgages,
leaces, Judgements, executions conveyance or conveyances
dowries widdoe Rights titles or intrest what soever ; And
further more yᵉ sd. Joseph Baily and alce his wife for our
selves our heires executors, administrators and asignes
doth covenant promise and grant too & with the sd. Jams
Smith his heires executors, administrators and asignes that
yᵉ sd. Joseph baiely and alce his wife together with our
heairs executors administrators and asignes shall and will
warant and defend yᵉ afore mentioned land from any
maner of just Ritte tittle & claime or demand of any person or persons what soever in wittness whearof wee have
here unto set our hands and seals yᵉ daye and yeer above
written.

JOSEPH BAILY

signed, sealed and
delivered in yᵉ presence
of us.

 THOMAS SMITH
JEREMIAH SMITH

the mark of

ALCE × BAILY

The 20<sup>th</sup> of August 1688 the subscribers appeared before me and acknowledged this instrument to bee their ackt and deed.

EPENETUS PLATT<br>Justice of y<sup>e</sup> Peace.

*(Deeds, Vol. 1, p. 246-7.)*

---

## [THE CHICHESTER RECORD.]

[1686, Sept. 15.]

Jams Chichester sonn of Jams Chichester Juneir was Borne y<sup>e</sup> 15<sup>th</sup> of September in y<sup>e</sup> yeer 1686.

*(Surveys, p. 164.)*

---

## [THE MILLER FAMILY RECORD.]

[1686, Sept. 19.]

Jonathan miller sonn of Jonathan miller was Borne y<sup>e</sup> 19<sup>th</sup> of septembar in y<sup>e</sup> yeer 1686.

*(Surveys, p. 160.)*

---

## [DEED. JOHN JONES TO ABIEL TITUS.]

[1686, Sept. 24.]

This Indenture made y<sup>e</sup> fowr an twenteth day of septembar in the second yeare of y<sup>e</sup> Raine of our Soveran Lord James king of great brittan, france, & Irland &c: And in y<sup>e</sup> year of our lord Acording to the Computation of y<sup>e</sup> Church of England and in y<sup>e</sup> year of our lord one thousand six hundred eaightie and six: Betweene John Joens nesaquaĸe, alies Smithstowne with in y<sup>e</sup> bounds of Broke haven alis Seatoket in yᵉ Counte of Suffolke and province of new yourke in Americae husbanman and mary his wife of yᵉ one partie and abiel titus of yᵉ town of huntington upon Long Island within yᵉ Countie and province afore said husbanman of yᵉ other Partie Wittnesseth That yᵉ sd. John Joens and mary his wife for divers good causes and considerations us their unto moving but especially for & in yᵉ consideration of yᵉ sum of twentie five pounds of good & curant Pay of this province as it Paseth from man to man in hand secured before yᵉ insealing and delivering heer of have Alinated Barganed sould & confirmed and by these psents Doe alien Bargan sell and confirm from us our heairs excecutors administrators and Asignes unto Abiell titus his heairs excekutors administrators & asignes the south side of my home lott & orchard situate Lying and beeing in yᵉ town of Huntington afore sd Butting and pounding the north side with the haulfe lott of Jonathan wood yᵉ west end with yᵉ woods in commonage, as specified the frunt or east end to yᵉ street yᵉ south side wᵗʰ yᵉ lott of Jonathan Scuders————————————————————

——————————together with yᵉ fence or fences their too beelonging I say yᵉ south haulfe of my lott with my orchard equally to bee devided as wee can devide it in yᵉ midel of the lott yᵗ Each part may bee alike in breadth only if yᵉ east haulfe of perticion fence fall to bee Jonathan woods and the well fall in yᵉ south haulfe lott then yᵉ sd Jonathan wood have free libartie by purchase to turne his fence short to take in yᵉ well for yᵉ use of him self and heairs and sucsesors for ever but all other Rights & benifits of yᵉ sd. haulfe lott and orchard to Remaine and bee to yᵉ use and benifit of abiel titus his heairs and sucksesors to have and to hold for ever yeilding and Paing theirfore his anuall or yeerly proportion of what may belong to yᵉ Govermᵗ of this province and yᵉ sd John Jones and mary his wife doth for our selves & heairs exsecutors administraters and asignes Doe covenant promise and grant too and with y⁰ afore sd abiel titus that yᵉ sd. John Joens and mary his wife now is and stands firmly seazed of A good sure and perfitt estatte in yᵉ law of yᵉ sd. haulfe lott and orchard and hath good Right and law full athoritie to sell and convae the same and y⁰ sd. Johns and mary his wife for our selves our heairs exsecutors administrators and Asingnes Doe further covenant promise and grant too and with yᵉ sd Abiel tittus his heairs execukutors administrators and asignes yᵗ yᵉ sd orchard and haulf lott of land is free and cleer of and from all other and former bargans grants sales morgages leases judments exsecutions convance or convances dowries or widdoe Rights titles or intrest what soever and further more the sd. John Joens and mary his wife for our selves our heairs exsecutors adminestrators and asignes Doe further Covenant, promise and grant to and with yᵉ sd. abiel titus his heairs exsecutors administrators and asignes that yᵉ sd. John Jones and mary his wife shall and will defend yᵉ same from any maner of just Rights Clames or demands of any person or persons what soever as witnes our hands and seals the day and yeer above written.

signed, sealled and                           JOHN JOENS
in y⁰ presence of                             The ✕ of
   SAMUELL TITTUS              MARY JOENS
   JOSEPH BAYLY

This Indenture was acknowlegd this 4 day of octobar before mee    EPENETUS PLATT Justice of yᵉ peace 1686.

Memorandom The wᵗʰ in named Abiel titus is to have yᵉ free use of yᵉ well as is specified in Jonathan woods deed yᵗ is hee his heairs and sucsesors for ever bairing equall charge to wards y⁰ maintaince of yᵉ well this memorandum was write before the sealing and delivering p mee

                           JOSEPH BAYLY
witness
EPENETUS PLATT
JOSEPH BAYLY

That which is enterlined one yᵉ other side in yᵉ 19ᵗʰ and
20ᵗʰ line was misplaced in yᵉ enterling and soe had to bee
understood, the sum of which is this yᵉ south side with the
lott of Jonathan Scudder yᵉ north side wᵗʰ the haulfe lott
of Jonathan wood: This was written before signed. a true
coppe.

A True Coppy Compared wᵗʰ yᵉ originall yᵉ 20ᵗʰ of
octobaʳ: 1686

p mee Isaac Platt, Recʳ

*(Deeds, Vol. 1, pp. 215-6.)*

---

## [DEED. JOHN JONES TO JAMES CHICHESTER, Jʀ.]

### [1686, Oct. 4.]

This Indenture Made yᵉ fowrth Day of octobar in yᵉ second yeer of the Raine of our sovʳ Lord James the second
King of great Brittan france & Irland et rᵉ: and in yᵉ yeer
of our lord acording to the computation of yᵉ Church of
england one thousand six hundred eaightie and six Beetween John Joens of nessaquage alis smiths Towne with in
yᵉ bounds of brooke haven ales seatoaket wᵗʰ in yᵉ countie
of sufolke and province of new yourke in Americai husbandman and mary his wife of yᵉ one partie and Jams Chichester Junʳ of yᵉ towne of huntington upon Long Island
within the countie and province afore sd. husbandman of
yᵉ other partie. Wittnesseth That yᵉ sd. John Joens and
mary his wife for divers good causes and considerations
us heer unto moving butt especially for and in consideration of feifteene pounds curant Pay of this province in
hand paid before yᵉ insealling and delivering heer of Have
Bargoned alinated sould and confirmed and doe by these
pʳsents Bargon alien sell and confirme unto yᵉ afore said

James Chichester his heairs executors administrators and asignes three sertaine parcels of medow Land situate lying and being one y^e south side of Island within y^e bounds of huntington one a neck of meadow land comonly called or known by y^e name of y^e west necke which is by denomination an hundred pound Right of meadowe acording to y^e denomination or customs of y^e town of huntington Butting and bounding acording to y^e contents of these presents one parcell on the west side with y^e medowe of timothy conklin one y^e east side with the meadowe James Chichester afore said the north with y^e woods the south with the sound :. one partte or devision y^e south side with y^e medowe of y^e afore sd. Jams Chichester the north the woods frunting to y^e medowe of timothy Conklin the third part or devision with medowe Land belonging to timothy conklin not as yet devided I say all these parcels of medowe land before mentioned with all Rights and previliges that doth may or can belong or apertaine to y^e afore mentioned p^rmises upon y^e neck afore said Too have hould use occupie and Injoe all the afore Bargoned and granted p^rmises too Jams Chichester his heairs executors Adminestrators and asigens for ever yeeilding and paing therefore his yeerly and anuall proportion of what may be long to y^e goverment of this province and furthermore wee y^e sd. John Joens and mary his wife for our selves our heairs executors administrators and asigens doe covenant promise and grant too and with y^e sd. James Chichester that y^e sd John and mary his wife now is and stands firmly seised of a good sure and perfit estate in y^e Lawe of all y^e afore mentioned p^rmises and every part and parcel their of and hath good Right and lawfull athoritie too sell and convae the same and y^e sd John Joens and mary his wife for our selves our heairs executors Administrators and asigenes doth further covenant promise and grant too and with y^e said James Chichester his heairs executors administrators and asignes that y^e said medow land and every part and parcell their of is free from all other and formar bargans grants sales morgages leasses judgments executions convance or convances dowries, widdow Rights, tittles or interest what soever: and furthermore y^e sd John Joens and mary his wife for our selves our heairs executors adminestrators and asignes doe covenant promise and grant too and with y^e sd Jams Chichester his heairs executors administrators and asigns y^t the sd. John Jones and mary his wife together with our selves our heairs executors and administrators and asigns shall and will warant and defend y^e afore mentioned p^rmises from any maner of just Rights tittels claims demands of any person or persons what soever in wittnes whearof wee have heer untoo sett our hands and seals y^e day and year above written.

Signed sealed ad delivered In y^e prsence of us whose nams are heer to subscribed.

JOHN JOENS

the mark of

MARY × JOENS

    ABIEL TITUS
    JOSEPH BAILY

This Indenture was acknowledg before mee The day and yeer above mentioned.

EPENETUS PLATT, Justice.

A True Coppy of the origanal deed Compared by mee Isaac Platt Rec^r November y^e 18^th 1686.

    (*Deeds, Vol.* 1, *p.* 221-2.)

---

### [CHILDREN OF JOHN KETCHAM.]

[1686, Oct. 12.]

The Record of y^e Children of John Kicham senier, of thee towne of huntington

John his eldest sonn was borne y^e 29^th of septembar In y^e yeer of our lord 1674.

Thomas Kicham sonn of John Kicham, senier was Borne y$^e$ 13$^{th}$ day of May in y$^e$ yeer 1676.

Elizabeth Kicham daughter of John kicham was Borne y$^e$ 14$^{th}$ of Aprill in y$^e$ yeer 1678.

Phillip kicham sonn of John kicham was borne y$^e$ 8$^{th}$ day of may in y$^e$ yeer 1680.

david Kicham sonn of John kicham was borne y$^e$ 27$^{th}$ of march in y$^e$ yeer 1683.

mary Kicham daughter of John Kicham was borne y$^e$ 12$^{th}$ of octobar in y$^e$ yeer of our Lord Christ 1686.

(*Surveys, p.* 164.)

---

[TOWN MEETING.—" MEADOW SOLD AT AN OUTCRY."]

[1686, Oct. 14.]

At a towne meeting Legally warned the 14$^{th}$ of october 1686.

It was voated and agreed by y$^e$ towne that y$^e$ medowe in ye east neck should bee sould at an out cry or vandue for marchandable pay, To. witt beef Porke, wheat, Indian corne any or all of these at marchandble. price and hee y$^t$ bids y$^e$ greatest sum to have it, it is to bee sould by an inch of candle y$^e$ which medoe was sould to Insigne Jonathan Scudder to him and his heairs for ever. which bad y$^e$ last and bad eaighteen pounds ten shillings: which money is to be Paid att or before Crismas next insuing y$^e$ datte of it is to bee understood y$^t$ y$^e$ intent of y$^e$ towne was that Jonathan Scudder should have y$^t$ medowe hee bought of y$^e$ towne in y$^e$ east neck. for him selfe and his haires or asignes forever the same day above sd. was granted to Samuell titus seventeen acears of land at the head of hemstead hollow on the west sid hemstead path by the path side.

(*Town Meetings, Vol.* 1, *p.* 145.)

[TOWN MEETING.  TROUBLE BREWING WITH
GOV. DONGAN.]

[1686, Oct. 16.]

At a towne meeting Legally warned yᵉ 16ᵗʰ ocktober 1686.

It was voated and consented to by all yt Tho Powell &
Isaac platt shall if Isaac Platt bee able atend these Genteⁱⁱ
men apointed by the Governer to take acount of what
lands and medows is allredy Purchased and wee doe im-
pour them to ackt to yᵉ best of their discretion in our
behaulfe if Isaac bee not able to Ride then they toe are to
chuse another.

The day above written it was voated and consented to
yᵗ ye towne will not stand tryall about yᵉ ten pound demanded att yourke but Rather pay it if thay can not other
ways help it.*

the day above written it was voated. and consented to
yᵗ Jonathan Jarvise shall have his hundred pound Right of
land : noe medowe bee longing to it: equall from yᵉ first
devision in yᵉ town.

the day above written there was granted by yᵉ town to
Jonothan Jarvis six acers of land to wards his division in
ye east neck one yᵉ left hand of yᵉ Path joining to yᵉ feild

the day above written granted to nicolas Smith 1 three
acare of land, division land one yᵉ south side of yᵉ long
point over against Tho. Scudders feild it is upon ye west
necke.

-----

[*Gov. Dongan wants to know what lands Huntington has
bought of the Indians and what remains unpurchased.  He also
wants £10. This is the beginning of a contention between Gov.
Dongan and the town about taking another patent, which lasted
for several years, and during this time the relations between
Huntington and the Governor's office were, as the diplomatists
say, "strained."—C. R. S.]

October y$^e$ 16$^{th}$ 1686: At a town meeting voated and granted to Richard brush six acars of land joining to his land one y$^e$ east side y$^e$ millpond brooke upon y$^e$ west neck.

the day above written y$^e$ town granted tho: Higbe seven acars of land joing north east to y$^t$ land hee had of nicolas ellice which is layed out in a long hollow in y$^e$ east neck.

The day a bove written granted to John Kicham three acers of land at y$^e$ nor west end of y$^e$ cove swamp upon y$^e$ west neck.

The day afore sd. granted to John Samis too acars of land one y$^e$ top of y$^e$ hill joing to that hee had of Tho: Brush.

The day above sd. it was granted to Jeremiah Smith y$^t$ if hee will set up a mill within six months the town will grant him y$^e$ twelf Part of all corn that they shall bring him to grind at his mill and y$^e$ town not to bee att any charge about the cleering y$^e$ soill Right of his land.

The day above written ocktob$^r$ y$^e$ 16: 1686 att a town meeting it was voated & granted y$^t$ M$^r$ Joens shall have all that medowe one ye east side Cowharbor brook all betwixt Mr Woods lott there: and the cart Path going over the swamp hee is to have it for himself and his heairs for ever: All soe the same day above datted it was voated and granted that Mr Joens above s$^d$ shall have one acare of meddow at cow harbor on y$^e$, west side y$^e$ brooke or creeke opposite to his one y$^e$ other side to bee his own and his heairs for ever: hee Resighng up a gaine to y$^e$ towne what was granted him y$^e$ day afore sd of y$^e$ parsonage alottment and y$^t$ fowr acres Resignd to remaine to y$^e$ parsonage.

(*Town Meetings, Vol.* 1, *pp.* 145-147.)

[TOWN MEETING.]

[1686, Nov. 4.]

November y$^e$ 4. 1686. at a towne meeting Thomas Pow-

ell was chossen commitieman for this present year to goe
to Southhamton theire to ackt w^{th} y^e Rest of ye comitie
for y^e town of huntington: if: Tho. Powell faill then
Thomas Higbee is chosen to goe.

The same day Samuell titus was shossen townsmen if Joseph Whittman goe his intended viage.

(*Town Meetings, Vol.* 1, *p.* 140.)

## [TOWN MEETING.]

[1686, Nov. 10.]

Att a towne meeting november y^e tenth: 1686  It was
a greed upon by y^e generalitie of y^e Inhabitants that too
men should bee sent —— yorke in anser to y^e geverners
Letter ye men chosen by y^e towne for y^t purpose was Tho.
Powell and Isaac. Platt:

The day above written it was voated and granted y^t y^e
medew at Cold spring should bee sould to cleer y^e towne
of y^t debt due to Mr coolly att yorke and ye over plusse
to bee ye towns which m—— was att y^e same time sould
to Samuell Kisham for twentie five shillings more than
y^t debt to Mr coolly and Samuell Kisham is to cleer the
town of any charge y^t may arise upon y^e acount of y^e fore
mentioned debt and to pay y^e town twenty five shillings
in m——.

(*Town Meetings, Vol.* 1, *p.* 141.)

## [POWER TO ACT FOR THE TOWN GIVEN THOS. POWELL AND ISAAC PLATT.]

[1686, Nov. 16.]

huntington no——b^r: y^e 16^{th}: 1686
Thes may signefie to any whome it may conserne y^t wee

under written doe imply our nabours Tho: Powell and
Isaac Platt to ackt in y⁰ townes behaulfe acording to their
discresion for y⁰ good of y⁰ towne and what thay shall see
cause to doe in order to y⁰ towns good: wee in y⁰ behaulfe
of y⁰ the towne doe promise to stand to and confirme.

JAMES CHESTAR
JOSEPH WHETM—
THO. FLEET:
JOHN SAMMIS.

(*File No. 4.*)

---

## [TOWN MEETING. RESOLVE TO HAVE PALMER TAKEN IN.]

[1686, Nov. 24.]

November y⁰ 24ᵗʰ 1686.

At a towne meeting then legally warned it was voated
and granted yᵗ the towne would treat with y⁰ governer and
counsell in Referance to a new Pattent.

The day above written it was voated and granted yᵗ the
towne will give twentie pound for a pattent and twentie
shillings quitt Rent.

The same day above written y⁰ townemen by voat weare
impowered to procure y⁰ best helpe thay could to asist
them in Returning y⁰ townes propositions to Mr Graham*
in Relation to a new Pattent.

---

[*James Graham was a member of Gov. Dongan's Council
and one of the most learned and able lawyers in the Colony.
He seems to have supervised the draft of most of the grants
and patents made by Gov. Dongan. A few years later, (in 1689),
after Dongan had been retired and Leisler had usurped the
authoiity of governor, Graham was expelled from the Council,
and for writing a bold and manly letter he was thrown into
prison. After Leisler was executed for treason, Graham was
again made a member of the Council.—C. R. S.]

The day above written it was voated and consented
yᵗ Mr. Wood and thomas Powell should improve yᵉ best
of their abillities them selves: and take yᵉ best help thay
can to settle the south bounds of yᵉ north purchase of this
towne with yᵉ Indians and what thay shall doe in order .*
* * * to yᵉ promised wee doe promise to Ratifie and
confirme.

The same day above written november yᵉ 24ᵗʰ 1686. it
was voated and granted yᵗ Judge Palmer should bee taken
in a pattenttee with us only in Refarance to soill Right of
yᵗ land eastward of Cowharbor butt not to have any intrest in yᵉ towns Right wẻstward from Cowharbor the
towne Reserving to them selves their own intrest from
Cowharbor east ward.†

The day a bove written it was voated and consented
that thomas Powell and Isaac Platt shall goe to yorke in
order to the taking of a pattent when need Requires it:
and upon fallure of eather of them the townsmen to chuse
another to goe

(*Town Meetings, Vol.* 1, *p.* 149.)

---

## [CONCERNING THE PROPOSED PATENT FROM GOV. DONGAN.]

[1686—Probable Date.]

Right worshipfull Sir.

We having Receved by our messengars Isaac Platt and

---

[†Judge Palmer's patent, dated about 1686, and the Indian
deed accompanying it, are on record in the office of the Secretary of State, in Albany. They cover the territory about
Northport and Crabmeadow. As the Indians had already
sold the same land several times and received their pay in
trinkets and "fire water," and as the same premises were covered
by the Nichols patent to Huntington of 1666, this paper title
has never amounted to much. It probably scared the people
of Huntington into offering "to take Judge Palmer in," with
the promise that they "reserve their own interest." Palmer
seems to have been taken in in a Pickwickian sense.—C. R. S.]

Tho: Powell from ye governer and counsell an order datted octobar y$^e$ 18$^{th}$ 1686 wherein it was ordered the un-
purchased lands within our township should bee purchased
and in complyanse with y$^t$ order wee thought meett to
present a few lins to your worship y$^t$ you would bee
pleased to bee asistant to us in this matter and to present
in our behalfe to his excelency y$^e$ governer our humble
petition which is this: yt wee may have license from his
exsclency : to purchase of y$^e$ Indians proprietors so much
land lieing north ward of our south medows as may be
convenent yt is haulf a mile or their about from an Indian
path y$^t$ lyeth aganst y$^e$ sd meddows and for y$^e$ other part
of y$^e$ sd. order yo$^r$ worship may understand y$^e$ towne are
willing to comply with y$^e$ sd order hoping his exselency :
will bee pleased to take in to his searios consideration y$^e$
state and condition of y$^e$ town and y$^e$ lownes of our estates
which by Reason of y$^e$ incapasitie of y$^e$ plase is not like to
bee much augmented our lands being barren and y$^e$ part
of it not fit for tillage yet not withstanding we are willing
to alow 20$^{lb}$ to his exselency yt our lands may bee confirmed for y$^e$ future and 20 shillings quit Rent which wee
hope considering y$^e$ premises his excellency well exsept of
and if it please god to move your hart to bee instrumentall
in our behalf to bee helpfull to us in this trancattion it will
bee a strong ingagment of us unto yo$^r$ worship : wee should
have waited upon his exselency w$^{th}$ more speed but wee
can not prevaille w$^{th}$ y$^e$ Indians to come with us till y$^e$
spring soe hoping yo$^r$ worship wil bee pleased to bee asistant to us wee take leave and Rest your humble servant for
and in y$^e$ behalfe of y$^e$ towne

ISAAC PLATT.

Sir, wee hope to make honorable satisfaction for yo$^r$ asist-
ance in y$^e$ premises

(*File No.* 7.)

## [THE JUDGE'S RATE.]

[1686, Nov. 26.]

Mr Epenetus platt : after due respectes presented to you, These lines is to request you, if your colecter have payed your Judges rate to you according to his warrant, and also the Coleckter of Smith Town, that then you would be pleased to deliver the monnie to my brother, John Howell, and his resept; with this my order shall be your full discharge as witness my hand.

South hampton this 26 of November 1686.

EDWARD HOWELL Tresurer<br>for the Countie of Suffolk

Huntington the 29 of novemer 1686.
then received of Epenetus Platt the sum of four pound three shilings & seven pence the proportion of the town of huntinun to pay to the Judes, I say Received by me.

JOHN HOWELL.

(*File No.* 58.)

------

[1686, Dec. 7.]

John mathews of this town departed this Life the 7[th] day of desember 1686.

(*Town Meetings, Vol.* 1, *p.* 142.)

------

## [INVENTORY OF THE GOODS OF JOHN MATHEWS.]

[1686, Dec. 11.]

An account taken of the estate of John mathews deceased

Apprized by phillip udall and John Scidmore Se^r the eleventh of desembar 1686.

| Imp^r | lb. | s. | d. |
|---|---|---|---|
| one Iern kettle and tramell, att | 00 | 12 | 00 |
| It, a horse att | 02 | 05 | 00 |
| It, an old Cowe | 02 | 00 | 00 |
| it an old chest and other small things | 01 | 00 | 00 |

owned by us ⎫ This account was
PHILLIP UDALL ⎬ exsepted of as le-
JOHN SCIDMORE ⎭ gall

(*Deeds Vol.* 1, *p.* 210.)

---

[LANDS OF REV. ELIPHELET JONES.]

[1686, Dec. 22.]

Whereas it a pears y^t M^r Eliphalet Jones hath a grant of: 20: acres of land wheare hee thinks good to take it wee have acordingly layd out unto him 14 acars on y^e west neck forty Rod broad along by the path going to horse necke one y^e east side y^e Path a little beyond the head of y^e cove swamp the lenth is 56 Rod Running east-ward, And wee have alsoe laid out to y^e said Mr Eliphalet Jones foure aceres and a haulf more joing to his home lotte of y^e which four acars and a halfe 3 acars was layd out formerly and is now fensed and improved soe theire Remains still one acare and a halfe more to bee Layd out of the said 20 acars granted by the towne: this wee wittness by subscribing our hands desemb^r y^e 22^d 1686

JOSEPH WHITTMAN
SAMUELL TITTUS

p. mee Isaac Platt Rece^r

(*Town Meetings, Vol.* 1, *p.* 147.)

## [ESTATE OF JOHN MATHEWS, Sen.]

[1686, Dec. 29.]

Knowe all men by these p'sents that wee John Mathews
of fresh pond neck within yͤ bounds of huntington upon
Long Island within yͤ countie of Suffolke and province of
new yorke in Americae husbandman and John Scidmore
senʳ of yͤ same place countie & province husbandman am
bound and firmly obliged unto Isaac platt and Jams Chichester both of yͤ town of huntington in the Countie of
suffolke and province afore said comisinors for yͤ towne in
yͤ full and intire some of five pounds 17 shillings silvar
curant pay of this province to bee paid to yͤ said comisinors
their heairs exsecuters administrators or asighns upon not
performing the under written condition of this obligation
for which wee bind us our heairs executors administrators
and asighnes firmly by these presents in wittness where of
wee have here unto set our hands and seals yͤ twentie nine
day of desembar in yͤ second yeer of his maᵗⁱᵉˢ Raine and
in yͤ yeer of our lord one thousand six hundred eaightie
six.

The condition of this p'sent obligation is such that if the
above bounden John Mathews and John Scidmore thay or
either of their heairs executors administrators or asignes
shall from time to time observe and keep such directions
or orders in paieing to yͤ creditors of John Mathews Deseased if any apeer the full and wholle vallue of all yͤ estatte
yᵗ yͤ deseased left acording to yͤ prizall of it with in ten
dayes next after thay shall Reseive their order either from
Isaac Platt or James Chichester wherby neither thay nor
their heairs executors or assignes may bee damnified butt
yͤ end of yͤ law atended this obligation beeing performed
and keept acording to yͤ true intent and meaning heer of
it to bee voayde and of noe efeckt or elce to stand Remaine

and bee in full powr force and vertue

JOHN

Sighned and delivered                    The marke ☓ MATHEWS
in yᵉ presence of                                of
    PHILLIP UDALL                      JOHN SCIDMORE.
    JOSEPH BAILY
A True Record of yᵉ origanall bond p mee

Isaac Platt Recʳ

Janaware yᵒ 3ᵈ :—16⁸⁶₈₇.

    (*Deeds, Vol.* 1, *p.* 211.)

---

[DEED. NICHOLAS SMITH TO THOMAS
SMITH.]

[1686, Dec. 30.]

This Indenture made yᵉ thirtieth day of desembar in the
second yeare of yᵉ Raigne of our soverʳ Lord Jams King
of great Brittan france and Irland etcʳ and in yᵉ yeare of
our Lord acording to yᵉ Computation of yᵉ Church of
England one thousand six hundred eaightie six Betweene
Nicolas Smith of yᵉ towne of huntington upon Long Island
in yᵉ countie of Suffolke and Province of new yourk in
Americai Carpender and mary his —— of yᵉ one ptie and
Thomas smith of yᵉ same towne countie and Province Carpender of the other Partie, Wittnesseth that yᵉ sd. Nicolas
Smith and mary his wife for divers good causes and considerations uss their unto moving but especialy for & in
consideration of a valliable some in hand Reseved by which
wee acknowlege our selfes to bee fully satisfied contented
and Paide before yᵉ ensealling and delivering of these
pʳsents by yᵉ sd. Thomas Smith Hath granted allenated
sould and confirmed and doe by these pʳsents fully clearly
and absolutly grant allinatte bargain sell and confirme unto

y° a fore sd Thomas Smith my dwelling house, orchard,
gardin out housing home lott sittuate Lying and being in
y° towne of huntington afore sd. frunting west to the
meetting house north to y° hie way east to y° Lotte of
thomas weeks, south with the lotte of y° widdowe Cory
now in y° tenure or ocupation of the afore said nicolas
smith the Lott containg three acars bee it more or less
containg one hundred pound Right in devition of com-
manage Acording to y° custome of y° towne of huntington
together with all woods under woods comans of pastures
what soe ever doth to y° same belonging or apertaing to
y° sd. house or teniment by devision or by any other way
or means what soever to have and too hould for ever all
y° said afore mentioned p'mises with their apurtinances;
exsept the dwelling house orchard and barne whome y°
afore said nicolas smith doth Reserve to him selfe for his
natturall life and y° life of mary his wife, if him the said
nicolas smith or mary his wife see cause to make use of it
them selves & during which time and tearme the a fore
said nicolas smith shall fence it of from y° Lott begining at
y° east end of y' house Runing strait to a peare tree and
from thence too widdowe Corys fence butt if y° afore said
nicolas smith and mary his wife chance to Remove out of
y° towne then y° sd. Thomas smith shall poses ocupie and
injoe y° dwelling house, orchard and barne as free as any
of y° Rest of y° p'mises: Butt if y° said nicolas and mary
his wife make use of it for their lives then after their
deseace to Remaine and bee as y° other afore mentioned
p'mises to y° only use and behoufe of ye afore said Thomas
smith his heairs exsecutors administrators and asignes and
y° above said nicolas smith for him self his heairs executors
administrators and asignes that att the sealling and delivering heer of hee then was the solle and Lawfull ———— of
all y° afor said p'mises and am lawfully seased of and in
the same and in every pa^t· and Parcel thereof in mine owne
Right and the said Thomas smith his heairs executors ad-

ministrators and asignes: shall and may by force and
vertue of these p^rsents from time to time and att all times
heer after Lawfully peacably and quitly have hould use
ocupie and Injoe the afore granted p^rmises with all their
apurtenances exsept before exsepted free and cleerly
aquitted and discharged of and from all and all maner of
fines gifts grants leases morgages jointurs dowries tittles of
dowries widdowe Rights judgments executions entailling
and of and from all other tittels trubles and incumberances
what soe ever had made commited wittingly or willingly
sufered or don by y^e said nicolas smith or by any other person or persons whatsoever lawfully claiming from by or
under him y^e sd nicolas smith or by his means or assent or
private procurment and y^e said nicolas smith his heairs and
asigns and all and every other Person and persons what
soever lawfully claiming from and under him shall and will
warant and for ever defend by these p^rsents the afore
mentioned p^rmises only Reserving what belongs his ma^tie:
in this province in wittnes whearof we have heer unto
sett our hands and seals the day and year above written.

of
The marke X SMITH
NICOLAS
of
The marke X SMITH
MARY

signed sealed and
Delivered in presence of
WILLIAM JARVICE
JOSEPH BAYLY
This above written indenture was acknowlegd by nicolas
smith and his wife this 14^th day of february 168⅘ before
mee EPENETUS PLATT Justice of Peace.

A True Coppy of y^e origanall deed Compared by mee
Isaac Platt Rec^r
ffebraway y^e 22^d: 168⅘.
(Deeds, Vol. 1, pp. 223-4.)

## [DEED. JOHN GREEN TO JAMES BETTS.]

[1687, Jan. 31.]

This Indenture made y$^e$ thirtie first: or y$^e$ Last day of Januare and in y$^e$ second yeer of y$^e$ Reaigne of our Soveran Lord James y$^e$ second king of great brittan france and Irland and acording to y$^e$ computation of y$^e$ church of england 168$\frac{6}{7}$: Between John Green of y$^e$ town of huntington in y$^e$ Countie of Suffolke in y$^e$ Province of new yourke in Americai husbanman of y$^e$ one partie: and Jams batte of y$^e$ towne of Hemsted in y$^e$ queens countie & Province afore said one y$^e$ other Partie: Wittnesseth y$^t$ y$^e$ said John green and elizabeth his wife for divers good causes us theire unto moving but especlially for & in y$^e$ consideration of sixty pounds in good and curant Pay of this province all redy in hand before the insealing heer of hath granted alined barganed: sould and confirmed. and by these presents doth fully cleerly and absoluttly grant allien bargan sell and confirme unto y$^e$ said Jams batte all that farme upland and medowe which was formerly asigned to mee from Jonathan Harnett lying between Crabmedowe and fresh pond: I say I doe with y$^e$ consent of elizabeth green my wife: sell and make over unto y$^e$ above said Jams batte of hemsted. to him his heairs executors adminstrators and asignes: and from mee my heairs exsecutors administrators and asigns I by these p$^r$sents confirme unto y$^e$ afore sd. batte all y$^t$ farme tenement or plantation now in y$^e$ tenure or occupation of y$^e$ sd. green or of his asignes, of thirtie acars of land and medowe or their abouts bee it more or lesse with all Rights preveleges and apurtinances their unto belonging as dwelling house barne stable orchard gardin fruit trees fences of all sorts and what soever doth belong to y$^t$ farme with three acars of Land Lying upon Crabmedow necke upon y$^e$ point called martins vinyard the westermost point to bee included in this bill of

saill bounded one y⁰ east with samuell kichams land : one
y⁰ west with y⁰ cove one y⁰ south with y⁰ hie way one y⁰
north with y⁰ sound the other Part of y⁰ land yᵗ is a bove
mentioned is bounded as followeth one y⁰ south side with
y⁰ comans one y⁰ north with y⁰ medowe of y⁰ sd green sum
Part of it, y⁰ other Part of it with John Inkersons medowe
and a peece of coman medowe yᵗ lyeth against y⁰ Land of
y⁰ sd. Green one y⁰ east with a creeke yᵗ Runeth betwixt
y⁰ sd. Green and John Scidmore and y⁰ west side with y⁰
comans : to gether with all coman of pasture or what soe
ever doth at present belong or heer after shall to y⁰ sd
p^rmises : y⁰ Indian Right only to bee exsepted which I y⁰·
above sd. Green doe not sell, I doe by these p^rsents make
over and sell and allien all my Right title & intrest in ye
above sd. p^rmises to y⁰ above said batte to him and his
heairs to have and to hould forever with all y⁰ above sd
and granted p^rmises with all and every their Rights mem-
bars and apurtinances to y⁰ same belonging or apertaing
unto y⁰ sd. Jams batte his heairs exsecutors and asignes to
y⁰ only proper use and be hoofe of y⁰ sd. Jams batte and
y⁰ heairs and asignes of y⁰ sd. Jams batte for ever and y⁰ ·
sd. John Green for him selfe his heairs executors and administrators doe covenant promise and grant by these
p^rsents yᵗ att the time of y⁰ ensealling heer of I am y⁰ sole ·
and lawfull owner of all y⁰ afore said barganed p^rmises and
am lawfully seaised of and in y⁰ same and in every part
and parcell theirof in my owne Right the Indians claime
onely to bee exsepted and y⁰ sd. James batte his heairs executors and administrators and asignes shall and may by
force and vertue of these p^rsents from time to time and att
all tims for ever heer after Lawfully peacably and quiatly
have hould use occupie posses and Injoe y⁰ above granted
pmises with theire apurtinances free and cleer and cleerly
aquitted and descharged of and from all and all maner of
former and other gifts grants Leasses morgages jointures
dowres, tittle of dower judgments exsecutions entaills and

of and from all other tittles trubles and incumberances what so ever had made committed or wittingly or willingly suffered or done by y^e^ sd. John Green or by any other person or persons what soe ever lawfully claiming from or under him y^e^ sd. green or by his means assent privattly or procurment, and y^e^ sd John green his heairs and asignes and all and every other person or persons what soever Lawfully claiming by from or under him him them or any of them: shall and will warrant and for ever defend by these p^r^sents In wittnes wheareof I y^e^ said John Green have heer unto sett my hand and seale y^e^ day and yeer first above written.

signed, sealled
and delivered
in prsence of us.
PATRUKE FFALCONER
JAMS SMITH

of
the marke X JOHN
GREEN.
of
the mark X GREEN
ELIZABETH

This above said Indenture was acknowledged before mee by John green and his wife Elizabeth green this twentie forth of febrawary $168\frac{6}{7}$.

EPENETUS PLATT Justice of peace.

A True Coppy of y^e^ origanall deed Compared by me Isaac Platt Reco^r^ march y^e^ 9^th^ $168\frac{6}{7}$.

(*Deeds, Vol* 1, *pp.* 225-6.)

---

## [JOHN INGERSOLL WARNED.]

[1687, Feb. 17.]

Huntington february y^e^ 17^th^ $16\frac{86}{87}$.

John Inherson wee are informed y^t^ you have given entertainment to a man and a woman and too children and have reseved them into yo^r^ famalie and have not acted therein acording to law wee underwritten doe advise you to send him, his wife and children out of this township as you will answer y⁰ penalty of y⁰ Law in yᵗ matter: hereof you are to take notice.

ISAAC PLATT

JAMES CHICHESTER

*(Town Meetings, Vol. 1, p. 142.)*

---

## [CHILDREN OF TIMOTHY CONKLIN.]

[1687, Feb. 20.]

Martha Conklin dafter of Timothy Conklin was borne y⁰ 20ᵗʰ of octobar in y⁰ yeer 1668.

Timothy Conklin was borne y⁰ 16ᵗʰ of desembar in y⁰ yeer 1670.

John Conklin sonn of Timothy Conklin was borne the 14ᵗʰ of march 167⅔.

Thomas Conklin was borne y⁰ 10ᵗʰ of march in y⁰ yeer 16$\frac{74}{75}$.

Jacob Conklin was borne y⁰ 15ᵗʰ of march 167⅖.

Elizabeth Conklin was borne y⁰ 15ᵗʰ of June 1679.

Rebecka Conklin daughter of timothy Conklin was borne 10ᵗʰ of Januare in y⁰ yeer 16$\frac{80}{81}$.

Mary Conklin daughter of timothy Conklin was borne y⁰ 10ᵗʰ of June in y⁰ yeer 1684.

Cornelius Conklin was borne y⁰ 20ᵗʰ of februwary in the yeer of our Lord Christ 168⅘.

*(Surveys, p. 158.)*

---

## [TOWN MEETING. CONCERN ABOUT THE PATENT.]

[1687, March 11.]

At a towne meeting march y⁰ 11ᵗʰ 168$\frac{6}{7}$ it was voated and

consented to y$^t$ all those persons y$^t$ doe not pay their preportion of y$^e$ charge expended about procuring a Pattent a
cording to time and speice ingaged shall have soe much of
their Land sould att an out cry : as will make sattisfaction
for their preportion with all charges rising upon their
negleckt.

The same day voted y$^t$ James Chichester shall goe to y$^e$
south for Thomas powell to come up to goe to yorke in
order to y$^e$ procuring of a Pattent and if thomas come not
James chichester shall be paid for his time & exspence.

march y$^e$ 11$^{th}$ 168$\frac{6}{7}$ att a town meeting it was voated and
consented to by all that thomas Powell and Isaac Platt are
left to their libirtie in procuring a pattent Capt. fleet is to
asist in it what he can and y$^e$ towne doth ingage to confirme
what any too of them shall doe in order to y$^e$ prmises.

(*Town Meetings, Vol. 1, pp.* 149-150.)

---

## [ISAAC PLATT'S BILL AGAINST THE TOWN.]

[1687, March 15.]

March y$^e$ 15$^{th}$ 168$\frac{6}{7}$.

The towne d$^r$ to Isaac Platt upon y$^e$ Pattent acount for
my Journie to Yorke my selfe & horse a : 11 : days for my
selfe, 2$^s$ : 6$^d$ per day : for my horse standing at y$^e$ fery soe
Long att sallt hay, was much abated of his flesh, y$^e$ towne
did all wayes in such casses alowe 9$^s$ : both 9 : to 01$^{lb}$ 16$^s$ 06$^d$
my self and horse a day to oyster Bay w$^{th}$ M$^r$ }
Wood to see their Pattent, and when wee }
came home y$^e$ Remainder of y$^e$ day spent at } 00   04   00
Capt fleets about y$^e$ Pattent. }

y$^e$ next day spent tell noon about y$^e$ Pattent } 00   01   03
in writing to Mr graham our propositions }

$\frac{1}{2}$ a day spent at M$^r$ Woods to view y$^e$ pattent   00   01   03 more time spent about $y^e$ pattent and exspense upon Swaneme, 3 quarts sider, 2 meals, meat ,87.     00   02   09

John & horse a day to make out $y^e$ bounds    00   04   00

for 1 : Journey to yourke, 1 : day spent to gett mony to carie : and Looking of writtings : 5 days gon    01   02   00

neer a day spent att Mr Woods $w^{th}$ swaname and Tho : Powell to discourse about $y^e$ bounds.    00   02   06

more expense upon Swaneme before hee went out of $y^e$ town, 3 meals, meat 3qts. sider.    00   02   07

for exspense upon $y^e$ $Gen^r$ Steuerd when hee came for Cattell, and time spent to see if I could provide any for him while he was gone east ward.    00   03   06

for $\frac{2}{3}$ of a day att $Cap^{tt}$ ffleets wth Tho : Powell to sett $y^e$ accounts to writtes abouts $y^e$ hides & wheat    00   01   08

8'8 April $17^{th}$ :

$\frac{1}{2}$ a day spent about $y^e$ Pattent, 3 times    00   01   03

going to gustis Platts about it in $y^e$ $\frac{1}{2}$ day    00   04   00

John sent to give Tho : Powell notice to goe to yourke with Justis platt himselfe and horse sent to Thomases farme—    00   06   03

for my trouble in getting in $y^e$ mony, to time spent at many tims about $y^e$ pattent to $y^e$ vallue of two dayes & a $\frac{1}{2}$ $y^t$. was not charged before.

| | s d | | | |
|---|---|---|---|---|
| | | 4 | 13 | 6 |
| Reserved of pattent mony | 10 : 9 | | | |
| more Reseved | 17 : 3 | | | |
| more Reseved of Walter Noakes | 01 : 6 | | | |
| for gathering the mony | | 0 | 10 | 00 |
| for makeing $y^e$ Rat for defraying all charg. | | 5 | 3 | 6 |
| all charge | | | 2 | 6 |

(*File, No.* 52.)

## [DEED. JOHN GOLDING TO RICHARD GILDERSLEEVE Jr.]

### [1687. April 2.]

This Indenture made the second day of Aprill in y^e third
yeer of the Raine of our Sov^r Lord James the second king
of great Brittan france & Ireland et cet^r: and in the yeer
of our Lord According to y^e Computacon of y^e Church of
England one thousand six hundred eaighty seven: Beetweene John Gouldin of fresh pond necke with in the
bounds of huntington in y^e counte of Suffolke and province
of new yourke in Americaie husbanman and grace his wife
of y^e one partie and Richard Gildersleeve Jun^r of Hemsted
upon Long Island with in the queens countie and Province
afore said of the other partie husban man, Witnesseth, that
y^e said John Gouldin & grace his wife ffor divers good
causes and considerations us there unto moving Butt more
especially for and in y^e consideration of y^e sume of sixty
pounds in silver coyne Passable in this Province or Part in
other Pay answerable theire unto in hand secured before
y^e ensealling and delivering heer of have Bargoned sould
alinated and confirmed and by these p^rsents from us our
heairs executors administrators and asignes doe allien bargon sell and confirme unto the aforsaid Richard Gildersleeve his heairs exsecutors, administrators and asignes all
and singular that part of my farme that I now lives in
uussed ocupie and Injoe containg twentie twoo acors of
upland and six acares of medowe as it was Laid out by
order of y^e towne of huntingten bee it more or lese sittuate
lying and beeing one fresh Pond necke Butting and bounding viz. that p.sell that y^e house stands one—the east end
with y^e Land of John Scidmore se^r: the north side by y^e
sound the west end south side with y^e hie way yt leads yt
to Crab medowe the other Parcell of upland lying south
ward from y^e dwelling house bounding east with a high

waye that leadeth to Jonathan Lewice the south with the woods in comanige or hill allsoe six acers of medowe land bee it more or lese lying and beeing in y$^e$ north east corner of Crab medowe Bounded one y$^e$ west side with y$^e$ medowe of John Scudemore sen$^r$ the north with y$^e$ way with in y$^e$ beach y$^e$ south with y$^e$ medow of Jonathan leuice or a creeke we say all our Rights tittle and intrest unto all and singular the afore said Comodations together with all housing out housing barne orchards, gardens, fences fruit trees that is standing or growing upon y$^e$ Premises or any part or Parcel their of which Right in the and to y$^e$ premises was by an order of assizes booth Governer & counsell setled according to y$^t$ order by and with y$^e$ consent of y$^e$ towne of huntington : wee say all our Right in and to the same to gether allsoe with all wayes watterings, watter courses comans, commons of Pastures surbery woods under woods unt the same belonging or in any wise apertaing To have and to hould the said granted and bargoned premises and apurtenances unto the said Richard gildersleefe his heairs excecutors administrators & asignes for ever, yeelding and paing therefore his yeerly and anuall p$^r$portion of what may belong to Goverment of this Province, a nol wee y$^e$ afore said John gouldin and grace his wife with our heairs executors administrators and asignes doe covenant promise and grant too and with y$^e$ said Richard gildersleeve that y$^e$ said John Gouldin and grace his wife is and stans firmly seaised of a good sure & perfit estate in the Law of the said lands and medowe acording to y$^e$ order afore Resighted and doth further covenant Promise and grant y$^t$ all y$^e$ Resighted p$^r$mises is free and cleer from all other former bargans, grants, sales morgages leasses judgments exsecutions convaance or convances, dowries widdowe Rights tittels or intrest what soe ever and the said John gouldin and grace his wife doth further covenant promise & grant with theair heairs and asignes to and with the said Richard gildersleeve his heairs excecutors

administrators and asignes that the saide John Gouldin and
grace his wife their heairs excecutors adminestrators and
asignes shall and will warant and defend y⁰ said granted
p^rmises with y^e apurtenances from any maner of any just
Right tittle claime or demand of any person or persons,
claiming from by or under us or our heairs or from any
other person or persons what soe ever in wittnes wheare
of wee have heer unto sett our hands and seals the day and
yeer above written.

JOHN GOLDEN.
the mark of
GRACE ✕ GOULDEN.

signed sealled and de-
livered in y^e presence of us.
    the marke of
ALLES ✕ BAYLY
JOSEPH BAYLY.

The subscribars John gouldin and grace apeared before
mee this 24th of June 1687 and acknowleged this to bee
their ackt and deed.

EPENETUS PLATT.

A True Coppy of y^e origanall deed compared p. mee
Isaac Platt, Reco^r

June y^e 28^th 1687.
        (*Deeds Vol.* 1, *pp.* 233-4.)

---

## [TOWN MEETING.  JUDGE PALMER PUT OUT.]

### [1687, April 4.]

Att a towne meeting Aprill y^e 4^th 1687 Samuel Kicham
was Legally chossen constable.

The day above dated James Chichester sen^r John Kicham
and Isaac Platt weare chossen comitieners

Att y^e same time M^r Wood, Capt fleet and Thomas Powell was chossen to bee asistant to y^e three comitieners when desired by them.

The day above datted John weeks was Legally chossen coleckter to gather all Ratts made in this town that is to say Countie Ratte and towne Ratte or Ratts and Mr Joenses fiftie pound a year.

The day above datted Aprill y^e 4^th 1687: it was voated and granted by y^e generallitte of y^e towne that Mr Eliphalet Jones shall have fiftie pounds a year dully and yearly Paid him in curant merchandable pay as it passeth from man to man amongst us and that all persons y^t are Rattable in this towne shall pay their due preportion of y^e same for their persons and estates.

The day above written it was seriusly considered and voated y^t Judge Pallmer shall not bee admitted as a pattentee in our pattent.

The day above datted was granted to Phillip Udall and Jonathan Luise twentie acers of land to each of them between bread en chees hollow and crabmedowe hollow if it prove within our line thay have libartie to go to y^e east side of the hollow.

the same day above datted was voated and granted to timothy Scuder seven acars and a haulfe of land for devision Land lying about 20 Rods or polls from y^e reer of his home Lott lying east from his home lotte.

The same day above written was granted to Jonathan Scudder twentie acars of land lying one y^e east side of y^e hoge pond one y^e cowe necke y^t Leads to eattons neck beach.

The same day above sd. was granted to Capttie Baily ten acars of land on y^e north side of stony brooke Path on y^e top of y^e hill.

(*Town Meetings, Vol.* 1, *p.* 155.

## [TOWN MEETING,]

[1687, April 4.]

Aprill the 4[th] 1687 at a towne meetting was granted to timothy Scudder fower acars and a haulfe of devission land The which Land was laid out acording to y[e] towns grant in the place specified Runing east and west fiftie Rod: the east end thirtie fowr Rod in breadth the west end twentie Rod in breadth:

Laid out by Captt Joseph Bayly survaer.

A True Record of what was given in to mee to Record.

p mee Isaac Platt<br/>Recor[r]

*(Deeds, Vol. 1, p. 74.)*

At a towne meeting Aprill y[e] 4[th] 1687 their was granted to Samuell tittus ten acars of division land lying joining to timothy Conklins land y[t] lyes on y[e] north side of Jonathan Scuders.

Aprill y[e] 4[th] 1687: it was voated and consented to by y[e] major Part of y[e] towne that noe hogs or swine of any sort shall goe upon y[e] commons after y[e] 19[th] of may next ensueing y[e] datte heer of and who soever doth sufer any swine to goe att libertie upon y[e] comons after y[e] day above datted after a second warning of them it shall bee lawfull for any person to kill them and who soever kills them shall bring them to y[e] constable and y[e] constable is to bee acountable to ye towne for them for what hee can make of them. butt if it bee a great acorne year people may have libertie to turne them out, to y[e] common after indian corn is all gathered in: till crismus: it to bee understood y[t] y[e] libertie of turning swine on to y[e] common after indian corn is in is only for this present year and not for y[e] future.

S. ARNOLD<br/>J. E. CORAIN<br/>EPENETUS PLATT

*(Town Meetings, Vol. 1, p. 157.)*

## [LANDS OF JOHN SCIDMORE, JR.]

[1687, April 14.]

The bounds and Limits of a Peece of salt medowe sould by John Golden of y^e fresh Pond husbandman unto John Skidmore Junior of the said ffresh Pond Husbanman as followeth, vict : The medowe of Edward Bunce one y^e west. The beach and sound one the north. The medowe of Richard Gilderslieve east. The maine creeke of Crab medowe Southly : Laid out and Posesion given by John goldin both by Turfe and twigg unto John Scidmore above said the 14th of Aprill 1687.

In Wittnes of us
SIMAN LANE
1687
JONATHAN LUICE
(*Deeds, Vol.* 1, *p.* 213.)

A True Coppy of the origanall p mee
Isaac Platt, Reco^r
Aprill y^e 28th 1687.

---

## ⌈CONCERNING PATENT FROM GOV. DONGAN.⌉

[1687.]

queries about our Patent :

1st. that y^e trustees may have Power to call y^e free holders to gether as thay shall see occation.

2nd. that wee may hold our lands in free and common sossage acording to y^e maner of east greenwich in y^e County of kent within his ma^ties Realme of england and that y^e quit rent wee Pay bee in full of all rents or former received rents services acknowledgment & demands whatsoever as is worded in y^e 3^d Pagge of y^e draught of the pattent.

3d. Whither theire bee not grants with in the bounds of y^e Pattent unknown to us besides them to Bryants and Loyde. again

Whether the faillure of any Partickeler forfitt y<sup>e</sup> Pattent
or not.

(File No. 5.)

---

## [LETTER OF ISAAC PLATT TO Mr. GRAHAM CONCERNING THE PROPOSED PATENT.]

[1687, April 18.]

Huntington Aprill 18<sup>th</sup> 1687.

S<sup>r</sup> after Respeckts, presented these are according to order and my promise when last with you : to send you word
of som perticelers which wee desire should bee in our Pattent which are as followeth ist : That we may have Libertie to disposse of our land according to our ushall way &
method formerly pracktist in our towne and y<sup>t</sup> noe partickeler Persons in our towne or else wheare shall have
libertie to Purchase any lands within our bounds or limmits
of y<sup>e</sup> Pattent with out y<sup>e</sup> consent of y<sup>e</sup> majoretie of y<sup>e</sup> towne.

nextly y<sup>t</sup> upon our taking of a generall pattent noe person
or persons in y<sup>e</sup> limits of it shall bee compeld to take any
Pertickel Pattent or Pattents.

nextly : That our towne and thay only shall have libertie
to Purchase haulfe a mille northward of y<sup>e</sup> old Indian Path
y<sup>t</sup> lieth a long a gainst our meddows soe far as our meddowe exstends east and west.

nextly. that y<sup>e</sup> three comissiners with y<sup>e</sup> towns men yeerly
chossen to carie one towne afairs may have libertie to call
a towne meeting as acasion may Require.

nextly
    that y<sup>e</sup> Benifitt of our Pattent shall bee to y<sup>e</sup> Pattenttees
y<sup>t</sup> are to bee mentioned to them their asosiats their heairs,
successors and asigns for our and for y<sup>e</sup> bounds of our

Pattent wee Refur you to y^e old Pattent which I left with you and as for quitt Rent wee have all Redy signified in writting to yo^r worship.

now sir our dependance is upon yo^r worship and hops in you : y^t you will doe for us in y^e p^emises as if y^e cace ware. yo^e owne and if you please to serve us with a Ruf draught of it y^t wee may see it wee shall send up soan to have it. confirmd and wee yo^r servants shall not for gett your kindnes butt hope wee shall make honest satisfaction to yo^r. worship for yo^r pains and care in y^e premises not else att present butt Rest your humble servant in behaulfe of y^e towne.

ISAAC PLATT<br>Towne Clarke.

(*File No. 6.*)

---

## [THOMAS SCIDMORE'S LAND.]

[1687, April 28.]

Thomas scidmore 7 acers of Land Lying by y^e west side of a hollowe that Leadeth to eatons necke with a Rocke in y^e entering of y^e hollowe.

A true coppy of what Capt. Baily gave mee in writting to Record for Thomas Scidmore.

April y^e 28^th 1687.

p mee<br>Isaac Platt, Rec^r

(*Deeds, Vol. 1, p. 132.*)

---

## [LANDS OF PHILIP "UDALL" AND JONATHAN LEWIS.]

[1687, April 29.]

Wee whose names are under written have Land out for

phillip udall* twentie acars of land ten acars in bred and
cheese hollowe, being fortie Rod square and ten acars at
the end of crab medowe hollowe neer a place called y⁰ hog
pond fortie Rod square.

Allsoe twentie acars to Jonathan Luice three acers on
y⁰ west side of his home Lott and seventeen acars in bred
en cheese hollowe on y⁰ south side of phillip Udall only a
way of fowr Rod wide beetween phillip udalls land and
Jonathan Luices land; wee say the towns Rights of y⁰ land
above said: wee have laid out to y⁰ persons afore said this
29ᵗʰ of Aprill 1687.

JOSEPH BAYLY<br>THOMAS POWELL

A true Record of what was given in to mee,

Isaac Platt, Recoʳ

(*Deeds, Vol.* 1, *p.* 125.)

## [DEED. DAVID SCUDDER TO STEPHEN JARVIS.]

[1687, May 23.]

This Indenture made y⁰ 23ᵈ day of may 1687 in y⁰ third
yeer of the Raine of our sovʳ: Lord Jams the second king
of great brittan france & Irland ets cets. and in y⁰ yeer of
our Lord Acording to the Computation off y⁰ Church of
England one thousand six hundred eaightie six seven between david scuder, of nessaquage River with in y⁰ Pattent of Huntington upon Long Island in y⁰ Countie of Suffolke and Province of new yourke in americai husbanman

[*I think Philip "Udall" came to Huntington from Flushing,
as the name appears in the early records of that Town. He
was not here long before the date of the above record.—C.
R. S.]

and mary his wife of the one Partie and Stephen Jarvice Jueneir of y[e] same towne countie and Province afore said husbanman of y[e] other Partie: wittnesseth: that the said david scuder and mary his wife for divers good causses and considerations us theire unto moving butt more especially for and in y[e] consideration of y[e] sum of nine pounds in good Pasable Pay of this province in hand Reseved and Payed by Thomas higbee before y[e] ensealling and delivering of these p[r]sents have bargoned allinated sould and confirmed and by these p[r]sents from us our heairs executors administrators and asignes doe allen bargon sel and confirme unto y[e] afore said stephen Jarvice his heairs executors administrators and asignes all that parcell of medow Land of ours sittuate lying and beeing on y[e] south side of y[e] Island one a necke of medow comonly called or knowne by y[e] name of y[e] haulfe necke by estimation too acars bee it more or lesse: or y[e] haulfe proportion of that peece of medow lying on y[e] east side the afore said haulfe necke y[t] was between my brother Jonathan Scudder and my selfe, butting and bounding as specified the north with y[e] woods in comonadge the west with y[e] medowc of Samuel kicham the east by the Creeke to have and too hould the afore said granted medow land with what Rights or preveliges may in any waies belong unto y[e] same free and firme unto said Stephen Jarvice his heairs executors administrators and asignes or as firme as can bee made by any deed or convance what soe ever exsept it bee y[e] yeerly and anuall proportion of what may belong to the government of this province, and y[e] said david Scudder and mary his wife for our selves our heairs executors, administrators and asignes doe covenant promise and grant too and with the said Stephen Jarvice that the said david scudder and mary his wife now is and stands firmly seised of a sure and perfit estate in y[e] law of y[e] afore said medow land before Resighted and hath good Right and lawfull authoritie to sell and convaye the same and y[e] aid david scuder and

mary his wife doth further Covenant promise and grant
too and with the said Stephen Jarvice his heairs, executors
administrators and asignes y$^t$ the afore said medow land is
free from all other former bargens grants salles morgages
leases Judgments executions convance or convances dowries widdowe Rights tittles or intrest what soever and
y$^e$ said david Scudder and mary his wife doth for our selves
our heairs executors administrators and asignes further
Covenant promise and grant too and with the said stephen
Jarvice his heairs and asignes that the said david scudder
and mary his wife shall and will defend and warant the
said granted p$^r$mises frrm any maner of Just Right tittle
claime or demand of any person or persons Claiming by
from or under us or our heairs or from any person or persons what soever in wittnes wheare of wee have heer unto
sett our hands and seales y$^e$ day and yeer above written.

DAVID

The marke of &times; SCUDDER

of

The marke &times; SCUDDER

MARY

signed sealled. and
delivered in the presence of

JOHN KICHAM

NATHANILL WILLIAMS

The with in mentioned indenture was acknowleged y$^e$
day and yeer above written by the subscribers before mee.

EPENETUS PLATT

Whearas it is specified that the payment of nine pounds
mentioned was Paid by thomas higbee which was in full
for the meddow land purchased of david scudder as more
att Large is specified by the within mentioned :

I the said Thomas higbee doe acknowlege by these
p$^r$sents to have Reseved of Stephen Jarvise Jun$^r$ the within
purchaser the full and wholle sum with in mentioned to
my content as wittnes my hand this 25$^{th}$ day of aprill in

y^e third yeer of his maties Raine and in y^e yeer of our lord
1687.

signed and                                          THO. HIGBEE
delivered in the
presence of
   THO. FFLEETT
   EDWARD HIGBEE

A True Coppy of y^e origanall deed Compared by mee
                              Isaac Platt
                                Reco^r

Septem^r y^e 27^th 1687.
   (*Deeds, Vol. 1, pp. 237-8.*)

---

[DEED. DAVID SCUDDER TO NATHANIEL
WILLIAMS.]

[1687, May 23.]

This Indenture made the twentie third day of may in y^e
third yeer of the Raigne of our Sov^r Lord Jams the second
ƙing of great Brittan france and Irland Defender of y^e faith
et cet^r : and in y^e yeer of our Lord Acording to y^e Computation of y^e Church of england one thousand six hundred
and eaightie seven.  Betwene David Scudder of nesaquage
within the bounds of huntington upon Long Island with in
y^e Countie of sutolke and Province of new yourke in americai husbanman : and mary his wife of y^e one Partie and
nathaniel Williams ot y^e same towne, Countie and Province
of y^e other Partie, Wittnesseth that the said David Scudder & mary his wife for divers good causes and considerations us their unto moving but more espeeshally for & in
consideration of a valliable sum in hand Reseved before the
ensealling and delivering heer of have Bargonned allinated
sould and confirmed and by these presents Doe from us
our heairs exsecutors administrators and asignes Doe allien

Bargon sell and confirme unto y^e aforesaid Nathanell Williams his heairs executors administrators and asignes : all y^t parsell of medowe Land of ours sittuate lying and beeing one y^e south side of this Island one a necke of meddow commonly called or knowne by y^e name of y^e great necke or for a more cleer destinktion y^e haulf neck : Butting and bounding as specified one y^e east side with y^e medowe of Richard williams y^e south end with y^e sound the west side with y^e medow of Jonathan Scudder the north end with the woods in comonage : wee doe acknowledge all and singular that Parcell of medowe bounded as aforesaid wee have estranged from us our heairs exsecutors, administrators and asignes unto nathaniell Williams his heairs, executors and asignes Too have and too hould for ever all and singular the afore granted p^rmises yeelding and paying therefore his yeerly and anuall proportion of what may belong to y^e goverment of this Province and wee y^e said david Scudder and mary his wife for our selves our heairs exsecutors administrators and Asignes : Doe covenant promise and grant too and with y^e said Nathaniell williams afore said that y^e said David Scudder & mary his wife now is and stands firmly seaised of a sure and perfit estate in y^e Law of y^e said medowe land afore Resighted and have good Right and Lawfull Athoritie too sell & convae y^e same and the said david scudder and mary his wife Doth further covenant promise and grant too and with y^e said nathaniell williams his heairs executors administrators and asignes that the aforementioned medowe land : is free from all other former bargans grants saills morgages Leasses judgments executions convance or convances Dowries widow Rights tittels or intrest what soe ever further more, the david scudder and mary his wife doth for our selves our heairs executors administrators and asignes doth covenant Promise and Grant : too and with y^e afore said Nathaniell Williams his heairs executors administrators and asignes that the saide david scudder and mary his wife shall and

will warant and defend the afore granted p^rmises from any
maner of just Right tittle claime or demand of any Person
or persons claiming by from or under us or our heairs or
from any Person or Persons what soe ever : in wittnes
whear of wee have sett too our hands and seals y^e day and
yeer above written.

                                        of
signed sealled and             The marke ✕ DAVID
ddl : in the p^rsence of us            SCUDDER
   JOHN KECHAM                 The marke ✕ MARY
   THOMAS BRUSH                        SCUDDER
The within written Indenture was acknowledged by y^e
Subscribars the day and yeer above mentioned before mee,
                               EPENETUS PLATT.
A True Coppy of y^e origanall deed Compared p mee
                               Isaac Platt Reco^r.
   may y^e 24^th 1687.
   (*Deeds, Vol.* 1, *pp.* 227-8.)

---

[TOWN MEETING.  JUDGE PALMER IN AGAIN.]

[1687, June 6.]

At a town meeting June y^e 6th 1687
It was voated and consented too that Judge Pallmer shall
bee taken in as trustee in our Patent with us only in Referance to y^e soill Right of that Land betwixt operhoweseck
and fresh pond the town Reserving to themselves their
own Right of hearbige and medowe in y^e afore said Land :
not alltering any thing y^t y^e govement hath done in
Refarance to y^e setlment of y^e farmes upon that Land.
allsoe y^t Judge Pallmer shall not himself or any of his
successors from by or under him by virtue heerof lay any
claime or have any intrest in our bounds westward of
y^e bounds before mentioned namely opechowseck which is
a small brooke Runing into y^e mill brooke.

An exchange of Land between Samuell Ketcham and
nathanill willams eight acars of Land which y⁰ sd Samuell
Ketcham had in y⁰ west feild for twelve acars at y⁰ spring
southward :

The same day it was ordered yᵗ y⁰ towns men may have
libertie to make chose of home thay plese to give them
advice in matters partaing to y⁰ pattent.

[This part of a leaf was cut from a volume of Court
Records forming old Book No. 3, and inserted here in the
revision in the year 1873.]

(*Town Meetings, Vol.* 1, *pp.* 152-4.)

---

## [DEED. MARY MILLER TO JAMES CHICHESTER.]

[1687, July 1.]      [Abstract.]

This Indenture made the first day of Jully 1687, betwene
Mary Miller wife of Jonathan Miller and James Chichester
Junr. Witnesseth said Mary Miller having power by her
first husband's will, and in consideration of a considerable
sum of money in hand paid have granted alinated barga",ed
and sould and confirmed unto the said James Chichester
Junʳ his heirs, executors, administrators or assignes two
acars of land lying on y⁰ north side of y⁰ aforesaid James
Chichesters home lot joining to it frunting to y⁰ highway
and y⁰ rear frunting to y⁰ woods bounded on y⁰ north by
y⁰ land of John Teed with all rights & priveledges that
doth at present belong to said land, with full covenant and
warranty of title. In witnes whereof I have hereunto set
my hand and seale.

Witness

his marke

NICKOLAS ✕ SMITH
SARAH SMITH

her marke

MARY ✕ MILLER

Acknowledged Feb. 25, 1689 before
EPENETUS PLATT Justice of the Peace.
(*Deeds, Vol.* 1, *p* 303.)

## [JOSEPH WOOD AND NATHANIEL FOSTER EXCHANGE LAND.]

[1687, July 26.]

This Writting wittneseth that wee Joseph wood and Nathaniell foster sen[r] both of Huntington have made an exchange of Land as followeth; first I y[e] said Joseph Wood doe by these p[r]sents deliver and give posesion unto nathaniell foster sen[r] all my Right and tittle that I have in a tracte of Land Containeing fower acers more or lese together with y[e] grant I had of the towne of Running my fence in to y[e] watter it lying one y[e] east side of stone brooke harbor

Secondly I the saide nathaniell foster sen[r] doe by these p[r]sents deliver and give possesion unto Joseph wood afore sd in exchange and leiu of the land afore said fower acars and a haulfe of land in the east feild joyning to John weekes one the east: by land of the said foster one y[e] west butting one the south to land of Epenetus Platts and on y[e] north by the higheway as wittnes our hands this 26[th] of y[e] 5 mo: called Jully 1687.

THOMAS POWELL                          NATHANIELL FOSTER
his                                              JOSEPH WOOD
JONATHAN X MILLER
mark

A True Coppy of what was given in to mee to Record p mee Isaac Platt Reco[r] Jully y[e] 27[th] 1687.

(*Deeds, Vol.* 1, *p*. 230.)

## [LAND DIVISIONS IN THE EASTMOST NECK.]

[1687, July 27.]

A Record of Captt fleetts meddowe upon y⁰ eastermost necke att south.

The necke of meddowe by estimation fortie acars belonging to Captt Thomas ffleett : Joseph Wood, Samuell wood nathaniel ffoster & Edward Higbee all Containing ten Hundreds, each mans proportion lying and beeing as followeth : first Captt ffleett five Hundred or twentie acars which is y⁰ one haulfe lying one y⁰ east side the necke streching west ward from the creeke fivety twoo Rodd from thence south ward near the east side of a little swampe in y⁰ meddowe with some bushes in it & soe Ranging to y⁰ sound, the south and east bounds the sound & creeke as hie northward as the Indian Path.

This Record is a true coppy as it is given in to mee.

Isaac Platt Reco^r

second.

Joseph Wood six acars fifteen Rodd west ward from Capttin fleets line soe holding that breadth to y⁰ sound.

thirdly

Samuell wood six acers fifteen Rodd westward from Joseph woods line soe holding that breadth to y⁰ sound.

fourth,

Nathaniell foster and Edward higbee eaight acars and is twenty two Rodd from Samuell woods line west ward which Reaches y⁰ Creeke one y⁰ west side : which creekr is their west bounds their south bounds ye sound, theie north bounds butting to y⁰ woods, and so they doe all.

A True Coppy of what was given in to mee to Record p mee

Isaac Platt, Reco^r

Jully y⁰ 27^th 1687.

(*Deeds, Vol.* 1, *p.* 233.)

## [CHILDREN OF JONAS WOOD, JR.]

[1687, Aug. 11.]

Elizebeth wood the dafter of Jonas wood Jun^r born in the month of february the 26 day the year 1668.

phebee wood borne in the 14 of may in the yeer 1671.

martha wood borne in the month of Jenewary the 29 daye in the yeare 167$\frac{5}{4}$

John wood borne the 15 day of aprill 1677

Jeremiah wood borne the 18 day of agust in the yeare 1679.

Jonas wood y^e son of Jonas wood Juner born the 8 day of desember 1681.

Timothy wood borne the 17 day of July in the yeare 1683.

An wood dafter of Jonas wood Borne in the month of Augost y^e 11 day in ye yeare 1687.

(*Surveys, p.* 158.)

---

## [TOWN MEETING.]

[1687, Sept. 20.]

At a towne meeting septem^r y^e 20^th 1687 Mr Wood Tho: Powell & Isaac Platt weare Legally chossen asessors for y^e three haulf pence upon the pound ordered by the Gover^e and Counsell.

The day above s^d was granted to James batte twentie acars of land y^e towns Right in it: adjoining to the south and west of his land not to predudise hie ways or wattering places for cattell.

The day above sd. was granted to Jonathan Wood six acars of land upon y^e east side of y^e path att y^e haulfe mile hill joining to y^e north side of sargent tittus land.

The day above sd was granted to John Scidmor Juner twentie acars of Land y$^e$ towns Right in it in bredd en cheese hollow from y$^e$ path y$^t$ leads to sunken medow to y$^e$ way that cattell goe over y$^e$ swamp above phillip udalls not to prededece hie ways or watering places for cattell.

The day above written was grantted to Jonas wood Junor five acars of land adjoining to his owne in the south hollow.

The day above sd was granted to Jonathan Jarvise and Jonathan miller libertie to dige a wel upon y$^e$ common.

The day above sd was granted to Captt fleet and william broderton each of them twentie acars of land a pees between the fresh pond and Crabmedow thay to clear y$^e$ towne of all demands of Indians or any other as all that have grants of land in y$^e$ towne bounds eastward of y$^e$ mill are to doe though not exprest in y$^c$ severall grants to them.

The day above sd. was granted to Edward bunce fortie acars of land upon y$^e$ south side of y$^e$ hog pond hee to have it as Captt fleet and all other farmers have.

The same day abov sd. was granted to John Kisham four acars of land att the reer of his home Lott.

The day above sd. was granted to nicolas Smith too acare of land joing to his land one y$^e$ west side y$^e$ harbor.

The day above sd was granted to John Teed five acare of Land at y$^e$ hed of y$^e$ hollow that coms from y$^e$ pipe staves in y$^e$ east necke.

The day a bove sd was granted to stephen Jarvise junr. too acars of land east ward of y$^e$ path joing into y$^e$ east neck oposite to James Chichesters Sen$^r$

(*Town Meetings, Vol. 1, p.* 156)

September y$^e$ 20$^{th}$ 1687 at a towne meeting Capt thomas fleet, thomas Powell and Isaac Platt were chossen to carie on all matters Relating to the finishing of their Pattent.

(*Town Meetings, Vol. 1, p.* 150.)

At a town meeting.

September y$^e$ 20$^{th}$ 1687 it was voated and granted that what parcels of medowe are at y$^e$ harbor of either side shall be sold at an out cry to y$^e$ hiest bider to defray Publicke charges y$^t$ is to say soe much of them as shall bee ajudged by men apointed for y$^t$ purpose to be convenient to bee sould.

(*Town Meetings, Vol.* 1, *p.* 157.)

---

## [RECORD OF LANDS OF DAVID SCUDDER AND THOMAS SCIDMORE.]

[1687, Sept. 26.]

Septem$^r$ y$^e$ 26$^{th}$ 1687.

A Record of y$^e$ medowe of david scudder att Crab medow a peece of medowe bounded one the east with y$^e$ meadowe of Jonas Vallentine and the west side by Thomas scidmores medowe, Runing from y$^e$ beach to y$^e$ maine creeke.

A nother peece of medow of david scudders att Crab medowe bounded with Thomas scudders medowe one y$^e$ west side and by Thomas scidmores medowe one y$^e$ east side, Runing from the upland to y$^e$ maine Creeke.

A Record of the medowe of thomas scidmore at Crab-medowe y$^e$ day above sd. Septem: y$^e$ 26$^{th}$ 1687.

A Peece of medow Runing from the beach to the maine Creeke bounded by david scuders medowe of each side east and west: A nother peece of medow of Thomas Scidmores upon y$^e$ south side of Crab medowe bounded by y$^e$ medowe of Jams batte one y$^e$ east side & by y$^e$ medow of david scudder one the west.

A True Record of what was given in to mee by y$^e$ above

sd. david scudder and Thomas scidmore the day and yeer
a bove written.

Isaac Platt

Reco<sup>r</sup>

(*Deeds, Vol.* 1, *p.* 235.)

---

## [A BILL OF ITEMS OF CHARGES.]

[1687, Oct. 5.]

Huntingtons due from y<sup>e</sup> Countie Octobar : y<sup>e</sup> 5<sup>th</sup> 1687

An acount of what charge hath been expended about y<sup>e</sup>
souldiers y<sup>t</sup> came with Cappt : seardam : att : 6<sup>d</sup> : p. meall &
2<sup>d</sup> p. nights Lodgin : 6<sup>d</sup> p. horse for one night : att their Return these y<sup>t</sup> brought backe the horses : for : 2 : nights and
a day 1<sup>d</sup> for each horse Pastering and for a horse going
neer to Hemsted with them prest for y<sup>e</sup> servise 2<sup>d</sup> :

| | lb. | s. | d. |
|---|---|---|---|
| due to Captt Platt upon y<sup>e</sup> acount above mentioned | 03 | 00 | 02 |
| due to Leutt Jónas Wood | 00 | 09 | 04 |
| due to Insighne Jonathan Scudder | 00 | 09 | 04 |
| due to SargentTho : weeks | 00 | 03 | 04 |
| due to John weeks | 00 | 07 | 02 |
| due to Mr Jonas wood | 00 | 04 | 10 |
| due to Isaac Platt | 00 | 03 | 04 |
| due to Thos. Whitson | 00 | 03 | 04 |
| due to John Brush | 00 | 07 | 04 |
| due to Joseph Wood | 00 | 03 | 04 |
| due to nicolas smith | 00 | 01 | 08 |
| due to Joseph Whittman | 00 | 08 | 04 |
| due to Thos. brush | 00 | 05 | 04 |
| due to Richard brush | 00 | 02 | 10 |
| due to Samuell Wood | 00 | 03 | 04 |
| due to Robart kellam | 00 | 02 | 10 |
| due to Saml. Kicham | 00 | 02 | 02 |

| | | | |
|---|---|---|---|
| the Constable demands for his truble | oo | 05 | oo |
| due to Jams Smith | oo | 04 | 04 |
| due to Tho: Powell | oo | 01 | 08 |
| due to Abiell titus | oo | 06 | 04 |
| due to Sargent titus | oo | 03 | 04 |
| due to Captt. Joseph Bayly | oo | 03 | 04 |
| due to John Samis | 01 | 01 | oo |
| " " Tho: Scudder | oo | 02 | 08 |

John Samis his horse Prest to Southhould for
Abraham Whitthaire . . . . . oo 15 oo
John Samis and John Wickes Grand Juriemen
att ye last court of sessions . . . 02 14 oo
Octobr: ye 20th 1687 John Scidmore Junr killed
an old woolfe . . . . . . 01 10 oo
for a hue and cry sent to oysterbay by ye Constable, Saml Kicham . . . . oo 02 06
An old woolfe was kild ye Last yeer by Stephen Jarvise &
Robart Cranfield which was given in to ye Clarke by John
Wickes then Constable: but ye Clarke falling sick it was
omited and not sent to ye Comittie ye last yeer there fore
ought to bee paid for this yeer.*

(*File No. 18.*)

---

### [LAND SURVEYED TO EDWARD BUNCE.]

[1687, Oct. 12.]

A Record of Land Laid out for Edward Bunce by the
Survaors of the towne as followeth.

Laid out for Edward Bunce Acording to the towne
grant the towne Right in fortie acars of land ling on the

---

[*These charges probably arose out of a general training of
militia. The "hue and cry sent to Oyster Bay" was probably
for the capture of a runaway slave or servant, as the law then
specially authorized it in such cases.—C. R. S.

South side of the hoge pond Containing eaightie eaight east and west and seventie too Rod north and southardly october yᵉ 12: 87.

JOSEPH BAYLY
THOMAS POWELL

A true Coppy of what was given in to mee to Record p mee Isaac Platt

Recorᵈ

(*Deeds*, Vol. 1, *p.* 206)

---

## [ORDER OF COURT OF SESSIONS CONCERN- ING ASSESSMENTS.]

[1687, Oct. 20.]

to yᵉ Comissioners of the town of Huntington.

At a Cowrte of sessions held at southold october the 20ᵗʰ 1687 : ordᵉed that you send and Impower an Assessor out of your town to meet with the Rest of the Assessors of the County at yᵉ town of Southold upon the second wensday of November next: and to bring with him an auᵗ of what charg of the County doth arise in your town then and thare with the Rest of the assessors to Assess the County for the Requisett Charges that shall come before them for the year past and bring with him a Lest of the estates of your town

p Curiam John Howell Clerk.

(*File, No.* 9.)

---

## [LETTER. MR JAS. GRAHAM TO TOWN CLERK OF HUNTINGTON.]

[1687, Nov. 7.]

N. Yorke Nov. 7 1687

Mr Platt

This Bearer the Gvoʳ Steward goes on purpos

upon the Island to provide Cattle for his excell eys servic,
yeu may doe well to accomedate him at a reasonable price,
and it will be allowed yeu per his excell<sup>ey</sup> upon the acct.
of yer Patent

Yer Frind & truly

JA. GRAHAM

*(File, No. 3 )*

---

## [DEED. JOSEPH BAILEY TO JOHN GREEN.]

[1687, December 18.]

To all expian people to whome these p<sup>r</sup>sents shall come
knowe yee : that I Joseph Bayly of the towne of Huntington
upon Long Island in y<sup>e</sup> Countie of Suffolke and province of
new yourke in Americai husbanman and allso his wife have
demised granted allinated and made over unto John Green
Ju<sup>r</sup> of the towne Countie and province afore said all that
house lott that y<sup>e</sup> said Joseph bayly Bought of nicolas
ellice that was estranged by John finch sen<sup>r</sup> to y<sup>e</sup> sd. ellice
by a deed of giuft I say by these p<sup>r</sup>sents wee doe give grant
and make over from us our heairs executors Adminstrators
and assignes unto y<sup>e</sup> said John Green his heairs exceutors
administrators and asignes too have and to hould for ever
that Lott sittuatte lying and beeing in huntington the
Land of John Green sen<sup>r</sup> one y<sup>e</sup> north side the frunt the
hie way that Leadeth to the harbor the south side the land
of Edward Higbe with one hundred pound Right of
Comanige there too : in Consideration of which y<sup>e</sup> said
John green Jun<sup>r</sup> is to serve Joseph Bayly and alse his wife
eaight yeers and a haulf from the day of the datte heer of
and att y<sup>e</sup> end and exspiration of his time Acording to the
tenor of his indenture : to enter posses and injoe the said
Lott and a hundred pound Right of comanage with out
Lett hinderance or mollestation of Joseph Bayly or allce

his wife or any other person or persons claiming Right
tittle or intrest by from or under them in wittnes wheare
of wee have heer unto sett our hands and seals the eaighteen day of Desembar in yᵉ third yeer of his maties Raine
and in the yeer of our Lord one thousand six hundred
eaigtie seven.

JOSEPH BAYLY
of
signed sealed and delivered          the Mark × ALLCE
in the presence of                            BAYLY
   THOMAS HIGBEE
   STEVEN JARVICE Junʳ
Januare yᵉ 10ᵗʰ 168⅘ then apeered before mee the subscribars and acknowledged the above said Instrument to
bee their ackt and deed.

EPENETUS PLATT
Justice Peace.

Memorandam. I promise my aprentice time and land to
plant a nurssarie for providing for an orchard for him
yᵉ sd. aprentice and time to plant them within his time as
wittnes my hand the day above mentioned.

JOSEPH BAYLY
   Januare yᵉ 23ᵈ 1687 A True Coppy of yᵉ originall deed
of gift

p mee Isaac Platt
Recoʳ
(*Deeds, Vol.* 1, *p.* 239.)

---

## [AGREEMENT BETWEEN JOHN ADAMS AND JONATHAN ROGERS.]

[1687, Dec. 22.]

decembʳ yᵉ 22ᵈ 1687
These Presents witness an agreement beetween Jonathan

Rodgers and John Adams in Relation to y$^e$ saw mill : That is to say if y$^e$ towne and Jonathan Rodgers agree about new terms conserning y$^e$ saw mill, then I John Adams doe in gage to Resigne up my Right in y$^e$ say mill upon the terms following y$^e$ sd. Jon$^n$ Rodgers to pay ten pound in pay as it passeth from man to man and y$^e$ choise of 2 maires y$^t$ y$^e$ sd. Jonathan Rodgers hase Runing at y$^e$ south.
Wittnes ISAAC PLATT
    JONAS PLATT

                JONATHAN ROGERS
                JOHN ADAMS.*
(*File No. 14.*)

---

[DEED. JOSEPH BAILEY TO JONATHAN LEWIS.]

[1688, Jan. 23.]

This indenture made the twentie third day of Januare in the yeer of y$^e$ Raine of our Sovr. &c and in the yeer of our Lord &c one thousand six hundred eaightie eaight nine betweene Joseph Bayly of ye towne of Huntington within ye Countie of Suffolk and province of new yourke in america husbanman and alce his wife of the one partie and Jonathan Luice of the same towne Countie and province of y$^e$ other partie wittnesseth, That y$^e$ sd. Joseph baily & alce his wife for &c and in y$^e$ consideration of the sum of fortie six pounds in curant passable paie in hand secured beefore the ensealling and delivering heer of : Have Bargoned alinated sould and confirmed &c unto the afore sd. Jonathan Lewice all that my twentie acars of upland sittuate lying and beeing on a necke of land commonly called and knowne by

---

[*As John Adams had been granted the right to build a sawmill on the stream at Cold Spring, this record probably refers to it.—C. R. S.]

the name of fresh pond necke with in y^e bounds of huntington part of the twentie acars to take up beeing not laid
out nor the place nomenated, the Land Laid out and improved bounded east with y^e comon that joins to y^e fresh
pond one the north and west with the Land of thomas
scidmore one the south with a high way that parts phillip
udalls lands and it : it beeing the upland of a haulfe farme
and by denomination A hundred & fiftie Right acording to
the custome of grants of land by the towne of huntington :
and the towne of huntington was ordered to settle ten
farmes betweene Cow harbour and nessaquage River by
order of the governer and counsell at a Court of asize in
y^e goverment of governer Lovelace, this afore sd. land being part of one of these farmes together with one hundred
and fiftie pound Right of comonidge with all Rights previlidges and apurtenances y^t the towne of huntington could
confirme unto y^e sd. apurtenances to have and to hold the
sd. granted and barganed premises and apurtenances unto
the sd. Jonathan Lewice his heirs &c forever only the sd.
Jonathan Lewise is to cleare the Rite of comanidge if any
truble doth arise there in, wee say all our Right title and
intrest in and too the afore granted premises with all it
apurtenanses as housing fenses lands devided or undevided
that doe or shall in any wise belong or appertaine to
y^e same to have hould occupie and injoe forever yeelding
& paying therefore his anuall and yeerly proportion of
what may belong to the goverment of this province and
the sd. Joseph Baily and alce his wife doth for our heairs
&c further covenant promise and grant too and with the
sd. Jonathan Lewise his exsecutors &c that y^e sd. haulfe
farme of upland with all its Rights of comanige is free from
all other former bargans grants &c what soever furthermore the sd. Joseph Bayly and alce his wife for our selves
our heairs exsecutors administrators and asignes promise
and grant too and with the sd. Jonathan Lewice his heairs
&c that at any time or times heareafter upon Request made

the sd. Joseph Baiely and alce his wife shall and will bee Reddy to give all other and further securities which he or his learned counsell in y$^e$ law shall think fitt and furthermore the sd. Joseph baily and allce his wife doth for our selves our heairs &c doe promise and grant too and with the sd. Jonathan Lewis his heairs &c to defend the sd granted prmises with their apurtenances exsept before exsepted from any maner of just Right, title, claime, or demand of any parson or persons claiming by from or under us or our heairs or from any person or persons what soever in wittnes where of wee have to this p$^r$sent Indenture sett to our hands and sealles the day and yeer above written.

signed and
delivered in the
presents of us

JOSEPH BAILY
the mark of
ALLCE × BAILY

NATHANIELL FFOSTER
ZOPHAR BEECH
(*Deeds, Vol.* 1, *p.* 260-1.)

[DEED. EDWARD HIGBEE TO JOSEPH BAILEY.]

[1688, Feb. 4.]

This Indenture made y$^e$ fourth day of febrawary in y$^e$ third yeer of the Raine &c and in ye yeer of our Lord &c one thousand six hundred eighty eight nine. Betweene Edward Higbee of Horse necke alles queens Village upon Long Island within y$^e$ queens countie and province of new yorke in america and Abigall his wife of y$^e$ one partie and Joseph Bailly of y$^e$ towne of huntington upon Long Iland in y$^e$ countie of suffolk and province afore sd. husbanman of y$^e$ other partie : Wittnesseth, that y$^e$ sd. Edward Higbee husbanman with Abigall his wife have for divers good causes and considerations &c for & in y$^e$ consideration of ye sum of thirtie pounds in good marchandable pay of this

province as it passeth amongst men, viz : winter wheat at
five shillings p bushell and Indian corne at too shillings
six pence p bushell beefe at two pence p pound Round,
porke at three pence p pound or other pay answerable
there unto. Have bargoned allened sould and confirmed
and by these prsents doe allen sell & confirme from us our
heairs exsecutors administrators & asignes : unto y$^e$ afore
sd Joseph Baily his heairs &c, all my home Lotte and orchard with proffitt of enlargment as may be added their
unto att y$^e$ Reare of y$^e$ sd. lotte acording too any order or
pracktice made observed or made use of in y$^e$ towne of
huntington which lotte & orchard, sittuate lying and beeing in huntington afore said, Butting and bounding as
specified and described the east side with y$^e$ home lotte of
thomas Whiston y$^e$ frunt or south end next to hieway that
Leadeth to y$^e$ harbour y$^e$ west and northwest side part
with y$^e$ afore sd. hieway and y$^e$ other part with y$^e$ lott of
the sd Joseph Baily made over to John green Jun$^r$ y$^e$ north
or north east ends y$^e$ woods in comanige together with
what wayes watterings, fences, hedges, woods underwoods,
fruit trees, timbar with what profits and Revenews is upon
the afore said orchard and lotte with what in largment as
can bee added at y$^e$ Reare or nore or nore east end thear
of not prejudicing y$^e$ hie way : this afore said lott with all
its Rights and previlidges was formerly in y$^e$ tenure or ocupation of John finch senior, and y$^e$ sd finch allinated to y$^e$
sd Edward Higbe and y$^e$ comanage there of the sd edward
higbee Reserveth to his owne proper use : only the lott &
orchard with what profits and conveniences as afore mentioned wee y$^e$ said edward higbee and abigall his wife
have allinated and estranged from us our heairs executors
administrators and asignes unto the afore sd. Joseph baily
his heairs executors &c To have and to hould use, ocupie
and injoe for ever firmly and freely or as firmly as can bee
made by any deed or convance whatsoever : yeeilding and
paying their fore his anuall proportion of what may bee

long to y^e goverment of this province and wee y^e said edward higbee and abigall his wife doth for our selves our heairs executors administrators and asignes doth covenant promise & grant to and with the sd. Joseph Baily his heairs &c That y^e sd Edward Higbee with abigall his wife now is and stand firmly seized of a good sure & perfitte estate in the law grantted and hath good Right & lawfull athoritie to sell and convae the same furthermore the sd. Edward higbee and abigall his wife doth for our selves our heairs &c doth covenant and promise too and with y^e sd. Joseph baily his heirs &c that y^e sd. orchard and lotte is free of and from all other former Bargens grants, saills, morgadges &c or intrest what soe ever ; furthermore y^e sd edward higbee and abigall his wife doth for our selves our heairs &c covenant promise & grant too and with y^e sd. Joseph his heairs &c that at any time hear after upon Request made the sd Edward higbee and abigall his wife shall and will bee Reddy to give all other and further securitie as hee or his learned counsell in y^e Law shall thinke fitt : and the sd. edward higbee and abigall his wife doth for our selves our heairs executors administrators and asignes doe covenant promise and grant to and with y^e sd Joseph Baily his heairs executors &c that hee y^e sd edward higbee his heairs &c shall and will warant and defend the sd. grantted and barganed orchard and lott with its inlargements from any maner of just Right, tittle or claime or demand of any person or persons claiming by from or under us or our heairs or from any other person or persons what soever in wittnes wheare of wee have to this present Indenture set too our hands and seales

signed sealled and                    EDWARD HIGBEE
delivered in the pre-
sence of

ZOPHAR BEETH
EPENETUS PLATT

(*Deeds, Vol.* 1, *pp.* 278-9.)

# [DEED. RICHARD SMITH TO ROBERT ARTHUR.]

[1688, March 17.]

This writting witnesseth an Agreement beetwen Richard Smith, seneir and Robart Arthur both of Smith towne in Suffolk Countie; first Richard shall deliver into y$^e$ posession of Robart one hundred acers of Land one y$^e$ east side of the fresh pond unshemamuke, fower score polle Long by the pond side and sixty pole by the cleft taking in all medowes marshes and swamps within that compase to the maine Runn of watter y$^t$ Runs out of y$^e$ pond and in to y$^e$ pond and to take up y$^e$ Resedue of wood Land with in 3 quarters of a mile of the same in a pcece whear Robart shall chuse it not intrenching on my daughters farme allsoe Richard is to build a house att his charge of 20 feet Long 18 foot broad, 11 foot stood to be framed groun seled, Clabborded and shingled & 2 door casces this where Robart shall direct on y$^e$ sd. Land as allsoe Robart shall have libertie of comonidge for all sorts of creturs and timber for his owne uses and under brush: privelidge of fishing fowling and hunting to have and to hould to y$^e$ sd. Robart his heairs executors administrators and asignes for ever and wattering places on the west side nesequake River all which Richard Smith doth bind him selfe his heairs executors administrators and asignes for y$^e$ sd. Robart arthurs quiet and peaceble enjoement clear from any morgage salle or forfiture whatsoever or any molestation what soe ever from mee and my heairs and all clames whatsoever in case any thing nessesary to make this Legall bee wanting it shall bee suplyed by a Learned counsel att law by another deed. I Richard Smith with consent of my wife doe asigne y$^e$ full contents of this bill to Robart arthor to have & to hould for ever. The house to be finished within a yeare.   March y^e 17^th 168⅞

Witnes                                    RICHARD SMITH
JONATHAN SMITH                     SARAH SMITH
JOHN MURWIN                          her ✕ mark
JOSEPH ACERLY

Whereas Robart arthur was indebted to Richard Smith
20^lb due in novembar I doe aquitt and discharge from all
debts dues and demands due before this day
    March y^e 17^th 168⅞              RICHARD SMITH
        *(Deeds, Vol. 1, p. 245.)*

---

## [RICHARD SMITH TO ROBERT ARTHUR.]

[1688, March 24.]

Memorandum the 24^th of March 168⅞ Richard Smith did
deliver season & posesion of thirtry acars of land 60 polls
by the clift and 80 polle by the pond side unto Robart
arthor in presence of John Jones and Thomas hulse and is
in part of one hundred acars in y^e bill one the other side
and soe runing to y^e runn y^t runs into the pond and out of
the pond which is the maine Run the bound marke south
ward is a chesnutt tree and a pible stone by it, and y^e east
bounds is a hamake of bay bushes and a rocke.
THOMAS HULSE
JOHN JOENS
    *(Deeds, Vol. 1, p. 245, B.)*

---

## [DEED.  JAMES BETTS TO JOHN INGERSOL.]

[1688, March 26.]

This indenture made the twentie sixth Day of march in
the third yeer of the Raine of our souv^r Lord James y^e

second King of great brittan ffrance & Ireland defender of
the faith et cet$^r$ and in y$^e$ yeare of our Lord acording too
the Church of england one thousand six hundred eaightie
eaight Between James Bets of Crab medow with in the
bounds of Huntington upon Long Iland with in y$^e$ Countie
of Suffolk and province of new yourke in America husbandman of the one partie and John Ingersolle of the same
towne Countie & province husbandman of the other partie
wittnesseth that the sd. James Batte have and doe for divers
good causes and considerations me there unto moving butt
more especially for and in consideration of y$^e$ sum of eaight
pounds in hand Reseved before the ensealling and delivering
hear of Have allinated barganed sould and made over from
mee my heairs executors Administrators and asignes I say
I doe by these p$^r$sents Allen Bargan sell & make over from
mee my heairs executors administrators and asignes all
my Right title & intrest in & too a parcell or poynt of Land
sittuate lying and beeing on a necke of Land comonly called
or knowne by y$^e$ name of Crabmeadow necke on y$^e$ nor
west poynt there of which point of land is called & known
by y$^e$ name of martens vinyard containg in quantetie seven
acars & a haulfe bee it more or les butting and bounding
nore and nore west with y$^e$ sea east & south with the Land
of John Inkersolle I say all my Right tittle & intrest in &
too y$^e$ same I have allinatted convaied wholy and clearly
made over from mee my heairs executors administrators
and asignes unto the aforesaid John Ingersolle his heairs
executors administrators and asignes Too have and to
hould for ever only y$^e$ said John Ingersoll to pay y$^e$ yeerly
annuall parportion of what belongs to y$^e$ goverment of this
province : furthermore I y$^e$ sd. James bets doth further
covenant promise and grant too and with y$^e$ aforesaid John
Inkersolle his heairs executors administrators and asignes
y$^t$ the afore mentioned Land & every part & parsell is and
shall bee continoed cleare of and from all and all maner of
former grants bargens salles morgages executions convance

or convances widoe Right or any incombrence what soe
ever and I y<sup>e</sup> said James bate my heairs executors administrators and asignes doe further covenant promise & grant
too and with the afore sd. John Ingersolle his heairs executions administrators and asignes y<sup>t</sup> the sd. James Batte his
heairs and successors shall and will from time too time and
for ever heare after save harmles and endemnified the afore
sd. John Ingersolle his heairs and succesers of and from any
person or person whoe 'may or shall Lay any Just claime
Right title or interest unto y<sup>e</sup> afore mentioned Land or any
part or parsell there of in witnes wheare of I have hear
unto set my hand and sealle y<sup>e</sup> day and year above written.

JAMS BETS

signed sealled and delivered
in the Presence of
SAMUELL KETCHAM
SYMAN LANE.
1688
Aprill y<sup>e</sup> thirtie apeared before mee Jams Batte and acknowledged the above sd. indenture to bee his ackt & deed.

EPENETUS PLATT
Justice peace.

A True Coppy of y<sup>e</sup> origanall deed compared by mee

Isaac Platt

Jully y<sup>e</sup> 19<sup>th</sup> 1688                                   Reco<sup>r</sup>
*(Deeds, Vol. 1, pp. 243-4.)*

---

## [TOWN MEETING.]

[1688, April 2.]

At a towne meeting Legally warned Aprill y<sup>e</sup> 2<sup>d</sup> 1688.
the day above s<sup>d</sup> Abiel tittus was chossen Constable.

the day above written Joseph whittman John Samis and
Isaac Platt weare Legally chossen commissinors.

the day above written Joseph whittman was chossen to bee a sealler of Leather that is Putt to saile.

the day above written John wood was chossen a gager of casks.

the day above written Robert Kellam did propound to the towne for twentie acars of Land joing to his land upon y$^e$ cove necke on y$^e$ west necke frunting east ward ty y$^e$ harbor it was granted y$^t$ noe other person should have it from him.

the day above written was granted to Captt fleett Mr wood and Samuel wood to take up their division of Land seven acars and a haulf to a hundred wheare thay shall see cause to doe it : not to hinder hie wayes & wattering Placees for Cattell : allsoe y$^e$ same grant is to all y$^t$ have not taken up acording to y$^e$ division mentioned.

The day above s$^d$ was granted to Richard Gildersleeve twentie too acars of land six or eight acars of it at the head of Claboard hollowe and y$^e$ Remainder of it beetwixt. william broderton and his owne Land facen against Crab medowe.

The day above written was granted to thomas Scidmore twentie acars of Land in bred en cheese hollow joining to the north side of Phillip udalls Land and twentie acars more of land was granted the same day to thomas scidmore one the north side of the hoge pond upon Crabmedowe necke.

(*Town Meetings, Vol. 1, p. 159.*)

---

# [DEED. EDWARD HIGBEE TO JOSEPH WOOD AND STEPHEN JARVIS.]

[1688, April 4.]    [Abstract.]

This Indenture made the 4 of Aprille 1688 Betwene

Edward Higbe and Joseph Wood & Stephen Jarves Jun'
Witnesseth that yᵉ sd. Edward Higby and abigall his wife
for yᵉ sume of ten pounds curant mony Hath given granted
barganed sold Released & Confirmed unto yᵉ sd. Joseph
wood & Stephen Jarves their heyres & assignes forever, all
his allotment share or pice of upland situate upon yᵉ east
necke, bounded by yᵉ high way & yᵉ land late in yᵉ tenure
of James Chitester senʳ towards yᵉ north east southest by
yᵉ land late in the occupation of thomas scuder yᵉ march
or medow and harbour south west & north west by
yᵉ Land late in yᵉ tenure of Stephen Jarves senʳ & containing about twelve acers more or less, with all priveledges
to have and to hold for ever. With full covenant &
warranty of title. Signed & sealed

Witness                                    EDWARD HIGBE
  THOMAS POWELL
  THOMAS HIGBEE
             Acknowledged April 4, 1688.
                ANDREW GIBB, Justice.

(*Deeds, Vol.* 1, *pp.* 348-9.)

[DEED. EDWARD HIGBEE TO THOMAS
HIGBEE.]

[1688, April 17.]

This Indenture made yᵉ seventeenth day of aprill in yᵉ
fourth yeer of the Raigne of our soverein Lord Jams the
second by the grace of god king of england scotland
ffrance & Ireland king defendʳ of yᵉ faith &c. and in the
yeare of our Lord God one thousand six hundred eaighty
and eaight Between Edward Higbee of queens village in
queens countie upon Long Island in yᵉ province of new
yourke in America yeoman of yᵉ one part and Thomas
Higbe of Huntington in yᵉ Countie of Suffolk upon Long

Island afore saide yeoman of y$^e$ other part wittnesseth that
y$^e$ saide Edward Higbee and with y$^e$ approbation & consent of abigall his wife testified her beeing a party by her
sealling and delivering of these p$^r$sents for and in consideration of y$^e$ sume of twenty pounds currant mony of new
yourke to them in hand paid by y$^e$ sd. Thomas Higbee the
receipt where of thay doe here by acknowledg. themselves and each of them to bee theire with fully satisfyed
contented & paid and there of & of every part & parsell
there of dothe by these p$^r$sents aquit & discharge the sd.
Thomas higbee his heairs executors and administrators:
for ever Hath given granted barganed and sold allined,
Released & confirmed & doe by these p$^r$sents freely cleerly
and absolutely give grant bargaine and sell allien Release
& confirme unto y$^a$ sd. Thomas higbee his heairs & asignes
for ever all their share piece parsell or allotment of medowe lying and beeing upon santepaug necke at y$^e$ south
side of Long Island within y$^e$ town ship of huntington
afore sd. being bounded by the upland & woods north
ward y$^e$ medowes in y$^e$ tenure of Capt. Epenetus Platt
east ward southward the bay or sound & by the medowe
in y$^e$ occupation of Jonathan Rodgers west ward containing eight acres more or lesse together with all the preveleges & apurtenances their unto belonging or in any wise
apertaining and all y$^e$ estate, right, title, claime, property
& hereditaments of them y$^e$ sd. Edward higbee & abigall
his wife in & to the sd. medowe & all other y$^e$ above
granted p$^r$mises To have and to hold the sd. trackt peice
share and allotment of medowe and all other above barganed p$^r$misses to him the sd. thomas higbee his heairs &
asignes for ever to y$^e$ only proper use benefitt & behoofe
of him the sd. thomas higbee his heairs & asignes for ever
and y$^e$ sd. Edward higbee doth hereby, covenant and
grant to & with y$^e$ sd. thomas Higbee y$^t$ hee the sd. thomas
higbee his heairs & asignes shall and may now and att all
times heer after for ever quietly & peacably have hold oc-

cupy poses and injoe y^e sd. piece or allotment of meddowe ground and all other afore mentioned p^rmises as his & theire free estate of inheretence in fee simple free & cleare & freely & clearly aquitted exonerated and discharged of & from all former & other guifts grants bargains sales morgages dowers entailes judgments executions Rents, taxes imposions or other titles or incumberances whatsoever had made comitted or suffered to bee dune by the sd. Edward higbee at any time or times before y^e ensealling of these prsents & that y^e sd. Edward higbee stands now at y^e time of ensealling heer of fully & freely seized and possessed of y^e sd. medowe & appurtenances as of his owne right of demesne in fee simple and y^e sd. Edward higbee and abigall his wife for them selves theire heairs executors administrators, or asignes doth hereby further covenant & promise to and with the sd. thomas higbee his heairs & asignes the sd. peice or allotment of medowe ground and apurtenances to the said Thomas higbee his heairs & asignes to warrant & defend against all persons claiming the same or part or parcell there of by from or under the sd. Edward higby his heires executors administrators or asignes or either of them or any other persone by & with the consent approbation or procurment of them or either of them as allsoe upon y^e Reasnable Reqest & proper cost & charges of y^e sd Thomas higbee his heairs or asignes to seale & deliver any other or former deed or convaance for the confirming & sure making of y^e sd. peice of medow & prmisses as y^e sd. thomas higbee his heairs & asignes shall bee advised & procure to bee drawne by his or their counsel learned in y^e Law In Witness wheare of y^e sd parties have here unto sett their hands & seales att huntington y^e day & yeer first a bove written.

signed & delivered          EDWARD HIGBEE
in presence of.          the mark of

JONAS WOOD          ABIGALL HIGBEE
JOHN GRAY.
    (*Deeds, Vol.* 1, *pp.* 252-3.)

[DEED.  ANDREW GIBB TO EDWARD HIGBEE.]

[1688, Aprill 17.]

To all Cristian People to whome these p'sents shall come
Andrew Gibb of brooke haven in y<sup>e</sup> countie of Suffolk
upon Long Island sendeth Greetting Wheareas the sd
andrew gibb by vertue of a judgment of Court obtained
at a court of oyer and terming held at south hampton on
the second wednesday ot novenber which was the second
yeer of our Lord the King that now is and in the yeer of
our Lord one thousand six hundred eaghtie and six was by
the sherif of y<sup>e</sup> sd Countie putt in to quiet and peacable
possesion of a sartaine orchard home Lott & other Lands &
meddowes their unto belonging with in the township of
huntington in y<sup>e</sup> Countie afore sd. latte in the tennor &
occupation of Edward Higbe. Now knowe yee that I,
the sd. Andrew gibb for & in consideration of thirtie
Pounds currant money of this Province to mee in hand
Paid by Edward higbe of queens village in queenes countie
upon Long Island yoeman the reseipt whereof I doe here
by acknowledge and my selfe there with to be satisfied and
contented have granted released quitt claimed & confirmed
& doe by these p'sents grant release quitt claime & confirme
unto y<sup>e</sup> sd. Edward higbee his heaires & asignes for ever
all my right tittle intrest & posesion in and to y<sup>e</sup> sd. orchard
and home lott & other lands & meadowes their unto be-
longing or in any wise appertaining To have & to hold to
him y<sup>e</sup> sd. Edward higbee his heairs & assignes for ever to
the only proper use benifitt & behoofe of him y<sup>e</sup> sd. Edward
higbee his heairs & asignes for ever In wittness whereof I
the sd. andrew Gibb have here unto sett my hand & fixed
my seale att Huntington y<sup>e</sup> seventeeth day of Aprill in
y<sup>e</sup> fourth yeare of y<sup>e</sup> Raigne of our soveraine Lord James
y<sup>e</sup> second King of England &c ano: dom : 1688.

ANDREW GIBB

sealled & delivered       1688.

in p$^r$sents of

 John Gray

 Thomas Higbee

 A True coppy of the origanall Releacm$^{tt}$ Aprill y$^e$ 19$^{th}$ 1688.

          p mee Isaac Platt, Rec$^r$

  *(Deeds, Vol 1, p. 240 )*

---

## [TITUS, LEWIS AND KETCHAM FAMILY RECORDS.]

 [1688, May 1.]

 Mary tittus y$^e$ eldest daughter of Abiell tittus was borne y$^e$ 12 of march in y$^e$ yeer 16$\frac{73}{74}$

Rebecka tittus y$^e$ 2$^d$ daughter of abiell titus was borne y$^e$ 21$^{st}$ day of ocktobar in y$^e$ yeer 1676

Abiell tittus y$^e$ eldest sonn of abiel tittus was borne the 15$^{th}$ of march in y$^e$ yeer 167$\frac{8}{79}$

Henry tittus sonn of abiell tittus was borne the 6$^{th}$ of march in y$^e$ yeer of our Lord 16$\frac{81}{82}$

John tittus sonn of Abiell tittus was borne the 9$^{th}$ Aprill in y$^e$ yeer 1684.

Hester kicham daughter of Samuell kecham was borne the 4$^{th}$ of Jully in y$^e$ yeer 1687.

sibbill Luice daughter of Jonathan luice was borne in the yeer of our Lord upon y$^e$ 20$^{th}$ day of october 1685.

Jonathan Luice sonn of Jonathan Luice was borne y$^e$ first day of may in y$^e$ yeer of our lord 1688.

  *(Survey, p. 154.)*

## [LEVY OF TAXES BY GOVERNOR DONGAN
## AND COUNCIL.]

[1688, probable date.]

A Bill for y⁰ Raising one haulf peny per pound of all persons estates : Reall and personall throughout y⁰ Province.

Bee it Inackted and it is heer by Inackted, established and ordained by his Exelency y⁰ gover. by and with the advise and consent of his majies Counsell for this province of new yorke y' for y⁰ suport of the goverment of his maji⁰ˢ sd. province at or before y⁰ first day of may next ensuing a forsaid Ratte or tax of one haulfe peny in y⁰ pound upon y⁰ estats Reall & personal of all and singular y⁰ free houlders & inhabitants of this his ma'ᵗⁱᵉˢ Province shall bee Imposed and asessed Raised and Levied and y' for y⁰ due and more Regular assesing and Leving y⁰ Ratte or tax a fore sd. the asesors for y' time being of all and every y⁰ Sities, towns maners & liberties Respecktively within this provinse who are or shall bee for y⁰ asesing y⁰ Publick charge of oath Respecktive, sitty, towne or maner & Liberty afore sd : having first taken oath before any his ma'ᵗⁱᵉˢ Justisces of y⁰ pease, well trully, and equally to asesse all and every y⁰ free holders and Inhabitants within their liberty and heerby Required and by vertue of this ackt are & shall bee sufficiently authorized and empowered at or before y⁰ first day of Septembar to assemble and meet to gether at such place as to them shall bee thought convenient and then and their shall well truly and equally acording to their severall estats Ratte and asess y⁰ free holders and inhabitants of y⁰ sd. Citties, towns maners & Liberties for the which thay are asesers Respecktively and that such Ratte & asesment soe made and assessed in maner afore sᵈ- shall bee forth with delivered by y⁰ sd. asessers to y⁰ coleckter for y⁰ time being of each Citty, towne, maner and liberty afore sd. by him to bee coleckted levied & Reseved acord-

ing to such Ratte and assessment so to him delivered as
afore sd. whoe for his trouble and Pains in leveing and
coleckting y$^e$ same shall take and Reseive twelve pence in
y$^e$ pound for all and every such sum and sums of mony
soe by him to bee coleckted in manor a fore s$^d$. which s$^d$
sum or sums of mony soe by him Coleckted and Reseved
shall all with possible speed y$^t$ is to say within five months
at furthest after such Ratte or asessment shall come to his
hands bee paid to y$^e$ sheriffe for the time being of every
the Countie whare such Citty towne, maner or Libertie
shall bee or ly and to bee transmitted to new Yourke to
his ma$^{ties}$ Coleckter and Recever of his Revenue their as
such offlcer or officers as shall by his exclency y$^e$ gov$^{ernr}$ bee
Impowered to Reseve the same at or before y$^e$ s$^d$. first day
of may now next Insuing who shall bee alowed all his
charges and disbursments hee shall exspend for all such
sum or sums of mony soe by him transmited as afore sd.
and be it further enacted by the athoritie afore sd. that the
produce of y$^e$ Countee shall bee taken and Reseved by
y$^e$ Coleckters and sheriffs herein before named for coleckting Reseving or transmiting the s$^d$ Ratte or tax att y$^e$ prises
heerin after exprest y$^t$ is to say good sweet marchandable
wheat at 3$^s$ and Indian corne at 1$^s$ and six pens p bushell
good marchantable porke att 2$^{lb}$ 2$^s$ p barill and beef att one
pound 4$^s$ p barrell and not other wise: and further bee it
inackted ordained by the authority afore sd. y$^t$ if any Person or persons within this province whoe shall bee asesed
and Ratted in maner before exprest shall negleckt and Refuse to pay and satisfie and Pay y$^e$ severall and Respecktive
sums of mony hee or thay shall bee soe Ratted and assessed
uppon y$^e$ exspiration of fourteen days after and demand
their of made it shall and may bee lawful for every such
Coleckter by warant from any too of his map$^{ties}$ Justisces
of y$^e$ peace of y$^e$ Countie wheare any such person or persons
shall hapen to Reside or such estate shall lye who by vertue of this ackt have powr to grant such warant to levy

yᵉ same by distres and sale of such defaulters goods and chattells, Resurving yᵉ over plus yᵉ charge and exspence of such disstres and salle being first deducted to the owners of such goods & chattls if any such over pluss happen to bee: and further bee it enackted and ordained by the athoritie afore sd. that if any of the persons in this ackt mentiond for yᵉ Ratting, assessing Coleckting Reseving, paying and transmiting yᵉ sum or sums of mony Ratte or tax heer in before exprest to bee a assesed, Ratted and taxed shall delay negleckt, Refuse or deny to doe, performe ex-secute and full fill yᵉ severall and Respective duties and ackts heer in before mentioned and exspresed to bee dune, performed, exsecuted and full filled and theirof shall Law-fully bee convickted before any of his majᵗⁱᵉˢ. Courts of Record within this province who by vertue of this ackt have and shall have power and athoritie to heer try and de-termine yᵉ some hee or they shall sufer such paine by fine and Imprisonment as by the disscretion of any of yᵉ Jus-tises of any of yᵉ sd. Courts shall be adjudged: Provided allways yᵗ this ackt nor any clause or thing therein con-tained shall loos force valliddittie or efeckt in yᵉ law butt only untill yᵉ first day of may which will bee in yᵉ yeer of our lord one thousand six hundred eaighty and nine any thing in this ackt contained to yᵉ contrary heer of not with standing.

THO: DONGAN
NICO BYARD
FFREDRICK FFILLIPS
ANTHO: BROKHOLLS
JE        COURTLAND
J. BAKHOR
By Counsel and
of his excelency
Js. SWINTON.

*(File No. 20.)*

## [DEED. JOHN BETTS TO JEREMIAH ADAMS.]

[1688, June 18.]

This in Denture made y^e eaighteene day of June in the third yeer of the Raine of our Sov^r Lord James the second King of Great Brittan france and Irland, defender of the faith etc & in y^e yeer of our lord acording to y^e computation of y^e Church of England one thousand six hundred eaighttie eaight: Between John beets of y^e towne of Huntington with in y^e countie of Suffolk and province of New yourke in America husbandman and abigall his wife of y^e on partie and Jeremiah Adams of the same towne countie and province husbanman of y^e other partie Witnesseth that y^e saide John Beets and Abigall his wife have for divers good causes and considerations us there unto moving but more especially for and in y^e consideration of the sum of three score pounds in hand secured before the ensealling and delivering heer of of passable pay of the province, have Bargoned Allinated sould and confirmed and by these p^rsents from us our heairs executors Administrators and assignes doe allen Bargen sell and confirme unto the afore said Jeremiah adams his heairs executors administrators and asignes all our Right tittle and intrest in and too part of a farme sittuate Lying and beeing one a necke of Land Comonly called or knowne by the name of Crab medowe necke with all the Rights of medowe land y^t doth belong or apertaine to y^e same as allsoe six acers of up land that was exchanged with thomas Scudder by Jacob walker which exchange was that Jacob walker should take the sd. six acars att crabmedow out of y^e sd. thomas scuders Right of Land: wee saie all our Right tittle and intrest unto all y^e afore mentioned lands and medowe with all Rights and previliges that doe in any wise to the same or any Right or intrest that might or could belong to our heires bee it by what kind or nature soe ever,

wee saie all the afore mentioned lands and medowes to
gether with all housing out housing orchards, gardens,
pastures, fences that is upon any part or parsel of y$^t$ land
situate and being one Crabmedowe necke as afore sd
Butting and bounding the Land of edward bunce one
y$^e$ west side the land of John Ingersoll one y$^e$ nore east the
norwest the woods in comanidge the south east the hie way:
wee saie all the afore named lands and medows with all its
Rights and previlidges wee have fully and freely or as
fully and freely as possably can bee made over by any deed
or convance what soe ever from us our heairs executors
administrators & assignes unto the afore mentioned Jeremiah adams his heires executors administrators and asignes
too have and to hould for ever the sd. bargoned and
granted p$^r$mises with its apurtinances yeelding and paing
y$^e$ anuall p.portion of what belongs to the government of
this province and the sd. John Beets and abigall his wife
for our selves our heairs, executors administrators and
asigenes Doe covenant promise and grant too and with
y$^e$ sd. Jeremiah Adams his heairs executors administrators
and asigens that y$^e$ said John Beets and abigall his wife
now is and stands firmly seaized of a good sure and perfitt
estate in y$^e$ law of all the afore mentioned Lands and medows and hath good Right and lawfull authoritie to sell and
convae the same and allsoe doth further covenant that
y$^e$ sd lands and medowe and every part and parsil thereof
is free and clear of and from all former bargons grants
sales morgages, leasses, Judgments executions convaance
or convances, doweries, widow rights, tittles or intrest
what soe ever all soe I y$^e$ said Jeremiah Adams doe covenant promise and grant that I my executors administrators
or asignes shall from time to time and at all times cleer
and pay all just demands for y$^e$ soyle Rights of the afore
mentioned premises as is more at large exprest in huntingtons oblygation to all those said farmes wheare by the
afore said John beets nor his sucksessors bee not endemni-

fied ffurthermore wee the said John beets and Abigall his
wife doth further Covenant promise and grant that wee
our heairs executors administrators and asignes will save
harmeless and endemnified the sd. Jeremiah adams his
heairs executors administrators and asignes of and from
any person or persons that shall lay any just claime to any
Right tittle or intrest to the towne of huntingtons grant to
y$^e$ whole farmers as at large is exprest in their covenant in
wittnes whereof wee have sett too our hands and seals to
this present indenture.

signed, sealed                                  JOHN BEETS
and delivered in                                     the mark of
the presents of                                 ABIGALL $\times$ BETTS
   THOMAS TAILOR
   JOSEPH BAYLY
   The scubscribars have acknowledged y$^e$ above sd. to bee
their act, and deed before mee this 18$^{th}$ of June
                   EPENETUS PLATT
                   Justice of y$^e$ peace.
   A True coppy of the origanall deed compaired y$^e$ 17$^{th}$ of
Jully 1688
      p mee Isaac Platt, Reco$^r$
     (*Deeds, Vol.* 1, *p.* 241-2.)

---

[DEED.   RICHARD SMITH TO JONATHAN
LEWIS.]


[1688, Ang. 1.]

Wheras The towne of Huntington hath given Jonathan
Luice seventeen acars of Land in bred an cheese hollowe
y$^e$ which is claimed by Richard Smith of Smithtowne sen$^r$
These prsents wittnes that I y$^e$ said Richard Smith doe
make over all my Right tittle and claime to y$^e$ said land

from mee & my heairs unto y^e sd. Jonathan Luice to have and to hold to him his heairs or asignes for ever and have Reseved content ffully for y^e same to my content, witnes my hand & seale this first of August 1688.

signed Sealed de-                    RICHARD SMITH
livered in presence
of : WILLIAM FFANCY
        his × mark
    MARY × ARTHOR
        her mark

A true Coppy of y^e origanall compared by mee this 12^th of Septem^r 1688

Isaac Platt Rec^r.

(*Deeds, Vol. 1, p. 125.*)

---

## [THE DONGAN CHARTER.*]

[1688, Aug. 2.]

The People of the State of New York by the Grace of God free and independent, To all to whom these presents shall come, Greeting : Know y^e that we, having inspected the records remaining in our Secretary's Office do find

[*Though clothed in a mass of veribage, much of which, under a change of government, has become in a measure obsolete, the Dongan charter was an important paper to the town. It confirmed the title acquired under the Nichol's grant of 1666, giving the same boundaries. Those who occupied lands under former grants by the town were to hold them. Lands not granted by the town to individuals were to be held in common. The town was erected into a public municipal corporation, invested with all the rights of a township; nine trustees were named who were to hold title to the town's common lands and were given power to manage and convey the same. The town was to pay the Governor annually twenty shillings quit-rent, and a sum was exacted by him for the grant of the charter, which was afterwards the subject of much contention. This is the beginning of the office of Town trustees, none having previously existed and no proceedings of trustees are found in this book.—C. R. S.]

there recorded in Lib. Pat. 6, page 360, certain Letters
Patent in the words and figures following, to wit : Recorded for the Towne of Huntington, Thomas Dongan, Capt,
Generall and Governour-in-Chief of New Yorke and Territories depending thereon, in America under his most
sacred Majesty, James y$^e$ second, by y$^e$ Grace of God
King of England, Scotland, France and Ireland, Defender
of y$^e$ faith, and to all to whom these presents shall come,
sendeth Greeting :

Whereas Richard Nicolls, Esqr., Governor-Generall
under his then Royall Highness James, Duke of Yorke
and Albany, etc., now his present Majesty of all his Terri-
toryes in America, did by a certain writing or patent
under his hand and seale bearing date y$^e$ thirtyeth day of
November, in y$^e$ eighteenth yeare of the reigne of ye late
Soveraign, Lord Charles y$^e$ second, etc., of blassed memory, etc., in y$^e$ year of our Lord God Sixteene hundred
sixty-six, by virtue of y$^e$ com'$^n$. and authority unto him
given by his s'd then Royall Highness now his present
Majestie as aff'd, I ratifie, confirme and grant unto Jonas
Wood, William Leveradge, Robart Seely, John Ketcham,
Thomas Scidmore, Isaac Platt, Thomas Joans, and Thomas
Weeckes, as Patentees in ye behalfe of themselves and
their associates, the Freeholders and Inhabitants of y$^e$
Towne of Huntinton, scituate, lying and being within this
Governm'nt upon Long Island in the County of Suffolk,
now in the Tennoure and occupation of severall Freeholders and Inhabitants there residing, who having there-
tofore made lawfull purchase of the lands thereunto belonging, have likewise manured and improved a considerable part thereof and settled a competent number of fami-
lys thereupon all y$^e$ lands y't already had been or thereafter should be purchased for and on the behalfe of y$^e$ s'd
Town of Huntington, whether from the Natives Proprietors or others within y$^e$ Limitts and Bounds herein expressed ; that is from a certain river creek on y$^e$ West

commonly called by the Indians by y$^e$ name of Nackqua-
tack and by the English the Cold Spring, to stretch eastward to Nesaquas River, on the North to be bounded by
y$^e$ Sound, runing betwixt Long Island and y$^e$ Maine, and
on y$^e$ South by the Sea, including therein nine severall
Necks of meadow ground, which tract of Land, together
with y$^e$ said Nine Necks thereunto belonging within y$^e$
bounds and Limitts afores'd, and all or any Plantations
thereupon, are to belong to the said Towne of Huntington
as allsoe all Havens Harbours, Creeks, Quarries, Wood-
lands, Meadows, Pastures, Marsh's, Lakes, Fishing, Hawking, hunting and fowleing and all other proffits, Commod-
itiys, Emoluments and Hereditamts to y$^e$ said land and
premises, y$^e$ Limits and Bounds aforementioned, described
belonging or in anywise appertaining, to have and to hold
all and singular, ye said Lands and Necks of Lands, Hereditam'ts and premissess with their and every of their appurtenances and every part and parcell thereof to ye said
patentees and their associates, their Heires, Successors
and Assigns forever and did likewise thereby confirme and
Grant unto y$^e$ sd Patentees and theire associates, their
heires Successors and Assigns all ye privledges belonging
to any Towne within this Governm't and y$^t$ y$^e$ place of
their present Habitation should continue and retaine y$^e$
name of Huntington, by wch name it should be disting-
uish'd and knowne in all Bargains and Sales Deeds,
Records and writeings, they y$^e$ said patentecs and their
Associates, their Heires, Successors and Assignes rendering and paying such Dutyes and Acknowledgments as
then were or thereafter should be constituted and established by y$^e$ Lawes of this Collony under y$^e$ obedience of
his Royall Highness his Heires and Successors, as by ye
said patent entered and recorded in ye Secretarys Office
att New Yorke, relation being thereunto had, may more
fully and att large appeare, and whereas y$^e$ free holders of
y$^e$ said Towne of Huntington have made application unto

mee y$^t$ I would Grant and Confirme y$^e$ premises by Patent under y$^e$ Seale of y$^e$ province to them their Heires and Assigns forever: Now know yee y't I, ye said Thomas Dongan, by virtue of ye power and authority to mee derived from his most sacred majestie affores'd in pursuance of the same for and in consideration of y$^e$ Quitt rent hereinafter reseived and other good and lawfull considerations mee thereunto moving have Given, Granted, Ratified and Confirmed, and by these presents doe Give, Grant, Ratify, and Confirme unto Thomas Fleet, Senior, Epenetus Platt, Jonas Wood Senior, James Chichester Senior, Joseph Baily, Thomas Powell Senior, John Joan, Isaac Platt, and Thomas ————, Freeholders and Inhabitants of Huntington, herein erected and made one Body Corporate and publique and willed and determined to be called by y$^e$ name of y$^e$ Trustees of y$^e$ Freeholders and Comonalty of y$^e$ Towne of Huntington and their successors, all ye above recited Tracts of Land within ye Limitts and Bounds aforesaid, together with all and singular ye Houses, Messuages, Tenements, Buildings, Mills, Milldams, fencing, enclosures, Gardens, Orchards, fields, pastures, woods, underwoods, trees, timbers, feedings and Common of pasture, meadows, marshes, swamps, plaines, Rivers, Rivoletts, waters, Lakes, Ponds, Brooks, Streams, Beaches, Quarries, Creekes, Harbours, Highways, and Easments, fishing, hawking, hunting, and fouling, mines, mineralls (silver and gold mines excepted) and all franchises, proffits, commodityes and Hereditaments whatsoever to y$^e$ said Tracts of Lands and premises belonging or in any wise appertaining or therewithall used, accepted, reputed or taken to belong or in any wise appertaine to all intents and purposes and constructions whatsoever, as alsoe all and singular y$^e$ rents, arrearages of rents, issues and proffits of y$^e$ said Tract of Land and Premises heretofore due and payable: to have and to hold all and singular ye before cited Tract of Land and premises within y$^e$

bounds and limits afforementioned, with their and every of
theire appurtenances unto y⁰ said Thomas Ffeet senior,
Epenetus Platt, Jonas Wood senior, James Chichester
senior, Thomas Powell, senior, Joseph Baily, Thomas
————, John Samnes and Isaac Platt, Trustees of y⁰
Freeholders and Comonalty of y⁰ Towne of Huntington
and their Successors forever to and for y⁰ severall and
respective uses following and to noe other uses, intents
and purposes whatsoever, that is to say as for and concerning all and singular ye severall and respective parcell of
Land and Meadows, part of y⁰ granted premises in any
wayes taken up and appropriated eighter by Pattent under
ye hand of any of his Majestys Governors in this Province
and sealed with y⁰ seale thereof or by perticular divisions
and allotments before y⁰ day of y⁰ date hereof unto y⁰
severall and respective present Freeholders or Inhabitants
of y⁰ said Towne of Huntingtown by vertue of y⁰ before
recited Deed or Patent to y⁰ use and behoofe of y⁰ said
Freeholders and Inhabitants respectively and to their severall and respective Heires and Assigns forever and as for
and concerning all and every such parcell or parcells,
Tract, or Tracts of Land, remainder of y⁰ granted premises, not taken upp or appropriated to any perticular person or persons by vertue of y⁰ before recited Deed or
patent, to y⁰ use and behoofe of y⁰ present Freeholders
and Inhabitants and their Heires, Successors, and assigns
forever in proportion to their severall and respective settlements, Divisions and allotments as Tenants in common
without any manner of Lett, Hinderance, or Molestation
to be had or reserved upon pretence of joynt Tennancy or
survivorshipp, anything contained to y⁰ contrary in anywise notwithstandin, alwaies, saveing to his most sacred
Majestie aforesaid, his Heires and successors, ye several
rents and Quitt-rents reserved, due and payable from severall persons inhabiting within y⁰ Limitts and Bounds
afforesaid by vertue of former Grants to them made, and

Given and alsoe saveing to his most sacred majestie aforesaid, his Heirs and Successors, all ye Necks of Land y$^t$ lye
to the South within y$^e$ limitts and Bounds aforesaid, and
ye Lands to y$^e$ Northward of y$^e$ same, y$^t$ remaines unpurchased from y$^e$ Native Indians, anything contained herein-
to ye contrary in any wayes not withstanding to bee holden
of his said majestys, his Heires and Successors, in free
and common soccage according to ye manner of East
Greenwich in ye County of Kent, within his Majesties
Realme of England, yielding rendering and paying therefore yearly and every yeare from henceforth to our Soveraigne Lord ye King, his Heires & Successors or to such
officer or officers as shall be appointed to receive ye same,
one Lamb or five shillings lent money of this province upon ye five and twentyeth day of March att New Yorke,
in full of all rents or former reserved rents, services, acknowledgements and demands whatsoever, and further by
vertue of ye power and authority to mee the said Thomas
Dongan, Given as aforesaid, and in persueance of y$^e$ same,
and for ye reasons and considerations above recited I have
Willed, determined, declared and granted, by these presents, due, will Determine, Declare and Grant y$^t$ y$^e$ said
Inhabitants and Freeholders y$^e$ freemen of Huntingtown
afforesaid, comonly called by y$^e$ name of y$^e$ freeholders
and Inhabitants of y$^e$ Towne of Huntington, or by whatsoever Name or names they are called or named, and their
Heires and Successors forever henceforward are and shall
be one Body corporate and Politique in Deed and Name
by y$^e$ name of y$^e$ Trustees of y$^e$ Freeholders and Com-
monalyty of y$^e$ Towne of Huntingtown one Body Corporate and Politique in Deed and Name, I have realy and
fully for his said Majesty, his Heirs and Successors, erected
and made Ordained, Constituted and Declared by these
presents, and y$^t$ by y$^e$ same name they have succession
forever, and y$^t$ they and their Successors by y$^e$ Name of
y$^e$ Trustees of y$^e$ Freeholders and Commonallity of y$^e$

Towne of Huntingtown be and shall be forever in future
times persons able and capable in Law to have, perceive
and receive and possess not only all and singular y⁰ premises, but other meassuages, Lands, Tenements, priviledges,
Jurisdictions, Franchizes and Hereditament of whatsoever
kind or species they shall be, to them and their Successors
in fee forever or for y⁰ tenure of a Yeare or Yeares or
otherwise whatsoever manner itt bee, and also Goods,
Chattles and all other things of what-soever Name, Nature,
Quality or Species they shall bee and alsoe to Give, Grant,
release, aliene, assigne and Dispose of Lands, Tenements,
Hereditaments and all and every other thing and things,
act and acts, to doe and execute by y⁰ Name aforesaid,
and yᵗ by y⁰ same name of Trustees of y⁰ Freeholders and
Comonality of y⁰ Towne of Huntington to plead and be
impleaded, answer and be answered unto, defend and be
defended, they are and may be capable in whatsoever
place and places and before whatsoever Judges and Justices or other persons, officials of his said Majesty's, his
Heirs and Successors in all and all manner of Actions,
Plaints, Suites, Complaints, Causes, Matters and demands
whatsoever of wᵗ kinds, quality and species y⁰ same bee
in manner and forme as any other of his Majestys Leidge
people within this province can or are able to have, require, receive, possesse, enjoy, retaine, Give, Grant,
release, aliene, assigne and dispose, pleade and be impleaded, answer an be answered unto, Defend and be defended,
doe Permitt and Execute and for y⁰ better Inableing y⁰
Trustees of ye Freeholders and Commonality of y⁰
Towne of Huntingtown aforesaid in doeing and executing
all and singular y⁰ premises, I have Willed, Granted and
determined, and by these presents Doe, Will, Grant and
determine that from henceforward and forever hereafter
y⁰ said Trustees of the Freeholders and Commonality of
y⁰ Towne of Huntingtown Doe and may have and use a
Comon Seale wch shall serve to execute y⁰ causes and af-

fairs whatsoever of them and their Successors, and further
I will and by these presents in y<sup>e</sup> behalfe of his said Majestye, his Heirs and successors that henceforward and forever
more there be and shall be Trustees of the Freeholders and
Commonality of y<sup>e</sup> Towne of Huntington aforesaid to be
chosen and elected in these presents hereafter is mentioned
who shall bee and shall bee called y<sup>e</sup> Trustees of the freeholders and commonality of y<sup>e</sup> town of Huntingtown and
they and their Successors shall and may at all convenient
times hereafter upon a publique summons from any three
of y<sup>e</sup> trustees aforesaid for the time being, assemble and
meet together in y<sup>e</sup> Towne House of y<sup>e</sup> said Towne or in
such publique place as shall be from time to time appointed,
to make such Acts and orders in writing for y<sup>e</sup> more or-
derly doing of y<sup>e</sup> premises as they, y<sup>e</sup> said Trustees of y<sup>e</sup>
freeholders and Commonality of y<sup>e</sup> Towne of Huntingtown,
afforesaid, and theire Successors, from time to time, shall
and may think convenient, soe always as y<sup>e</sup> said Acts and
orders be in noe way repugnant to y<sup>e</sup> Laws of England and
of this province wch now are or hereafter may be established, and that they be not in anywayes against y<sup>e</sup> true
intent and meaning of these presents, and alsoe I Will, Or-
daine and Determine y<sup>t</sup> all and singular y<sup>e</sup> afforsaid acts
and orders, from time to time, shall bee made and ordained
by y<sup>e</sup> vote of y<sup>e</sup> major part of y<sup>e</sup> said Trustees of y<sup>e</sup> Freeholders and Commonality of y<sup>e</sup> Towne of Huntingtown,
aforesaid, or at least by y<sup>e</sup> major part of such of them as
shall from time to time assemble and meet together in
manner as afforsaid, so allways as there be not fewer
in number than six of the Trustees present at such
meetings soe to be holden as afforesaid, and for y<sup>e</sup> better Execution of this Grant in this Behalfe I have assigned, Nominated, Created, Constituted and made, and
by these presents Doe Assigne, Nominate, Create, Constitute and make Thomas Fleet, Senior., Epenetus Platt,
Jonas Wood, Senior, James Chichester, senior, Thomas

Powell, senior, Joseph Bayley,——, John Sammes, and
Isaac Platt, to stand to bee the first Modern Trustees of yᵉ
Freeholders and Commonallty of yᵉ Towne of Huntingtown, to continue in yᵉ afforesaid office from and after yᵉ
date of these presents untill yᵉ time yᵗ others bee elected
and chosen in their stead, according to yᵉ manner and
forme hereinafter expressed, and morever I doe by these
presents, for and on yᵉ behalfe of his most sacred majesty
afforesaid, his Heirs and Successors, appoint yᵗ yᵉ Trustees
of yᵉ Freeholders and Commonality of yᵉ Towne of Huntingtown and Clerke within yᵉ Towne of Huntington aforesaid, ye yearly chosen on yᵉ first Tuesday of May forever,
viz.: Nine Trustees of yᵉ Freeholders and Commonallity of
yᵉ Towne of Huntingtoun, one Clerke, one Constable, and
two Assessors in such publique place as yᵉ Trustees for yᵉ
time being shall appoint and direct, and yᵗ yᵉ Trustees,
Constables, and Assessors be chosen by yᵉ majority of
Voices of the Freeholders and freemen of yᵉ Towne of
Huntington afforesaid ; and whereas there is an Act of yᵉ
Generall Assembly of this province entiteiled an Act for
defraying of yᵉ publique and necessary charge of each
respective Citty, Towne and County throughout this province, etc., wherein amongst other things it was enacted
and provided yᵗ annually and once every yeare there
should be elected a certaine number out of each respective
Citty, Towne, and County, throughout this province, to be
elected and chosen by yᵉ major part of all yᵉ Freeholders
and Freemen, which certaine number so duely elected
should have full power and authority to make a assessment
or certaine Rule, within their respective Cittyes, Towns
and County annually, and once every yeare, which assessment and certaine rate soe established as afforesaid should
be paid unto a certain Treasurer, who should be chosen by
yᵉ Major part of all yᵉ Freeholders and freemen of each
respective Citty, Towne and County as afforesaid, and
whereas yᵉ said Towne of Huntington is to be regulated

in y$^e$ premises according to y$^e$ Tennure and effect of y$^e$
afforerecited Act of Assembly : Now know y$^e$ likewise y$^t$ I
have given and granted and by these presents Doe Give
and Grant, for and on behalfe of his said Majesty, his
Heires and Successors, unto y$^e$ sd Trustees of y$^e$ Freeholders and Commonallity of y$^e$ Town of Huntingtonn, and
their Súccessors forever, y$^t$ said Trustees for the time being
shall be Commissioners of y$^e$ said Towne to execute and
officiate in y$^e$ sd. office to all intents, constructions and
purposes whatsoever, and further y$^t$ sd. Trustees, as Commissioners of y$^e$ said Towne shall have forever from time
to time and at all times hereafter, and by such wayes and
means to Leavy and Impose such sume and summes of
Money as they shall think fitt for y$^e$ defraying y$^e$ necessary
and publique charge of y$^e$ said Towne, and for y$^e$ more
Orderly doeing thereof, they shall and may from time to
time give such directions unto y$^e$ Assessors Yearely to be
chosen for the sd Towne, how and after y$^t$ manner to pro-
ceed in their Assessmts for such sumes of money as afforesaid, on y$^e$ Estates of each of y$^e$ respective inhabitants and
freeholders of y$^e$ sd. Towne, and y$^e$ sd Sumes when soe
raised and unto y$^e$ hands of y$^e$ Treasurer of y$^e$ sd. Towne
as afforesaid, to Order y$^e$ payment, Disbursement and Dis-
posall of to such persons and to and for y$^e$ uses aforesaid,
in such manner as to them shall seeme convenient, and
further y$^t$ all and singular y$^e$ Acts and Orders of y$^e$ said
Trustees in y$^e$ premises shall be certified under y$^e$ said
common seale signed by y$^e$ President of y$^e$ said Trustees
for y$^e$ time being, who is allways first to be chosen of y$^e$
said Trustees, or in his absence by any other two of y$^e$ said
Trustees of w'ch y$^e$ Treasurer and y$^e$ Assessors of y$^e$ said
Towne, for y$^e$ time being and all other persons, are to take
due notice, and lastly, I Give and Grant for and on behalfe
of his said Majesty, his heires and Successors, by these
presents to all and every person and persons and to whatsoever person subject to his said Majesty, his Heirs, and

Successors, free and lawfull power, and abillity and
authority that they or any of them any Messuages, Tenements, Lands, Meadows, feedings and pastures, Woods,
Underwoods, rents, reversions, services, and other Hereditaments whatsoever which they hold of his said Majestie,
his Heirs, and Successors, unto y$^e$ aforesaid Trustees of y$^e$
freeholders and Commonality of y$^e$ Towne of Huntingtonn,
and their Successors, shall and may Give Grant, Bargain,
Sell, Allienate, to have and to hold and enjoy unto y$^e$ said
Trustees of y$^e$ Freeholders and Commonallity of y$^e$ Town
of Huntingtonn, and their successors forever, yielding
and paying therefore unto his said Majesty his Heirs and
Successors, on y$^e$ said five and twentyeth day of March,
yearely and every yeare forever, y$^e$ full and just sume of
twenty shillings, curr't Money at New Yorke ; wherefore
by vertue of y$^e$ power and authority aforesaid, I doe Will
and Command for and on behalf of his said Majesty, his
Heirs and Successors, y$^t$ y$^e$ aforesaid Trustees of y$^e$ Freeholders and Commonallity of y$^e$ Towne of Huntingtonn
and their Successors, have, held, use and enjoy all y$^e$
liberty, Authority, customes, orders, ordinances, franchizes,
acquittances, Lands, Tenements, and Hereditaments,
Goods and Chattle aforesaid, according to y$^e$ Tenoure and
effects of these presents, without y$^e$ lett or Hinderance of
any person or persons whatsoever. In Testimony whereof
I have signed these presents with my Handwriting,
caused y$^e$ same to be recorded in y$^e$ Secretary's office and
y$^e$ seale of this his Majestys province to be thereunto
affixed, this second day of August in y$^e$ fourth year of his
Majestye Reigne and in y$^e$ yeare of our Lord one thousand
six hundred eighty and eight.

May it please your Excellency, The Attorney Generall
has perused this Grant and finds nothing therein contained
prejudiciall to his Majesty Interest. Examined August y$^e$
1688 W. NICOLLS. Att a Councill held att Fort James in
New York, August y$^e$ 2. 1688, Present His Excellency y$^e$

Governour, Major Antho Brockholls, Major Gervis Baxter, Major Frank Philips, Major S. V. Cortlands. This Pattent was approved of GEO. BREWERTON.

All which We have Exemplified by these presents.

In Testimony whereof We have caused these our Letters to be made patent and the Great Seal of our State to be hereunto affixed. Witness our trusty and well beloved George Clinton, Esquire, Governor of our said State General and Commander-in-chief of all the Militia and Admiral of the Navy of the same, at our City of New York the thirteenth day of September, in the year of our Lord One thousand seven hundred and ninety three and in the Eighteenth year of our Independence.

GEO. CLINTON. [L. S.]

(*File No.* 70.)

# INDEX OF DEEDS.

# REVERSE INDEX OF DEEDS:

| | GRANTEE. | GRANTOR. | PAGE. |
|---|---|---|---|
| 1688, June 18, | Adams, Jeremiah | John Betts, | 529 |
| 1658, May. 14, | Andrews, Samuel | Indians, | 15 |
| 1659. Feb. 1, | "    " | " | 20 |
| 1681. Mar. 25, | Arthur, Robert | George Baldwin, | 290 |
| 1688, Mar. 17 | "    " | Richard Smith, | 516 |
| 1668, July 16, | Bailey, Joseph | Jonas Wood, | 126 |
| 1682, Nov. 15, | "    " | Nicholas Ellis, | 349 |
| 1688, Feb. 4, | "    " | Edward Higbee. | 513 |
| 1665, Mar. 6, | Baldwin, George | Thomas Mathews, | 64 |
| 1680, June 26, | "    " | "  Brush, | 263 |
| 1681, Mar. 25, | "    " | John Finch, | 290 |
| 1687, Jan. 31, | Betts, James | " Green, | 480 |
| 1680, Jan. 26, | "  John | Jacob Walker, | 256 |
| 1684, June 28, | Brush, John | Benjamin Smith, | 395 |
| 1681, July 19, | "  Richard | Abial Titus, | 312 |
| 1684, June 25, | "  Thomas | Thomas Smith, | 394 |
| 1686, June 28, | "    " | David Scudder, | 444 |
| 1668, July 11, | Bryan, Alexander "  and Richard } | George Baldwin, | 124 |
| 1684, Nov. 13, | "    " | William Jones, | 403 |
| 1679, Oct. 27, | Bunce, Edward | John Jones, | 250 |
| "    "  27, | "    " | Abial Titus, | 251 |
| 1681, May 1, | Chichester, James Jr. | Benj. Jones, | 293 |
| "  June 20, | "    "    " | James Chichester, Sen., | 298 |
| 1686, Oct. 4, | "    "    " | John Jones, | 464 |
| 1687, July 1, | "    "    " | Mary Miller, | 500 |
| 1663, July 7, | Corey, John | Jonas Wood, | 48 |
| 1685, Apr. 10, | Davis, Richard | Edward Ketcham, | 426 |
| 1665, May 12, | "  Samuel | Caleb Wood, | 66 |
| 1665, June 24, | "    " | "    " | 71 |
| 1681, July 15, | Ellis, Nicholas | John Finch, | 310 |
| "  Nov. 13, | "    " | "  .  "  Sen., | 323 |

www.ingramcontent.com/pod-product-compliance
Lightning Source LLC
Chambersburg PA
CBHW071351290326
41932CB00045B/1419